Intellectual Property Management

Contributions to Management Science

H. Dyckhoff/U. Finke
Cutting and Packing in Production and Distribution
1992. ISBN 3-7908-0630-7

R. Flavell (Ed.)
Modelling Reality and Personal Modelling
1993. ISBN 3-7908-0682-X

M. Hofmann/M. List (Eds.)
Psychoanalysis and Management
1994. ISBN 3-7908-0795-8

R.L. D'Ecclesia/S.A. Zenios (Eds.)
Operations Research Models in Quantitative Finance
1994. ISBN 3-7908-0803-2

M.S. Catalani/G.F. Clerico
Decision Making Structures
1996. ISBN 3-7908-0895-4

M. Bertocchi/E. Cavalli/S. Komlósi (Eds.)
Modelling Techniques for Financial Markets and Bank Management
1996. ISBN 3-7908-0928-4

H. Herbst
Business Rule-Oriented Conceptual Modeling
1997. ISBN 3-7908-1004-5

C. Zopounidis (Ed.)
New Operational Approaches for Financial Modelling
1997. ISBN 3-7908-1043-6

K. Zwerina
Discrete Choice Experiments in Marketing
1997. ISBN 3-7908-1045-2

G. Marseguerra
Corporate Financial Decisions and Market Value
1998. ISBN 3-7908-1047-9

WHU Koblenz – Otto Beisheim Graduate School of Management (Ed.)
Structure and Dynamics of the German Mittelstand
1999. ISBN 3-7908-1165-3

A. Scholl
Balancing and Sequencing of Assembly Lines
1999. ISBN 3-7908-1180-7

E. Canestrelli (Ed.)
Current Topics in Quantitative Finance
1999. ISBN 3-7908-1231-5

W. Bühler/H. Hax/R. Schmidt (Eds.)
Empirical Research on the German Capital Market
1999. ISBN 3-7908-1193-9

M. Bonilla/T. Casasus/R. Sala (Eds.)
Financial Modelling
2000. ISBN 3-7908-2282-X

S. Sulzmaier
Consumer-Oriented Business Design
2001. ISBN 3-7908-1366-4

C. Zopounidis (Ed.)
New Trends in Banking Management
2002. ISBN 3-7908-1488-1

U. Dorndorf
Project Scheduling with Time Windows
2002. ISBN 3-7908-1516-0

B. Rapp/P. Jackson (Eds.)
Organisation and Work Beyond 2000
2003. ISBN 3-7908-1528-4

M. Grossmann
Entrepreneurship in Biotechnology
2003. ISBN 3-7908-0033-3

H.M. Arnold
Technology Shocks
2003. ISBN 3-7908-0051-1

T. Ihde
Dynamic Alliance Auctions
2004. ISBN 3-7908-0098-8

J. Windsperger/G. Cliquet/G. Hendrikse/M. Tuunanen (Eds.)
Economics and Management of Franchising Networks
2004. ISBN 3-7908-0202-6

Klaus Jennewein

Intellectual Property Management

The Role of Technology-Brands in the Appropriation of Technological Innovation

With 62 Figures
and 22 Tables

Physica-Verlag
A Springer Company

Series Editors
Werner A. Müller
Martina Bihn

Author

Dr. Klaus Jennewein
T-Mobile International AG & Co. KG
Group Strategy
Landgrabenweg 151
53227 Bonn
Germany
klaus.jennewein@t-mobile.net

ISSN 1431-1941
ISBN 3-7908-0280-8 Physica-Verlag Heidelberg New York

Cataloging-in-Publication Data applied for
Library of Congress Control Number: 2004109407

Physica-Verlag is a part of Springer Science+Business Media

springeronline.com

Softcover design: Erich Kirchner, Heidelberg

SPIN 11011996 88/3130/DK-5 4 3 2 1 0 – Printed on acid-free paper

With love to my wife
Amélie and my son Léo

„Ein hohes Kleinod ist der gute Namen“

‘A valuable gem is the good name’

(Friedrich Schiller,1759-1805)

Preface

Innovation is a source of competitive advantage. In other words, firms may leverage innovation to generate rents, at least temporarily. And this is intended to be a self-sustained business model: part of the rent extracted from the market may be re-invested into new technological developments which in turn permit additional innovations, thus regenerating the sources of rents. This is the positive loop of innovation.

In this sense, business would be a permanent hunt for innovations, in search of rents.

Yet, innovations need to be protected if firms want to benefit from rents over long periods of time. However, the strategic management literature tends to suggests that patents are a weak protection against aggressive imitators. Secrecy may help but we also know that technology ends up leaking in most cases. Speed in new developments to cut "time to market" may be another way of protecting the technological advance of the firm. But again, this may not be enough as start-ups may out-compete the established firm in the race for innovation.

This is where Dr. Klaus Jennewein's key idea comes into the picture. The core of his thesis is that brand equity may be combined to technological protections such as patents to build a multi-layer, complex, intricate shield to protect the sources of rents against competitors and imitators.

Dr. Jennewein presents two detailed case studies which remarkably feed into his argument. One case is Bayer's aspirin. How come a drug company is still able to extract rent from an innovation which was first introduced to the market over a century ago? How come Bayer still has a dominant market position when the patent protection disappeared so long ago? How come producers of the generic molecule were unable to win against the pioneer of Aspirin?

The second case study tells us the story of the routers of Cisco Systems in the network business. There we see how a newcomer, a start-up, was able to build a long-lasting competitive advantage, based on systematic effort to leverage technological innovation, while carefully building and defending the reputation of the company, its products and its services. As a result, Cisco became the *de facto* standard in the profession, meaning both innovative technologies and reliable services. The technology received the backing of the brand name, and vice versa. When Cisco was badly in need of technological expertise, the name of Cisco helped the company attract and retain the best talents, including through a campaign of acquisition of targeted companies.

In the tradition of grounded theory, Dr. Jennewein actually builds from these two in-depth, rich and detailed case studies to present a life cycle model. The model shows how intangible technological assets may be intertwined over the years with brand equity to build a long lasting protection to innovations. He shows how the start-up firm focuses on bringing a new technology to the market and enjoys a temporary monopoly, that of the innovator. More innovations – mostly process and then incremental innovations – are generated as the start-up consolidates its position as a recognized pioneer. Interestingly enough, this recognition brings along an emerging brand name which is going to become increasingly important as imitators come into the picture. The brand name helps sustain market shares and significant margins, yielding enough returns to invest in new developments. When radical innovation strikes again, the company is now an incumbent. It cannot fully rely on its technological capabilities, as these are only partly relevant to the new context. The incumbent thus primarily relies on its brand name which helps the company bridge over towards the new technological paradigm.

In a way, K. Jennewein is celebrating the wedding of the patent with the brand, the technology with the market reputation, the engineer with the marketer. Dr. Jennewein further suggests to organize the corporation in such a way that this marriage be successful. Instead of letting the development Engineer deal with technology in his unit, the Lawyer at the headquarters deal with patent and other forms of technological protections, the Marketer in his marketing departments deal with brands, K. Jennewein recommends to pursue an integrated intellectual property strategy. He insists to show that the multilayer shield to protect the innovations must be crafted by a coordinated team working hand in hand over the years. This is actually not what I observe in most companies today. To our opinion, this is the core contribution of this book.

This is a brilliant and convincing book with many concrete implications for both business practitioners and academics in the field.

Prof. Dr. Thomas Durand
Ecole Central Paris

Prof. Dr. Alexander Gerybadze
Universität Hohenheim, Stuttgart

Acknowledgements

> *"On ne voit bien que par le cœur. L'essentiel est invisible pour les yeux"*
>
> Antoine de Saint-Exupéry

According to the currently ongoing scientific discussion in the field of strategic and in particular technology management, intangible assets and especially intangible technological assets represent the most important strategic asset for business corporations. However, although the given high strategic importance of intangible assets, many authors criticise the inefficiency of the existing system of intellectual property right protection. Empirical studies have clearly revealed that singular patent right protection does generally not enable companies to efficiently and effectively appropriate the returns of their intangible technological assets. The growing awareness of the shortcomings of legal protection rights has encouraged the investigation of alternative protection modes with a mostly technological focus. On the other hand, the investigation of the role of company specific market based assets in the appropriation of returns of intangible technological assets has been almost entirely neglected by research, so far.

This lack of research has motivated the here presented investigation of the role of brand equity in the appropriation of intangible technological assets. The investigation reveals by an empirical and theoretical analysis the complementary relationship between technological and market based assets, and shows how this relationship affects the ability of companies to appropriate the returns of technological innovation. The investigation is placed at the intersection of strategic management, technology management, and the management of brand equity and builds upon the resource based view.

A major endeavour such as this work which has been handed in as PhD thesis at the University of Hohenheim at Stuttgart and the Ecole Central Paris would never have been possible without the support and guidance of many people which I want to thank here.

The research was undertaken during my time as PhD student at the Centre of International Management and Innovation at the University of Hohenheim and the Laboratoire Stratégie et Technologie at the Ecole Centrale Paris. My first and greatest debt of gratitude is to Prof. Dr. Thomas Durand and Prof. Dr. Alexander Gerybadze my two PhD supervisors. It was their creative and professional opinion as well as the sufficient freedom which have inspired and enabled the realization of this endeavour. Prof. Dr. Bertrand Quélin of Ecole HEC as well as Prof. Dr. Helmut Kuhnle and Prof. Dr. Ulrich Schwalbe at the University of Hohenheim I want to thank for their constructive questions and remarks.

Next I have to thank the companies and research institutes that enabled through their cooperation to realize the empirical investigations and to gain further empirical evidence. Here I want to thank in particular Mr. Michael Chmilewski of Bayer AG, Mr. Harald Zapp of Cisco Systems GmbH, Mr. Robert Chanezon of Rhodia SA, Mr. Jean Moulin, Mr. Jochen Maser, and all the others who gave so generously of their time. I want to particularly show appreciation to Mr. Ulrich Schmoch of the Frauenhofer Gesellschaft at Karlsruhe for extremely valuable support and help in searching and processing of the patent and trademark data. His generous help in accessing the needed data-bases and encouraging discussions considerably contributed to the success of the extensive econometric investigation.

I also owe a great debt of gratitude to my colleagues at the Centre of International Management and Innovation at the University of Hohenheim and at the Laboratoire Stratégie et Technologie at the Ecole Centrale Paris. In particular I want to thank my friend and former colleague Michael Stephan for the inspiring and reassuring discussions. The mutual support, above all during the data mining and data processing process, has probably helped the both of us to avoid some major frustration. I also would like to express my thanks to Miss Barbara Ungerer and Miss Fatiha Gunelli, who have always been a source of encouragement and were of great help to master the bureaucratic hurdles encountered during the binational doctorate studies. Last but not least, I want to thank Nuria Martin, Eric Pfaffmann and Wolfgang Burr for the good co-operation and cheerful time.

I reserve the last acknowledgement for those who really made this research project possible – my wife and my parents. To Amélie, Anneliese and Martin I owe the greatest debt. The constant support, encouragement, and reassurance made it all worthwhile. To all of you, my thanks and love.

Klaus Jennewein

Contents

List of Abbreviations

adj. R^2	adjusted coefficient of determination
A&D	acquisition and development
AG	Aktiengesellschaft / public company
APC	Alien Property Custodian
approx.	approximately
ASA	acetylsalicylic acid
AMA	American Medical Association
AVVID	application, voice, video, and integrated text
BTO	Benelux Trademark Office
CEO	chief executive officer
CICD	Corporate identity and corporate design
CTO	chief technology officer
cf.	confer to
chap.	chapter
cp.	compare with
DM	Deutsche Mark / German Mark
DPA	Deutsches Patentamt / German Patent Office
e.g.	for example
EoS	economies of scale
EPO	European Patent Office
EU	European Union
FDA	Food & Drug Administration (USA)
ISP	Internet service provider
ICGS	International Classification of Goods and Services
i.e.	that is
IOS	Internetworks Operating Systems
IP	Internet Protocol
IPC	International Patent Classification
IPO	initial public offering
M&A	merger and acquisition
MNE	multinational entreprise
N.A.	not available
NIH	not-invented-here-syndrome
OTC	over the counter drugs/self-medication drugs
p./pp.	page/pages
PC	personal computer
PCT	Patent Co-operation Treaty
R&D	research and development
resp.	respectively

ROI	return on investment
RTA	revealed technological advantage
sect.	section
SCA	sustainable competitive advantage
TM	trademark
TRIPS	trade related aspects of intellectual property rights
UK	United Kingdom
unpubl.	unpublished
U.S.	United States of America
USPto	U.S. patent and trademark office
VoIP	Voice over Internet Protocol
WIPO	World Intellectual Property Organisation

I The New Era of Intangible Assets

In the 21st century the most valuable strategic resources for business enterprises will no longer be physical assets such as land, machines, etc., as it was the case in the beginning of the 20th century, but rather intangible assets such as knowledge, know-how, and intellectual property rights.[1] Moreover, various authors have stated that in order to be successful in most industries, companies need to have a competitive advantage on technological grounds which enables them to offer superior products. In particular technological progress has continuously accelerated over the last century so that the average duration of product-life-cycles and even technology-life-cycles has been considerable reduced. This increasing technological progress has not decreased, but rather increased the strategic importance of technological expertise. Therefore, companies are forced to constantly learn, create, and update new technological competencies, as well as unlearn obsolete procedures in order to be able to remain competitive in a world characterised by rapid technological progress. Accordingly Nonaka (1991) stated:

> *"In an economy where the only certainty is uncertainty, the one sure source of lasting competitive advantage is knowledge. When markets shift, technologies proliferate, competitors multiply, and products become obsolete mostly overnight, successful companies are those that consistently create new knowledge, disseminate it widely throughout the organization, and quickly embody it in new technologies and products."*[2]

However, the creation of new technological know-how and knowledge which improves existing products and is supposed to give the inventing company a competitive edge on the market, necessitates considerable investment. On the other hand, technological assets represent intangible assets that generally show the qualities of *public goods* of non-rivalry, non-excludability, non-abrasion in use, and high fixed cost in production. These characteristics of immaterial valuables render the appropriation of the returns generated by these assets particularly difficult or even impossible.[3] As we know, companies will only invest in the creation of new information and knowledge if the marginal return on additional

---

[1] Cp. Teece, D. J. (2000); Teece, D. J. (2000a), chap. 1.

[2] Nonaka, I. (1991), p. 96.

[3] For a more detailed discussion of the public good characteristics of intangible assets and their influence on the appropriation of returns generated by these assets see chap. III.1.

knowledge exceeds or at least equals the marginal cost of production.[4] Hence, the higher the costs of production and appropriation of the returns the higher the marginal cost and thus the lower the overall output. Consequently, if companies cannot appropriate the returns of their immaterial assets, marginal returns are low and hence they will be reluctant to invest the resources necessary for their creation and in turn endanger the company's competitive advantage and thus survival in the long-term.

On the other hand, the increasing globalisation of the economy as a whole, the non-transferability of intangible assets across open markets that is due to the public good characteristics of these valuables, and the increasingly shorter product and technology life times create increasing interest of managers and scientists alike on multinational enterprises. The *multinationality of an enterprise* is perceived per se as a strategic advantage vis-à-vis competitors since it gives the company an advantage in recognising, seizing, and exploiting new innovative market based as well as technological trends in a multitude of different national and regional markets. Consequently, a company bestowed with an international organisational network is supposed to show advantages in acquiring and creating new know-how, knowledge, and competencies with respect to companies only active on a national or regional level.[5]

In the ongoing discussion of the economic role of intangible assets and the globalisation of the economy the aspect of the *international appropriation of economic returns* generated by intangible assets is at the centre of interest. Companies are reluctant to invest in the generation of intangible assets when a sufficient appropriation of the potential returns generated by these assets is not warranted. Therefore, the complete technological development would come to a complete halt if companies do not have the possibility to protect and thus exclude third parties from the use of their immaterial assets and consequently generate some economic returns that justify the initial investments. In the fundamental discussion of the possibility of companies to exclude actual and potential competitors from using their intangible achievements, authors have predominantly focused on the possibility to place legal patent rights which bestow the owner with a legal monopoly right on the use of the subject matter of the patent for a limited period of time. The growing awareness of the *inefficiencies of such patent rights* in the real world has encouraged the investigation of alternative protection modes with a mostly technological

---

[4] Cp. Magee, S. P. (1977).

[5] For a more detailed discussion of the advantages of multinational enterprises see chap. III.2 and IV.1.2.

focus, e.g., lead-time advantages or company specific complementary technological competencies. Alternatively, the investigation of the *role of company specific complementary market based assets* in the appropriation of the returns generated by intangible technological assets has, however, been almost entirely neglected, so far.

Our research was motivated by the insufficient investigation of the possibilities of how companies can ensure an efficient and effective appropriation of the returns of intangible technological assets which are broadly claimed to be of utmost importance for the continued existence of companies. Thus, our investigations intend to analyse the role of *market based assets*, and here in particular *brand equity*, in the appropriation of the returns generated by intangible *technological assets* in the long-term. Companies are recognising brand equity increasingly as a corporate asset of utmost strategic importance, where single brands can attain market values of a multiple of the companies' book values.[6] Hitherto, research in the field of brand equity has principally concentrated on the analysis of the role of brand equity for companies active in consumer goods markets, and has largely neglected to investigate the role brand equity plays in general, and in particular in the appropriation of economic returns for *technology intensive firms*. However, before entering the empirical and theoretical discussion of the role of brand equity in the sustained appropriation of the returns of intangible technological assets, we will further specify the problem investigated in our research work and in particular point out the role of intangible assets for business enterprises and the economy as a whole, as well as specify the problem of appropriation in chapter I.1 which is of central importance in the knowledge-base economy. Subsequently, we will specify our research focus and terminology used in our analysis in chapter I.2 before presenting the overall structure of the thesis in chapter I.3.

I.1 Problem Development

This section outlines the general field of intangible assets, their role in the economy in general, as well as for the individual business enterprise, and clearly specifies the problem of appropriation immanent to any immaterial technological asset. This problem is at the core of our research. Scientists such as List, Hayek, or Arrow have already perceived the *general*

[6] Cp. Hatch, M. J. & Schultz, M. (2001).

economic importance of immaterial valuables in the early 20th century.[7] Hayek, for example, pointed out in his studies the problem of the efficient utilisation of existing information and knowledge in society which are not concentrated in one single person but are rather dispersed over a large number of individuals.[8] Arrow, on the other hand, already stressed the difficulty of non-appropriability of the returns generated by intangible assets because of their public good characteristics which leads to an under-investment of the free economy in such assets.[9]

In the following sections we are going to point out the importance of immaterial assets which we consider to consist of information and knowledge, for the present economy and business enterprises.[10] We first analyse the transformation of the general economy towards a knowledge-based economy. Building on this general discussion the resulting consequences for business enterprises that result from the so called "third economic revolution" are depicted.

I.1.1 General Economic Significance of Intangible Assets

The late 19th and early 20th century were dominated by the industrial revolution which considerably augmented wealth in Europe due to increased productivity in industrial production. This increase in productivity had been, as discussed by Adam Smith in his famous book "The Wealth of Nations," rendered possible by the availability of new machines, the accumulation of specialised capabilities, and the opening of national markets which significantly lowered trade barriers.[11] Nowadays, the wealth of nations and entire regions depends increasingly on *accumulated knowledge and its effective and efficient utilisation.* As List already perceived in 1841, the national income does not only depend on

---

[7] Cp. Freeman & Soete (1997), chap. 2; Hayek, F.A. (1945); Arrow, K. J. (1962a, 1962b, 1969).

[8] "The economic problem of society is thus not merely a problem of how to allocate 'given' resources - if 'given' is taken to mean given to a single mind which deliberately solves the problem set by these 'data'. It is rather a problem of how to secure the best use of resources known to any of the members of society, for ends whose relative importance only these individuals know.", Vgl. Hayek, F.A. (1945), S. 519-520.

[9] Cp. Arrow, K. J. (1962a).

[10] For a detailed definition of the different forms of intangible valuables see in particular chap. III.1.

[11] Cp. Freeman, C. & Soete, L. (1997), chap. 2.

the employment of physical capital but also on the utilisation of the prevalent immaterial valuables:

> *"In opposing to this reasoning, Adam Smith has merely taken the word capital in that sense in which it is necessarily taken by renters or merchants in their book-keeping and their balance sheets. ... He has forgotten that he himself includes (in his definition of capital) the intellectual and bodily abilities of the producers under his term. He wrongly maintains that the revenues of the nation are dependent only on the sum of its material capital."*[12]

The importance of immaterial assets in the generation of revenues stressed by List has considerably increased since the mid 19th century. Today the access to scarce natural resources, e.g., coal, ore, or petrol, and to factors of production such as machines no longer has the central importance it had had at the beginning of the 20th century. Prices for raw materials have continuously declined throughout the past century and factors of production such as machines but also natural resources are globally available at constant quality and uniform competitive prices. In the 20th and 21st century which have been characterised by an increasing globalisation of the economy, the creation and utilisation of immaterial assets are of utmost importance in the determination of the wealth of nations.

These new insights have lead to so called "*new growth theory*," which does not perceive physical assets at the basis of national economic growth and national income, but rather knowledge and capabilities of the workforce of a country.[13] The appearance and increasing recognition of the new growth theory which reveals the formation of the workforce as the elementary factor in the determination of economic growth and wealth, have initiated a fundamental change in public policies in most industrialised and even developing countries.[14] Moreover, public authorities endeavour to warrant a sufficient supply of the economy with intangible technological assets.[15]

---

[12] Freeman, C. & Soete, L. (1997), p. 296.

[13] For a detailed discussion of immaterial assets in macro-economic growth theory see Romer, P. M (1986); Grossman, G. M. & Helpman, E. (1990), Stiglitz, J. E. (1999a).

[14] Cp. Dunning, J. H. (1994).

[15] For a detailed discussion of the role of public authorities in the generation of intangible assets and innovation see in particular Freeman, C. & Soete, L. (1997), chap. 16.

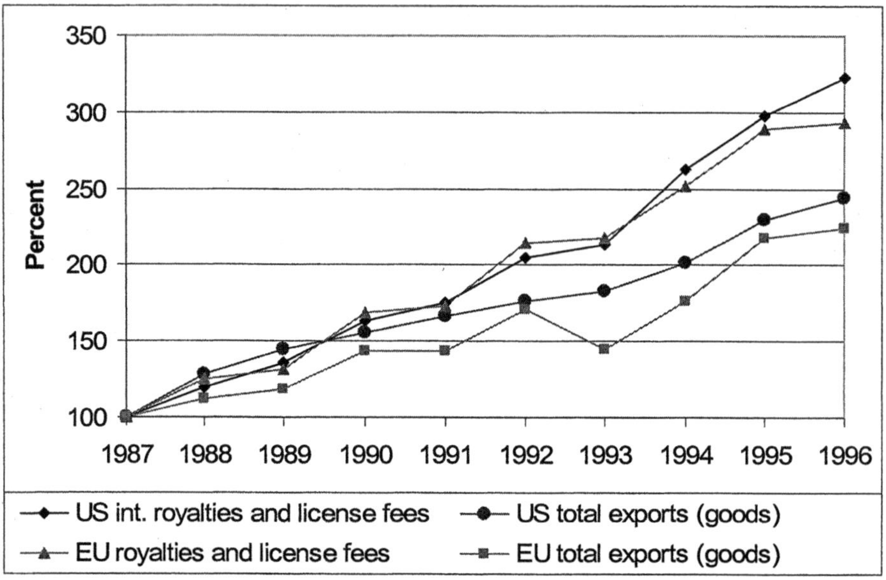

Source: OECD (1998).

Figure I.1: Development of the international trade in immaterial assets

This change towards a knowledge-based economy has not only become apparent on the national level, but has also a considerable influence at the level of business enterprises. The development of the international trade in immaterial assets has, for example, disproportionately increased with respect to the growth in the international trade in physical assets. As figure I.1 illustrates, income from royalties and licensing fees have risen in the US and EU between 1987 and 1996 by 222 and 192 percent, whereas income from exports of physical goods have only increased over the same period of time by 145 and 124 percent, respectively. Building on these general findings we discuss the role of intangible assets on the company level in the following section I.1.2.

I.1.2 Role of Intangible Assets in Business Enterprises and the Central Problem of Appropriation

The above described economic changes do not only influence the competition on a national or regional basis, but also considerably modify the global economic environment surrounding business companies. Consequently, the success of companies in the 21st century will no longer depend on the access to factors such as land, raw-materials, and physical capital but is rather determined by the effective and efficient generation, acquisition of new intangible assets and their profit maximising utilisation. As already pointed out above, natural resources and physical assets can be acquired on the global market at competitive prices and consequently these factors of production do no longer confer a company a defendable competitive advantage.

The success of companies is and will increasingly depend upon technical invention and innovation and hence on the generation, acquisition and utilisation of intangible asset such as knowledge, know-how, patents, trademarks, and information, for example. Moreover, the increasing economic globalisation, the ever faster technological development, as well as the appearance and establishment of new media such as the Internet have increased competition in most product markets over the past decades. The *Internet*, for example, enables companies to enter national markets and offer their products to a large number of consumers without even establishing a subsidiary. In addition, the Internet enables consumers to directly compare offers from different companies in various national markets and thus to choose the most attractive offer with search-costs that approach zero. If a company wants to remain successful in such globalised markets, characterised by fierce competition, shortening product- and technology-life-cycles, it has to *possess advantages and capabilities that are company specific and cannot be easily imitated, replicated, substituted or acquired* on the market by other companies.

As illustrated in figure I.2, the value of the immaterial assets of the selected companies outweighs by far the value of their physical capital as stated in the companies' balance sheet.[16] In the case of Yahoo, for example, a provider of Internet-portals and search machines, the market value of the company was in December 1998 5400% higher than the company's actual equity capital stated in the balance sheet. Even in the case of Cisco Systems the market value was still 20 times the company's stated equity capital and in the case of Bayer more than 50% of the company's market value can be attributed to the company's intangible holdings.[17]

[16] Cp. Hall, R. (1997); Sveiby, K. E. (1997), chap. 1.

[17] It has to taken into consideration that the actual market value of the company is also influenced by general disturbances. For a detailed discussion of the determination of the value of intangible assets see chap. III.1.

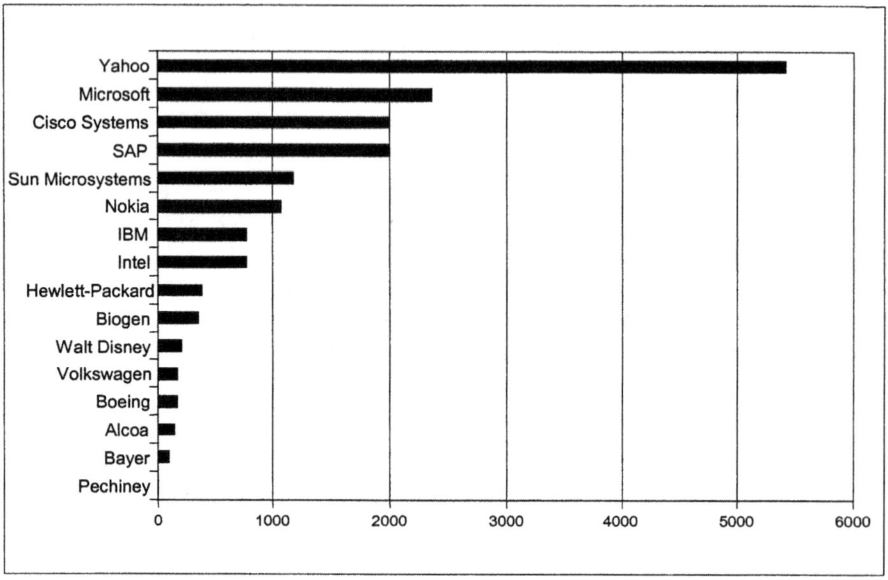

Source: Company reports; Hoover database (www.hoovers.com).

Figure I.2: Value of immaterial assets in business enterprises[18]

It is argued that company specific intellectual assets represent one possibility to establish a strategic advantage vis-à-vis competitors.[19] Such intangible valuables can, in general, not be acquired on an open market and, moreover, companies have to invest considerable resources in their creation. These immaterial assets show, however, the *characteristics of collective goods* which render the appropriation of the returns generated by these assets extremely difficult or even impossible. However, if companies cannot appropriate the returns of the intangible assets generated by considerable investments in R&D, for example, enterprises will be reluctant to invest private resources in their creation. Such an under-investment in the generation of intangible assets would, however, not only endanger the competitiveness of the individual company or national economy but would bring the whole economic development to a halt.

Thus, the appropriation of the returns is at the core of the discussion of the knowledge-based economy. The fundamental importance of the appropriation problem becomes particularly apparent by the considerable efforts of public authorities in *most nations to establish a system of*

[18] The bars indicate the value of the companies' intangible assets in relation to their equity capital indicated in the companies' balance sheet (fiscal year 1998). The relationship was calculated on the grounds of Dec. 1998 stock quotes.

[19] For a more detailed discussion see chap. III and IV.

intellectual property rights which has the aim to enable the inventor to appropriate a sufficient part of the returns generated by his invention in order to justify the extremely risky investments in the creation of new intangible assets. These intellectual property rights, e.g., patents and trademarks, bestow the owner with a legal monopoly over the covered intangible assets and thereby enable him to appropriate a better part of the returns generated by his immaterial assets. However, intellectual property rights in general and in particular patents with respect to intangible technological assets are not as effective in practice as is often believed in theory.[20]

Various authors have *heavily criticised the prevailing system of intellectual property rights* because of its limited effectiveness and the high costs of implementing and upholding protection. However, these authors have mostly regarded one isolated protection mode, e.g. patents, and did not take the complementary nature of the different existing protection modes available to companies into consideration.[21] In spite of the broad and fundamental critique on the current system of intellectual property rights, the considerable research on the effectiveness of patent right protection that revealed the insufficiency of patents in the protection of intangible technological assets,[22] and the ongoing discussion of the central importance of immaterial assets in generating competitive advantage, the *general problem of the appropriation of intangible assets has been largely neglected*, so far. Moreover, the past discussion on appropriation mostly focused on the protection of intangible assets by singular intellectual property right protection leading to an immediate economic return measured in monetary terms. However, in order to fully understand the problem of appropriation and thus to be able to efficiently and effectively appropriate the returns of intangible assets a more holistic view of the topic is needed. In our view appropriation is not only concerned with the protection of existing immaterial assets but, as described by Morin (1988), also includes the functions: optimisation, enrichment, stocktaking, evaluation, and supervision (cf. figure IV.6).[23]

Furthermore, the *complementary nature* of the different existing intellectual property rights as well as alternative modes of protection have to be taken into consideration if a company wants to ensure the effective

---

20 For a detailed discussion of the different intellectual property rights and their shortcomings see chap. III.3.

21 Cp. Erickson, G. & Jacobson, R. (1992), Thurow, L. C. (1997).

22 See in particular chap. I.2.1 and III.3.

23 For a more detailed description of the model established by Morin (1988) see chap. IV.1.2.1.

appropriation of the returns of its intangible technological assets in the long-term. Thus, as described above and discussed in detail in chapters III and IV, a company may fail to recuperate its investments made in new product and process technologies and/or may not be able to benefit of the invention in the long-run by merely considering patent right protection in its technological management.

Consequently we can claim, if intangible assets are a '*company's most valuable asset*,' as stated by Steward (1994), a company has to ensure an efficient and effective protection of its immaterial valuables that enables it to appropriate the returns generated by these assets in the long-run.

I.2 Field of Investigation and Terminological Specification

As outlined above, the appropriation of returns generated by immaterial valuables is central to the discussion of intangible assets as an economic resource. If companies cannot appropriate the returns of their intangible valuables they are not prepared to invest the considerable resources necessary for their creation. Such an under-investment would not only reduce the competitiveness of the individual firm, but would also considerably slow down or even bring to a complete halt the general economic development. Consequently, legal authorities have established a system of intellectual property rights in order to enable innovative companies to appropriate, at least in theory, a better part of the returns generated by their intangible assets. These intellectual property rights show, however, in reality considerable shortcomings in the protection of intangible technological assets. Various investigations in the past revealed, on the one hand, the significant importance of patent protection in appropriating the returns generated by the use of the subject matter of the patent. On the other hand, the investigations pointed out major shortcomings of patent protection which severely limit the possibility to generate sufficient economic returns in order to justify the investments necessary to generate intangible technological assets.

In the following section we will briefly summarise the findings of previous investigations of the relationship between patent rights and innovative efforts and the effectiveness of patent right protection in appropriating the returns of a technical invention in the long-term. Even though the findings of the mostly econometric investigations have revealed considerable limitations and deficiencies of patent right protection in assuring the appropriation of the returns, most studies have merely concentrated on patent protection as the only effective means to appropriate the returns. Building on the results of these investigations on the effectiveness of patents in enabling a company to appropriate the returns of the investments in new intangible technological assets, we present and discuss the findings of the rare investigations which have analysed the role of complementary market based assets, and particularly brand equity, in the appropriation of the returns of intangible technological assets. The discussion of previous research work will help us to further specify the research focus of our work that will be pointed out in detail in section I.2.2. Finally, we give some terminological definitions and specifications in section I.2.3 which have the aim to facilitate and clarify our subsequent discussions.

I.2.1 Survey of Previous Research Work in the Field of Appropriating Intangible Assets and the Role of Brand Equity

The protection of intangible technological assets with the aim to exclude other companies of the use of knowledge in question and thus to appropriate a better part of the returns generated by the utilisation of the knowledge, as well as the output measurement of companies' innovative activities have been subject to a multitude of investigations.[24] These analyses have, however, generally focused only on patent right protection and *entirely neglected other alternative and complementary modes of protection*. In addition to the disregard of alternative protection modes and the resulting singular inspection of the relationship between the input variable 'R&D expenditures' and the output variable 'patent filings,' most studies entirely neglected the facts that not all intangible technological innovations are patentable, and neither are all patented innovations economically useful nor do they guarantee their legal owners a perfect appropriation of the returns.[25]

Nevertheless, past analyses revealed a strong correlation between companies' R&D expenditures and patent filings. Econometric investigations such as Pakes & Griliches (1984), or Bound, Cummins et al. (1984) revealed a *strong and significant relationship between companies'*

[24] Cp. Kamien, M. I. & Schwartz, N. L. (1974); Kitch, E. W. (1977); Pavitt, K. (1982); Griliches, Z. (1984); Mansfield E. (1986); Basberg, B. L. (1987); Narin, F., Noma, E. et al. (1987); Cockburn, I. & Griliches, Z. (1988); Griliches, Z. (1990); Caves, R. E., Whinston, M. D. et al. (1991); Berkowitz, L. (1993); Patel, P. & Pavitt, K. (1995); Almeida, P. (1996); Ernst, H. (1998).

[25] For a more detailed discussion of the patentability of innovations and quality of patents see chap. III.

R&D expenditures and patent filings. Moreover, Griliches & Mairesse (1984), Griliches (1984b), and Clark & Griliches (1984) have revealed a positive link between a company's R&D investments and its productivity growth, as well as market value. These results indicate that a company's investments into R&D activities can be valued as investments into intangible assets which are subsequently protected by patent rights.

The findings of Mansfield, Schwartz et al. (1981) and Levin, Klevorick et al. (1987) on the effectiveness of patents in protecting technological innovations and companies' choice of preferred protection mode have, however, been largely ignored in the discussion of the appropriation of the returns of intangible technological assets. The econometric investigations of Mansfield, Schwartz et al. (1981) revealed that although patents are deemed to significantly increase imitation costs, with considerable variations between the different industries, 60% of the patented innovations in the sample had been *imitated within 4 years* after their introduction. Accordingly, Levin, Klevorick et al. (1987) and Arundel & Kabla (1998) have shown in their analyses that even though companies assume patents to considerably increase imitation cost in most industries, patent protection is perceived as *least efficient protection mode* in the case of process innovations. Furthermore, although product patents were found to be significantly more efficient as product patents, companies still regarded lead-time, learning curve, and sales and service efforts as more effective protection mechanisms as patent rights. Accordingly, Arundel & Kabla (1998) have stated:

> *"Patents are relatively unimportant compared to alternative appropriation methods such as lead time advantages or technical complexity in sectors that produce complex products that are costly to copy, or where high investment costs and expertise levels create entry barriers that limit competition from new entrants, such as in aerospace."*[26]

Nevertheless, it has to be recalled that considerable differences in the effectiveness of patents prevail with respect to the industry in question, type of innovation, as well as national origin of the company.[27]

Hence, these studies have clearly shown that the singular consideration of patent rights in the protection of immaterial technological assets *cannot be regarded as sufficient*. Although the results of the independently performed investigations are significant and coincide, they have been largely ignored in the discussion of the strategic importance of intangible

[26] Arundel, A. & Kabla, I. (1998), p. 129.
[27] Cp. Levin, R. C., Klevorick, A. K. et al. (1987); Arundel, A. & Kabla, I. (1998).

assets. Moreover, the role of *complementary market based assets*, such as brand equity, distribution channels, etc., in the protection and appropriation of the intangible technological assets have been mostly neglected, so far. On the other hand, a vast discussion of the strategic importance of market based assets and in particular brand equity has evolved over the past years largely independent of the technology management discussion.[28] Only very few authors have seen some *coherence between the topics of brand equity and technology management*.[29] Pettis (1995a), for example, clearly pointed out the strategic importance of market based assets and in particular brand equity for companies active in technology based industries.

Although brand equity is nowadays perceived as one of the most valuable assets of companies, and especially the *brands of technological companies* which are among the most valuable brands of the world,[30] the investigation of the potential relationship between technological proficiency and brand equity has been almost entirely disregarded, so far. In particular the role of market based assets in the protection of existent idiosyncratic intangible technological assets, as well as in their generation and acquisition has, hitherto, been largely ignored. Up to now, *only one empirical investigation* of the potential link between technological innovation and trademark protection has been carried out by Allegrezza & Guarda-Rauchs (1999) which has revealed promising results.

The *econometric analysis of Allegrezza & Guarda-Rauchs (1999)* is based upon survey data collected in 1996 for the Benelux Trademarks Office (BTO). The data set includes the responses of some 1600 companies headquartered either in Belgium, Netherlands, or Luxembourg and focused in particular on *small and medium sized companies*. With the available data the authors performed a logit multiple regression analysis with the aim to explore on an ad hoc basis the factors influencing a firm's decision to file for trademark registration at the BTO. The results indicate, among other things, a positive and statistically significant correlation between the dependent variable trademark deposits and the firm's size, its

[28] See in particular Aaker, D. A. (1989, 1991, 1992, 1996, 1997); Kapferer, J. N. & Thoening, J. C. (1994); Richards, I, Foster, D. et al. (1998); Srivastava, R. K., Shervani, T. A. et al. (1998); Farquhar, P. H. (1989); Geobbels, R. (1997, 1998); Kapferer, J. N. (1999); Interbrand, (1999a); Esch, F. R. (2000).

[29] See particularly Pettis, C. R. (1995a, 1995b); Tibesar, A. (1996, 1997, 1998); Goebbels, R. (1998); Allegrezza, S. & Guarda-Rauchs, A. (1999).

[30] Cp. Badenhausen, K. (1996); Interbrand (1999); Khermouch, H., Holmes, S. et al. (2001).

R&D efforts and belief in its competitors' ability to imitate its products, as well as the company's export orientation.[31]

Thus, the findings of the econometric analysis have clearly shown a link between a company's investments in R&D, and consequently in the generation of new technological assets, the inventing companies' concern about the ready ability of competitors to imitate its products, and the likelihood to file for trademark registration. Nevertheless, the investigation of Allegrezza & Guarda-Rauch (1999) shows considerable shortcomings and limitations because of the *lack of an appropriate theoretical framework* underlying the econometric investigations and the *structure of the data set*. The data only considered small and medium sized companies of the Benelux countries and, in addition, only contained binary data indicating if a company had filed for trademark registration during the investigated period or if the company had undertaken some investments in R&D. However, no analysis of the direct correlation between the absolute figures of the companies R&D expenditures and trademark filings, indicating if higher R&D expenditures lead to higher trademark filings, has been undertaken.

I.2.2 Main Focus of the Thesis

Building on the existing frameworks of technology management and brand equity and the concepts of intangible assets, we further investigate the interplay between intangible technological assets and brand equity, and in particular the *role brand equity plays in appropriating the returns generated by a company's specific intangible assets* which has been almost entirely neglected, so far. In particular our research sets out to analyse the strategic role of brand equity in complementing patent right protection of innovative technological assets and hence in enabling a company to effectively appropriate the returns of its intangible valuables in the long-term. However, we largely omit the ongoing discussion of auditing intangible assets in business enterprises for management control motives and concentrate on the appropriation of intangible technological assets.[32]

In this respect, we do not perceive the term 'appropriation' as merely protecting already existing intangible technological assets and seizing of the current economic returns, but rather take a holistic view[33] of the term

[31] Cp. Allegrezza, S. & Guarda-Rauchs, A. (1999).

[32] See Eggington, D. A. (1990); Brooking, A. (1996, 1997); Edvinsson, L. & Malone, M. S. (1997); Srivastava, R. K., Shervani, T. A. et al. (1998).

[33] See for a detailed discussion of the holistic view of the term appropriation chap. IV.1.2.1.

including the role of currently existing intangible technological, as well as market based assets in the generation and acquisition of new and the protection of existing technological assets. This investigation necessitates a detailed analysis of the characteristics and the different types of intangible assets, as well as the various sources of immaterial technological assets. Thereby we base our work on already existing frameworks which we further develop and specify. Building on this initial step we develop and establish a theoretical model of complementary brand equity in the appropriation of the returns of companies' intangible technological assets.

In order not to diverge into other interesting fields not directly related to our research focus, we will formulate a core research-question specifying our exact research intent. The *central research question* of our investigation is:

> *Which relationships exist between a company's brand equity and its technological proficiency and how does established brand equity influence a company's ability to appropriate the returns generated by its current and future intangible technological assets and hence which strategic role does brand equity play in complementing patent right protection for intangible technological assets?*

The above stated core research-question can be decomposed in four basic questions. Thus, according to our core research-question the investigation has the aim to reveal: 1) the *role of intangible technological assets* and the *efficient and effective appropriation of their economic returns* in order to ensure the success of technology based companies; 2) the importance of *market based brand equity in enabling technology based companies* in *effectively appropriating the returns of existing intangible technological assets*; 3) how technology based companies *build new and foster existing brand equity* and the role of companies' technological competencies in this process; and 4) the *contribution of existing brand equity to companies' ability to uphold and/or build new technological competencies*. These questions and the general assumptions drawn from the analysis of previous empirical investigations, as well as theoretical discussions lead to our general research hypothesis:

> *Established market based brand equity which can efficiently be built with the help of a company's specific technological capabilities, gives the company a strategic advantage vis-à-vis competitors not having established brand equity at its disposal and thus enables the company to better appropriate the returns generated by its intangible technological assets.*

These central questions, of which further basic questions can be deduced, as well as the general research hypothesis guide our research and thus should be kept in mind throughout our work. Moreover, the aim of these research-guiding questions is to *limit our field of investigation* in order to allow for a thorough analysis and not to slide into other, although not less interesting fields of research. Thus, as can be deduced from the central research questions, the unit of investigation is the *company level*, where we focus our analysis on the role of *brand equity* in the appropriation of the returns of *intangible technological assets*. Consequently, we are aiming to unveil the role of brand equity in dependence of a company's technological expertise and hence do *not* endeavour to examine the role of brand equity in companies not active in *technology based industries*. Furthermore, the starting point of our investigation presents a technological advantage of a company and hence, special attention is paid on how companies can achieve an efficient and effective appropriation of the returns of these technological assets in the long-run. As a consequence, we analyse the role brand equity plays in the appropriation of the returns of technological assets and how companies can build brand equity with the help of technological assets and thus largely neglect other, perhaps not less important initial sources of brand equity, e.g., marketing expenditures, entrepreneurial luck, etc.

I.2.3 Terminological Specification

Our investigation builds upon the research findings presented in section I.2.1 and will expand the discussion of the appropriation of intangible technological assets by the aspects of brand equity. In order to facilitate and clarify our discussion, as well as to enable us to classify our work within the ongoing discussions in the field of strategic and technological management, this section specifies some terms of fundamental importance for the upcoming discussion. However, this section is kept very brief since most definitions evolve from our theoretical discussions in chapters III and IV, where they are discussed in greater depth.

Our theoretical discussion of the appropriation of economic returns stemming from intangible technological assets builds upon the *resourced based view*. The resource based view defines a company resource as anything that represents a *strength or weakness* of a company.[34] Barney (1991) more clearly defines a *strategic resource* according to four attributes:

> "... *a firm resource must have four attributes: (a) it must be valuable, in the sense that it exploits opportunities and/or neutralizes threats in a firm's environment, (b) it must be rare among a firm's current and*

[34] Cp. Wernerfelt, B. (1984).

> *potential competition, (c) it must be imperfectly imitable, and (d) there cannot be strategically equivalent substitutes for this resource that are valuable but neither rare or imperfectly imitable."*[35]

These attributes which equally apply to physical as well as immaterial resources of a company, do also determine the *strategic importance* of resources. However, until further specification of the term strategic importance and strategic resource in chapter IV the above presented definition of Barney is used.

Moreover, the discussion of a companies' *competencies* has obtained an increasing importance in the strategic and technology management literature. Unfortunately no universal and uniform definition of the term has been established yet, but rather diverse interpretations are used in the literature. Even though we have tried to minimise the use of the term 'competence' we cannot completely avoid its utilisation in our discussion. This is in particular due to the close interrelation between the terms competence and *knowledge* which will be defined and discussed in detail in chapter III. Thus, in order to clarify our discussion we establish in this section a working-definition of the term competence which is used coherently in the subsequent chapters. However, we do not establish a definition of the term competence that is independent of the definitions established before and hence do not contribute to the diversity of existing definitions, but rather adopt the definition established by Sanchez & Heene. Accordingly, Durand & Guerra-Vieira (1997) have stated:

> *"By competence, we thus mean not only all forms of available assets, capabilities and knowledge, know how and skills, technologies and equipment in the organization, as most of the existing literature would suggest, but also the coordinated deployment of the above assets and capabilities."*[36]

Although the definition of the term competence may seem at this point of the discussion as somehow isolated, the centrality of the term competence will become clearer in the subsequent chapters. Furthermore, by establishing a clear and uniform definition in an early phase of our discussion we hope to obviate any confusion and facilitate our argumentation.

Concerning the terms '*brand equity*' and '*appropriation*,' which are of central importance to our discussion, no coherent and precise definitions have yet been established. Thus, our theoretical discussion tries to

---

[35] Barney, J. (1991), pp 105-106.

[36] Durand, T. & Guerra-Vieira, S. (1997), p. 81 and cp. Sanchez, R. & Heene, A. (1997).

establish a general definition of the term brand equity and further elucidate what should be understood under the term appropriation in chapter III and IV. However, in order to facilitate the upcoming theoretical discussion, as well as to avoid confusion and misinterpretation of the upcoming empirical analysis, the *definition of brand* equity established by Richards, Foster et al. (1998) is used which perceives a brand as:

> *"...a part of our lives, where its personality represents a promise and a set of values that are supported by benefits, features and functions that deliver that promise."*[37]

Hence, until further specification, the term brand equity summarises any association people in general hold about a certain name or trademark. These associations are built by the specific characteristics of the products and services to which the name has been attached and furthermore, people perceive the name as a promise of the products and services related to the specific name to meet these associations. Consequently, brand equity is not only the legal right to use a name in one's business but moreover includes any associations, feelings, etc. people attach to the specific name or trademark.

Finally, regarding the term *appropriation*, the discussion adopts the perception of Tidd, Bessant et al. (1997), who perceive appropriation as a firm's *capacity to benefit commercially* of its investment in technology.[38] Chapter IV then tries to enlarge this perspective and establish a more holistic view of the term appropriation that better accounts for its strategic role.

I.3 Research Structure

The book is structured into 6 chapters (cf. figure I.3) which gradually work their way down to a model of complementary brand equity for the sustained appropriation of intangible technological assets, with a final empirical investigation of the most important theoretical assumptions, as well as a first econometric investigation of an integrated form of the established model in chapter V. Chapter I gives an introduction to the general field of appropriation, presents the most important studies undertaken in the specific field, depicts the insufficiencies of the current status-quo of scientific research, and points out the main research focus of our investigation.

---

[37] Richards, I., Foster, D. et al. (1998), p. 47.

[38] See in particular Tidd, J., Bessant, J. et al. (1997), chap. 4.3.

Chapter II outlines the strategic role of brand equity on the basis of the case examples Bayer-Aspirin and Cisco Systems. The two case studies have the aim to introduce into the field and further clarify the intent of our research by presenting some initial empirical evidence. The two cases are meant to complement each other. Whereas the case Bayer-Aspirin points out in detail the changing strategic role of brand equity in the pharmaceutical, and in particular in the over-the-counter drugs industry, over a period of more than 100 years, the case Cisco Systems focuses on the strategic role of brand equity in a fast-cycle industry, characterised by business-to-business relations, and where merely 10 years of historical track are available. Both case examples, also placed in distinct industries and depicting different time periods, clearly stress the utmost strategic importance of brand equity in appropriating returns initially generated by technological assets. Moreover, the subsequent theoretical chapters refer to the case examples presented in detail in chapter II in order to illustrate and clarify the theoretical discussion.

The subsequent theoretical chapter III is divided in three principal subchapters. Chapter III.1 points out the particular characteristics and establishes a clear-cut definition of the different forms of immaterial assets which has the objective to facilitate and clarify the discussion. The second subchapter aims at indicating the major sources of intangible technological assets in business enterprises. This discussion primarily focuses on the generation of intangible assets by R&D and learning-by-doing, the external sources of licensing and M&A activity, as well as by co-operative forms of immaterial asset generation, e.g., informal knowledge trading.

Finally, the last subchapter of chapter III points out the most important protection modes of intangible assets. Herein we differentiate between legal modes of protection, e.g., patent rights, trademarks, as well as petty-patents, and further possibilities of protection which are of more organisational nature, e.g., trade secrecy, lead-time advantages and complementary resources. Section III.3.1 points out the major differences between trademarks and brand equity and gives a brief definition of brand equity which will clarify the argumentation of the subsequent chapter IV.

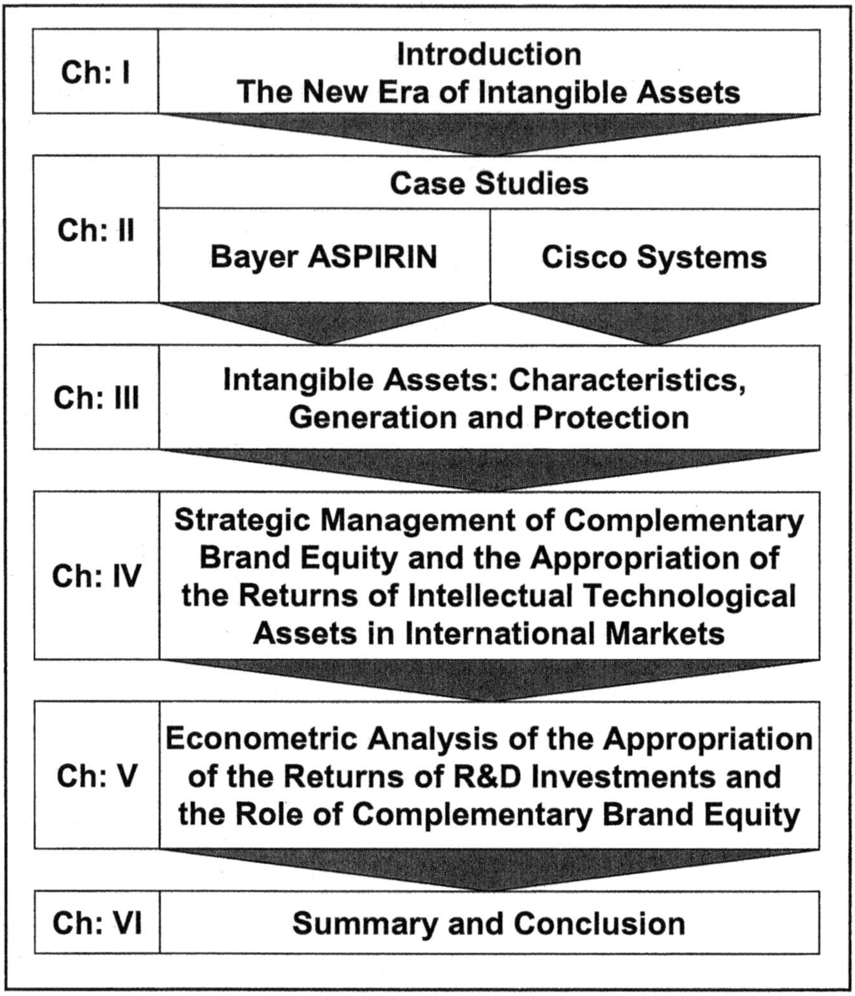

Figure I.3: Overall structure

Chapter IV which is subdivided in four principal sections, takes a strategic regard on intangible assets and in particular brand equity. After a general discussion of the strategic role of intangible technological assets, as well as central problems of these assets in generating a competitive advantage in chapter IV.1, chapter IV.2 points out the important role of complementary brand equity in protecting intangible technological assets, as well as in appropriating the returns of these assets in the long-run. The theoretical discussion of chapter IV.1 and IV.2, as well as of chapter III, in combination with the initial empirical findings of chapter II lead to the formation of a general model of complementary brand equity for the sustained appropriation of intangible technological assets in chapter IV.3. This model integrates the findings of the previous chapters and points out the strategic role of complementary brand equity in the appropriation of the returns of intangible technological assets along the technology-life-cycle. Section IV.4 touches upon the topic of how companies can allocate responsibility for brand equity and technological assets in order to ensure its efficient management. Moreover, the subchapter points out the principal organisational forms of how companies can allocate brand equity and technology responsibility and align the strategies across the business unit and product division level. Finally, the balanced scorecard concept is further develop so as to allow for an integration of the company's brand equity and technological visions at the process level.

Chapter V is organised in 4 subchapters and envisages the econometric investigation of the theoretical foundations established in chapters III and IV, as well as presents an initial attempt to statistically verify the model of complementary band equity established in chapter IV.3. In chapter V.1 the methodological proceeding and the major sources of data, as well as their ascertainment are pointed out. The subsequent chapter V.2 then presents the findings of our descriptive and econometric investigations that are discussed in chapter V.3. Although a comprehensive and full verification of the established model has been limited by problems of operationalisation and the lack of precise and comparable data, the analysis represents the most extensive econometric investigation exploring the relationship between technological invention and market based assets. Thus, even though the econometric investigation cannot verify the established model per se, it nevertheless considerably contributes to the general understanding of the relationship between technological and market based intellectual property rights and verifies central theoretical assumptions underlying the model of complementary brand equity. Thus, chapter V establishes a sound foundation of econometric evidence in the field of complementary brand equity on which further theoretical as well as empirical research can be built.

The book closes in the final chapter VI with a comprehensive discussion of our general research findings and indication of the results' impact on research and practice. Moreover, the chapter points out the scope and need of further research in the general field of brand equity and in particular with respect to the role of brand equity in the appropriation of returns of intangible technological assets.

II Case Studies on the Appropriation of Intellectual Assets

This section studies two specific cases with the aim to clarify the exact focus of our research and exemplify the strategic role brand equity plays in technology intensive industries. Consequently, the case examples should not be perceived as means of validating a certain theory nor as a description of the particularities of the pharmaceutical Bayer Aspirin or the company Cisco Systems, but rather as an important initial empirical example specifying the question of the strategic role of brand equity in technology based industries and thus clarifying our research intent. Thus, the case studies represent a central initial step in our theory-building process. Moreover, the two cases contribute to the development of an approach which explains the general strategic importance of brand equity in the appropriation of the revenues generated by certain technological innovations in the long-term. Although the two cases are situated in two distinctively different industries and both case studies focus on different time periods, they show considerable convergence with respect to the importance of company specific technological capabilities in building brand equity and subsequently the role of existing brand equity in the companies' competitive positioning in the market in question.

Before presenting the empirical analysis we first clarify our methodological proceeding in the two cases in section II.1, e.g., choice of cases and data ascertainment, as well as validity and reliability of the results and hence if our findings can be generalised. The subsequent sections II.2 and II.3 present and discuss the results of the investigations. It should be kept in mind that both analyses represent descriptive case studies unfolding a sequence of specific occurrences within a certain period of time. The last section of chapter II opposes the two cases, analyses if the research hypotheses are confirmed or rather vitiated by the case results, and discusses general findings which clarify the subsequent theoretical discussions presented in chapter III and IV.

II.1 Methodology of the Case Studies

II.1.1 Choice of Case Examples

Our research has the intent to analyse in detail the role of brand equity in the appropriation of returns of investments in R&D that has so far been neglected in the ongoing discussion of strategic management of technology, wherein the aspect of appropriation is of central importance. In this context the choice of case examples has the objective to present *polar cases* which depict extreme circumstances that constantly accentuate the point of interest. Accordingly, Eisenhardt (1989) has pointed out:

> *"The cases may be chosen to replicate previous cases or extend emergent theory, or they may be chosen to fill theoretical categories and provide examples of polar types. While the cases may be chosen randomly, random selection is neither necessary, nor even preferable. ... given the limited number of cases which can usually be studied, it makes sense to choose cases such as extreme situations and polar types in which the process of interest is 'transparently observable.' Thus, the goal of theoretical sampling is to choose cases which are likely to replicate or extend the emerging theory."*[1]

Consequently, a deliberate selection of extreme cases which draws attention to a special phenomenon that cannot be sufficiently explained by existing concepts, has to be preferred to a random choice of empirical examples. With regard to our special research focus, the cases Bayer Aspirin and Cisco Systems are two extreme examples which vividly point out the strategic importance of brand equity in appropriating the returns of technological innovations in the long-run. Bayer Aspirin has the special advantage of analysing an extremely long history of more than 100 years, as well as the extreme accentuation of the brand immanent advantages of a pharmaceutical not only sold as an ethical but also as an over the counter (OTC) drug. Moreover, due to the expropriation of the Bayer AG in various nations due to German warfare in World War I and II and the subsequent vanishing of the trademark Bayer Aspirin in several national markets, or the continuation of the trademark by another company provide good insight into general aspects of brand management, as well as the importance of established brand equity in Bayer's present Aspirin business. On the other hand, Cisco System is an example where no long historical track is available and which is, in contrast to Bayer Aspirin, located in a fast-cycle industry characterised by business-to-business relations. Nonetheless, the case Cisco Systems imposingly illustrates the central role of brand equity and idiosyncratic technological strengths not only as a substantial market entry barrier for potential competitors, but also as an important asset in the acquisition of new, highly skilled employees. Thus, the two cases do not only present two polar cases but, in addition, complement each other with regard to the period, as well as the industry of

[1] Eisenhardt, K. M. (1989), p. 537.

investigation. This has the aim to strengthen validity and allow for generalisation on a high conceptual level.[2]

The choice of the two case examples was based on a certain prior theoretical knowledge about the exact field of investigation. According to Yin (1994) such prior understanding of theoretical knowledge is needed in the choice of adequate case studies. The prior theoretical understanding has been established by reviewing previous research and focusing of the thesis which has led to the establishment of a central research guiding question.[3] Building on this knowledge we can deduce from our core research question and general research hypothesis of chapter I, several research hypotheses with the aim to keep our attention during the case-study investigations on those fields that are central to our research, to structure and guide information ascertainment, in particular with regard to expert inquiry, as well as to clarify our field of investigation in the subsequent case studies and thus facilitate the appraisal of the collected information. The research theses of chapter II are:

1. A company can efficiently and effectively establish brand equity with the help of company specific technological advantages that create a perceivable consumer benefit.
2. Existing brand equity bestows the company with a sustainable advantage which continues to exist even though the initial technological advantage has been lost due to successful imitation of competitors.
3. Incremental improvements of the technology and adaptations of the product's characteristics which create a perceivable improvement of consumer utility, influences consumers' associations and thus reinforce and/or alter existing brand equity.
4. Existing brand equity bestows a company with considerable advantages with respect to the recruitment of new, highly skilled employees, as well as in accessing alternative sources of technological knowledge external to the company in question.
5. Existing brand equity can effectively be used by the company in question to attain advantages in related fields of technology and client relationships.

II.1.2 Data Ascertainment and Specific Sources of Information

In the investigation various different sources of information have been used, whereof the most important has been semi-structured face-to-face

[2] Cp. Eisenhardt, K. M. (1989).
[3] Cp. Yin, R. K. (1994), chap. 1 and 2.

and telephone interviews with various employees of the companies, as well as of external organisations knowledgeable about the case in question.[4] These interviews took place during the period from May 2000 to August 2001 and lasted between 60 to 150 minutes, each. The individual questioning was prepared beforehand and a questionnaire was established which had the aim to guide and structure the interview and thus prevent a digression of the interview in other attention-grabbing topics not directly related to our research. In certain cases interviewees entirely refused to answer or give detailed information about a certain question. In these cases we proceeded with the next question. The principal aim of the multiple questionings which sometimes treated identical topics, had been to obtain different perspectives and opinions of various experts about the issue and thus to acquire a broad understanding of the case in question. Moreover, for each case example one interview partner, with an extensive knowledge about the specific case, agreed to verify the accuracy and truthfulness of the information given in the final study.[5]

Other important sources of information represented scientific and general publications in related fields, as well as documents which the companies put to our disposition. The most important secondary sources represented company and/or product biographies (e.g., Mann, C. D. & Plummer, M. L. (1991); Bunnel, D. (2000)), annual reports, and Internet pages about the company and/or product in question. Information stemming from secondary sources are marked and specified in the case studies.

II.1.3 Methodological Proceeding and Validity of Case Studies

The analysis of the information gained through face-to-face and telephone interviews started by a detailed transcription of the results within four days after the interview. However, as Yin (1994) pointed out, such information gained through interviews can be subject to problems of bias, poor recall, and poor or inaccurate articulation.[6] Thus, we have opposed the information gained through the individual interviews as well as with

[4] A total of 9 interviews with 10 interviewees of different organisations have been conducted.

[5] In the case of Bayer Aspirin Mr. Chmilewski, Bayer Marketing Europe, and in the case of Cisco Systems Mr. Zapp, Marketing Director Europe, reviewed the specific case.

[6] Cp. Parkhe, A. (1993), p. 249.

information from secondary sources.[7] The *triangulation* of information clearly revealed a convergence of the statements with respect to our subject of investigation. Moreover, by comparing information of different source of evidence stronger substantiation of our findings has been achieved.

The overall quality of any empirical analysis, and thus of case study research, is generally determined by the two criteria of validity and reliability.[8] The validity criteria can be further distinguished into construct, internal, and external validity. To meet the test of *construct validity* a precise research focus has to be established and the correct variables of investigation have to be determined. *External validity* is, on the other hand, achieved when the results of a case investigation can be generalised. *Internal validity* is given when all relevant factors determining a certain outcome have been included in the research design. Finally, the test of *reliability* in the context of case study research is passed if later investigators, following exactly the same research procedures in conducting the same case study as an earlier researcher, attains the same results and conclusions as the initial investigator. Thus, in order to achieve reliability the researcher has to document as thoroughly as possible the process followed in his investigation.

In the subsequent case studies we have tried to comply the tests of validity and reliability by establishing a clear research focus and formulation of research hypotheses building on the specification of our research in chapter I. Moreover, by using multiple sources of evidence we ensured not to omit important variables and factors, or even investigate variables that are not important for our investigation.[9] Last but not least, in order to attain reliability we conducted two extensive case investigations, documented all conducted interviews, and archived the protocols, as well as any other company document or article. Information from secondary sources are marked in the cases and the exact source specified in the respective footer.

Nevertheless, case study research does only represent one of several different approaches to theory development and testing. Accordingly, Parkhe (1993) stated:

> "*... no single approach to theory development, including case studies, is self-sufficient and capable of producing a well-routed theory that simultaneously maximises the research quality criteria of construct*

[7] This comparison of information of different sources is called *triangulation*. Cp. Eisenhardt, K. M. (1989); Parkhe, A. (1993); Yin, R. K. (1994), chap. 4.

[8] Yin, R. K. (1994), chap. 2.

[9] Cp. Eisenhardt, K. M. (1989).

> *validity, internal validity, external validity, and reliability. It was therefore argued earlier that the various approaches to theory development in our typology complement and reinforce each other."*

Therefore, we examine our initial results and conclusions drawn form the case studies, as well as further theoretical developments outlined in the subsequent chapter III and IV by a final extensive econometric analysis in chapter V. By doing so we aspire to further increase validity and reliability of our empirical investigations and thus substantiate our theoretical elaboration on the relationship between technological strengths and market based brand equity.[10]

II.2 Case-Study: Bayer Aspirin

II.2.1 Company and Product Profile

Bayer AG, established in 1863 by Friedrich Bayer and Johan Weskott, represents one of the early German dye companies which successfully extracted natural dyes during the second half of the nineteenth century. Around 1880 Bayer AG (officially known at that time under the name 'Farbenfabriken vormals Friedrich Bayer & Co.') experienced an economic downturn because of competitors' ability to easily invent around the subject matter of existing patents. This was primarily due to a peculiarity of the German patent law that enabled an inventor to only protect the production process but not the product itself by patent right. Consequently, Bayer was forced by the mounting competition in the dyestuff industry to diversify in other related industries. Duisberg, who was at that time head of Bayer's research and patent program, decided to expand the company's business into pharmaceuticals. In 1888 Bayer's researchers were successful in turning para-nitrophenol, a waste product of the company's dye manufacturing, into acetophenetidin, a fever and pain reducing drug, sold under the trademark 'Phenacetin'. It was the first time that a private business had conceived, developed, tested, and marketed a pharmaceutical and thus marked the outset of the modern drug industry.[11] A few years later, in 1899, Bayer launched a new pharmaceutical under the

---

[10] "Perhaps 'grand' theory requires multiple studies – an accumulation of both theory-building and theory testing empirical studies." Eisenhardt, K. M. (1989), p. 547.

[11] Cp. Mann, C. C. & Plummer, M. L. (1991), chap. 1; Freeman, C. & Soete, L. (1997), chap. 4.

generic name Aspirin.[12] This pharmaceutical which later turned out to be 'the pharmaceutical of the 20th century,' is nowadays not only sold as an ethical drug in the field of the prevention of second heart attack and stroke, but also as an analgesic OTC drug known in most countries in the world.

At present, the Bayer AG is an international chemicals and healthcare company employing some 120,000 people world-wide. Total group sales amounted to some US$ 14 billion in fiscal year 1999, whereof approximately 50% were attained within Europe and 30% in North America.

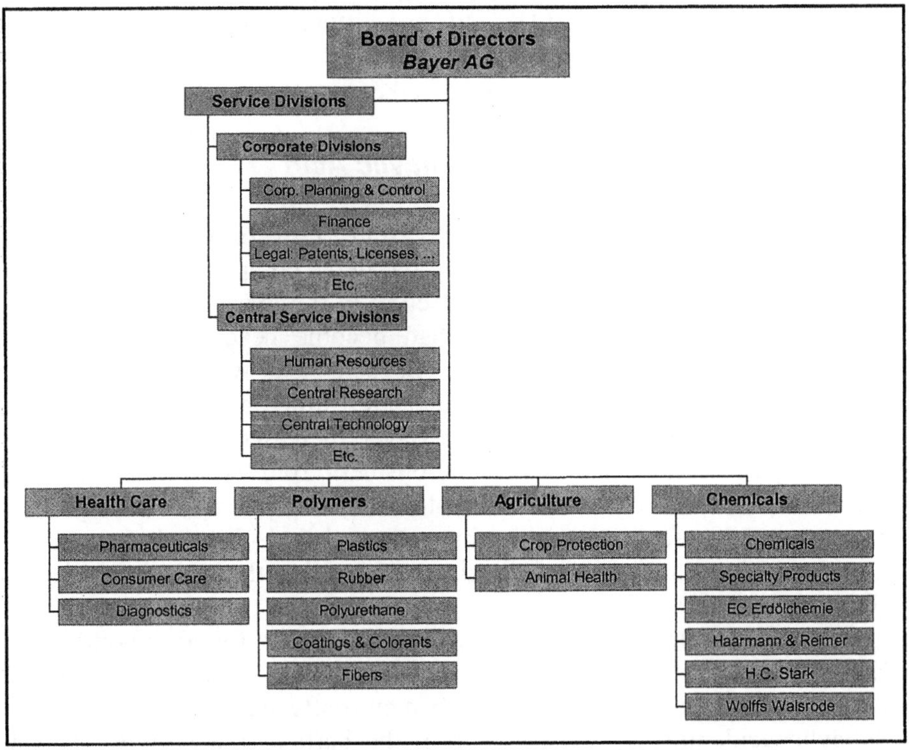

Figure II.1: Organisation of the Bayer AG

The company subdivides its business, after the de-merger of the Agfa-Gevaert-Group in May 1999, into the four business segments: Health care,

[12] Due to the different trademarks used in different countries and regions, e.g., Bayer promotes its ASA products in France under the trademark 'Aspirine du Rhône,' or in Argentine, Italy, or Spain under the trademark 'ASPIRINIA'. Our discussion uses the term 'Bayer Aspirin' as a synonym for the different trademarks used by Bayer AG in the various national markets.

agriculture, polymers, and chemicals (see figure II.1). Of these four business segments, polymers represent the most important segment with an annual turnover of some US$ 4.7 billion followed by health care with almost US$ 4.3 billion in 1999.[13] As illustrated in figure II.1, Bayer AG structures its business into four global business segments and one central service division which again is subdivided into corporate divisions, e.g., corporate planning and control, finance, or legal, patents, licensees, insurance, as well as corporate service divisions, e.g., human resources, central research, or central technology. Moreover, in fiscal year 1999 Bayer spent a total of some US$ 2.3 billion on R&D whereof more than 60% was spent in the field health care, 20% in agriculture, 13% in polymers, and 7% in chemicals.[14] Thus, R&D intensity of Bayer's health care business amounted to some 32% in the year 1999.

II.2.1.1 The Innovation: Acetylsalicylic Acid

As was pointed out above, Bayer's decision to diversify its business into pharmaceuticals was mainly driven by the fierce competition the company encountered due to weak patent protection in the dyestuff industry. After its initial success, Duisberg, who had become head of the company, significantly increased the number of scientists working in Bayer's research labs, employing by 1890 ninety full-time chemists. By doing so the list of new drugs developed by Bayer increased rapidly and Bayer decided to separate its pharmaceutical business from the dyestuff business. Moreover, the pharmaceutical laboratories were split up in two parts: a pharmaceutical section developing new drugs, headed by Arthur Eichengrün, and a pharmacological section testing the new drugs, led by Heinrich Dreser.[15]

One of the first tasks assigned to the newly found laboratory of Eichengrün was to develop a version of salicylic acid with fewer side effects than the products which had been currently available on the market. Salicylic acid, initially extracted from the bark of the willow-tree, had already been known since the Antique, an even Hippocrates recommended the use of 'Spirea' bark to better all kinds of pain and fever. In 1763 Edward Stone presented a report on the successful treatment of 50 patients suffering from fever with the extracts of the Salix-bark to the Royal Society at London. The Italian pharmacist Francesco Fontana finally isolated in 1825 for the first time the active substance of the bark and

[13] Cp. Bayer annual report (2000).
[14] Cp. Bayer annual report (2000).
[15] Cp. Mann, C. C. & Plummer, M. L. (1991); Kohl. F. (1997).

called it "Salicine" according to the Latin name of the willow-tree. In 1853 the French chemist Charles-Frédéric Gerhard was the first to exactly analyse salicylic acid and to already produce a crude form of acetylsalicylic acid which, however, remained unexploited because of Gerhard's early death. Building on Gerhard's analysis of the salicylic acid, Hermann Kolbe at the University of Marburg succeeded in 1859 to synthesise pure salicylic acid. The production process of the salicylic acid was further improved by Heyden, a scholars of Kolbe, which allowed for large-scale production and considerably lowered production cost. Although, salicylic acid was commonly used for the treatment of infections and rheumatism at that time, it was accompanied by bad taste, provoking nausea, and causing the decomposition of the lining of the stomach and thus rendered a long-lasting treatment of patients difficult.[16]

Building on these previous findings, Eichengrün assigned the young chemist Felix Hoffmann to search for a similar drug, but with lesser side effects than salicylic acid. It happened that Hoffmann's father suffered from chronic rheumatism that physicians tried to ease by subscribing sodium salicylate which had seriously damaged his stomach. Felix Hoffmann thus pushed to find a remedy easing his father's pains. In order to enhance the characteristics of salicylic acid, he tried to acetylate salicylic acid, a broadly known method of refining pharmaceuticals (see figure II.2). He succeeded in doing so on October 10, 1897 and described a method of producing a *pure and durable form of acetylsalicylic acid* (ASA) which was improved over the forms described earlier by Gerhard and Karl Kraut, a German chemist who reported in 1869 a progress on Gerhard's initial synthesis in the chemical production of a crystalline form of ASA. The chemical production process described by Kraut was, however, not pure and still contained free salicylic acid.[17]

---

[16] Cp. Bayer (1983,1996); Rhône-Poulenc (1995); Alstaedter, R (1997); Marseille, J. (1999).

[17] Cp. Mann, C. C. & Plummer, M. L. (1991), chap. 1; Kohl, F. (1997); Alstaeder, R. (1997); Schreiner, C. (1999); Zündorf, U. (2001).

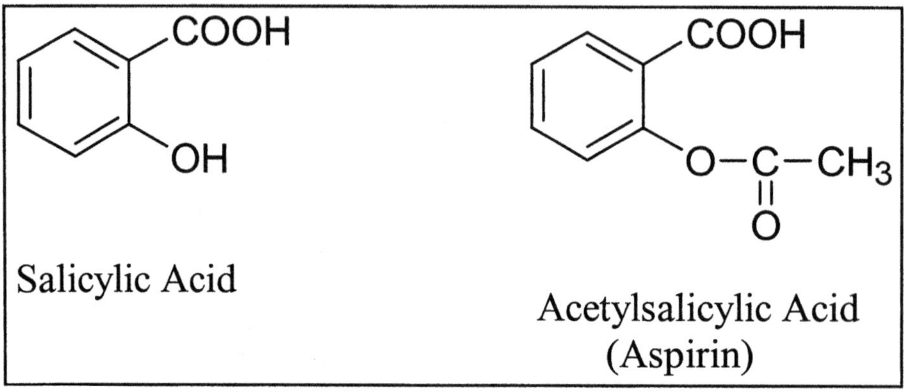

Figure II.2: Salicylic acid versus acetylsalicylic acid

The further development and the official testing of the pure and durable form of acetylsalicylic acid discovered by Hoffmann, however, was delayed until 1898 by the rejection of ASA by Bayer's pharmacological section. Nevertheless, Eichengrün tested the ASA on himself and gave samples to doctors in hospitals to test the new pharmaceutical, although Heinrich Dreser judged ASA as worthless. The overwhelming success of ASA in the pharmacists' trials due to its good effectiveness in reducing the discomfort of pain and fever, as well as its low side effects, in particular with regard to salicylic acid and related products available on the market, created considerable company internal attention for the invention. The good results of pharmacists and the positive pharmacological report, commanded by Duisberg himself from an external expert, finally broke Dreser's resistance against acetylsalicylic acid and Bayer finally announced in summer 1899 the appearance of a new pharmaceutical.[18]

The Beginning of a Success Story

With the decision to launch a new pharmaceutical on the basis of the active substance ASA Bayer tried to file for patent right protection. However, due to the lack of novelty Bayer did not succeed in broad patent protection with the sole exception of the USA. In addition to patent right protection Bayer did not call the new drug by its chemical name, but by a brand name, just as in the case of the previous drugs Phenacetin and Heroin, an applied in 1899, two years after Hoffmann's initial invention, in Germany and USA for trademark protection for its name: *Aspirin*. The name represents a composition of the Latin name of the willow tree "Spiraea"

[18] Cp. Mann, C. C. & Plummer, M. L. (1991), chap. 1.

and the 'A' standing for Acetyl.[19] Bayer easily obtained *trademark protection* in almost all countries in the world due to the name's genuine nature.[20]

In March 1899 Bayer started the production of Aspirin in its Eberfeld plant and initially sold the new pharmaceuticals as a powder in 250 gram bottles (see figure II.3). Furthermore, at that time the promotion of a new drug was not directly done through media, but by sending free samples to pharmacists and professors testing the new drug and publishing any new findings about its effectiveness. Thus, *scientific publication* and *word-of-mouth* of Aspirin's effectiveness was one of the most important means of promotion. Unfortunately for Bayer, however, end consumers did not come into contact with either the company name nor the product name Aspirin, since druggists weighted the powder and put the prescribed amount of ASA into neutral paper sachets.

In the early 20th century Bayer was the only company knowing how to produce pure ASA in large quantities and at a reasonable price. Although, no significant threat from competitors existed at that time, Bayer had problems with druggists diluting or even completely substituting the white Aspirin powder by other white powders, e.g., flour. Bayer's response was immediate: In 1900 the company launched *Bayer Aspirin in tablet-form* containing 500mg ASA (cf. figure II.3). By doing so, druggists did not have the possibility to dilute Aspirin powder and, in addition, companies trying to imitate Aspirin products were put at a disadvantage since they did not know how to put ASA in tablet form because of the extreme instability of the active molecule. Moreover, each tablet was stamped with the Bayer-Cross and the packaging clearly showed the Bayer and the Aspirin name. Thus, by the market launch of Aspirin tablets end-consumers came into contact and became familiar with the trademark. This process of establishing the trademark 'Aspirin' and achieving consumer awareness received a considerable boost by *several serious influenza epidemics in Europe* within the early years of the 20th century. Physicians all over Europe prescribed in considerable quantities Aspirin and consequently large numbers of consumers came into contact with the Bayer-Cross and the brand name Aspirin. The consumers' intense direct contact with the brand and its good effectiveness built broad awareness and strong positive associations. Thus, the trademark Aspirin rapidly achieved international

---

[19] In the discussion the name Bayer Aspirin is used to represents all Aspirin brands of Bayer in the various national and regional markets, e.g., ASPIRINA, Bayaspirina, or Aspirine du Rhône.

[20] Cp. Schreiner, C. (1999).

awareness so that its name and its field of application no longer had to be explained.

Source: Bayer AG

Figure II.3: Bayer Aspirin® bottle around 1899 and Aspirin tablets in 1904

Because of the tremendous success of Aspirin in Europe,[21] Bayer decided to take Aspirin to the USA. In 1905 Bayer started its Aspirin production in Rensselaer, Albany, and in 1909 Bayer already achieved almost 30% of its world-wide Aspirin sales in the US market. Bayer also introduced its product in most other continents where the South American market turned out to be particularly interesting with 330 million tablets – or 100 tons – of Aspirin sold by 1929, per annum.[22]

II.2.2 Appropriation Regime and Intellectual Property Constellation

After having recognised the magnitude of Hoffmann's invention, the Bayer company tried to file for patent protection on the improved production process for ASA and trademark protection for the name Aspirin, wherever possible. *Patent protection* was, however, only available in countries that disregarded the fact that acetylsalicylic acid had been invented years before by the chemists Gerhard and Kraut. And even though the German and British patent offices had initially granted Bayer

---

[21] Bayer evaluated Aspirin's success in 1906: "Aspirin has in the decade since its introduction become so popular that it is unsurpassed by any other drug. Surely it is not an exaggeration to say that it is today the most used and beloved medicine we manufacture.", Mann, C. C. & Plummer, M. L. (1991), p. 28.

[22] Cp.Schreiner, C. (1999).

patent right protection, they later denied Bayer the right. The Royal Court of Justice in Britain, for example, argued that the initial patent document was so obscure that "none of the experienced counsel engaged in this case had ever seen [one] like it."[23] The only country that granted Bayer a patent and upheld its decision over the entire lifetime of the right, although various companies filed suite against this decision, was the USA. The US Patent Office (USPto.) granted Bayer the exclusive right to manufacture, import, and sell ASA in the US for a period of 17 years on February 27, 1900.[24] Thus, any other channel of ASA in the USA represented illegal imports or patent infringements which Bayer indefatigably prosecuted so that in 1914 *only* 27% of the Aspirin sold in the US market was counterfeit.

On the other hand, Bayer's attempt to achieve *world-wide trademark protection* of the name '*Aspirin*' had not been a problem since it was a genuinely new name. Thus, in 1899 Bayer registered 'Aspirin' in the USA and Germany and finally in the year 1906 as an international trademark. This policy of pharmaceutical companies not to call the drug by its chemical name, but rather by a protected genuine name dates back to the success of Hoechst with its pharmaceutical sold under the trademark 'Antipirine,' which had been launched in 1883. However, this policy of marketing pharmaceuticals under protected names was heavily disputed by medical associations because physicians did often not know the active molecule and thus did not prescribe the drug under its generic but rather by its trade-name. Consequently, druggist had to sell the more expensive product associated with the trademark and could not vend a cheaper generic product.[25] Thus, the allowance to launch new pharmaceuticals under a registered genuine name represented, according to the American Medical Associations (AMA), the extension of patent right protection:

> *"...it has been impossible in this country for anybody except Bayer Company to manufacture or sell acetylsalicylic acid. ... Needless to say, the American people have been made to pay exorbitantly for the monopoly our patent office granted this firm. ... Not content with the iron-bound monopoly which it had been granted through our patent laws, the company attempted further to clinch its exclusive rights by giving the preparation a fancy name, "aspirin," and getting a trademark on this name."*[26]

[23] Mann, C. C. & Plummer, M. L. (1991), p. 36.
[24] Cp. Zündorf, U. (2001), pp. 36-40.
[25] Cp. McTavish, J. R. (1987).
[26] Mann, C. C. & Plummer, M. L. (1991), p. 38.

Although Bayer was not able to file for patent protection with the sole exception of the US market, the company was able to hold imitators under control due to its *proprietary process knowledge*. It appeared extremely difficult to produce pure ASA in large quantities and, in addition, it appeared almost impossible to competitors to press ASA into tablet form. The main problem of imitators presented the high instability of the active molecule in contact with humidity. Thus, Bayer was the only company at that time knowing how to produce ASA in pure form and high quantities at a reasonable price, and to even press the drug in tablet form. Furthermore, Bayer's *US patent document* on Hoffmann's ASA production process was so *confusing and obscure* about important details of the process that not even specialist chemists could understand the exact process of production described in the document. Nevertheless, first imitators of ASA products came up in Europe using different production processes like the Société Gillard, Monnet et Cartier in France, later known as Socété Chimique des Usines du Rhône which started its production of ASA powder in 1902 and succeeded eight years after the market launch of the Bayer Aspirin tablets to produce ASA in tablet form.[27] However, during the early years of the 20th century the main threat for Bayer did not represent companies imitating its ASA products but rather people dissolving Aspirin powder with flour and people smuggling Aspirin form Europe, Mexico, or Canada, where no patent protection existed and hence Bayer Aspirin was sold at considerably lower prices, to the USA where Bayer had the legal monopoly until February 1917.[28] Bayer fiercely enforced its legal property rights by prosecuting any smuggling and trademark infringement.

In 1914 the US market had grown so important for Bayer's business that Duisberg, at that time CEO of Bayer, decided to set up the *Bayer Corporation* which subsequently became the *legal owner of all patent and trademark rights* of the Bayer group in America. Furthermore, with the approaching expiration of patent protection in the USA and the threat of competitors entering the US market, e.g., Dow Chemicals and Monsanto, Bayer decided not only to promote the drug to doctors, pharmacists, and drug companies, as it was quite common at that time, but also directly to end-consumers. Bayer started, in particular in the US market, to advertise its product in order to make the Bayer name known to consumers, as well as to link up the company name with that of Aspirin. This *marketing campaign* of Bayer, at that time unknown to the pharmaceutical sector,

[27] Cp. Rhône-Poulenc (1995).

[28] In most of Europe the Bayer Aspirin price was less than one-tenth, and Canada still one-third of the price it sold in the USA. Cp. Mann, C. C. & Plummer, M. L. (1991), chap. 2.

instantly caused opposition by the American Medical Association (AMA) and Bayer subsequently agreed to the proposition of the AMA to limit its advertisement to the packaging of the product and the tablets which were all stamped with the Bayer-Cross. This agreement, however, was only of short duration and Bayer continued its extensive marketing campaign in the fall of 1916.[29]

When finally the patent expired on February 17, 1917, Bayer had succeeded in establishing a strong brand name which had become a word of use in everyday life, and the pharmaceuticals application area, as well as it effectiveness did not have to be explained to anyone anymore. In addition, most consumers, druggists, and even physicians did not know that Aspirin was made of a drug called acetylsalicylic acid but they regarded Aspirin as if it was the name of a drug in its own right. Thus, when competitors entered the US market in spring 1917, most people did not know they could buy an identical product sold under another trademark at significantly lower prices.[30]

II.2.2.1 From Technological Invention to a Global Brand

Hoffmann's invention allowed for a large-scale production of ASA and thus the provision of patients suffering from rheumatism, headaches or even inflammation with an *effective drug with relatively low side effects* with respect to other drugs which had been in the market in the late 19th and early 20th century. Thus, ASA excelled any other competing product in the market and achieved widespread use as an anti-rheumatic, anti-pyretic, anti-inflammatory, analgesic, and was even prescribed in the treatment of hay fever and diabetes. Moreover, the occurrence of various influenza epidemics in Europe and North America during the first quarter of the 20th century and the broad use of pharmaceuticals based on ASA in their treatment, as well as large-scale public announcements in newspapers of how people can effectively cure the flu with the help of a good rest, warmth, and 'Aspirin,' made the drug and its merits known to a vast majority of the European and North American population.[31]

---

29 Cp. Mann, C. C. & Plummer, M. L. (1991), chap. 2.

30 Cp. Mann, C. C. & Plummer, M. L. (1991), chap. 14.

31 The newspaper 'Kölner-Stadtanzeiger' recommended its readers on March 6, 1924 to cure influenza with rest, warmth and Aspirin: "Sobald man sich krank fühlt, lege man sich ins Bett mit einer Wärmeflasche an den Füßen, trinke brühenheißen Kamillentee oder auch Grog, um tüchtig zu schwitzen und nehme täglich drei Aspirin-Tabletten. Befolgt man diese Regel, so wird man in den

These obvious advantages of ASA products, as well as Bayer's dominant position due to its company specific knowledge in ASA's production process, and, with regard to the US market, its legal monopoly in manufacturing and distributing any product containing ASA, enabled Bayer to rapidly establish its trademark Aspirin and build a reputation as the initial innovator. These brand-building efforts were further reinforced by the market launch of Aspirin tablets which were stamped with the Bayer-Cross and packaged in tubes clearly displaying the company, as well as the product name (cp. figure II.3). Moreover, the invention of the Aspirin tablets considerably simplified the dosage of ASA and made false labelling of other white powders as Aspirin extremely difficult. However, not only consumers benefited of the advantages of Aspirin tablets but also Bayer AG which was able to reinforce its already dominant position because it was the only company capable of producing ASA in tablet form for almost a decade. All these factors contributed to the rapid spread of ASA usage and thus to the familiarisation of large numbers of consumers with the merits of ASA which they subsequently associated with the trademark Aspirin. The success of Bayer Aspirin was, however, not restricted to Europe and North America. Aspirin was introduced in almost *every region of the world* during the early years of the 20th century and consequently, the trademark Aspirin obtained rapid notoriety and became a word of daily use in almost any household throughout the world.[32]

Facing the approaching date of patent expiration in the USA in 1917, Bayer focused its attention on its trademark Aspirin which would continue in existence. Thus, the company commenced around 1914 with an advertisement campaign promoting its products directly to end-consumers and by doing so hoped to increase consumers' familiarity with the Bayer name, reinforce their awareness about the trademark Aspirin, and link up the two names.[33] This advertisement campaign which represented a radical break with the pharmaceutical industry's history of product promotion and enraged medical associations and physicians, further increased and strengthened consumers' awareness about Bayer Aspirin.[34] However, in

meisten Fällen nach wenigen Tagen wieder gesund sein.“ Altsaedter, R. (1997), p. 9.

[32] Cp. Bohle, F. (1988).

[33] All the advertisements contained the following sentence: "The Trade-Mark 'Aspirin' (Reg. U.S. Pat. Off.) is a guarantee that the monoacetic acid ester of salicylic acid in these tablets is of the reliable Bayer manufacture." McTavish, J. R. (1987), p. 357.

[34] Cp. Mann, C. C. & Plummer, M. L. (1991), chap. 2.

summer 1914 Bayer was surprised by the outbreak of the *First World War* which was going to completely change Bayer's global Aspirin business.

II.2.2.2 Bayer Aspirin in the Inter- and Post-War Period

The shots at Sarajevo in 1914 entirely altered Bayer's global Aspirin business. With the beginning of war in Europe Britain immediately put an embargo on Germany and, in addition, enemy nations put any German firm active on their territory into a *trust*, initially planning to return them after the fighting would have ended. The USA, Bayer's most important market for Aspirin, entered the war on April 6, 1917. For several months nothing really changed for Bayer's US business until October 1917 when the *office of the Alien Property Custodian* (APC) was established in order to take over the control over any enemy property and to seize enemy-owned intellectual property rights, i.e., patents and trademarks. Bayer was, however, not immediately concerned of the appearance of the APC because it had previously established 'good relationships' with the chairman of the APC board.[35]

Confronted with the changed business environment, Bayer Corporation did no longer try to please the AMA and thus intensified its advertisement campaign communicating that only *Bayer Aspirin was genuine* and that any imitation or substitute was implicitly or explicitly dangerous. Moreover, Bayer was afraid of losing its exclusive rights to the word Aspirin and thus intended to convince the public to distinguish between Aspirin from Bayer and Aspirin from any other company and consequently to explicitly demand the Bayer brand from their doctors and pharmacists. At the same time Bayer tried to fiercely *enforce its legal rights on the name* Aspirin and commenced to sue any company using the name Aspirin for trademark infringement.[36] However, only a few months after Bayer's patent on ASA had expired in the USA, worst came to worst and by June 1918 the company was under the control of the APC and within a few months the whole Bayer management was arrested for violations of the 'Espionage and Trading with the Enemy Acts.' In addition, in March 1918 the US Congress amended the 'Trading with the Enemy Act' enabling the APC to sell enemy property to Americans.[37]

A few weeks after the armistice of November 1918 which signalled the end of the First World War, the APC announced to *auction Bayer Corporation's properties* on December 12, 1918. Several parties were

[35] Cp. Mann, C. C. & Plummer, M. L. (1991), chap. 2.
[36] Cp. McTavish, J. R. (1987).
[37] Cp. Mann, C. C. & Plummer, M. L. (1991), chap. 2.

interested in Bayer's US properties which not only included one of America's largest chemical plants at Rensselaer, but also a collection of patents and drug trademarks, Bayer Aspirin being the most valuable. This desperate situation of Bayer grounded on the fact that Bayer Corporation in the USA had not been using licenses for patent and trademark rights from Bayer AG in Germany, but rather owned the legal rights on most patents and trademarks for the North and South American markets. The APC sold the company to the most bidding company, *Sterling Products Inc.*, a small patent medicine company, for US$ 5.31 million. Sterling immediately sold the dyestuffs part of Bayer for US$ 2.5 million to the Graselli Chemical Company of New York. Furthermore it combined the former pharmaceutical activities of Bayer in the division Winthrop Chemical Company which subsequently registered the name Bayer and the Bayer-Cross in Latin America.[38] The Aspirin business, however, was kept as a distinct unit. Finally, Sterling purchased in July 1920 the trademark and patent rights of Bayer which had been confiscated in the United Kingdom during the war, and thus acquired the intellectual property rights of Bayer in various countries of the world that had been under British control.

Although the owners of the Bayer Corp. and the associated Aspirin trademark had changed in various countries, the principle struggle to uphold trademark protection for the name Aspirin was, however, in almost all markets the same. Due to German warship Bayer AG had not only lost its properties in the USA and the UK, but also its legal rights on the Aspirin name in various enemy nations, e.g., France and associated territories, or Australia, where the trademark had subsequently been declared to a public term.[39] Furthermore, many nations were thinking about declaring Aspirin to a generic name that could be used for any product containing ASA produced by any company.

The Two Bayer Companies

Sterling Products Inc., whose profits had risen from US$ 800,000 pre-war figures to over US$ 2 million in 1919 due to the acquisition of Bayer's US

[38] Cp. McTavish, J. R. (1987), Mann, C. C. & Plummer, M. L. (1991); N. A. (1994); Schreiner, C. (1999).

[39] «Il est généralement admis que la marque Aspirin est tombée dans le domaine public à la suite du traité de Versailles du 29 juin 1919. Une de ses clauses prévoyait en effet l'expropriation de nombreux brevets ou marques allemandes. Mais avant la Première Guerre mondiale, le mot Aspirine était déjà considéré comme un terme générique désignant l'acide acétylsalicylique.» Marseille, J. (1999), p. 134.

pharmaceutical business, intended to sell ASA under the name Bayer Aspirin associated with the Bayer-Cross all over the world.[40] However, the company had serious problems in producing the drugs which it had acquired, and the sophisticated production facilities at Rensselaer appeared as an impressive technological miracle. Moreover, the previous German supervisors and managers had been jailed or deported so that nobody knew how to run the machines or operate the facilities efficiently. Last but not least, Sterling's employees could not understand Bayer's patent document which was meant to specify Hoffmann's production process of ASA, but was rather perceived by chemists as a marvel "of obfuscation."[41] Thus, Sterling's only possibility to get the needed process knowledge and to keep its Aspirin business going was to ask the previous owner of the facilities for help, the Bayer AG at Leverkusen. However, Sterling had not been the first company to ask for aid at Leverkusen, Grasselli Chemical Company which had purchased Bayer's dyestuff business, had similar problems.

Duisberg, CEO of Bayer AG, was astonished by the request of Sterling Products Inc. for help in the production of Aspirin:

> *"Duisberg regarded Sterling's purchase of Bayer's name as a kind of theft and wanted his property returned. Many people had synthesized acetylsalicylic acid over the years, but only one firm had created Bayer Aspirin."*[42]

Bayer management in Germany realised that this request was a good *opportunity to regain some influence on the American Aspirin business*. In October 1920 Bayer finally succeeded in establishing a treaty with Sterling that allowed Bayer to sell acetylsalicylic acid and products based on ASA under the name Aspirin and the company name Bayer associated with the Bayer-Cross over a period of 50 years in Latin America jointly with Sterling Products. In addition, Sterling transferred its trademark rights for the Latin American countries to Bayer. However, a few month before the 'Latin American Treaty' was signed by the two companies, Judge Learned Hand declared on May 1920 Sterling's US trademark 'Aspirin' on the consumer level as a *generic name*, indicative of any ASA product.[43] Thus, Bayer Aspirin was now only Sterling's Bayer brand of Aspirin in the USA. In 1923 the two companies signed another contract, the so called '*Weiss-Treaty*,' which clearly divided up the world into three regions: One where Sterling was the single owner of the rights on the name Bayer and the

---

[40] McTravish, J. R. (1987).

[41] Cp. Mann, C. C. & Plummer, M. L. (1991), chap. 3.

[42] Mann, C. C. & Plummer, M. L. (1991), p. 58.

[43] Cp. Mann, C. C. & Plummer, M. L. (1991), chap. 4; N.A. (1994).

Bayer-Cross, these were all British territories such as Great Britain, Australia, New-Zealand, South Africa, etc., and the USA, a second region represented by the Latin American countries, where both companies, Bayer AG and Sterling Products Inc., could use the Bayer name and symbol. The last region included all remaining countries, e.g., continental Europe, most African countries (except countries under French control) and Canada, where Leverkusen had the exclusive rights on its company name and symbol. Furthermore, Bayer AG agreed to give Sterling *technical help in producing Aspirin* for the US market in return for half of the US profits.[44]

The I.G. Farben Trust and Bayer Aspirin in the War and Early Post World War II Period

Duisberg, who was fascinated by the big American trusts, arranged meetings with the directors of BASF and Hoechst which finally led in 1925 to the merging of the three companies and the 'Aktiengesellschaft für Anilinfabrikation,' the present Agfa-Gevaert-Group, into the *I.G. Farben trust*. The I.G. which had become in 1926 Europe's biggest and the world's fourth largest business enterprise, extended the agreements fixed with Sterling in the 'Weiss-Treaty' on all pharmaceuticals of I.G. Farben and *closely co-operated* with Sterling Products Inc. on a global scale. Both companies acquired together firms and shared profits, as well as management tasks and at last Bayer AG even acquired 50% on Winthrop.

Moreover, the companies focused on fiercely fighting infringers in those countries where Aspirin was still a valid trademark, and in those countries where Aspirin had been declared a generic name they tried to convince consumers that only Bayer Aspirin is genuine Aspirin having significant advantages with respect to Aspirin products offered by other companies. In effect, the substance produced by the Bayer AG was at that time substantially superior in its quality so that the Bayer name and the Bayer-Cross were perceived by customers as a *sign of high quality*. By the end of 1929 Latin American consumers only consumed 100 tonnes of Bayer Aspirin annually which corresponded to some 330 million tablets.[45] And although Sterling was initially reluctant to heavily advertise in the USA, the Bayer Aspirin brand continued to prosper despite its high price, minimal promotion, and mounting competition because of the significant accumulated power of the name. Finally, in the early 1930s Sterling started

---

[44] Cp. N.A. (1994).

[45] Schreiner, C. (1999).

to broadly advertise Bayer Aspirin and by 1936 it had become the fourth-biggest radio advertiser in the USA.[46]

The co-operation of Sterling Products Inc. and Bayer AG continued until the USA officially entered the Second World War in 1941. Within the same year the US ministry of justice judged Sterling capable of violation of the *antitrust laws* and immediately annulled any agreement between Sterling and Bayer without even hearing Bayer AG. Moreover, Sterling was declared *exclusive owner of all mutually held international properties*, e.g. patents, trademarks, and shared participation in third companies. Thus, Bayer AG had again, just as in the case of the First World War, lost its rights on the company name Bayer, the Bayer-Cross, and the trademark Aspirin in most national markets.[47] In other enemy nations, where Leverkusen had still been the official owner of the rights, its properties were seized as a consequence of German warfare.

After the Second World War had ended in 1945, the I.G. Farben trust was split up in three independent companies BASF, Hoechst and Bayer. Around 1949 Bayer recommenced to advertise Bayer Aspirin in those countries where it had not lost the right on its company name and perhaps even on the trademark Aspirin, e.g., Germany, Argentine. Furthermore, Bayer AG tried to regain ownership on its international trademark rights by *taking legal action* and appealed against the ruling of the US ministry of justice in 1941 which had declared Sterling as the exclusive owner of any mutually held properties, including international patent and trademark rights. However, in 1962 Bayer AG lost its litigation in the USA and thus any hope to regain ownership on its international trademarks by legal measures.

In addition, in the 1950s several new brands of ASA appeared on the US market which entered in direct competition with Bayer Aspirin on the market for analgesics. These *new brands*, e.g., Anacin of American Home Products Inc. or Bufferin of United Drug Inc., claimed to be better than Aspirin, and spent huge amounts of money on communicating their advantages (e.g., Anacin's advertisement budget amounted to some US$ 15 million in the mid 1950s). However, these companies entirely missed out to tell consumers that these new brands were basically Aspirin with a few added ingredients.[48] In other markets even the substance ASA was attacked by analgesics based on the substitute substance *acetaminophen* which was already known since 1878. Acetaminophen was supposed to be superior in the treatment of pain because it did not cause gastrointestinal

[46] Cp. Mann, C. C. & Plummer, M. L. (1991), chap. 9.
[47] N.A. (1994).
[48] Mann, C. C. & Plummer, M. L. (1991), chap. 10.

bleeding like ASA which could, although extremely rarely, upset stomachs. On the other hand, however, acetaminophen is ineffective in the treatment of inflammation. Nevertheless, in some countries, e.g., France and Britain, promotional activities have succeeded in convincing consumers that analgesics based on acetaminophen are better tolerated than Aspirin since they do not cause gastrointestinal bleeding and thus do not upset stomachs.[49] In 1955 McNeil Laboratories, a small US based pharmaceutical company, was granted FDA approval for acetaminophen for the treatment of children. The drug was subsequently launched as an ethical drug under the trademark *Tylenol.* In 1958 McNeal applied for FDA approval for an adult version of its drug Tylenol, aiming to sell it to people who are allergic to ASA. However, before FDA approval was granted, McNeal was acquired by a company called Johnson & Johnson Inc.

II.2.2.3 The Revival of Bayer Aspirin

Even though competing brands of ASA aggressively attacked Bayer Aspirin in almost all national markets, Sterling Products and Bayer AG had a *reassuring share of the global analgesic market*. Moreover, although acetaminophen had already proved successful in a few national markets and Tylenol had made it by 1965 onto the list of the two hundred most frequently prescribed pharmaceuticals in the USA, ASA was perceived as the *dominant drug* which could not be made up by any other competing substance. However, by the end of 1977 *Tylenol* sales had overtaken the sales of any other analgesic brand in the US market and replaced Bayer Aspirin, whose market share had fallen to 10%. Sterling's response was the launch of an acetaminophen based drug under the name Bayer Non-Aspirin. However, US consumers' association of the Bayer name with pure, high quality Aspirin was so strong that they became confused by hearing that Bayer was suddenly no-longer Aspirin. The brand was a complete failure with a market share of 0.3% and was subsequently withdrawn from the market.

The response of Sterling Products Inc. and Bayer AG to the attacks of new Aspirin brands and alternative drugs was, during the early post World War II period, only moderate. Both companies were predominantly

[49] The advertisement campaigns were so successful that the marketing director of Winthrop ascertained in the early 1960s: "If you were in Britain in the fifties and asked for aspirin, it would be 'Good God are you trying to kill yourself?' Aspirin was not only a poison, but it would burn a hole in your stomach!" Cp. Mann, C. C. & Plummer, M. L. (1991), p. 189.

occupied by the legal battle between them, and *Leverkusen's aspire to regain the international rights on its company name* and the Bayer-Cross. A partial success of Bayer AG in its battle represented the company's purchase of the international rights on its name and symbols for US$ 2.8 million in 1970. This purchase, however, excluded the rights on the name Bayer and the Bayer-Cross in the USA and Canada. In 1978 Leverkusen bought *Miles Laboratories*, the makers of Alka-Selzer, and finally paid in 1986 US$ 25 million for the right to use the name Bayer[50] for its American holding which subsequently was renamed to 'Bayer USA Inc.'[51]

In June 1985, however, for all US producers of Aspirin products worst came to worst, when the FDA obliged pharmaceutical companies to put warning labels on all products containing ASA pointing out a possible *link between ASA and the Reye's syndrome*. The Reye's syndrome is a serious but rare illness which strikes children in the aftermath of a viral infection. The market response was immediate and pronounced; in 1979 Bayer Aspirin still had a 20% share of the US market for children's analgesics and Johnson & Johnson's Tylenol owned 40%, by 1985 Bayer's market share had fallen to less than 10% and Tylenol had almost 60% of the market. By the end of 1986 Bayer Aspirin's market share of the US analgesics market was down to merely 6%! In 1988 *Eastman Kodak* purchased Sterling Products for US$ 5.1 billion and thus became the owner of the Bayer name and symbol in the USA. The new owner of Sterling sued Leverkusen in 1990 for deliberate infringement of the agreements settled in 1986 and in 1992 the Bayer AG lost again virtually all rights to its company name and symbol in the USA due to the ruling of a New York district court.

In the early 1990s Bayer AG had regained control over its own name and the Bayer Aspirin business in all countries except for pharmaceuticals in the USA and Canada. However, the global Aspirin business had significantly changed. Since the beginning of the World War II, several *competing substances* had appeared on the market for analgesics, e.g., acetaminophen or ibuprofen, many countries had declared the *trademark Aspirin to a generic term* that any company could use for its ASA products, and finally the name Aspirin had received in various markets a *negative reputation* for causing gastrointestinal bleeding and even provoking ulcer. Nevertheless, Bayer Aspirin's *market position* was still dominant, although threatened by competition, in those countries or regions where Bayer Aspirin was continuously available over the last 80 to

[50] The trademark Bayer Aspirin was excluded from the deal and thus only Sterling Products Inc. could sell Bayer Aspirin on the US market.

[51] N.A. (1994).

90 years, where many wrong or qualitatively bad products had been on the market and the Bayer name was perceived as a guarantee of high quality, i.e., Africa and South America, and/or where Bayer still had exclusive rights on its trademark Aspirin.

However, the 1980s turned out to be the crucial turning point for the substance ASA in general and the product Bayer Aspirin in particular. In 1978 the New England Journal of Medicine published an article which revealed the findings of Prof. Barnett about ASA's *risk reducing influence by apoplexy*. The article pointed out that ASA could reduce the risks of severe harm or even death by stroke in general by 31% and in particular by men by an astonishing 48%. Moreover, the new Bayer Aspirin tablets containing vitamin C recaptured market share due to the tablets faster pain releasing effect and increased tolerance. In addition, in 1982 Prof. Vane of the Royal Physicians College in London received the *Nobel Price* of Medicine for the finding of ASA's and thus Aspirin's inhibiting effect on the production of certain prostaglandin groups. Approximately at the same time Bryan Smith and Jim Willis discovered the effect of ASA in *preventing the agglomeration of platelets* which generally causes thrombosis. By 1983 the so called Lewis-Study was published which revealed that the *risk of heart attack* of people with an unstable angina pectoris was reduced by taking ASA by a significant 50%.

Known as the *Physicians Health Study*, in 1988 one of the largest ever conducted medical experiments was started, involving 22,071 volunteers. Fifty percent of the participants took a tablet containing 325 mg of ASA every day, the other half took a placebo – a tablet that resembled the ASA tablet but did not contain any active substance. Over four years a committee of physicians monitored the health of each of the volunteers until December 1987, when they had the unequivocal result that the group taking ASA experienced *47% fewer heart attacks* than the group taking the placebo.[52] Because of these highly significant findings the study was halted three years early and so to give all participants the possibility to benefit of the results.

The publication of the results in the New England Journal of Medicine triggered an enormous response in media and gave the slackening ASA business some new impetus and in particular Bayer Aspirin which was the most familiar brand and synonymous with the drug. In the Western World heart attacks represented the leading cause of death and alone in the USA 500,000 people died by heart attacks a year.[53] Moreover, in order to keep the risk of heart attack low, one does have to *consume ASA continuously*

---

[52] Cp. Schreiner, C. (1999).

[53] Cp. Mann, C. C. & Plummer, M. L. (1991), chap. 1.

over several years and not only once in a while as it is the case in the treatment of headache or inflammation. Thus, the prevention of heart attacks represented a business worth several billion of US$, although in many countries ASA had only received indication for the treatment of *second hard attacks*, e.g., USA, Germany, France and Australia. Further research on ASA revealed that the mechanism of how ASA effects the human body and in particular the blood-cells is much more complicated than initially thought by Prof. Vane. It appeared that acetylsalicylic acid has an inhibiting affect on the cyclooxygenase which exists in two variations in the human body – isoenzyme 1 (COX1) and 2 (COX2). While COX1 inhibits the agglomeration of platelets (causing thrombosis), COX2 becomes active in inflamed tissue. ASA has on both isoenzymes an inhibiting affect and thus, as illustrated in figure II.4, is effective in fighting pain, infections, and thrombosis, although, in order to inhibit COX2 a higher dosage of ASA is necessary.[54]

Another important finding represented the *colon-cancer preventing effect* of ASA, published in 1991. According to a study, realised by the American Cancer Association, the consumption of ASA reduces the risk of colon-cancer by 40%. However, Aspirin has not yet received therapeutic concession for the treatment of colon-cancer because information about the exact dosage, risks and benefits, as well as exact fields of application are hitherto not available.[55] Nevertheless, the effect on the image of ASA products, and in particular Bayer Aspirin, had been considerable by triggering a broad discussion and pointing out the *drug's specific advantages* vis-à-vis competing substances, e.g., acetaminophen and ibuprofen.

In early 1994 the US business activities of Bayer AG brightened up by the decision of the Court of Appeal to quash the 1992 verdict of the New York district court and thus the company regained the *right to use its company name in its US business* with the sole exception of the Aspirin business. In May 1994 Eastman Kodak put Sterling Products for sale and in August the pharmaceutical company SmithKline Beecham acquired the company's international self-medication-business. Bayer AG in turn negotiated with SmithKline Beecham to take over Sterling's US OTC business including all rights Sterling was still holding on the name Bayer and associated symbols in the USA.[56] In September 1994 Bayer finally acquired Sterling's US OTC business from SmithKline for US$ 1 billion

[54] Cp. Altstaedter, R. (1997); N.A. (1998).
[55] Cp. N.A. (1997); Altstaedter, R. (1997); Schreiner, C. (1999).
[56] Cp. N.A. (1994).

and on April 3, 1995 renamed its US subsidiary Miles into *Bayer Corporation*.[57]

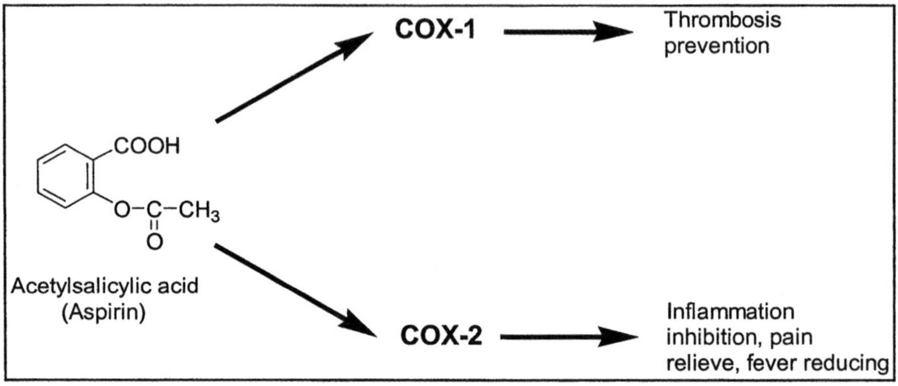

Figure II.4: The mode of action of ASA

Thus, by September 1994 Bayer AG in Leverkusen had regained exclusive rights on its company name and the Bayer-Cross in all countries and henceforth is the only company in the world that can sell Bayer pharmaceuticals and consequently Bayer Aspirin. In 1999 Bayer AG celebrated the *100th birthday* of the registration of the trademark Aspirin at the 'Kaiserliche Patentamt'[58] in Berlin. However, how had Bayer Aspirin's international market position evolved over the 100 years since its market launch and what remained of the mighty Bayer Aspirin empire of the early 20th century?

Present Market Positioning of Bayer Aspirin

The market of analgesics, fever and infection drugs had considerably changed since the initial market launch of Bayer Aspirin in 1899. On the one hand, new *competing substances* had been discovered such as ibuprofen or acetaminophen which have specific advantages with regard to ASA, and, on the other hand, the *field of indication* of ASA has been substantially enlarged into the field of thrombosis and here in particular into the prophylaxis of second heart attacks. Nevertheless, Bayer Aspirin still represented in the year 2000 the *second most important analgesics brand* in the world with a global market share of approximately 10-20% after Johnson & Johnson's Tylenol (cf. Table II.1). Tylenol's leading

[57] Cp. Bayer Annual Report (1994); Jeannet, J. P. & Hennessey, H. D. (2001), chap. 2.1 – 4.1.
[58] 'German Emperor's Patent Office.'

market position was, however, merely based on the pharmaceutical's dominant position in the US market which represented the single most important market in the world, accounting for approximately 35 to 40% of global analgesic sales. Moreover, Bayer Aspirin's sales growth significantly exceeded the overall growth of the analgesics market in the past years. As illustrated in figure II.5, the value of the global analgesics market had increased by 50% from 1987 to 1994, whereas Bayer Aspirin's sales volume had risen by almost 150% over the same period.

With the exception of North America and Asia, Bayer Aspirin still occupies today a leading position in the analgesics market in all world regions although competitors have succeeded in imitating Bayer's production process and alternative ASA brands have appeared in most national markets which have acquired substantial parts of the markets. In addition, the Bayer AG was, at the end of the 20th century, no longer present on all national markets, but had *withdrawn its Aspirin products* from individual national markets, e.g., France or Great Britain. Thus, the international market for analgesics had turned into an *extremely fragmented market* with numerous competitors on the individual national level.

Although ASA has faced severe competition in the market for pain relievers by new substances, global ASA production had constantly increased over the years to an estimated 40,000 tons of ASA produced globally per annum which represented some 80 billion of ASA tablets in 1999.[59] Bayer Aspirin, the most well known ASA brand, benefited from the rising ASA consumption and in 1997 Bayer AG Aspirin sales amounted to of some US$ 550 million. Although Bayer AG still has a *leading position on the analgesics market* with its Bayer Aspirin brand in all world regions except North America and Asia, the company does no longer occupy a dominant position as it did before the First or even Second World War. Nowadays, Bayer's picture of the global analgesic market is much more diversified, not only from the point of view of national competitors but also from a point of view of Bayer Aspirin market coverage and from its positioning in the individual national markets.

Today the different national markets can be classified into three distinctive country groups. The first group represents those countries where Bayer Aspirin still occupies a *dominant market position* with more than 30% market share. This is in particular the case in those countries where Bayer still owns its exclusive right on the trademark Aspirin and/or the brand Bayer Aspirin has been continuously available over the whole 100 year period. Such national markets are, for example, Germany where

[59] Marseille, J. (1999).

Bayer still has between 30 to 40% of the national market for analgesics or Argentine, the country with the highest per capita consumption of Aspirin in the world, where Bayer Aspirin sales account for more than 50% of total national analgesic sales (cf. Table II.1).

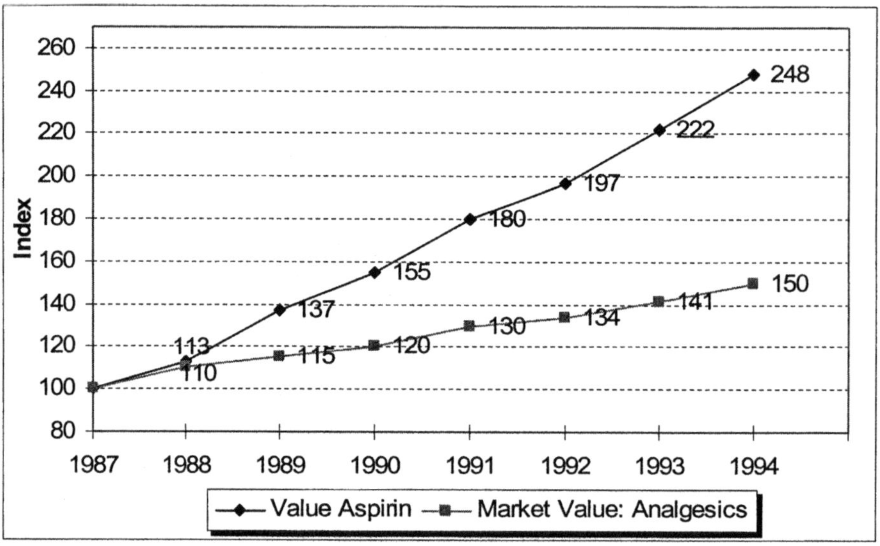

Source: N.A. (1995).

Figure II.5: Index of world-wide analgesics sales: Bayer Aspirin® vs. total analgesic market

The second group is composed of countries where Bayer still is present with its ASA products, however, the company has lost its exclusive right to the trademark Aspirin and thus represents *just the Bayer brand of Aspirin* competing with other Aspirin brands of several different competitors and/or ASA products are perceived as inferior or even 'dangerous' with respect to competing drugs, e.g., USA. The last group of countries is composed of those national markets where Bayer has *completely abandoned the market* for ASA products, e.g., Great Britain and most Eastern European countries.

Although the analgesics market represents still the most important market for Bayer Aspirin products, the *market for the prevention of heart attacks* has become of increasing importance, even though ASA has received in most markets indication for the treatment of second heart attacks only. In the US market, for example, the market for the prevention of second heart attacks has become important and accounts for a significant share in Aspirin sales. A third market which may be of utmost importance in the future for ASA, is the market of *cancer treatment and particularly colon cancer*. Thus, producers of ASA products are convinced that the future of the 'drug of the 20th century' has just begun.

Table II.1: International analgesic market shares of Bayer Aspirin (2000)

Region / Country	**Market Size** (percentage of global analgesic market)	**Market Share of Bayer Aspirin®**
EU	30-35 %	< 20 %
• Germany	5 %	30 - 40 %
USA	40-45 %	< 10 %
Latin America	20 %	> 30 %
• Argentine	N.A.	> 50 %
Asia	10 %	Marginal
World	~ US$ 8 billion	10 – 20 %

II.2.3 Persistent Market Share

Although the drug ASA is already known since the antique and the pharmaceutical Bayer Aspirin celebrated its 100th birthday in 1999, it still is today one of the most sold OTC drugs in the world and Bayer Aspirin the second most important analgesic brand after Tylenol holding a market leader position in most world regions except North America and Asia. In a few national markets Bayer has even been able to uphold its dominant position over the 100 year period even though patent protection was never in place or has expired a long time ago, and the production process of the substance ASA has become broadly known and can be readily imitated by any pharmaceutical or chemical company. Hence, the Bayer AG has long since *lost its technological advantage* and in some countries even the exclusive right to the trademark Aspirin. However, why did other companies not enter the lucrative ASA market and if they did so could not out-compete the Bayer AG?

The Bayer AG has been the *first company* to recognise the specific advantages of the drug ASA and has been able to produce the substance in pure form and large quantities at a reasonable price, and thus initially had a substantial advantage vis-à-vis competing companies. This technological advantage and the superiority of the drug with respect to other products available on the market at that time enabled Leverkusen to rapidly gain market share on a global scale. The rapid spreading of Bayer Aspirin was reinforced by several strong influenza epidemics in Europe and North America. Moreover, the invention of the ASA tablet packaged in tubes displaying the company and product name in 1900 and the coinage of the tablets with the Bayer-Cross brought the consumers into direct contact with the *brand 'Bayer Aspirin.'* The brand attained immediately broad awareness due to the monopoly like position of Bayer's ASA products and consumers attached their positive experiences with the drug to the brand Aspirin. However, the technological advantage of Bayer did not represent a lasting advantage on which the company could build in the long-run. Because no patent protection was available for Bayer, competitors succeeded already in 1902 in producing ASA, although they had initially not been able to imitate the more efficient production process used by Bayer.

The superiority of the drug and the initial technological advantage, although relatively short-lived, enabled Bayer not only to rapidly establish a strong global brand but also to set up a *global distribution network* for its pharmaceutical products. Moreover, the head-start of Bayer, the global presence of Bayer Aspirin products, and their dominant market share enabled the company to benefit of substantial *learning curve effects* which subsequently reduced production cost, improved product quality, and triggered new incremental innovation. These incremental innovations in turn offered consumers perceivable advantages in comparison with competing products. Aspirin tablets, for instance, facilitated the dosage of ASA with respect to ASA powder, or the first soluble Aspirin tablet facilitated the taking of the drug and thus reinforced the image of the brand Bayer Aspirin as an efficient and innovative pharmaceutical.

II.2.3.1 Bayer's Sustainable Strategic Advantage: The Trademark Bayer Aspirin

Although the initial advantage of Bayer was based on the *company specific technological knowledge* on how to produce pure acetylsalicylic acid in large quantities at reasonable costs, the *trademark 'Aspirin' attained early strategic importance*. This was particularly the case in those countries where Bayer did not achieve patent protection of its process invention, but even in the USA the trademark Aspirin was promoted and perceived by Bayer as an extremely long-lasting and important strategic asset. In certain countries the positive associations attached to the trademark Aspirin, as well as the consumers' awareness created and reinforced by promotional activities were so strong that consumers and even physicians were not certain if Aspirin really contained the identical drug as other ASA products not produced by Bayer and thus not sold under the trademark Aspirin. Moreover, the company name and the Bayer-Cross represented in the early years of the 20th century an *important guarantee* against low quality or even mislabelled ASA products in all countries and even kept its reassuring function over the decades, particularly in those countries where a high risk of fraudulent labelling existed, e.g., Latin America and Africa.

With Germany being at the verge of war in the years 1912 to 1914, the Bayer AG perceived the danger of losing its exclusive rights to the trademark Aspirin in several enemy nations. In anticipation of the consequences of such an expropriation Bayer tried to establish a strong link between its corporate name and the trademark 'Aspirin' and thus to transfer the customers' associations held about the trademark Aspirin on the brand '*Bayer Aspirin.*' These efforts concentrated in particular on the pronunciation that only Bayer Aspirin was genuine Aspirin and that the Bayer name guaranteed for superior quality, other Aspirin brands, on the other hand, may be of inferior quality and/or even harmful. However, the brand building strategy did not bring the expected success, since most enemy nations did not only seize and often declared the trademark Aspirin into a generic term, but also confiscated any other tangible and intangible properties including Bayer AG's rights on the corporate name and symbols. A few countries, e.g., USA, Australia, France and Great Britain, even sold any pre World War I properties of Bayer AG to domestic companies.

Although Leverkusen could regain some control over its foreign Aspirin activities during the inter-war period due to its company specific technological knowledge, the outbreak of the Second World War nullified any previous effort. Thus, Bayer had *lost its exclusive rights on its company name, symbol, as well as most trademarks* in many national markets. The two world wars did, however, not only bereave Bayer of its Aspirin business in most enemy nations, e.g., USA, Australia, France, United Kingdom, and associated colonies, but also created a competitor competing with the original Bayer under the same corporate name and symbols – Sterling Products Inc. The co-existence of the two Bayer companies on the international Aspirin market continued until 1970 when Leverkusen bought the international rights on its corporate name and symbols excluding, however, the rights in North America. Bayer AG finally regained its exclusive rights on its corporate name and symbols in the North American market at the end of 1994. The company had, however, permanently lost its trademark Aspirin in many nations.

The *utmost strategic importance of the brand* Bayer Aspirin became particularly apparent in the second half of the 20th century. In those countries where Bayer Aspirin has been permanently available to consumers over the entire 100 year period and/or Bayer still has its exclusive rights on the trademark Aspirin, e.g., Germany, Spain, Italy, and most of Latin American countries, the company still occupies a *leadership position* in the analgesic market. In Germany, for instance, Bayer Aspirin still had a 40% stake in total ASA turnover in 1996 although the standard Bayer Aspirin product was more than 300% more expensive than the cheapest offer on the market.[60] On the other hand, the position of Bayer Aspirin products is considerably weaker in those national markets where the trademark Aspirin has turned into a generic name which can be used by any company for its ASA products, and where the brand has not been sufficiently fostered over the past years because of the legal quarrels between Sterling Products Inc. and Bayer AG. In these national and regional markets, e.g., North America, Bayer Aspirin is still present, but faces fierce competition by multiple national Aspirin brands and even ASA's general position on the market for analgesics is substantially weakened or even threatened by competing drugs. In the US analgesics market, for example, Johnson & Johnson's brand Tylenol, a pharmaceutical based on acetaminophen, has overtaken Bayer Aspirin and occupies a dominant position on the national analgesic market. Finally, in those national markets where the Bayer Aspirin brand was not present at all over a period of several years and consumers have become acquainted with national Aspirin brands, e.g., France and former colonies, Bayer has no intent to re-enter these national markets directly because of the *lack of strategic advantage* vis-à-vis the established national competitors. Since the end of the First World War most chemical and pharmaceutical companies have the knowledge to produce pure ASA in large quantities, and thus Bayer AG no longer has a significant technological advantage which is readily perceivable by consumers.[61]

In France and its former colonies, for example, Bayer AG had not been present with its ASA based analgesics products until 1997 when the company acquired the ASA business of Rhône-Poulenc Rorer. Even today, Bayer is still selling its ASA products in these countries under the brand *Aspirine du Rhône* which is one of the most important ASA brands in French speaking countries, and not under the brand Bayer Aspirin. This is due to the fact that the name Bayer is not associated by consumers in these countries with the name Aspirin or the pharmaceutical industry in general, but rather with the chemical industry.

Nevertheless, Bayer Aspirin still has, more than 100 years after its initial market launch, a considerable *strategic advantage* in those markets

---

[60] N.A. (1996).

[61] Although the knowledge how to produce ASA in pure form and high quantities is nowadays considered as basic technological knowledge, ASA molecules produced by Bayer AG still show a qualitative advantage which is, however, only perceivable under laboratory conditions and not by consumers.

where the brand Bayer Aspirin has been permanently available with regard to competing ASA and even Aspirin brands. In most of these markets consumers still associated the brand Bayer Aspirin with genuine Aspirin, good quality, familiarity, and high innovativeness, whereas competing ASA brands are perceived as low priced imitations. Thus, even though all ASA products are today of almost identical quality, consumers still perceive Bayer Aspirin as superior and, as Chmilewski of Bayer brand management pointed out: "*Perception is reality*!" In addition, the brand Bayer Aspirin and its relatively higher price positively influences the vendors' sales argumentation. This is particularly true in those countries where Aspirin is exclusively sold in pharmacies. The relatively high demand for Bayer Aspirin products obliges pharmacies to have the brand in its stock and moreover, the considerably higher absolute margins of Bayer Aspirin products for the pharmacy reinforces the vendor's endeavour to sell Bayer Aspirin instead of a lower priced, alternative ASA brand.[62] Thus, Bayer does not only have an advantage vis-à-vis competing pharmaceuticals due to the broad awareness, high customer loyalty and consumers' perception of superiority of the brand Bayer Aspirin, but also due to the established global distribution network, as well as the readiness of distributors to hold a stock of those pharmaceuticals which are in high demand and to promote in particular the pharmaceutical that shows the highest absolute profit margin.

II.2.3.2 Innovations Nurturing Existing Brand Equity

Bayer AG was able to establish its strong brand Bayer Aspirin which still benefits of broad global consumer awareness, and an image of high quality and innovativeness because of its initial monopoly like position due to the company's specific technological knowledge and patent protection in the US market. In addition to its initial advantage, Bayer succeeded in continuously improving product quality and ease of utilisation and has thereby *cultivated and strengthened its innovative image* over the years (cp. table II.2). Moreover, the superior quality of Bayer Aspirin with respect to competing products until about the 1920s created a strong consumer loyalty towards the company name Bayer, and in particular the

---

[62] In Germany, for example, Bayer Aspirin is only sold in pharmacies and the general price mark-up of the pharmacy is in the order of range of 50% of the purchase price. Consequently, a pharmacy is more inclined to promote a Bayer Aspirin 0.5 tablet at a price of DM 0.34 per tablet than a comparable ASS-ratiopharm 500 at a price of DM 0.08 per tablet and thus absolute revenues of DM 0.17 vs. DM 0.04 per tablet, respectively.

brand Aspirin. Thus, the *brand* which was immediately of high strategic importance due to the absence of patent right protection, enabled Bayer AG, in combination with the consumers' lack of knowledge about the pharmaceuticals active substance and hence comparability with other ASA products sold under different brands, to dominate the market. Hence, even though competing companies had acquired the knowledge of how to produce pure ASA in large quantities by 1915, consumers and pharmacists had been reluctant to change to other brands because they did generally not know the exact differences between the various brands.

The uniformity of the consumers' associations across the different national or even regional markets changed with the appearance of the two Bayer brands. In those markets where Sterling Products Inc. served the market with Bayer Aspirin products until the last quarter of the 20th century, e.g., USA, the brand Bayer Aspirin is perceived as familiar, homy, well proven, but rather outdated analgesic. This is due to ASA's image of being an inferior or even harmful drug that may causes stomach complaints with respect to acetaminophen or ibuprofen in the respective markets. In contrast, those markets which have been permanently served with Bayer Aspirin by Leverkusen, the brand has the image of being a familiar, well proven, effective, and innovative pharmaceutical. The *diverging associations* of consumers about the brand Bayer Aspirin in the different national analgesic markets, even though Bayer Aspirin's basic characteristics are identical over all markets, is due to the efforts of the two companies to further improve and ameliorate its Aspirin products.

Bayer AG has been the only company continuously investing considerable resources into research and development in the field of ASA. As table II.2 reveals, Bayer AG has succeeded in *continuously improving* the pharmaceutical by either reducing side effects, increasing effectiveness in the different application fields, or facilitating dosage and use of Aspirin products. These innovations in the field of galenica and effectiveness have been replenished by the discovering of new indications for ASA, i.e., heart attack prevention and possibly cancer. On the other hand, Sterling Products Inc. and even other producers of ASA products have followed a strategy of exploiting the currently existing technology without investing in the improvement of the drug's qualities.

R&D in the Field of ASA

Bayer AG which had been one of the early companies developing new drugs entirely within the company through organised R&D activities, is still one of the leading European companies with respect to R&D expenditures in the pharmaceutical field. In fiscal year 1999 Bayer had invested some US$ 1.38 billion in R&D activities in the field of pharmaceuticals.[63] Moreover, with respect to acetylsalicylic acid Bayer AG even represents the only company devoting significant financial resources to research and development. Thus, Bayer AG has occupied since the early 20th century a *technologically leading position* in the field of ASA and has defended its position throughout the century by significantly investing in R&D. Competitors, on the other hand, do generally not invest into R&D in the field of ASA, but follow a strategy of fast imitation if the market seems to be economically interesting. The company has, for example, been the first to offer ASA tablets which significantly facilitated the dosage of the drug and reduced the risk of false indication for consumers. Even before most competitors had imitated the ASA tablet, Bayer AG was already about to launch the soluble ASA tablet which further facilitated the taking of the drug (cf. table II.2).

Table II.2: Most important innovations of Bayer AG in the field of ASA

Year	Innovation	Advantage	Brand
1899	Acetylsalicylic acid (ASA)	Effectiveness, low side effects	Aspirin
1900	ASA tablet	Ease of dosage, reduction of consumer risk	Aspirin
1904	Soluble ASA tablet	Ease of utilisation	Aspirin
1971	ASA + Vitamin C effervescent tablet	Reduction of side effects, vitamin C	Bayer Aspirin + C
1992	Chewable ASA tablet	Ease of utilisation	Bayer Aspirin direkt Kau-tablette
1993	Enteric coated ASA tablets for the long-term treatment and heart attack prophylaxis	Effectiveness in the treatment of heart attacks, improved gastric tolerability	Bayer Aspirin Protect
2000	ASA tablets (two 500 mg tablets in twin-pack) for the treatment of migraine	Effectiveness in the treatment of strong pain	Bayer Aspirin Migraine

Source: Schreiner, C. (1999).

A more recent example presents the chewable ASA tablet that enables the consumer to use ASA in circumstances where no water is available and

[63] Cp. Bayer annual report (2000).

thus enlarges the range of application and facilitates the usage with respect to ordinary ASA which has to be dissolved in water. Although the innovation of the chewable ASA tablet was not patentable, as most of the incremental innovations in the field of ASA, competitors have not imitated the chewable tablet, yet. Hitherto, competitors do not possess the needed *process knowledge* on how to produce chewable ASA tablets and they are not certain if the market for chewable ASA tablets will be sufficiently large to justify the investments required to acquire the needed knowledge. On the other hand, Bayer AG is using its temporary lead to create positive associations with and broad awareness of its new product and thus establish or reinforce customer loyalty. Moreover, by continuously being the first to introduce incremental innovations in the field of ASA Leverkusen not only gets a head-start in acquiring customers in the new application areas but it also fosters its innovative image in the general field of ASA.

In-house R&D activities do, however, not represent the only source of innovation. Bayer AG also *supports and motivates external research* in the field of ASA by financing interesting research projects and conferring the 'Aspirin Award' to those scientists which have considerably contributed to the uncovering of interesting discoveries in the field of ASA. In addition, these research results are of extremely high marketing importance by keeping ASA and thus Bayer Aspirin in scientific and/or public discussion. Moreover, by financing interesting research projects Bayer AG assures that the publication of the results mentions the name Aspirin which is still closely associated in various nations with the company Bayer AG, and does not use the generic term acetylsalicylic acid or even ASA which puts competitors at a communication disadvantage.

Thus, by investing, supporting, and/or motivating company internal and external R&D in the field of ASA, Bayer AG has succeeded to defend its technology leadership position, foster its innovative image, and continuously improve its Aspirin products and thereby keep them competitive with respect to alternative drugs. Moreover, by motivating scientists to publish new findings in the field of ASA under the name Aspirin, Bayer AG has even succeeded in creating strong associations between new indications of ASA and the corporate name and the Bayer Aspirin brand. The strong link between the corporate name and the product brand in most countries may also explain the pronounced interest of Bayer in the development of the drug ASA and thus the Bayer Aspirin brand which still is undisputedly one of the most well known pharmaceutical brands of Bayer AG and significantly influences the overall image consumers hold about the company as a whole.

II.2.3.3 Bayer Aspirin in the 21st Century

As discussed above, ASA is no longer the drug of first choice in all countries, nor is Bayer Aspirin the undisputed leading brand in the analgesics market. Nevertheless, the brand is still the second most important international analgesics brand in the world after Tylenol and represents one of Bayer's most important pharmaceuticals. In fiscal year 1999, for example, Bayer Aspirin was the company's 3rd most important pharmaceutical in terms of sales with an annual turnover of some US$ 580 million (see table II.3). Moreover, the company estimates that the sales growth of Aspirin will lie above the average growth figures in the analgesics market and the importance of new fields of indication, i.e., prophylaxis of second heart attacks and stroke, will rise in importance for the drug ASA and thus Bayer Aspirin.

Table II.3: Bayer AG's most important health-care products in1999

Pharmaceutical	1999 Sales (US$ million)	Change to Previous Year
Ciprobay®	1,519	17%
Adalat®	1,021	6%
Aspirin®	580	6%
Kogenate®	377	-2%
Glucometer® Elite	354	18%

Source: Bayer annual report (2000).

Bayer, however, does not see the future of the drug ASA, and the brand Bayer Aspirin in particular, in the analgesic market, but rather in new fields of indication. In the USA, for example, the market of the prophylaxis of second heart attacks has already become extremely important for Bayer Aspirin and accounts for an increasing share of its sales in the market for analgesics which is dominated in the USA by Johnson & Johnson. However, Bayer tries to further extend the field of indication of ASA into the fields of first heard attack and even cancer prevention. The field of colorectal cancer prevention appears particularly interesting since the drug's effectiveness has already been proven in various studies.[64] Furthermore, in certain countries, i.e., Belgium, Greece and Italy, ASA has obtained approval from official authorities for the prevention of first heart attacks for certain high risk groups. Bayer's brand

64 Cp. Schreiner, C. (1999).

equity, representing the company's most important competitive advantage in the market for analgesics today, is easily transferred to these new markets by keeping the basic characteristics of the pharmaceutical unchanged, using the same trademark, as well as market appearance. Moreover, Bayer not only transfers the established brand equity and thus the consumers' association of familiarity, effectiveness, and good quality, but also builds on an established global distribution network.

The brand Bayer Aspirin not only bestows Bayer with a strategic advantage in new fields of indication of the drug ASA due to its ready transferability, but also facilitates the introduction of new incremental innovations in already existing markets, e.g., analgesics. This is in particular true for those markets where Bayer Aspirin is perceived as an innovative pharmaceutical, e.g., Germany, Argentine, or Spain. In these markets consumers perceive Bayer as the technology leader in the field of ASA *and thus are inclined to accept new incremental innovations* such as the effervescent ASA tablets containing vitamin C, the chewable ASA tablets, or the twin-packaged ASA tablets for the treatment of migraine, all launched under the trademark Bayer Aspirin. In the case of the Bayer Aspirin Migraine tablets introduced on the German market in June 2000, for instance, 70% of the pharmacies had already commanded the new product more than 6 month in advance of the initial market launch of the product and without even knowing the product's final success on the market. But, the *consumers' acceptance of new Aspirin products* is in these national markets extremely high since they know the brand from their youth and have accumulated considerable positive experiences over the past. Furthermore, the basic characteristics of Aspirin have never changed and the product has been permanently available on those markets and thus consumers use the brand Bayer Aspirin as a *reinsurance* for high quality, good effectiveness, and low side effects.

On the other hand, the pharmaceutical Bayer Aspirin is threatened by the appearance of new drugs excelling ASA in the different fields of indication. Monsanto and Merck & Co. have, for example, developed new pharmaceuticals which are generally referred to as '*Super-Aspirins*,' that use the cyclooxygenase 2 (COX-2) inhibitor as the active substance and thus concentrate entirely on the field of pain and inflammation without having the disadvantages of ASA (cf. figure II.4).[65] Although these new pharmaceuticals have already received market approval in various nations they will remain ethical drugs and more importantly extremely expensive for the next couple of years. Nevertheless, these Super-Aspirins represent a considerable threat for ASA products in the analgesic market. However,

[65] Cp. N.A. (1998).

the advantage of ASA and thus of the pharmaceutical Bayer Aspirin with respect to the new Super-Aspirins remains its cycooxygenase 1 (COX-1) inhibiting function which in turn explains the drug's effectiveness in the prophylaxis of heart-attacks.

Thus, Bayer Aspirin is threatened in its dominant position on the global analgesic market by COX-2 inhibiting drugs which are assumed to be more efficient in releasing pain, inflammation as well as fever, and in addition do not have the ASA specific side effects, i.e., attacking the lining of the stomach or the possible link to the Reye's syndrome.[66] Nevertheless, in the *medium term* these new drugs remain too expensive for large-scale employment and thus their utilisation will be limited to patients which have to consume large quantities of ASA over a prolonged period and thus are severely concerned of the side effects of ASA. Furthermore, because of insufficient experience, these Super-Aspirins will remain an ethical drugs for some years and thus Bayer Aspirin will not be directly concerned in the medium term since the pharmaceutical's most important market is the OTC analgesic market. Last but not least, ASA will remain the dominant drug for second heart attack, as well as stroke prophylaxis and may even receive indication for first heart attack prevention which has a significant influence on consumers' purchasing decision in the OTC analgesic market in favour of ASA drugs and hence Bayer Aspirin. In the *long-term*, however, the Super-Aspirins may become a more serious competitor for any ASA drug in the analgesic market due to their superior effectiveness and the prospect that with increasing process-knowledge in the production of the drugs and mounting competition prices will decline. Moreover, it can be assumed that the new Super-Aspirins will receive OTC approval in the future and consequently attack ASA in its most important market segment.

Thus, the future of Bayer Aspirin in the analgesic market is still open and the pharmaceutical still has a dominant position on the global market more than 100 years after its initial market launch and will probably be able to defend its market position in the years to come. Furthermore, new fields of indication, e.g., heart attack or cancer prophylaxis will open up new prospects which may be able to substitute for losses Bayer could experience in the OTC analgesic market due to the appearance of new, superior drugs. In addition, Bayer AG represents today the company with the most extensive knowledge and experience in the field of ASA and thus may be able to transfer its specific knowledge onto the related fields of COX-1 and COX-2 inhibitors and use its established global distribution network in launching a prospective new pharmaceutical. Although Bayer

---

[66] Cp. N.A. (1998).

will not be able to use the brand Bayer Aspirin for a new analgesic pharmaceutical based on another drug, and is probably not even willing to do so after the experience of Sterling Products Inc. with the brand Bayer-Non-Aspirin in the 1970s, it may be able to transfer some of the positive associations consumers attach to the brand Bayer Aspirin, i.e., good quality, effectiveness, etc., by associating the new pharmaceutical with the company name and associated symbols. Thus, even though the technology life-cycle of the drug ASA, and thus of the product Bayer Aspirin, has already passed its glory days in the market for analgesics, Bayer may still be able to transfer a part of its assets, e.g., technological knowledge, existing distribution channels, or a certain positive image consumers associate with the company name Bayer and the Bayer-Cross, and thus may have a certain advantage with its new pharmaceutical vis-à-vis competitors or at least facilitates the market launch of the new product under a new Bayer brand.

Conversely, the incidents of the Bayer pharmaceutical LIPOBAY which had lost market approval due to suspects of strong side effects with even mortal effects and had to be withdrawn from the market in the summer 2001. The loss of market approval for one of Bayer's pharmaceuticals with an extremely high growth rate and the preliminary proceedings taken by the Office of Public Prosecutor in various countries because of violation of the pharmaceutical law have severely damaged the reputation associated with the Bayer name in the pharmaceutical industry in general. The Bayer LIPOBAY scandal finally reached the dimension of Bayer thinking about completely selling its pharmaceutical branch and the leave finally turned as Bayer was the only pharmaceutical company able to readily offer an effective anti-anthrax drug: Bayer CIPROBAY. These incidents which occurred within a few months and their considerable influence on the reputation of the Bayer brand in the general market for pharmaceuticals and thus also on the product Bayer Aspirin tellingly illustrate the disadvantages of using corporate brands, as well as the extreme influence of isolated incidents on the general reputation of a company in a certain market and thus the vulnerability of established brand equity.

II.2.4 Discussion and Findings

The case Bayer Aspirin endeavoured to reveal how Bayer succeeded to sustain its dominant position on the global analgesic market and to still represent the second most important analgesic brand and by far the most important ASA brand in the world, more than 100 years after the initial innovation. Although, one has to keep in mind that Bayer Aspirin represents a specific case with a particular history, it nevertheless clearly points out the central importance of company specific technological knowledge and established brand equity in bestowing a company with a specific and lasting advantage which enables the company to appropriate a better part of the revenues generated by a certain technology. Moreover, the case revealed the outstanding importance of brand equity and company specific technological knowledge in appropriating the revenues of the initial innovation, acetylsalicylic acid.

Even though Bayer AG did not receive patent protection of its initial innovation in most countries, the company had during the first decade an almost monopoly like position due to its specific knowledge about the production process of ASA. Thus, already at the market launch of Bayer Aspirin, the trademark had an important strategic role, since it represented (with the exception of the US patent) the only legal protection Bayer had on its innovation. This strategic role of the trademark was considerably reinforced by the market launch of the ASA tablets stamped with the Bayer-Cross and packaged in tubes clearly displaying the company and product name. Thus, the dominant market position of Bayer due to the company's specific process knowledge, as well as the striking superiority of the drug with respect to competing substances not only led to a rapid global proliferation of the pharmaceutical, but also led to an immediate awareness of consumers about the brand Aspirin to which they attached their positive experiences.[67] Consequently, by the beginning of the 1920s when large numbers of companies succeeded in producing pure ASA, they were put at a considerable disadvantage since consumers, and often even physicians, were not able to evaluate the prevailing differences between the pharmaceutical Aspirin and other pharmaceuticals using the same drug, but being sold under alternative trademarks.

Although Bayer received patent protection in the USA for the invention of the improved production process of ASA, the company's specific process knowledge and the trademark had a comparable significance as in the other markets where no patent protection was available. This became particularly apparent by the acquisition of Bayer's properties by Sterling Products Inc. in 1918 and the company's inability to produce ASA even though it had Bayer's entire production facilities and Bayer's patent document describing the production process at its disposal. On the other hand, the utmost importance of the trademark Aspirin already during the early years of Aspirin's history can be deduced from Bayer's readiness to

[67] In the discussion the name Bayer Aspirin is used to represents all Aspirin brands of Bayer in the various national and regional markets, e.g., ASPIRINA, Bayaspirina, or Aspirine du Rhône.

help Sterling in using its production facilities in exchange for the right to use the name Aspirin in the Latin American countries, although Bayer perceived the acquisition of its properties by Sterling as theft.

Since then, the importance of the brand Bayer Aspirin has further increased in strategic significance because of the increased number of companies capable to produce pure ASA in large quantities. Thus, even though Bayer may still have an advance with respect to its technological knowledge about ASA with regard to competitors, today the only remaining significant strategic advantage of Bayer is its established brand Bayer Aspirin. This becomes particularly apparent by comparing those nations where the brand Bayer Aspirin has not been available over the past with those countries where the pharmaceutical has been permanently marketed either by Leverkusen itself or by Sterling Products. So is Bayer Aspirin still available in those markets where the brand has been available over the entire period, e.g., Germany, Spain, Argentine, but has completely disappeared from those markets where Bayer Aspirin had not been marketed over a prolonged period, e.g., Great Britain and most Eastern European countries. In addition, Bayer has lost in these countries any strategic advantage, since consumers became familiar with alternative brands and no longer associate the positive experiences with the Bayer brand of ASA and consequently Bayer does not intend to re-enter these markets directly with the Bayer Aspirin brand.

Thus, the brand represents today Bayer's only significant strategic advantage enabling the company, however, to defend its strong position on the global analgesic market by demanding considerably higher prices than comparable pharmaceuticals offered by competitors under alternative brands. Moreover, by extending the brand into new fields of indication, Bayer was able to transfer its image of good quality, effectiveness, and low side effects in these markets and consequently acquire considerable shares of these new markets, i.e., prophylaxis of heart attacks and stroke. A rough estimate of the considerable economic value the brand Bayer Aspirin has reached today is given by Bayer's willingness to pay US$ 1 billion in 1994, even though the company was free to use its corporate name and associated symbols in any market except the ASA business in the US market, where Bayer was already present with the brand Alka-Seltzer sold under the company name Miles.

Moreover, the diverging associations which prevail in the different national markets, can be perceived as an indication of the importance of incremental technological innovations in adapting the product to the current market needs and conditions and thus reinforcing the consumers' association and consequently fostering existing brand equity. As the case clearly showed, in those countries where Leverkusen has continuously been supplying the market with Bayer Aspirin, the brand is associated by consumers with good quality, effectiveness, familiarity, and innovativeness, whereas the same brand is perceived as familiar, well proved, but rather outdated and sometimes even dangerous in those countries where Sterling Products was serving the market. Thus, even though both companies were using the same trademark in selling almost identical products, Bayer succeeded in maintaining its innovative image over a period of more than 100 years. The striking difference between the two Bayer companies with respect to the pharmaceutical was Leverkusen's striving to continuously improve the pharmaceutical with respect to its taking, side effects, and even field of indication while Sterling Products neglected R&D in the field of ASA and entirely concentrated on marketing activities. Thus, whereas Bayer has been able to react to the threat of new emerging drugs in the analgesic market by further ameliorating its pharmaceutical, and subsequently launched the Bayer Aspirin Protect and Bayer Aspirin plus C tablets in 1992 and 1993 which have considerably less side effects than ordinary ASA, Sterling had to face competition with the already 90 year old ordinary ASA tablets. Consequently, Bayer succeeded by continuously improving its product and by swiftly using new findings about ASA's effectiveness in new fields of indication to maintain its innovative image and in consequence not only endorsed its dominant position on the ASA market successfully, but even on the analgesic market in general.

In conclusion, we can say that the brand Bayer Aspirin was and still is the most important strategic asset of the Bayer AG in the analgesic market. This strong, global brand has been established with the help of the company's specific technological knowledge and patent right protection in the USA. Companies missing a brand or technology advantage have not been able to seriously threaten Bayer Aspirin on the market for ASA although certain companies offered comparable product more than 300% cheaper than Bayer Aspirin. Furthermore, even though if the era of ASA and thus Bayer Aspirin in the analgesic market would approach its end, Bayer AG could still use its market based assets, i.e., existing distribution networks and consumers' awareness of the Bayer brand, as well as its technological knowledge of ASA and related fields to obtain an advantage vis-à-vis companies not possessing these assets. These lasting advantages for Bayer may explain the outstanding importance of the Bayer Aspirin business which is not only perceived by the company and even consumers as one isolated brand, but rather as an important image bearer for the whole Bayer group in the pharmaceutical industry. This image bearing role of Bayer Aspirin for the whole Bayer activities in the pharmaceutical industry has gained considerable importance because of the recent problems the company encountered with its pharmaceutical LIPOBAY and the considerable adverse effects the incident had on the corporate brand in that market.

In the next section we present the company Cisco Systems and analyse the specific strategic role of brand equity for the case in question. Although the company's history is much shorter than that of Bayer Aspirin, and the company is not active in the pharmaceutical industry characterised by relatively long product and technology life-cycles, but rather in the fast-cycle industry of network equipment, the initial sources of brand equity, its strategic role, as well as the principal brand management principles and the mutual complementarity of leading technological expertise and brand equity appear to be identical in the two cases.

II.3 Case Study: Cisco Systems

II.3.1 Company Profile

Cisco Systems, based in San Jose, California, has been established by Leonard Bosack and Sandy Lerner in 1984, who were attending Stanford University at that time. The two founders worked out a way how different computer networks could communicate via an electronic router. The possibility to communicate between different distant computer networks presented a solution to a growing problem at that time. Thus, a market for routers quickly developed and with the market the venture capital financed small company Cisco Systems.[68] Meanwhile Cisco Systems has turned into one of the most valuable companies with the 16th most valuable brand in the world in the year 2001. This remarkable success is not only due to the invention of a new technology but also to its ability to dominate the fast changing networking industry which is in general rather the domain of high-tech start-up companies, and to constantly deliver high quality products with a leading edge technology.

Today, Cisco Systems is an international company with total net sales amounting to some US$ 18.9 billion in fiscal year 2000. The most important fields of corporate activity are routers and switches with net sales amounting to US$ 7.6 billion and US$ 7.5 billion, followed by access and other activities with US$ 2.4 billion and US$ 2.8 billion, respectively.[69] The most important region with respect to Cisco Systems'

[68] Cp. Bunnel, D. (2000), chap. 1.

[69] Cp. Cisco Systems annual report (2000).

sales represents the Americas region, and here in particular North America, where some 63.5% of the company's net sales were attained. The region Europe, Middle East and Africa (EMEA) represents the second most important region where 23.5% of total sales were achieved in the year 2000 followed by Asia Pacific and Japan with 8.5% and 4.5%, respectively. With regard to the EMEA region the most important national market represents Great Britain, followed by Germany and France.

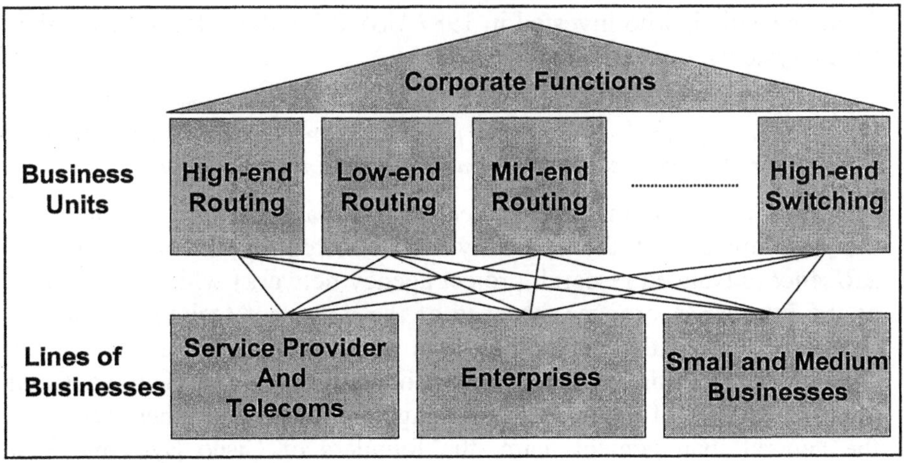

Figure II.6: Organisation of Cisco Systems

As illustrated in figure II.6, Cisco Systems is structured in business units which have global responsibility for the concerning technological field, and lines of businesses (LOBS) which have global market responsibility for the concerning customer group. In the year 2000 the company had some 60 business units which have been reduced during the year 2001 to approximately 30 business units, e.g., high-, low-, mid-end routing, as well as switching, wireless, etc., and three LOBS, i.e., Service Provider & Telecoms, Enterprises, and Small & Medium Businesses. Moreover, in fiscal year 2000 the company invested some US$ 2.7 billion in R&D which represents an increase in R&D expenditures of almost 63% with respect to the preceding year.

II.3.2 From the Computer Lab to the Global Leader in the Internet Economy

The invention of the router of Sandy Lerner of the Stranford University Business School and Leonard Bosack of the Computer Science

Department which was motivated by the fact that they could not communicate via e-mail because their departments used different computer networks, became an instant success.[70] The successfulness of Lerner and Bosack was due to the existing market need for routers able to connect distant computer networks of different nature and the focus of the newly found "cisco systems" (the lowercase c has later been altered into a capital C) on maintaining unique customer relationship, and high commitment to customer satisfaction. Accordingly, venture capitalist Don Valentine of Sequoia Capital, who invested in 1987 US$ 2.5 million for a 32% stake in Cisco Systems, pointed out:

> *"... Cisco in 1987 filled a desperate need. Customers were tearing the hinges off the door to get the products. I never met a company that entered the market in such a timely way with no competition."*[71]

Thus, Cisco Systems quickly became the market leader for routers and the development of the company was boosted by the *opening of the ARPAnet* (advanced research project agency network) which later evolved as the Internet. Moreover, because of the dominant technology of Cisco Systems' routers the technology was about to evolve as the *de facto standard* in routing. However, due to animosity with Sequoia Capital about the choice of the executive management team and other members of the general management team, the founders of Cisco Systems, Sandy Lerner and Leonard Bosak, left the company after John P. Morgridge had become the new president and CEO of Cisco Systems and the company had turned public in 1990. At that time Cisco Systems had already grown to a company with an US$ 4.2 million profit in fiscal year 1989.[72] Due to the strong effort of Cisco Systems to focus on customer satisfaction and strong customer relationships,[73] the company continued its high growth which obtained a further important impetus by the creation of the first *Internet browser* that was later marketed by the company Netscape Communications. This browser opened the Internet to a large number of potential users and consequently boosted the demand for network equipment and thus routers from Cisco Systems.

With the growing market for network equipment new companies entered the market and alternative networking technologies appeared, e.g., switching, which threatened Cisco Systems' 80% market share in the router business. Morgridge and John Chambers, Senior Vice President of

---

[70] Cp. Bunnel, D. (2000), chap. 1.

[71] Bunnel, D. (2000), p. 11.

[72] Bunnel, D. (2000), pp. 15-22.

[73] For a more detailed discussion see section II.3.2.2.

Wang Laboratories, who joined Cisco Systems in 1991 and who later turned out as Morgridge's successor as Cisco Systems' CEO in 1995, realised that Cisco Systems had to *diversify* and turn into a *full-line supplier* of network equipment if the company wanted to remain successful in the exploding market for network equipment in the future.

II.3.2.1 Cisco Systems: A Large Multinational with the Culture of a High-tech Start-up

Cisco Systems' management team was aware that the company could not attain the target of quickly and successfully entering new businesses with distinct technologies, e.g., switching, and to turn into a one-stop-selling position for network equipment by internal development. Moreover, market development has been too fast and uncertain in the networking field that management agreed that Cisco could not get into its envisaged position of a complete solution provider offering the latest technological developments in all fields by internal research and development activities, but rather has to follow a strategy of constant acquisitions. This is how Cisco Systems' *strategy of acquisition and development* (A&D) was born that has the aim to keep Cisco in a position to develop and market an increasing number of diverse networking products and standards within the company.

Cisco Systems which employed in 1993 some 1000 employees, realised that it could not out-compete small high-tech start-up companies in the diverse fields of technological innovation related to network equipment. However, an excessive acquisition strategy is inherently difficult and extremely risky since companies are often not perfectly complementary and thus acquisitions often entail the laying off of employees, clashing management styles and corporate cultures which again brings about the leaving of specialised employees of the acquired companies and the frustration of those who are staying. This *potential brain-drain* presents a particular problem since Cisco Systems endeavours to acquire new technologies and innovative products needed to uphold and extend its market position as a complete solution provider. Thus, it has been of utmost importance to ensure that the *employees* of the acquired companies would stay with Cisco Systems post acquisition in order to contribute their technological know-how and expertise, and/or finalise and launch the new product.

Strategy of Acquisition and Development (A&D)

Since the acquisition of the company Crescendo, a start-up company in the field of switching with US$ 10 million in revenues, for US$ 97 million in

1996, Cisco Systems has acquired numerous companies in various fields complementing what Cisco considers to be its core competencies. Since 1984 Cisco Systems has acquired some 70 companies, whereof most are located in the USA and particularly in the bay area. Although Cisco Systems has grown in the meantime to a large company with US$ 22.2 billion in revenues and employing some 38.000 people in fiscal year 2001, it has succeeded in a record-braking employee retention rate. In average 95% of the employees of the acquired start-up companies have stayed with the company post acquisition. In comparison, in the industry an average of 40% of the employees leave the company after acquisition. This *high retention rate* of Cisco Systems is claimed to be brought about by various factors of which the most important are: (1) the thorough evaluation and appraisal of the potential company though for acquisition, (2) the forthcoming manner of Cisco Systems and its representatives during negotiations, and (3) the meticulous integration of the company and its employees within the corporate network of Cisco Systems.

During the *period of evaluation* Cisco Systems sets out to check if the potential acquisition fulfils the five key selection criteria of sharing a common view and complementary product strategy, being culturally compatible with the specific corporate culture of Cisco Systems, if the acquired technology is critical to Cisco's customers and thus if the acquisition provides a long-term strategic win for all involved parties, i.e., shareholders, customers, employees, and business partners, and finally it has to be geographically desirable which means in, or close to the Silicon Valley or near its East Coast headquarters in North Carolina. Moreover, the company thought for acquisition obligatorily needs a product that is at least close to market launch. During the entire period of negotiations Cisco Systems asserts to pay attention to point out the *mutual benefits* of an acquisition and to proceed in a friendly and relaxed atmosphere. A hostile take-over is claimed not to be in the interest of Cisco Systems. Nevertheless, Cisco takes a close and meticulous look in order to ensure that the choice of company is a good one, that there are no hidden problems with respect to financial details, and if the employees of all levels could be integrated into Cisco Systems successfully. If all these steps are passed successfully, Cisco Systems starts the *integration of people and products* of the acquired company already before the acquisition is actually transacted.[74] In this integration process, however, Cisco stresses that people are put first in order to ensure the retention of the employees and thus the success of the acquisition. This is of extreme importance since Cisco Systems' aim is always to get hold of the

---

[74] Cp. Bunnel, D. (2000), pp. 64-75.

technological know-how of a company and thus its people and not the elimination of a direct competitor.

Furthermore, the success of the acquisition strategy is ensured through the advantages of which the acquired companies benefit through the integration in the Cisco Systems corporation. Since Cisco Systems principally focuses in its acquisition on small high-tech start-up companies which do have a technological advance in comparison with its competitors but lack a global marketing and distribution network and thus suffer from severe disadvantages in the market launch of its innovative products. Cisco Systems enables these start-up companies to considerably shorten *time-to-market* by giving access to its established global marketing and distribution networks, and its established customer relationships. Moreover, the acquired companies benefit of the *general advantages of large companies*, e.g., employment security and social benefits, enlarged budget for R&D. These advantages are accompanied by the possibility of the newly integrated companies to retain high freedom and technological responsibility and thus a *motivating and highly entrepreneurial environment* resembling that of a high-tech start-up company. The perpetuation of the start-up like culture ex-post acquisition is tried to be ensured by the manner how the new entity is organisationally integrated in the overall structure of Cisco Systems. First of all, since Cisco merely attempts to acquire companies that complement its current technological and product portfolio and the integration of most employees is clarified before the acquisition is actually executed, there remains no or only very little scope for uncertainty and fear. Furthermore, the maintenance of a highly motivating and start-up like working environment is supported by the *high autonomy and freedom* with respect to technological research and development the integrated companies enjoy. Acquired companies are often organisationally integrated within the Cisco Systems structure in the form of an independent business unit (cf. figure II.6). From a technological and product point of view, a *fast integration* of the products of the acquired companies is warranted by the use of an identical software, the '*Internetwork Operating System*' (IOS), that is uniform to all products of Cisco Systems. The identical software platform in turn guarantees an *optimal interoperability* of all individual products.

The persistent success Cisco Systems has shown in its acquisition and development strategy which aims to integrate relatively small high-tech companies that complement Cisco's actual technological and product portfolio and by doing so to remain ahead of its main competitors, can be attributed to the companies above presented *acquisition procedure*. Moreover, the company has managed to remain highly flexible and keep an entrepreneurial spirit resembling that of a small start-up company by keeping bureaucracy in check as well as giving the business units a high level of freedom, and thus to *combine the advantages* of a small high-tech start-up company with that of a large established multinational company. In addition, by keeping its entrepreneurial spirit, establishing a global marketing and distribution network, in combination with its open communication policy, Cisco Systems seems to have become an *acquirer of first choice* for high-tech start-up companies within the field of network equipment which is highly trusted and respected by actual and potential employees. The high trust of employees in the company and their empowerment, the specific corporate culture of Cisco Systems, as well as the issuing of stock options are identified as being of utmost importance in retaining and attracting new, highly qualified employees. Moreover, a considerable advantage of Cisco Systems has been its ability to pay for acquisitions by its own shares which has enabled the company to pay the outrageous amounts for even small start-up companies in the range of up to several billion US$.[75]

Internal Research & Development (R&D)

Although Cisco Systems follows a strategy of acquisition of companies with technological competencies complementing the actual competencies of the company, and having an interesting product in its development pipeline that is close to market launch, internal R&D activities play an important role. Internal R&D projects have two principal aims:

1. To finish the *development* and technologically *integrate* the products of the acquired companies, and
2. To keep Cisco Systems' business units at the *technological edge* in their respective technological field.

Thus, due to the high number of acquisitions, the increasing diversity of fields of corporate activity within the field of network equipment, the rising number of competitors within the different fields, and the rapid technological development has entrenched a high growth in corporate expenditures on R&D over the past years. In fiscal year 2000 R&D expenditures have reached a new all-time high of US$ 2.7 billion compared with US$ 1.7 billion in 1999, an annual increase of 62.6%.

[75] Cisco Systems has acquired, e.g., in fiscal year 1996 StrataCom Corporation for US$ 4,5 billion, in November 1999 Cernet Corporation for US$ 6.9 billion, and in June 2000 ArrowPoint Communications for US$ 5.7 billion. Cp. Cisco Systems annual report (2000) and see Bunnel, D. (2000), chap. 4.

Consequently, the overall R&D intensity of Cisco Systems with respect to net sales has increased from 13.7% in 1999 to 14.3% in fiscal year 2000.[76]

As has already been pointed out above, the individual business units have *full technological responsibility* for their respective technological field. Consequently, research and development projects, asked for by the three lines of businesses (LOBS), are prioritised in accordance with the LOBS as well as their potential market importance and carried out in the particular business unit (cf. figure II.6). Due to the strong influence of the LOBS on the R&D projects in the individual business units, Cisco Systems keeps a high focus on actual and current customers' problems and needs and does not aspire a technology push strategy. If, however, a new technology turns up that appears interesting for Cisco Systems' business, the company tries at an early stage to get involved with the leading companies in the new technology fields through equity participation or joint development projects, for instance, and, if mutually beneficial for the parties involved, acquire and integrate the new development. Cisco Systems appears to have successfully established a corporate culture that does not care about whether a product and/or technology was invented under the roof of Cisco Systems or if it was brought in by the acquisition of another company. All that counts is that it has to bring the company forward. The non-existence of the so called *not-invented here (NIH) syndrome*[77] is of utmost importance for the company so as to be able to follow a successful acquisition strategy in order to keep the company at the forefront of technological innovation in a rapidly evolving industry where smaller, more agile companies tend to be the ones with the most innovative technologies and a company's internal R&D cannot be fast enough to seize and develop any new trend.[78]

Align with Partner Companies

A third important pillar in the process of keeping Cisco Systems at the technological forefront in diverse technological fields represents the company's *alliances with partner companies*. Partnerships, however, are claimed to only represent a strategy of first choice in fields that *complement* Cisco's product and technology portfolio but which the company considers as being *too far from its own core competencies*.[79]

---

[76] Cp. Cisco Systems annual report (2000).

[77] For a definition of the NIH syndrome see chap. III.2 or Katz, R. & Allen, T. J. (1982).

[78] One calendar year represents seven "Internet years" in the networking for the Internet industry.

[79] Cp. Bunnel, D. (2000), pp. 122-132.

Furthermore, since the appearance of John Chambers as the CEO of Cisco Systems in 1995 any potential partnership is evaluated according to three principal criteria:[80]

1. It has to create customer benefit,
2. It has to generate a revenue stream of US$ 500 million to 1 billion per annum within a period of 3 years, and
3. It has to change the competitive landscape of both partner companies.

Thus, Cisco Systems has initiated various alliances with increasingly larger partners. For example Cisco entered an alliance with Hewlett-Packard in 1994 in the fields of ATM (asynchronous transfer mode) and LAN (local area network) switching technology in order to catch up with the technologically leading companies in these fields. The 1994 alliance with IBM presents another example of a successful partnership in the field of IBM mainframes that lasted until 1999. In the early 1990s IBM mainframes were in widespread use and by co-operating with IBM Cisco has become the leading company in the IBM networking market with an approximate market share of 75%.[81]

With respect to Cisco Systems *distribution*, the company completely relies on its partner companies. Cisco does not have a direct distribution and hence its products are only available via its partner companies, e.g., Hewlett-Packard, Siemens, or even Deutsche Telekom. One of its first partner companies that was acting as a reseller and service provider for Cisco Systems products was Hewlett-Packard (HP). Cisco Systems enlarged its initial co-operation with Hewlett-Packard in 1995 in the field of reselling and service provision and thereby gained access to HP's global distribution and service network which instantly enabled Cisco to offer its clients a 24-hour customer service. In the meantime, Cisco Systems has established own subsidiaries and its own customer-service network in the most important national and regional markets and has considerably enlarged the number of partner companies selling and servicing Cisco Systems products.

Moreover, with respect to *hardware production*, Cisco Systems today relies almost entirely on external partner companies with which the company works closely together and has integrated directly into its supply chain. Cisco Systems does not see its strengths in the production and distribution of networking hardware but rather in the product and especially software development, design, marketing and post-sales

[80] Bunnel, D. (2000), p. 123.

[81] For a detailed discussion of the various alliances Cisco Systems has joined over the past years see Bunnel, D. (2000), pp. 124-132.

services. Moreover, due to the almost complete outsourcing of production activities to partner companies, Cisco Systems has gained considerable flexibility with respect to the choice of technology since it does not have to invest considerable financial resources in specific production facilities which may later turn out as burdensome. Nevertheless, since Cisco Systems endeavours to be recognised by actual and potential customers for its good quality and highly reliable products it ensures a high quality of the products offered under its name through severe quality controls of its partner companies.

In these partnerships Cisco Systems tries to give its partners the impression of dividing the benefits of the partnership equally between the various partnering companies in the long-run and thus not to give the partner companies the feeling of being exploited which would have an adverse effect on Cisco's reputation. However, as Cisco has realised, in the short-run it is impossible to equally split the benefits of each individual transaction. Sometimes one partner will get the major share of benefits in one transaction but may lose out in another. Moreover, because of the fast technological development in the networking and computer industry partnerships have to be flexible and agile so that actions are often undertaken before formal contracts have been established. Consequently, a certain amount of *mutual trust* of the partners is of utmost importance for a successful and long-lasting co-operation.[82]

Even though acquisitions of high-tech companies are of primary importance in enlarging Cisco Systems' product and technology portfolio, as well as keeping pace with the rapid development of the networking industry, alliances and partner-ships do play an important strategic role in those fields which Cisco Systems does not consider to represent one of its core businesses. Partnerships can hence be found in various fields such as production, product support and sales, and operations. Nevertheless, Cisco Systems has shown an astonishing talent to take advantage of such co-operation agreements in order to successfully acquire, establish, and/or integrate technological as well as market based assets in the long-run and maintain its high flexibility.

II.3.2.2 Central Attributes of the Success of Cisco Systems

The development of Cisco Systems presents one of the most astounding success stories of the past decades which has been reflected in the rapid growth of the company that has reached up to 40% p.a., the overall market value of the company transcending an amazing US$ 300 billion in market

---

[82] Bunnel, D. (2000), pp. 122-132.

capitalisation in December 1999, and in the value of its corporate brand worth some US$ 17 billion.[83] Furthermore, Cisco Systems has become the global market leader for routers with an approximate 85% market share and over 80% of the data sent over the Internet is being transmitted through Cisco Systems equipment.[84] This is the more impressive if one considers that the company is only in business since 1984. The success of the company can in general be attributed to 5 principal aspects that are to a certain degree interconnected. These are in detail:

1. The talent to combine the advantages of small high-tech type companies with that of a large multinational company,
2. The aptitude to attract and acquire highly skilled employees and to retain these specialists,
3. The ability to provide customers with a complete network infrastructure,
4. The capability to offer a complete network with guaranteed full interconnectivity, and
5. Being at a position to influence and determine the industry's standards.

The section outlines the different aspects in detail and shows their utmost importance in determining the overall success of Cisco Systems. Moreover, as will be depicted, all aspects discussed subsequently show a close relationship with the company's initial technological innovation of the router, and the utmost importance the company attributes to meet any promises given either explicitly through employees of the company or implicitly through the company's image and reputation.

Combining the Advantages of an Entrepreneurial Start-up Culture with the Advantages of a Large Integrated Multinational Enterprise

Cisco Systems has managed to maintain a *culture and working atmosphere* that is generally associated with rather small high-tech start-up companies. This is claimed to be particularly due to the fact that Cisco is not a monolithic company but is subdivided into a large number of small groups, all trying to make their product a success.[85] This high-tech start-up culture is also reflected in the *organisational structure* of Cisco Systems. The company was composed of approximately 60 business units in the year 2000 which have been reduced to 30 business units in 2001. All business units have global technological responsibility for their respective field of activity (cp. figure V.6).

---

[83] Khermouch, G., Holmes, S. et al. (2001), pp. 44-55.
[84] Cp. Cisco Systems (1998).
[85] Cp. Bunnel, D. (2000), p. 99-105.

Thus, by granting the individual business units maximum responsibility and freedom with respect to their technological development, the individual business units have kept a start-up like culture characterised by high independence, spontaneity and flexibility with respect to technological development. On the other hand, Cisco Systems has grown over the years to a *large multinational corporation* with some US$ 18.9 billion in revenues in fiscal year 2000 which has an established global distribution and marketing network at its disposal. Consequently, Cisco can offer its various business units the security and stability which is not only reflected in the budget available for R&D but also in the social benefits for its employees that small start-up companies cannot provide. Moreover, the *established global distribution and marketing network* bestows the business units with a strategic advantage regarding the time-to-market vis-à-vis its main competitors which are in general small high-tech start-up companies. In addition, small start-up companies in complementary technological fields are attracted by Cisco Systems' structure which gives them immediate access to the advantages associated with large established companies with the possibility to maintain their start-up-like culture.

Thus, the organisational structure enables Cisco Systems to combine the advantages of a small high-tech start-up company with those of a large integrated multinational company and thereby gives the company a considerable strategic advantage in relation to its competitors. The established companies in its domain have in general not succeeded in staying flexible and agile and thus are not able to keep up with the technological development in the networking industry. Moreover, due the structure of research and development tasks given from the Lines of Businesses (LOBS) to the individual business units, Cisco assures a high focus on actual needs and problems of its customers (cf. figure II.6). On the other hand, the small high-tech companies which are perceived as having an advantage with respect to technological innovation, are put at a severe disadvantage with respect to time-to-market since they lack a global distribution network. Furthermore, by the ability to acquire and integrate small start-up companies with a technological innovation complementing its current products and technological expertise, Cisco System has a considerable advantage. This is in particular due to its ability to readily integrate the complementary products in its overall product offer, its reputation as an acquirer who allows the acquired companies to uphold its start-up like culture, and the trust of potential employees in Cisco not to loose their jobs post acquisition.

Internetwork Operating System

The ability of Cisco to easily and promptly integrate the new products and technologies offered by the newly acquire companies is due to the *universal software* used in all products of Cisco Systems. The software underlying all products which is called *Internetwork Operating Systems (IOS)*, guarantees the full *interoperability* of all products. The interoperability not only guarantees the customers the perfect working together of all products but also the availability of all services offered by the individual products at all levels. Consequently, a network composed of Cisco Systems products not only assures a high compatibility of the individual products making up the whole network, e.g., routers and switches, but also the full support of services at all levels of the network such as Voice-over-Internet-Protocol (VoIP) and security measures.

A domain that is of growing importance for Cisco Systems presents the IP-telephoning and in particular the market for telephone extensions. So far suppliers of integrated systems such as Alcatel or Siemens dominate the market for telephone extensions. If a company acquires such an integrated telephone system it is usually limited to voice services and more importantly it has to buy all equipment from the same company which is considerably more expensive than those of other companies, in order to be able to use all functions offered by the installed system. Nowadays, however, a movement towards a disintegration of the system of telephone extensions can be perceived. This development is a result of the growing needs of customers not only in voice but also in fields such as data and video services. The technological advance in the field of Internet protocol (IP) offers the possibility to respond to the new needs expressed by customers. Furthermore, the technology of Voice-over-IP (VoIP) not only considerably reduces the cost of phone calls[86] but also entrenches a disintegration of the whole system of telephone extensions that enables customers to use components of different companies that best suit their needs while still being able to use all functions of the overall system.

As illustrated in figure II.7, the currently prevailing integrated system of telephone extensions can be decomposed into the three principal fields of applications, network, and final equipment. Applications present certain functions of the telephone system such as answer-phone or mailboxes. The network is the backbone of the system that has to ensure the full availability of all services enabled through the installed applications. The final equipment presents the devices connected to the systems such as

[86] Communications over the Internet do only cause costs of the local connection to the Internet since the data transfer over the Internet is free of charge.

telephone sets and computers. In such an IP based telephone system the client can freely choose the applications that best suit its needs, the network, as well as the final equipment of different companies and still use all functions offered by its system. However, in order to be able to use all services and functions of the overall system, the different products composing the network have to perfectly work together and support the applications and the underlying services. Moreover, the interfaces between the applications, the network, and the final equipment have to be open and standardised.

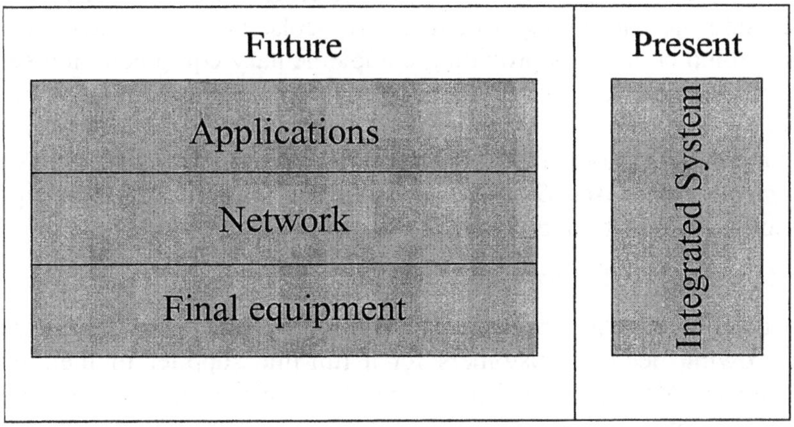

Figure II.7: System of telephone extensions

Cisco Systems which is currently the leading company in the market for VoIP networks can guarantee the full interoperability and thus availability of all services and functions of any one component within the overall network because of the uniform IOS software used in all of its products. Moreover, due to the disclosure and standardisation of the underlying structures, protocols, and interfaces in the field of 'application, voice, video and integrated data' (AVVID) between its network and the applications and final equipment, it enables other companies specialised in these fields to develop new applications and final equipment which perfectly integrate and complement its IP network. Moreover, Cisco Systems has licensed its IOS software to other network equipment manufacturers and thus has considerably increased the spread of its IOS software over the entire networking industry which has led to the establishment of its software as the *standard networking software*, enabling the interoperability of the different networking products.

Thus, Cisco Systems presents a formidable competitor in the field of IP networking equipment since it is in a position to provide all products needed to set up an entire network and guarantee the full interoperability of all components owing to the use of the identical IOS software. Moreover, competitors in the field of networking equipment are put at a severe disadvantage due to the strategy of Cisco Systems to keep its IOS *secret* and the *inability to reverse engineer* the IOS software. Because of the extremely fast development of the networking industry and hence Cisco's IOS software, as well as the increasing complexity of products and the integration of hard- and software, competitors would not be able to keep pace with the general development in the networking industry by following a strategy of reverse engineering. On the other hand, by disclosing the underlying structures, protocols, as well as interfaces Cisco has enabled companies providing complementary equipment and services, e.g., applications and final telephone equipment, to offer a large choice of products and services that perfectly respond to the diverse needs of customers in various fields. This *large offer of products and services complementing Cisco Systems networks* has reinforced and strengthened Cisco Systems leading position in the networking industry.

Customers' Trusted Full-line Supplier

When John Chambers became CEO of Cisco Systems in 1995 he realised the growing need of customers for a full-line supplier of their network equipment. Although the different products of various companies can be combined in a network, problems of *interoperability* have currently occurred and in general the products of the different companies do not fully *support the functions* each individual component of the network is offering. Consequently, a network composed of products from different companies may not guarantee full interoperability and thus severely limits the applications and functions of the overall network. An even more important disadvantage of network equipment provider concentrating on one particular product in the network is the extreme difficulty and cost of the clients to *service* a network composed of products from different companies. This is in particular due to the inability to trace back a particular problem to one individual product in the network and the expertise needed on products of diverse companies in order to be able to service the network. Furthermore, with regard to start-up companies clients encounter the risk that these companies may no longer exist when specific problems occur or if the products need repair and service.

Cisco Systems, on the other hand, has established itself as a *competent full-line supplier* by acquiring leading companies in most fields of networking equipment. Moreover, it can guarantee the full interoperability, as well as the availability of all functions offered by any of its products. Thus, Cisco Systems is one of the only companies able to offer *service-*

level-agreements regarding an entire network, ensuring the customer to obtain the agreed upon results within the fixed period of time. Other companies are usually not able to offer such service-level-agreements concerning the whole network since they do not know the problems of interoperability that may occur between the network components beforehand. In addition, Cisco Systems is, in contrast to its most important competitors, a large established company and thus is not endangered as most start-up companies to disappear in the near future. Consequently, Cisco is perceived as a full-line supplier of network equipment who guarantees perfect interoperability of its products and thus the availability of all functions offered by the individual components, e.g., security systems and VoIP.

Thus, although Cisco Systems may not be able to offer the most technologically advanced solution on the level of all individual components of the network, it still appears to beat most competitors by the *security* it can offer its clients concerning the prolonged existence of the company, and hence the ability to service its products, and the perfect working together of all individual products of the network because of the identical IOS software. Hence, competitors such as Juniper Networks, who presents the most important competitor in the market for high-end routing, are generally small high-tech start-up companies in the field of network equipment that are financed by venture capital. Consequently, the most important competitors are already put at a disadvantage by the *financial strength* of Cisco Systems signalled by the US$ 4.2 billion in cash reserves shown in its balance sheet. Thus, customers are certain that Cisco Systems will not disappear due to financial distress or may be acquired by another bigger company. Consequently, they can be sure that Cisco Systems' products will be serviced in the future and the company will be able to fulfil any guarantee and warrantee given.

Large Install-base and Standard Setting Company

The market for networking for the Internet equipment has been characterised by an extremely *high growth rate* since the appearance of the Internet and the Netscape browser, and an *astounding technological development* with the capacity of processors doubling almost every twelve months. Such a fast technological development is associated with a relatively high uncertainty and risk for customers since no clear and uniform technological standards have been established, yet. Hence, if a *technology standard* evolves after the purchase of the network has taken place, the companies may be stuck with the wrong technology that turns out to be incompatible with the new standard. In order to reduce such risks associated with the choice of the wrong technological system, customers usually stick to the products and technology of the market leader, who has the potential to establish a *de facto standard.*

Therefore, Cisco Systems has a considerable strategic advantage in new technological fields of the network equipment market where no technological standard has evolved, yet. This is due to its position of a *global market leader* and the *large install-base* of its network equipment with currently more than 85% of the router market and more than 80% of the data transferred over the Internet being transferred by Cisco Systems products.[87] Hence, customers already possessing a network composed of Cisco Systems products may wish to purchase the new technology from Cisco as well in order to assure the full interoperability of the new components. Moreover, Cisco Systems has evolved over time as the trend-setter in the networking industry due to its head start in the routing industry and the establishment of the IOS software as the *standard for the entire networking industry* just as Microsoft's Windows has evolved as the standard desktop operating system.

Thus, Cisco Systems appears nowadays to be in a position in which customers will even wait until Cisco Systems has launched its new product in a new technology field in order not to be locked in the wrong technological standard. In the case of the development of Layer 3 switching and Gigabit Ethernet products, for instance, Cisco Systems was lagging behind other competitors. Nevertheless, most customers were willing to wait and see what Cisco Systems offers would be like since most companies already had had Cisco Systems products installed. This tactic of customers to wait and see its new products coming out before making a choice is called FUD at Cisco Systems – fear, uncertainty, and doubt.[88]

On the other hand, the extreme dedication of Cisco Systems to customer needs and wishes which is reflected in an 85% *customer satisfaction rate,* has resulted in an extremely high loyalty of Cisco Systems' customers. The company tries to perfectly respond to actual customers' needs through its *lines of businesses* (LOBS) structure (cf. figure II.6). Each of the three LOBS concentrates on its respective customer segment, i.e., service provider and telecoms, enterprises, and small & medium businesses, and can thereby rely on the technical competency of the various business units. Furthermore, in the case of yet unresolved problems, the LOBS can charge a business unit with a research task. Thus, research and development activities are mostly *customer driven* and do in general respond to an actual customer need. On the other hand, the risk of parallel research within the different business units is reduced by the existence of a chief

[87] Cisco Systems (1998).

[88] Bunnel, D. (2000), pp. 132-134.

technology officer (CTO) who tries to be knowledgeable about the ongoing projects in the individual business units and to co-ordinate the research and development projects across all business units.

Another advantage of Cisco Systems, that is closely connected to its large install-base, presents the large amount of *complementary applications and equipment* offered by a multitude of independent companies. Because of the large amount of Cisco networks installed and the open standards, protocols, and interfaces a considerable amount of applications and equipment complementing Cisco's products have evolved over time. These complementary applications and equipment increase the possible choice and flexibility of Cisco's customers and thus augments Cisco Systems' products. The market of complementary applications and equipment has reached a further impetus by the strategy of Cisco Systems to license out its IOS software to even competitor network equipment producers. Through this *out-licensing strategy* Cisco has not only succeeded in establishing its IOS software as the standard in the networking industry but moreover has further expanded the market for complementary applications and equipment which has entrenched an increase in the offer and diversity of complementary services and products. This increase in the offer of complementary applications and equipment has finally resulted in a better match of the needs and wishes of individual customers and hence has considerably increased *customer utility*.

Human Resource Management

Last but not least, the established system of human resource management which is closely interrelated with the before mentioned aspects, bestows Cisco Systems with a considerable strategic advantage vis-à-vis other large multinational enterprises in the networking industry. Cisco Systems is perceived by actual and potential employees as a trusted and respected employer. Moreover, due to the *reputation as the global market and technology leader* in the Internet industry, Cisco Systems is perceived as a very interesting and challenging employer. This perception appears to give Cisco an advantage in recruiting specialist employees which is of particular importance in the highly competitive market for IT specialists.

The advantage in the recruitment process due to its position as a market and technology leader in the networking for the Internet industry is further reinforced by the ability to offer actual and potential employees to participate in the success of Cisco Systems by issuing *stock options*. This has been of particular interest due to the breathtaking development of the value of Cisco Systems' shares since the initial public offering (IPO) in February 1990 until the beginning of the so called 'dot-com' crisis in late 2000. Anyone who bought Cisco shares at the IPO for US$ 18 a share would have increased the value of its equity stake a hundredfold until 1999. Thus, stock options have bestowed Cisco Systems with an effective tool to attract and retain highly skilled employees. Moreover, Cisco was even able to offer below average salaries since employees were more interested in stock options than in their fix monthly salary.[89]

Apart from the reputational and financial aspects which may motivate actual and potential employees to stay with or work for Cisco Systems, the company has also communicated to cultivate a culture of openness and honesty with its workforce. This is particularly reflected in Cisco's effort to keep its employees informed about the latest corporate developments, as well as contact information, product data, etc. by the customised 'Cisco Employee Connection' (CEC) Web site. Moreover, the CEC presents an important tool in the integration process of new employees which has presented a particular challenge by up to some 1000 new employees per quarter.[90] Concerning the laying-off of actual employees, Cisco Systems has followed a strategy of avoiding any releasing of its workforce, and if no alternative possibility existed, as it was the case in the year 2001, Cisco has tried to get all employees having to leave the company a new job in one of the numerous partner companies or in one of its client companies.

In conclusion, Cisco Systems has attained its position of a global market leader and trusted full-line supplier, employer, and partner company through its technological and organisational innovations, as well as its proven reliability and honesty with regard to its external partners, employees, as well as acquired companies. Another principal contributor to the overall success has been Cisco Systems' focus on the actual needs and problems of its customers and its full dedication to customer satisfaction. The following section discusses in more detail the role brand equity plays for Cisco in maintaining a good relationship with its customers as well as employees.

II.3.3 The Multibillion Brand

The above outlined success factors, associated with the corporate brand Cisco Systems, together with Cisco Systems' advantage of having been an important innovator and the first to offer routers able to connect distant and different computer networks, have considerably contributed to the company's *notoriety* and *reputation as a technology and market leader.*

[89] Cp. Bunnel, D. (2000), pp. 102-105, 169-174.

[90] For a detailed description of the CEC tool see Bunnel, D. (2000), pp. 93-94, 141-145.

This has been in particular true for its main clientele which has been above all companies in the field of telecommunications (telecoms) and large enterprises. These companies have gained specific knowledge about the products and services of Cisco Systems and associate these past experiences with the company name. Over the last years Cisco has successfully expanded its business in the field of service providers and small and medium companies (cf. figure II.8). In this expansion strategy the established positive reputation and the high notoriety of the Cisco brand in the market for routing and switching has been of critical importance. Moreover, through the large install-base of Cisco products, the standard setting character of its products and services, the extreme focus on customer satisfaction, as well as its position as a global full-line supplier the name Cisco Systems has evolved as an important reinsurance for actual and potential clients.

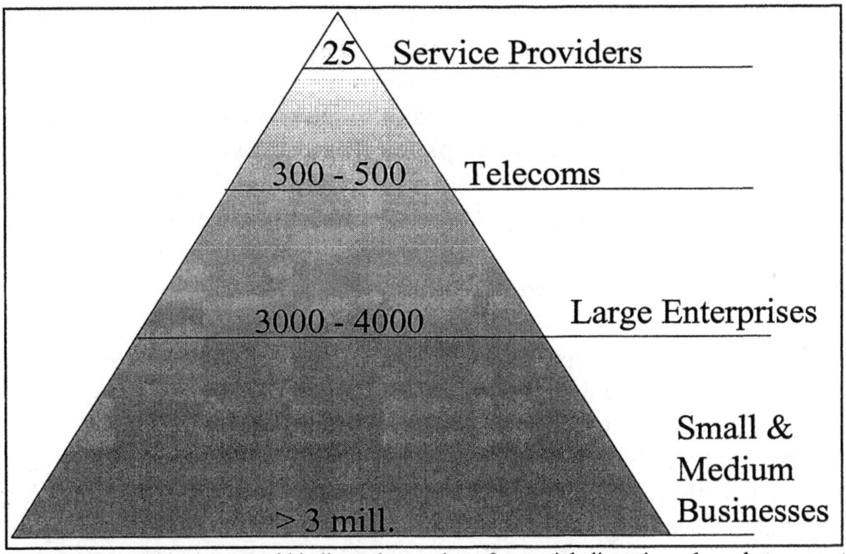

The numbers within the pyramid indicate the number of potential clients in each market segment.

Figure II.8: Cisco Systems' clients

If a company has to make a decision about the purchase of new networking equipment it faces on the one hand the risk of buying equipment from different companies that may not be fully compatible and thus the purchasing company may be stuck with a badly functioning network infrastructure and high network servicing and operating costs. On the other hand, even if the individual products would work together, the company cannot be sure at the time of purchase that it has chosen the right technological standard, or if the suppliers of the individual products will still exist when service and repair or a general update of the network equipment will be necessary. This is the more important since most companies in the market for network equipment are only relatively small start-up companies and thus are not endowed with cash reserves of several billion US$ such as Cisco Systems. Thus, by choosing a solution from Cisco Systems companies can considerably reduce any of these risks which are of decisive importance in deals that range in general from US$ 10 million to US$ 50 million and can even attain the order of magnitude of several hundred million US$ in the case of service-provider agreements. Accordingly, Cisco Systems' representatives claim: '*You can't get fired for purchasing our internetworking gear.*'[91]

Consequently, the *value of the brand* Cisco Systems, whose value was estimated by Interbrand at about US$ 17 billions in the year 2001 after US$ 20 billion in 2000,[92] is attributable to the *positive experiences and associations* attached to the corporate brand, as well as its high notoriety in the domain of network equipment. The positive experiences and associations of actual and potential customers are again brought about by Cisco Systems dominant market position, the standard setting character of its products and services, its complete offer of networking products whose perfect working together is assured through the identical IOS software, and last but not least the company's full dedication to customer satisfaction.

II.3.3.1 Leveraging Brand Equity

As long as Cisco Systems had entirely focused its activities on the service provider, telecommunications, and large enterprise market segments it did not need an active brand management. The positive reputation of Cisco Systems spread by word-of-mouth and thus the brand attained a high notoriety within the company's original markets just by its technological expertise, its strategy of a full-line supplier, and the high quality of its products and services. In addition, Cisco's brand grew stronger over the years though the company's continuous extreme focus on customer satisfaction and fulfilling the pledges given by its company name. Due to the low number of companies active in these segments, Cisco could easily contact and inform each individual company by mail and/or visits of representatives (cp. figure II.8). However, with the move into the *market segment of small and medium businesses* the role of brand management has considerably risen.

[91] Cp. Bunnel, D. (2000), p. 113.
[92] Cp. Khermouch, G., Holmes, S. et al. (2001), pp. 44-55.

Until 1998 the name Cisco Systems and the company's products and services were already known to most service provider, telecommunications, and large enterprises in the world. However, most small and medium sized companies were not familiar with the corporate name and the average consumer was unfamiliar with the name Cisco Systems and did not know what the company was actually doing. Thus, with the move downwards in the small and medium business market segment Cisco entered ground where it could no longer build instantly on its established reputation and moreover, the number of potential clients was too large in order to be able to contact any individual company either by mail or company representatives. Consequently, Cisco launched on August 24 a big-budget television *advertisement* featuring children from different cultures all over the world making the point that Cisco Systems is the dominant company in building the world's Internet infrastructure.[93] The aim was to establish the brand Cisco Systems as a broadly known household name, just as Intel did with its corporate brand by the Intel Inside brand building campaign.[94]

Table II.4: Most valuable brands in the technology industry in the year 2001

Rank	Brand	Brand Value 2001 (in US$ billions	Brand Value 2000 (in US$ billions)
1	IBM	52.75	53.18
2	Intel	34.67	39.05
3	Hewlett-Packard	17.98	20.57
4	Cisco Systems	17.21	20.07
5	Compaq	12.35	14.60

Source: Khermouch, G., Holmes, S. et al. (2001).

Thus, the larger the number of potential customers grew, the more important became the brand Cisco Systems. In addition, small and medium sized companies do not have the same possibility to collect information about the different offers of the various competing companies in the network equipment industry. Thus, the brand and its associated reputation is an effective and efficient *means to inform a vast number of potential customers* about the characteristics of the products and services offered.

[93] Cp. Graves, L. (1998a).

[94] For a detailed discussion see, e.g., Mirow, M. (2000); Cp. Pettis, C. R. (1995a), pp. 70-76; Pettis, C. R. (1995b); Aaker, D. A. (1996), pp. 12-13.

Consequently, the successful establishment of the Cisco brand has reinforced Cisco Systems' strategic advantage of its global marketing, distribution, and service network and is reflected in the economic value attributed to the brand. Cisco Systems was ranked by Interbrand as the 4th most valuable brand in the technology industry behind IBM, Intel, and Hewlett-Packard (cp. table II.4).

A further advantage that is partially related to the brand building strategy, as well as contributes to the establishment of the brand, is Cisco's volume *pricing strategy*. The longer Cisco has been in the market and the more renown the brand and the associated products and services became in the different market segments, the more products Cisco Systems was able to sell, and consequently was able to follow down the *experience curve* and take advantage of *economies of scale*. For example, in 1996 Cisco was able to reduce prices for its switches by 50%. Competing companies generally selling much small quantities were not able to produce at the same cost as Cisco did and were subsequently driven out of the market. The disappearance of competitors in turn further increased the demand and the spread of switches from Cisco Systems and thus further lowered their unit-production costs.[95] Moreover, due to the higher amounts of products sold to a larger number of different clients, more customers have come into direct contact with Cisco products and services and thus gained experiences which they subsequently associate with the brand.

II.3.3.2 Brand Strategies

With the sustained success of Cisco Systems and its prolonged position as the technology and market leader in field of routing and switching, the notoriety, positive reputations associated with the corporate brand, as well as its strategic importance have continuously increased. Reflecting the rising significance of brand equity, Cisco has followed several different strategies in order to foster and expand its brand equity based advantage. The first attempt was to establish different brands for different *market segments*. In the style of Intel's strategy of relying on different brands for different market segments, Cisco Systems tried to establish the brand '*Cisco-Pro*' for rather low-priced products in the small and medium business market segment.

The strategy of market segmentation through the establishment of different brands was, however, a complete failure. The market for network equipment is extremely transparent and thus potential client companies which are extremely well informed about prices and functions of the

[95] Cp. Bunnel, D. (2000), pp. 119-120.

different offers, were not sticking to the brand designed for the relevant market. Companies' main focus was on the overall functionality and quality of the network, as well as the security of the prolonged existence of the provider of the networking equipment in order to service and upgrade the installed hard- and software. Consequently, companies paid utmost importance on the *general reputation associated with the company* in general but did not pay any attention to the specific product brands. Having realised the profound understanding of the clients of the different product offers sold under different brands and the low brand loyalty on the product level, Cisco Systems reduced the functionality of the products sold under the low-priced brand 'Cisco Pro' in order to enhance the differentiation of brands and thus reinforce market segmentation. Although the strategy of product differentiation reinforced the market segmentation, the cost of product differentiation outweighed by far the benefits of market segmentation and multi-brand strategy. Moreover, considerable problems appeared with the maintenance of the different products showing differences vis-à-vis functionality and subsequently Cisco Systems completely abandoned the strategy of market differentiation and the brand 'Cisco Pro' and re-concentrated its efforts on the corporate brand Cisco Systems.

Since the mid 1990s Cisco follows another brand strategy that can be classified as an *ingredient-branding strategy*,[96] which is comparable with the Intel-Inside brand campaign.[97] Cisco Systems has realised the difficulty of companies receiving network services from an external service provider in evaluating the *quality of the service* before actually having singed the service provider agreement. Building on the reputation of highly powerful and reliable network products associated with its corporate brand, Cisco Systems allows service providers to display and use in marketing the '*Cisco Powered Network*' logo if their network is made up of at least 75% of parts stemming from Cisco and Cisco's partner companies. The 'Cisco Powered Network' logo in turn communicates potential client companies considering the outsourcing of their network infrastructure if the service provider has a powerful and highly reliable infrastructure at his disposal. The 'Cisco Powered Network' logo has evolved as an important means for service providers to signal potential clients its high quality network equipment and hence a high service quality. This is the more important

[96] For a detailed discussion of ingredient branding strategies see Theile, K. & Burr, W. (2000), Freter, H. & Baumgarth, C. (2000).

[97] For a detailed discussion of the Intel brand strategy see Mirow, M. (2000); Cp. Pettis, C. R. (1995a), pp. 70-76; Pettis, C. R. (1995b); Aaker, D. A. (1996), pp. 12-13.

since potential clients do not have any other possibility to evaluate ex-ante the quality of the service which in turn is predominantly influenced by the quality of the network, e.g., reliability, functionality, capacity, etc.

Consequently, by relying on its existing reputation as the leading provider of reliable and powerful network equipment, Cisco Systems has successfully established the 'Cisco Powered Network' logo as the standard for network equipment in the service provider industry. Moreover, due to the attention companies pay to the 'Cisco Powered Network' status in their outsourcing decision, service providers are not only obliged to buy their network equipment from Cisco Systems and its partner companies but also to advertise the fact that they use Cisco equipment. The advertising of the used network equipment of the service providers thus further reinforces Cisco's brand and the general importance of the logo 'Cisco Powered Networks' as an important reinsurance for powerful and reliable networking products and services. The brand building effect of service providers' accentuation of the fact that they use Cisco products is particularly due to the status of service providers which are perceived as especially demanding and expert users of network equipment.

The different brand strategies followed by Cisco Systems clearly show that the information carried by the brand Cisco Systems is not specific to a product or market but rather concerns information about the general quality of the network equipment and associated services, as well as information about the company in general. Thus, potential clients associate the brand Cisco Systems with highly reliable, technologically leading, and standard setting network equipment, as well as with a financially sound company dominating the networking for the Internet market. Accordingly, the brand Cisco Systems presents an important reinsurance for high quality networking products, as well as for a reliable supplier whose future existence is assured. This is of particular importance in *times of general economic uncertainty* which affects particularly relatively small and financially weak companies.

II.3.3.3 The Brand Cisco Systems in an Internet World

As described above, the brand Cisco Systems has evolved as the international standard brand for networking equipment and the Internet protocol (IP) based industry through its profound knowledge and leading solutions in this field, the ability to offer clients complete solutions with perfectly compatible products due to the uniform IOS software, as well as its head-start in the router industry. Consequently, the name does not only stand for solutions in routing and switching, although these domains are

Cisco's traditional and still principal fields of activity, but for any solution in the field of IP and thus including software solutions as well as new solutions in the field of VoIP.

Thus, the company Cisco Systems has an *advantage in entering new markets and fields* related to IP technology in comparison with companies lacking the positive reputation. This has become particularly apparent by the development of the VoIP technology. Although Cisco Systems has not been active in the market for telephone extensions previously, it has been able to rely on its established reputation in the field of network equipment and Internet protocol and thus successfully enter the market for IP telephone networks. Although Cisco is currently active in the field of final equipment, because no sufficient supply of IP telephone sets exists, Cisco does not have a specific advantage in this field and thus has no strategic interest in the market for final equipment, nor do clients associate the brand Cisco Systems with such equipment.[98] Consequently, Cisco Systems concentrates on the network equipment, as well as the definition of the general architecture of the system of telephone extensions based on IP, e.g., the interfaces between the applications running on the network as well as the final equipment connected to the network and using the applications installed. Cisco Systems has a strategic interest in these fields and perceives a strategic advantage vis-à-vis its competitors due to its accumulated expertise and experience in the field of network equipment and IP technology. Moreover, customers clearly associate the brand Cisco Systems with network equipment and ascribe the company a standard setting position.

This clearly shows that the Cisco Systems brand is an important asset in the market for network equipment and IP technology that bestows Cisco with a considerable strategic advantage. The advantage due to the established corporate brand plays a particular role in the phase of *first contact* with a new client. However, in order to uphold and foster the established brand and thus not to risk the emergence of a rather negative reputation, Cisco Systems has to permanently substantiate its technological excellence, and focus on customers' requirements, needs and problems and hence continuously certify the reputation associated with its brand. Accordingly, M. Krohmann, Technology-Manager at Cisco Systems Germany, pointed out:

> *"...the name Cisco Systems is certainly a 'door-opener' and creator of confidence, however, as soon as Cisco is in the business we have to fulfil the high ranking expectations of the clients through actual performance... ."*

---

[98] For an illustration of the system of telephone extensions see figure II.7.

Consequently, even though the established brand equity bestows Cisco Systems with a considerable strategic advantage with regard to competing companies in the field of IP technology, it has to constantly confirm its reputation through its actual products as well as services. Moreover, concerning future diversification strategies of Cisco Systems in new fields of corporate activities not directly linked to IP and/or network equipment may be extremely difficult if not impossible under the corporate name. This is because of the associations customers relate or rather do not relate to the brand Cisco Systems and hence may not even consider the brand in their purchasing decision in fields not related to the company's usual activities, e.g., final telephone equipment.

Thus, Cisco Systems has succeeded in familiarising a vast number of people with the company name and its activities by its position as an important innovator, its prolonged position as the market and technology leader in the global network equipment market and the IP based industry, its successful strategy of acquisition and development (A&D) that has established Cisco as a trusted full-line supplier, and its international advertisement campaign. The so established brand equity clearly bestows Cisco Systems with a strategic advantage vis-à-vis actual and potential competitors that do not have such an established market based asset at their disposal. The strategic role of the brand, and here in particular the brands function as a reinsurance for the decision maker, has further risen during the recent 'dot-com crises' and the financial distress of even large established companies in the networking equipment industry and the disappearance of numerous start-up companies with innovative networking solutions.

II.3.4 Discussion and Findings

The above presented case example Cisco Systems has clearly pointed out the strategic role of brand equity in the market for networking equipment which is characterised by business-to-business relationships. Even though Cisco Systems is still a relatively young company, in particular in comparison to Bayer AG presented in chapter II.2, brand equity and hence accumulated reputation plays an important strategic role. Furthermore, as has become apparent in the previous discussion, Cisco Systems has built its market based brand equity, worth some US$ 17 billion in 2001, chiefly through its technological expertise in the field of Internet protocol and its head-start in the router business. Marketing expenditures, although often assumed in theoretical discussion of being of central importance in building market based advantages, has only become a topic over the last few years. Moreover, the advertisement campaigns had merely the aim to establish the company's brand in new market segments and to transfer positive associations, e.g., technology and market leader in IP technology, that already existed in Cisco's initial market segments, i.e., service provider and large enterprises.

Thus, Cisco Systems possesses nowadays a strategic advantage in comparison with actual and potential competitors in the IP based industry due to its established brand equity. Actual and potential customers associate the name Cisco Systems with a competent full-line supplier of network equipment with standard setting technology whose dominant market position, leading technological expertise, and sound financial basis assures the future existence of the company. Such a reputation is of utmost importance in a market characterised by high technological uncertainties due to the rapid technological development and not yet established technological standards, as well as extremely high investments with an order of magnitude ranging from some US$ 10 million to several hundred million US$. Thus, companies investing considerable financial resources in their networking infrastructure make sure that the company delivering and installing its network equipment will continue to exist in order to service and upgrade the installed hard- and software in the future.

Moreover, the importance of the brand has further increased during the actual economic crisis that has in particular touched upon companies in the electronics and the Internet industry. Due to the disappearance of various high-tech start-up companies and the financial problems of even large multinational enterprises such as Nortel Networks and Lucent Technologies, companies have become increasingly aware of the problem of being stuck with network equipment worth several million US$ of a company that has ceased to exist. Consequently, the "dot-com" crisis and the news about financial distress of some of its most important competitors[99] has reinforced the position as well as reputation of Cisco Systems as the technology and market leader in the IP based industry whose prolonged existence is guaranteed.

On the other hand, the past experience has plainly revealed the importance of the corporate brand Cisco Systems in carrying important information for customers concerning the company in general. Customers do, however, not take individual product brands in their purchasing decision into consideration but rather associate the qualities signalled and information carried by the corporate brand with all products offered by

[99] The financial problems of some of the most important competitors of Cisco Systems has attracted considerable attention by media. See for instance Bermann, D. (2001); N.A. (2001a, b).

Cisco Systems. Moreover, the different products and their characteristics are easily comparable and hence customers are able to choose the products with the characteristics that best meet their needs before purchase regardless of the individual product brand. Concerning characteristics and associated risks that are more difficult to evaluate ex-ante purchase, e.g., general product and service quality, choice of right technology standard, continued existence of the supplier company, are, however, considerably reduced by the information carried by the corporate brand Cisco Systems. Thus, no matter of choice of the individual product brand, customers' associate these qualities with all products sold under the corporate brand and hence, all products associated with the brand Cisco Systems have to meet customers' expectation in order not to risk the deterioration of established brand equity. Consequently, customers choose their network equipment according to their needs and expect all products and services sold under the name Cisco Systems to meet the qualities associated with the brand in general, e.g., reliability and quality of network equipment, perfect interoperability of the different products, certainty about the prolonged existence of the company, etc., no matter if the individual product is sold under an individual product brand or not.

Furthermore, the market based advantage due to Cisco Systems' established brand equity is reinforcing itself over time. Through selling higher quantities of its products and services Cisco benefits of larger economies of scale and thus can produce at lower unit costs, as well as can spread development costs of new products over larger quantities sold. Thus, companies lacking brand equity are not able to offer their products at comparable prices or have to cut back on development costs which will put them at a considerable disadvantage in a market characterised by fast technological development.

However, the established brand equity gives Cisco Systems not only an advantage in selling its final products and services, but also in acquiring new technologies through co-operation agreements and acquisitions of small high-tech start-up companies. As has been shown above, Cisco cultivates an open culture that does not care about the source of new product and technological developments. Moreover, it has established itself as an 'acquirer of first choice' for small start-up companies due to its acquisition policy characterised by integrity and putting employees first. Cisco Systems' specific corporate culture allows the acquired companies to maintain their start-up like mentality by at the same time giving them instant access to the advantages of a large multinational company and perfect integration of products of the acquired company through the use of the identical IOS software. On the other hand, the name Cisco Systems and the associate reputation of a technological and market leader in the IP industry, as well as a trusted and competent co-operation partner has enabled Cisco to easily establish co-operation agreements with the leading companies in fields that the company does not consider to be at the core of its business.

Hence, the brand Cisco Systems can be said to represent an important strategic asset which enables the company to dominate the market for IP based networking solutions and thus appropriate a better part of the revenues generated in the IP industry. On the other hand, the brand not only gives Cisco a market based advantage making it a formidable competitor, but also bestows the company with an advantage in acquiring new technologies through acquisition of companies in complementary technological fields, as well as co-operation agreements in the field of technology development and/or new market segments. Consequently, Cisco is not only able to sell its products and services more profitably than most other companies in the network equipment industry, but is also able to acquire new technologies and develop new products more easily and cheaply than companies not owning a brand such as Cisco Systems. It remains, however, to be seen if Cisco Systems will be able to successfully continue its strategy of acquisition and development in order to remain at the leading edge of technological development in the network equipment industry although company shares, and thus Cisco's currency of acquisition, have considerably lost value during the actual crisis. Thus, will Cisco be able to continue its strategy with the help of its established brand equity and acquire technological expertise, as well as remain almost as flexible as a small start-up company due to its organisational form or will history repeat itself and a new, more agile high-tech company with a new technology will take the lead in the network equipment industry substituting for IP technology and thus rapidly build new brand equity and replace the currently dominating companies?

II.4 Contrasting the Two Cases

The above presented case studies Bayer Aspirin and Cisco Systems have the aim to further specify our research interest, point out the relationship between technological expertise and market based brand equity, as well as to give some initial empirical evidence about the strategic importance of brand equity for companies active in even technology intensive industries. Although the two case examples show some considerable differences with respect to the market analysed, dynamics of technological development, unit of investigation, etc., both cases have clearly pointed out the strategic relevance of brand equity. Bayer has succeeded due to its strong global brand Aspirin to dominate the ASA market over a period of more than 100 years even though it has never obtained widespread patent protection for its innovation. In the case of Cisco Systems, our discussion has clearly shown that brand equity is not only of importance in consumer markets but also in markets characterised by business-to-business relationships. Thus, both companies possess a strategic advantage in relation to actual and potential competitors in their markets that enables the two companies to better appropriate the revenues generated by their intangible assets in the long-run including brand equity and technological assets. Furthermore, both companies have an advantage vis-à-vis competitors in launching new technological innovation because of their reputation as innovative and technologically leading companies in their respective markets. In this respect it has to be stressed that both companies have built and fostered their market based and technology based competencies in close interrelation. Whereas in both cases the starting point presents a technological innovation, the long-run success of the two companies relies on the mutual influence of technological expertise and brand equity. Thus, on the one hand *brand equity was built and maintained by the companies' specific technological expertise and, on the other hand, the companies were able to defend their technologically leading position because of the established brand equity*.

Moreover, the different cases have revealed the different tasks and thus qualities of product and corporate brands for their respective clients. Whereas the product brand Aspirin stands for the good quality, reliability of products based on the active molecule ASA produced by the company Bayer AG, the corporate brand Cisco Systems applies equally to any product offered under the name Cisco Systems. Thus, the information carried by product and corporate brands are distinctly different and hence the choice of brand has do depend on the needs of the customers. If customers need specific information in their purchasing decision about the individual product, a product brand may be most adequate. If customers do, however, not differentiate between the different products offered by the company but rather associate the information carried by the brand with the company and its products in general, the corporate brand may be of utmost strategic importance. This has clearly been shown by the above presented strategy of Cisco Systems to offer its products under specific product brands. This strategy completely failed since customers associated the qualities of the brand Cisco Systems to all products sold under the corporate brand no matter of the individual product brand.

Thus, the five research theses of chapter II which have been presented in chapter II.1, have clearly been validated by the two case studies. *Thesis one*, putting forward the important role of a company specific technological advantage in establishing market based brand equity, has been substantiated by the findings of the two case studies. The Bayer AG as well as Cisco Systems have successfully established market based brand equity in their respective fields through an initial company specific technological advantage which has generated considerable utility for the respective customers. In the case of Bayer Aspirin, the success of the company and the brand has built on the companies' specific knowledge in the chemical production of pure acetylsalicylic acid (ASA) and the advantage of pharmaceuticals based on ASA with respect to other active molecules in use in the early 20th century. In the situation of Cisco Systems, the immediate success of the company can be attributed to the specific knowledge in the field of routers that enabled the company to offer a product that presented a solution to an important technical problem. Thus, due to Cisco Systems technological know-how and the utility generated by its products, the company quickly built brand equity and attained a dominant market position.

Theses two and three, attributing a long-lived strategic role to established brand equity in technology intensive industries that is maintained and fostered through incremental technological improvements, are evidently supported by both case examples. Both companies, Bayer AG as well as Cisco Systems, do have a considerable strategic advantage in their respective markets because of their established brand equity. Moreover, the brand equity based advantage of both companies has outlived by far the initial technology based advantage of the companies. As has been pointed out in the case Bayer Aspirin, although Bayer AG has rapidly lost its technological advantage since competitors rapidly succeeded in the imitation and/or replication of the production process of ASA, Bayer still dominates the over-the-counter market for ASA in most national and regional markets where the company has permanently possessed its product brand Aspirin. Furthermore, by continuous incremental innovation of the initial product which have created a perceptible advantage for customers, Bayer AG has successfully maintained and fostered its market based advantage. Thus, even more than 100 years after Bayer's market launch of Bayer Aspirin the company still holds a dominant position in various national and regional markets for ASA products and thus is able to benefit of its initial innovation. The same applies to Cisco Systems which has successfully built brand equity with its initial innovation in the field of network routers. Cisco Systems has continuously fostered its technological expertise and improved its products and thereby remained at the leading edge of technological development. Although nowadays more agile high-tech start-up companies may take the lead in certain technology fields, Cisco Systems has successfully defended its dominant market position with the help of its established brand equity and the successful strategy to position itself as a trusted full-line supplier of network equipment. Consequently, established brand equity can be said to present a strategic advantage that continues to persist although the company may has lost its initial advantage build upon intangible technological assets.

Although both case studies validate in general the *theses four and five* of chapter II.1, the case Cisco Systems may have been more explicit about the relationship between established brand equity and the ability of a company to recruit and retain highly skilled employees, as well as the ability of a company to attain advantages in related fields of technology due to its established market based assets. The company Cisco Systems has successfully managed to broaden its field of technological proficiency and market dominance in complementary IP based field through its strategy of acquisition and development. Thus, nowadays the name Cisco Systems is not only associated with Internet routers but stands for high quality and leading edge technology in the general field of IP technology and network equipment. In this diversification strategy the established associations held by customers, as well as actual and potential employees about the company Cisco Systems in general, and its products and services has been of decisive importance. The corporate status as a global market and technology leader in the network equipment industry, its reputation as a honest and respected employer that has managed to remain agile and combine the advantages of a start-up like culture with the benefits of a large multinational enterprise, as well as the possibility of the employees to participate in the success of the company through stock options bestow Cisco Systems with an advantage in acquiring high-tech start-up companies and retaining specialist employees, as well as in the recruitment of highly skilled employees from the market. Hence, it can be claimed that established brand equity plays an important role in attracting and retaining highly skilled employees and thus to maintain and foster the company's technological capabilities. Consequently, Cisco's established reputation has been of key importance in its diversification strategy that has the aim to establish and maintain Cisco Systems as a trusted full-line supplier of network equipment. Without the established brand equity, Cisco Systems would not have been able to follow its strategy of acquisition and development and thus to successfully diversify in various fields related to IP technology.

Thus, the presented case examples Bayer Aspirin and Cisco Systems, although presenting extreme examples of the strategic role of brand equity for companies in technology based industries, have further substantiated the initial hypothesis of chapter I stating a strong link between companies' market based brand equity and its specific technological aptitude, as well as an important role of companies' established brand equity in the ability of the company to appropriate the returns of its intangible technological assets. Hence, the case example Cisco Systems has clearly pointed out the importance of brand equity for a company active in high technology and fast cycle industry that is characterised by business-to-business relationships. Furthermore, the case study Bayer Aspirin has revealed the extreme persistence of market based advantages if managed adequately and consequently both cases indicate the important role of brand equity for enterprises in technology intensive industries and thus a need of a further theoretical and empirical analyses of the relationship between company specific intangible technological assets and brand equity, the role of market based assets in upholding technological expertise and the appropriation of the returns generated by technological assets, as well as the role of continued leading technological expertise and innovation in the respective fields in order to maintain and foster existing brand equity in the long-run.

The upcoming theoretical chapter III points out the general characteristics and establishes a classification of intangible assets within business enterprises, as well as discusses the most important sources of intangible assets and potential means of protection of these assets. The discussion of chapter III strongly focuses on intangible technological assets which are assumed to be of key importance in the process of building and preserving market based brand equity in technology based industries. Chapter IV then builds upon the theoretical foundations laid in chapter III and analyses the strategic role of intangible technological assets and the importance of their efficient protection and in this respect develops the specific role of complementary brand equity. The discussion of chapter IV finalises in a model of complementary brand equity for the sustainable appropriation of intangible assets. Throughout our discussion reference to the presented case examples is drawn in order to clarify and/or substantiate our discussion. Finally, in chapter V an initial econometric investigation of the underlying theoretical assumptions is performed.

III Intangible Assets: Characteristics, Generation & Protection

As shown in chapter I.1 and in the case studies on Bayer Aspirin and Cisco Systems in chapter II, intangible assets and in particular intellectual property rights play an ever increasing economic role in business enterprises, as well as in the economy in general. This rising role of intangible assets is reflected in the increasing number of international conferences and publications devoted to this subject. Some authors even talk of a "*knowledge based economy*" in which the economic success of companies and even whole nations are no longer dependent on the prevailing natural resources or geography, but rather on the generation and the application of immaterial assets.[1] In such a knowledge based economy in which the value of intangible assets surmounts by far the value of physical assets (cp. figure I.2), the protection of these immaterial assets and the appropriation of their returns play predominant roles.[2] In this chapter we discuss the characteristics of immaterial assets, their generation and/or acquisition, and the means of protection of these assets against imitation and replication with the aim of a sustainable appropriation of their returns.

In chapter III.1 we point out the central differences between physical and intangible assets. As is shown, immaterial assets represent so-called '*public goods*'. We analyse the characteristics of these public goods, and evaluate the influence these characteristics have on the appropriability and in turn on the generation of such assets in business enterprises. This analysis of the appropriability of intangible assets leads to a conceptual delimitation of human capital, intangible assets, and immaterial or intellectual property. Following the analysis of the special characteristics of intangible assets and property in companies, we outline in chapter III.2 the different possibilities to generate immaterial technological assets. Hereby we distinguish between two principal sources: Company external and company internal sources of intangible assets. In the case of the company external provision, we focus on the acquisition and the generation of intangible assets in co-operation arrangements. With respect to the company's internal generation of intangible assets, we concentrate our analysis on R&D activities, as well as on learning-by-doing. Hereunto we point out the determining role of the appropriability of intangible assets

---

[1] Cp. Nonaka, I. (1994), p. 14; Parr, R. L. & Sullivan, P. H. (1996a), p. 267; Grant, R. M. (1997).

[2] Cp. Edvinsson, L. & Malone, M. S. (1997), p. 1-10.

in the decision process of business enterprises in allocating resources for their generation.

With regard to the central role of the appropriation of the returns generated by intangible assets we discuss in chapter III.3 the possible protection modes that are available to companies to ensure the appropriation of their immaterial assets and thus to give these assets a strategic dimension. As will be pointed out, the appropriability can either be achieved through legal measures, e.g., intellectual property rights, or through alternative, organisational measures of protection.

III.1 Characteristics of Intangible Assets

III.1.1 Particular Characteristics of Intellectual Assets

Companies mostly possess a repertoire of physical and intellectual assets that has a decisive influence on their market values. Physical assets, such as machines, raw materials, half-finished and finished products, land, and buildings, are shown on the balance sheet with their current book value. Intangible assets are, however, in comparison to physical assets, neglected since they are not accounted for on a company's balance sheet.[3] Moreover, companies have problems in evaluating the exact value of their intangibles, since no efficient market for such assets exist and thus no competitive equilibrium prices are established. Before analysing the general characteristics of intangible assets, we have to establish an approximate classification of immaterial assets in companies. Subsequently, we discuss the special characteristics of these assets, whereby a special focus is put on their public-good characteristics. In section III.1.2 the terms intellectual capital and intangible assets are delimited and the correlation between the two terms, as well as human capital is illustrated. The delimitation of the different types of intangible assets should contribute to the reduction of the prevailing heterogeneity in the classification of immaterial assets in business enterprises and thus establish a uniform and coherent categorisation.[4]

---

[3] For a detailed discussion of the accounting of immaterial assets see Egginton, D. A. (1990); Goldfinger, C. (1994), S. 138-142.

[4] Cp. Johanson, U. (1999).

III.1.1.1 Qualification & Structure of Immaterial Assets

A company's market value can either be determined by its stock quote as in the case of a publicly traded company or by the alienation of the company. The value of the company is in any case primarily influenced by its financial, physical, and immaterial assets. The assessment of the value of the financial and physical assets of the company can be easily accomplished on the basis of the book values presented on the balance sheet. Immaterial assets, however, are not covered in a company's balance sheet, and in addition, there exists no efficient market for such assets which could determine an effective equilibrium price. The economic value of these intangible assets is, hence, only indirectly measurable. If the company is a public quoted stock company, the value of its immaterial assets can be evaluated by the difference between the value of the company on the balance sheet which is the value of the company's financial and physical assets, and the company's market value which represents the value of all assets owned and held by the company (see figure III.1). Another possibility arises with the alienation of a company or parts of a company, whereby the value of the immaterial assets is appraised by the difference between the company's book value and its purchase value.[5]

Accordingly, the value of the immaterial assets can only be determined by the difference between its market value and its book value. The value of the intangible assets is, however, still influenced by so called disturbance terms. Such disturbances are, for example, general changes in the global or national economic environment or the general psychology at the stock market which in turn influences stockholders' expectations and hence a company's stock price.

[5] Cp. Sveiby, K. E. (1997), S. 25.

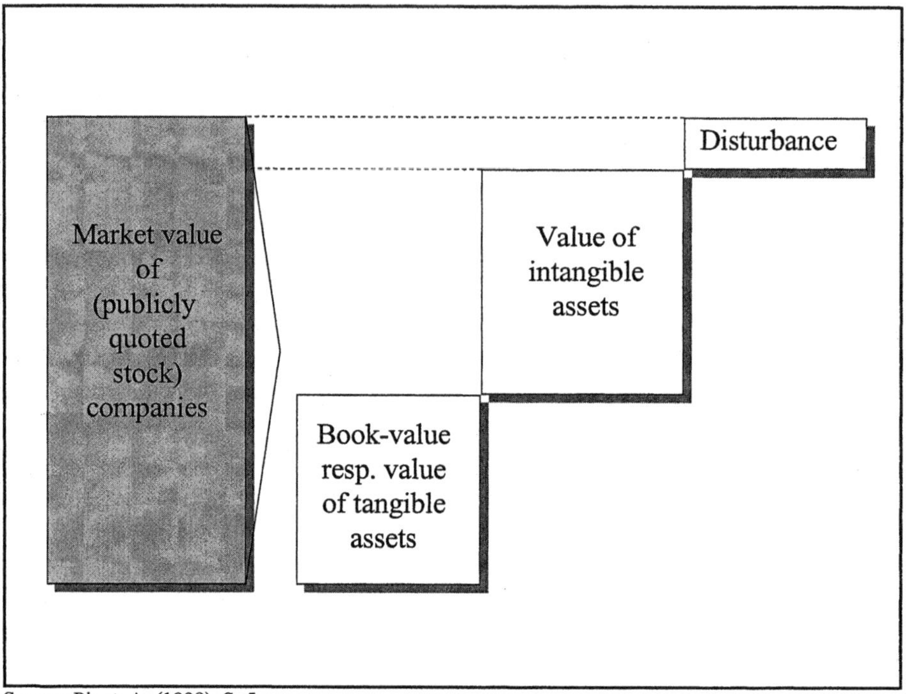

Source: Picot, A. (1998), S. 5.

Figure III.1: Determining the value of intellectual assets of a stock corporation

The value of a company's intangible assets which has been determined by the difference between the company's balance sheet value and its market value less the disturbance term, is composed of different types of intangible assets. Edvinsson & Malone (1997) have established, while elaborating an intellectual asset report for the Swedish insurance company *Skandia*, a classification of the company's intellectual assets.[6] According to this approach, the value of a company's intangible assets can be attributed to either human or structural capital. The structural capital can be further subdivided into customer and organisational capital which again can be decomposed into innovation and process capital (cf. figure III.2).

[6] Cp. Edvinsson, L. & Malone, M. S. (1997); Economist (1998).

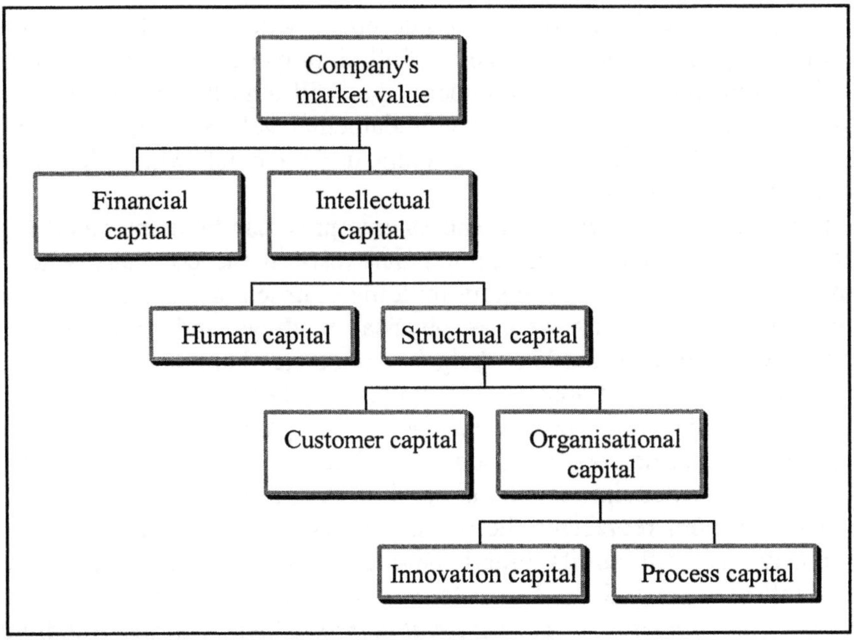

Source: Edvionsson, L. & Malone, M. S. (1997), S. 52.

Figure III.2: Plan of a company's market value according to Skandia

Types of intangible assets in companies

According to Edvinsson & Malon's segmentation of the factors contributing to the overall value of a company, intellectual capital can be defined as the *sum* of the organisation's established human- and structural capital (cf. figure III.2).[7] In this sense intellectual capital equals the term '*goodwill,*' which represents the value of all human and structural capital and thus all positive associations of the customers with the organisation and its trademarks and brands.[8]

In general, *human capital* can be defined as the capability of the employees to recognise and solve customers' problems.[9] Moreover, under the term human capital we subsume the corporate culture and the

[7] Cp. Edvinsson, L. & Malone, M. S. (1997), p. 10-15.

[8] "Il est symptomatique que les anglo-saxons appellent 'goodwill' cette différence entre le prix payé et la valeur nette comptable de l'entreprise. … Le goodwill comptable est l'évaluation monétaire du goodwill psychologique que la marque a su, à force d'effort et de temps, d'investissements et de constance focaliser sur son nom.", Kapferer, J. N. (1999), p. 20; for a more detailed discussion see also chap. IV.1.

[9] Cp. Sullivan, P. H. & Edvinsson, L. (1996), p. 254.

philosophy, since these assets are predominantly determined and sustained by the company's workforce. Thus, if all employees or at least a majority of the employees leave the company this will significantly influence or even entirely alter the company's fundamental values. Human capital is also commonly referred to as a company's capital which leaves the company at the end of the day.

The *structural capital* of a business enterprise can be demarcated vis-à-vis its human capital as the capital that rests in the company when all employees have left the company buildings. Structural capital is thus any codified knowledge, as well as physical holdings and properties of a company. Under codified knowledge we understand any knowledge which can be expressed and transferred in written or other recorded form, such as documents, sketches, processes, but also patents, trademarks, and organisational structures.[10] As shown in figure III.2, structural capital can be further divided into customer and organisational capital. The term *customer capital* represents the positive associations of customers with a company, as well as its brands and trademarks. Thus, a company's goodwill is expressed by the customers' commitment to these subjective values. The company's *organisational capital* which is further subdivided into innovation and process capital, comprises all those systems and devices in a company that enable, facilitate, and accelerate the transfer of knowledge and information within the company.[11] This can, for example, be a particular structure within a company that effectively increases the company's innovativeness as well as specific investments of a company which increase and facilitate the flow of information and knowledge between the individual employees within the organisation and hence permit the company to use its human and structural capital more efficiently. Such an investment is, for example, the establishment of a database (e.g., patent or customer database) with which the company's employees obtain easy and efficient access to existing information and knowledge in a particular field.

The linkage between human capital and structural capital is established by the mutual influence of these two capital blocks. The company's structural capital is established and maintained by a company's human capital. On the other hand, the better the company's established structural capital, the better its human capital's performance. The company's employees establish and represent the philosophy, culture, and structure of a company. Once these structures have been established in the company they will have a significant influence on the performance of its employees

[10] Cp. Lei, D. T. (1997); Nonaka, I. (1994); van Reekum, A. H. (1999), p. 77.
[11] Cp. Edvinsson, L. & Malone, M. S. (1997), p. 35.

which again affects the underlying corporate structures. It has emerged in the past, that companies which posses a particular innovative corporate culture, are more efficient in generating new products, processes, services, etc. than companies possessing a rigid organisation that emphasises the mere fulfilment of precisely defined tasks.[12]

If we go deeper into the analysis of intangible assets, we can see that the starting point of any intellectual capital is *knowledge* and *information*. In this sense information represent useful messages which can be the outcome of focused search and observation, as well as the result of accidental discovery.[13] Information thus corresponds to a flow of messages that supplement, restructure, or entirely alter the company's existing knowledge base.[14] In our work we adopt the definition established by Nonaka (1994) whereupon knowledge represents a justified true belief:

> *"... knowledge is conventionally defined as 'justified true belief' this convergence needs to be based on the 'justification' or truthfulness of concepts – justification determines the 'quality' of the created knowledge and involves criteria or 'standards' for judging truthfulness."*[15]

In the following section we analyse the characteristics of information and knowledge and depict its influence on the appropriability of the returns generated by these assets.

III.1.1.2 Public Good Characteristics of Intellectual Assets

As analysed before, information and knowledge are the basis of any intangible asset within companies. Information and knowledge resemble in the broader sense durable goods since present resources have to be invested in their establishment and once these assets exist, they will create a flow of revenues.[16] Consequently, a company's accumulated information and generated knowledge do have an economic value which can be used to generate a flow of revenues in the future.

---

[12] An innovative corporate culture mostly expels by its tolerant backing of new ideas and acceptance of mistakes which implies that mistakes of employees are not punished in a draconian way. A company which has become well known for such an innovative corporate culture is 3M. Cp. Nonaka, I. & Takeuchi, H. (1995), pp. 135-40.

[13] Cp. Arrow, K. J. (1969).

[14] Cp. Nonaka, I. (1994).

[15] Nonaka, I. (1994), p. 26.

[16] Cp. Magee, S. P. (1977).

As opposed to physical durables, in the case of immaterial assets further companies cannot be excluded from their exploitation. The increased use of the intangible assets diminishes the expected future flow of income for the "*inventor*".[17] However, we have to emphasise that the increased use of the immaterial assets will not reduce their overall economic value, but in fact, the returns generated by the asset in question are spread over several parties of which not all have contributed to their creation. Moreover, we have to distinguish public goods from *free goods*. Public goods are generally defined as goods that consumed by one person can still be consumed by another.[18] However, in order to be able to use a public good companies generally have to incur considerable costs, e.g., building up company internal competencies for their absorption and use. Thus, *immaterial assets do not represent free goods* which are defined as goods that can be absorbed, integrated, and used at no or negligible cost, since companies have to invest in internal skills to be able to absorb and use these public goods.[19]

Non-rivalry and Non-excludability

Information and knowledge and thus any type of intangible asset represents so called *public goods* which show the three critical characteristics of *non-rivalry*, *non-excludability*, and *high fixed costs* in their production.[20] Thus, due to the characteristic of non-excludability other parties cannot, or only under high costs, be excluded from the exploitation of the intangible asset in question. Moreover, the usage of the intangible asset in one company has no direct influence on the simultaneous utilisation of the same intangible asset in further companies. Hence, the *marginal cost* of using intellectual assets equals zero.[21] Consequently, companies can simultaneously use the same intangible assets without taking notice of the parallel usage.

Global Public Goods

All public goods show the characteristics of non-excludability and non-rivalry and hence zero marginal costs. Public goods can, however, be

---

[17] Under the term "inventor" we understand business corporations and individuals which are the first to have deliberately used or considered the information and/or knowledge in their acting.

[18] Cp. Begg, D., Fischer, S. et al. (1991), pp. 284.

[19] For a detailed discussion see e.g. Levin, R. C. (1988); Gambardella, A. (1992); Quintas, P., Lefrere, P. et al. (1997).

[20] Cp. Foray, D. (1995); Stiglitz, J. E. (1999b).

[21] Cp. Geroski, P. (1995); Liebeskind, J. P. (1996); Stiglitz, J. E. (1999b).

distinguished in two principal classes: *national* or *regional* public goods and *global* public goods. As Kaul, Grunberg et al. (1999a) have shown in their discussion, there exist three primary characteristics that classify global public goods. These distinctive characteristics are their universal validity in various, if not all nations and regions of the world, their general benefit has to apply to a large number of regions and nations, as well as to a broad spectrum of the world's population, and last but not least, global public goods have to satisfy the needs of current and future generations.[22]

There exist only very few goods which show all three characteristics. Stiglitz has identified five such global public goods, these are: International economic stability, international security (political stability), international environment, international humanitarian aid, and knowledge.[23] Specific types of knowledge fulfil the premises of global public goods which can be shown in an exemplary fashion on the case of knowledge about a metal-alloy.

The knowledge about the production of a particular metal-alloy which is exceptionally hard and corrosive-resistant, can be applied in all world regions and nations in the same manner as long as the used metal or metal ore has the same quality. Moreover, the metallurgical knowledge creates benefits for a vast number of individuals which can benefit of an exceptionally hard and corrosive-resistant metal-alloy by the increased use of the knowledge. Finally, the knowledge about the alloy not only serves the current generation, but also future generations which can built upon the already existent knowledge to develop new alloys that better satisfy the future needs. Then again, these characteristics do not apply to all kinds of knowledge and information. Geographical knowledge, for instance, can be appropriate and useful for a specific region, however, this knowledge cannot be readily used in other regions.

Thus, only specific types of knowledge and information and hence intangible assets classify as global public goods. However, for which types of knowledge and information do these characteristics of global public goods apply? These global intangible assets generally build on the laws of nature which show the characteristic of global validity. Thus, global intangible assets are predominantly based on technological, physiological, biological, pharmaceutical, mathematical, and economical principals. Hereunto we have to demarcate knowledge based on physiology, geography, and culture of a particular region since this knowledge is not uniform and thus cannot be readily transferred and applied in several world regions.

---

[22] Cp. Kaul, I., Grunberg, I. et al. (1999a), p. 10-12.

[23] Cp. Stiglitz, J. E. (1999b), p. 310.

Problem of Appropriating Immaterial Assets

A general problem of all public or collective goods constitutes the existence of a '*problem of provision*' which evokes from the characteristic of non-excludability. Companies investing in the generation of public goods can only partially appropriate the benefits generated by these assets. This phenomenon also applies to intangible assets within business enterprises and is described in *Arrow's problem of appropriability*. Since the inventor cannot exclude further parties from using his privately created immaterial assets, the assets' economic value for the innovator is reduced:[24]

> *"Information ... is also a public good in that once it is created, its use by the party who discovers it does not preclude its use by second parties. But in the case of privately created information, use by second parties reduces the private return on information by the first party."*[25]

The problem of appropriating intellectual assets creates a particularly severe economic problem in association with the generation of new immaterial goods. As already pointed out, the generation of intellectual assets is associated with high costs and thus companies have to invest significant resources in their generation. Consequently, in order to be willing to invest private resources, companies must be able to sufficiently appropriate the future stream of revenues created by these assets.[26] If the appropriation of these future revenue flows is not feasible, and hence other parties can reap a part of the revenues without having to incur the innovator's costs, no company would be willing to invest private resources in the creation of such assets.[27] This reduction of private resources for the generation of immaterial goods will result in a decline in the creation of new intellectual assets which will not only reduce the competitiveness of the individual company, but the economic progress as a whole will be endangered.[28]

---

[24] This phenomenon is known in microeconomics as the "free-rider-problem," which classifies companies and individuals that profit from existing public goods without having to incur the cost of provision as "free-riders". Cp. Pindyck, R. S. & Rubinfield, D. L. (1992), S. 665; Kaul, I. Grunberg, I. et al. (1999a); Liebeskind, J. P. (1996).

[25] Magee, S. P. (1977), p. 90-91.

[26] Cp. Lawless, M. W. & Fisher, R. J. (1990).

[27] The link between appropriability and the willingness of private parties to invest in the creation of intangible assets will be discussed in more detail in chap. III.3.

[28] Cp. Drucker, P. F. (1998); Mansfield, E., Schwarz, M. et al. (1981), Mokyr, J. (1998).

The problem of appropriation leads not only to a sub-optimal provision of the economy with immaterial assets, but also evokes the *non-tradability* of such assets on a free market. This phenomenon of non-tradability of intangible assets generates further social inefficiencies. The owner of an intangible asset can, accordingly, solely use the asset himself although there may exist other companies which can use his assets more efficiently. The problem of non-tradability results from the difficulty of ascertaining the real present value of these intangible assets. The inventing company owns a monopoly position on its internally generated intangible assets so that potentially interested parties do not know the assets and consequently cannot evaluate their economic value. If the inventing company, however, transfers its intangible asset for their evaluation to the prospect purchasers, the latter would have received the asset and hence could reproduce and use the information at low costs without having to incur a quid pro quo.[29] Consequently, the trade in intangible assets is not feasible in the absence of appropriation.

A solution to the above described appropriation and non-tradability problems represents legally enforceable intellectual property rights such as patents, trademarks, copyrights, etc.. However, as Arrow (1962b) has already stated:

> *"With suitable measures, information may become an appropriable commodity. However, no amount of legal protection can make a thoroughly appropriable commodity of something so intangible as information."*[30]

However, there do exist further possibilities for companies to increase the appropriability of intangible assets whereof the internalisation of their use and the registration of intellectual property rights represent but two.[31] On the basis of the internalisation of the use of intellectual assets we discuss the second distinctive characteristic of intellectual assets, their non-abrasion in use.

III.1.1.3 Non-Abrasion in Use

If a company uses its intellectual assets internally, the company not only takes advantage of the effect of increased safeguarding, but also of an effect which results from the non-abrasion of knowledge and information in their use. In contrast to physical assets, e.g., machines, the value of

[29] Cp. Arrow, K. J. (1962b).
[30] Arrow, K. J. (1962b), p. 615.
[31] For a detailed discussion see chap. III.3.

immaterial assets is not reduced but rather increased by their utilisation.[32] The increase in value of the intangibles through their use is due to their special nature. The human capital of a company represents with its inherent knowledge and information the starting point of any immaterial assets within the organisation. By using the *employees' know-how* a flow of information is generated which again influences the knowledge-basis of each individual employee and thereby renews and enlarges it. The know-how of a company which is represented by the totality of its employees, is preserved and renewed by its repeated utilisation. Furthermore, by using the already existing knowledge, new insights and information are created that again influence the current knowledge stock by updating, enlarging, or entirely altering it.[33]

If a company, however, does not use parts of its existing knowledge over a prolonged period, the company risks to lose the knowledge and thus to reduce its knowledge base and consequently endangers parts of its immaterial asset stock. This reduction of a company's knowledge stock is, on the one hand, provoked by the fluctuation of employees that carry a part of the company's knowledge. On the other hand, employees tend to forget parts of their know-how which they have not used for a long period of time. The phenomenon of '*forgetting*' is particularly pronounced in relation with knowledge that is difficult to articulate, transfer, and transmit, so called *tacit knowledge*, e.g., playing a musical instrument. For example, a piano virtuoso who is not cultivating his competencies by continuous repetition and application will not be able to hold his skills at a high level in the long-run.[34] This phenomenon of forgetting also applies to routines of companies that are not used over a long period of time. The more tacit and thus the less understood the knowledge in question, the more pronounced is the phenomenon in general.[35]

If employees, however, can use their know-how in the company's activities, the process of forgetting is not only brought to a hold, but in contrast to physical durables the value of the intangibles will be enhanced by their frequent utilisation. This rise in value is due to the process of learning and unlearning while using immaterial assets. If an employee uses, for example, his know-how to solve a specific problem or to perform a particular task, he encounters new, still unknown facts that will enlarge, update, or ultimately change his accumulated knowledge base. Moreover,

---

[32] Cp. Lei, D. T. (1997).

[33] Cp. Mokyr, J. (1998).

[34] For a detailed discussion of tacit and codified knowledge see Nonaka, I. & Takeuchi, H. (1995), chap. 3.

[35] Cp. Saviotti, P. P. (1998); Prahalad, C. K. & Hamel, G. (1990).

certain circumstances and relationships can be better understood due to frequent repetition so that these can be more easily codified or at least transmitted to other colleagues. So, we can summarise that the use of intangibles does not reduce their value as compared to tangibles because the knowledge base is updated and sustained by its utilisation.

The phenomenon of non-abrasion in use is not limited to tacit knowledge, but can also be transferred to codified or explicit knowledge. If we take, for instance, the case of an expiring patent, the general economic value of the patent will not decline because of the vanishing of the property right, but rather realises an increase due to its more widespread use in the economy.[36] However, in this case we have to distinguish the general economic value of the knowledge covered in the patent from the innovator's private value. The innovator who owns monopoly rights on the usage of the knowledge covered in his patent, will face the already described appropriation problem characterising public goods after the expiration of his patent. In the case of human capital based assets, a company faces the danger of the migration of its employees who carry the knowledge, since the company cannot declare its workforce as its private property. The only legal means companies possess to reduce the danger of knowledgeable employees leaving the company is to establish rigid and long-lasting labour agreements which increase the switching costs of the employees. However, such rigid contracts are only a second best solution, since they not only increase the switching cost for the company's employees, but also reduce a company's flexibility. In the following section we discuss possibilities how companies can extract non-codified, human capital based knowledge in order to obtain property- or at least holder-rights and consequently to increase the appropriability of these assets.

III.1.2 Human Capital, Intangible Asset, and Intellectual Property: A Definition

As pointed out above, companies cannot acquire legal property on their employees and thus on their inherent knowledge assets. However, as long as companies cannot obtain legal rights on intangible assets, the

[36] It is of crucial importance to distinguish between the general economic value and the private economic value of the intangible assets. In general the private value of the knowledge covered in a patent is severely reduced due to the expiring of the intellectual property right. However, the value for the society as a whole will be increased because of the more wide-spread use of the subject matter of the intellectual property right.

appropriation of the returns of these assets will be rather difficult. The reduced appropriability will result in a negative impact on the allocation of private resources for their creation.[37] The resulting sub-optimal generation of intangible assets not only adversely influences the prosperity of the individual company, but also the whole national, regional, or even global economic development. This significant role of the socially optimal provision of intellectual assets on the general economic development has so far justified the intervention of regulatory instances.[38]

In section III.1.2.1 we discuss the possibilities of how companies can create intangible assets with the help of their employees and how companies can extract the human-based knowledge in order to be able to obtain holder- or even ownership rights on these intellectual assets. We then establish a conceptual classification of human capital, intangible assets, and intellectual capital or property which aims at increasing the general comprehensibility of the discussion. The chapter closes with an upshot in section III.1.3.

III .1.2.1 Human Capital, Intangible Assets, and Intellectual Property

Due to the ever-increasing role of intangible assets, companies have to efficiently manage their immaterial assets in order to remain competitive in increasingly globalised markets. This implies that companies have to efficiently generate intangibles within their organisation, but also acquire externally created assets and to efficiently appropriate the revenues generated by these assets. The process of efficient appropriation and utilisation of intangible assets will have a decisive influence on the structure and the boundaries of the companies in the future. On the one hand, the corporate boundaries will become increasingly fluid since companies will increase their available intellectual basis and thus access intangible assets generated by external sources such as universities, public and private research institutes, and even other companies. On the other hand, the management of the human capital will further increase in significance in order to ensure an efficient company internal creation of intellectual assets. The human capital will represent the central factor of production and bearer of immaterial assets within business enterprises of the 21st century. Companies that realise the central role of their human capital on time and adjust their personnel management and corporate structures accordingly will have a competitive advantage in the knowledge

[37] For a detailed discussion see chap. III.1.1.2.

[38] Cp. Wright, B. D. (1983); Stiglitz, J. E. (1999a, 1999b).

based economy vis-à-vis those companies that still put their main focus on the management of tangible assets and regard human capital just as a cost factor.

Human Capital

The employees represent the knowledge basis of any business enterprise with which it can produce products and services, but also generate new intangible assets. The human capital is the basis of any economic activity, as well as the source of any immaterial asset and hence no company can exist without it.[39] The employees provide a company with their know-how and experiences which are in turn used in generating the company's output and thus it has been realised that employees' know-how usually represents a company's most important intangible asset.[40] By using the employees' know-how, new flows of information are created which will in turn influence the employees' knowledge base.[41] Yet, the know-how and experiences embodied in the company's employees only represent a part of the so-called human capital based assets of a company. Other important assets that have an impact on a company's success and which are embraced by the term human capital are the creativity, innovativeness, and the general skilfulness of the workforce (cf. figure III.3). Thus, a company's human capital can be defined as the sum of all assets associated with its employees.

These intangible assets embodied in a company's employees, however, represent not only the source of all products and services produced within the hierarchy, but also constitute the only source of new intellectual assets within the organisation.[42] The employees create by their acting structural capital which comprises several immaterial asset forms, e.g., customer-, organisational-, innovation-, and process-capital.[43] The stock of structural capital created by the human capital has, however, again a bearing on the effectiveness of the company's employees. The better the company's existing structural capital, the more efficient the employees in the creation of physical and intangible assets.[44] A company, for example, that possesses a corporate culture and structure which facilitates a rapid and efficient treatment of information and knowledge within the organisation, or possesses extensive databases and information systems that reduce the

---

[39] Cp. Sveiby, K. E. (1997), p. 26; Grant, R. M. (1996a).
[40] Cp. Hall, R. (1997); Grant, R. M. (1997).
[41] For a detailed discussion see chap. III.2.1.2, III.2.2.3, and figure III.15.
[42] Cp. Nonaka, I. & Takeuchi, H. (1995), p. 59.
[43] Cp. figure III.2.
[44] Cp. Edvinsson, L. & Malone, M. S. (1997), p. 35.

employees' search costs, will show an enhanced productivity of its human capital in the production of physical and immaterial assets.

Intangible Assets

In order to be able to efficiently appropriate and preserve intangible assets within an organisation, a company has to extract the ideas and know-how embedded in its employees.[45] The human capital can generate intellectual assets within a company by codifying its inherent know-how and experiences. The *codification* can take place by recording knowledge, for example, in databases, documenting employees' ideas and experiences in manuscripts and sketches, as well as by transferring knowledge and information by oral or action based communication to a large number of colleagues.[46] Hence, the term intellectual assets not only embraces all documents, sketches, manuscripts within a company but also the established corporate culture and structure which are defined by prevailing rituals, codes of conduct, and established structures, hierarchies, and procedures in a company. The culture and organisation of a company are not always codified in its original sense, but these assets are *more closely tied to a company per se as to any particular employee*.[47] If a particular employee or even a group of employees leaves a company, for example, this will merely have a marginal influence on the company's culture and structure since the knowledge is also embedded in the remaining employees. Thus, with regard to human capital intangible assets include the know-how and knowledge collectively held within the organisation, the company's culture and organisation, as well as any codified know-how and expertise. Intangible assets can thus be classified as those immaterial assets which are tied to a company and represents its holdings.

Intellectual Capital and Property

A company's intangible assets represent in general public goods on which the company itself possesses no *property rights* per se. Since a company cannot obtain ownership rights on knowledge, ideas, and experiences

---

[45] A well known example of unique knowledge lost by the death of a single man represents the story of the producer of the renown violins of Stradivarius. Stradivarius kept the process-know-how of how to produce his violins secret throughout his lifetime and the know-how disappeared with the death of the master. Cp. Seibert, G., Wandelberger, E. (1988), p. 4621.

[46] The codification of knowledge is defined as the transformation of experiences and information in symbolic forms. Cp. Teece, D. J. (1981), p. 83.

[47] Nonaka & Takeuchi speak in the context of codes, knowledge, etc., which have been established within a company but have not been codified from '*socialisation*'. Cp. Nonaka, I. & Takeuchi, H. (1995), pp. 62-70.

located in employees' brain not even if they are held collectively, the aim of any business enterprise has to be the extraction and codification of the employees' know-how and ideas to take possession of these assets.[48] However, in order to obtain a *strategic relevance*, the revenues of the intangible assets have to be appropriable. This can be achieved by obtaining legal property rights such as a patent, copyrights, etc. Thus, intellectual capital or property can be defined as those intangible assets of a company on which it holds *ownership rights* or which are *legally bound* to the company in question.

If a company tries to increase the appropriation of its intangible assets by trade secrecy, establishing complementary assets, or lead-time-advantages, we do not speak of a company's intellectual capital or property, but of its intangible assets or holding. By these *organisational means* a company can increase the appropriation of the revenues generated by its immaterial assets but it cannot assert any *right of ownership* on these assets. Thus, immaterial assets that are not legally bound to the company but appropriated by organisational arrangements do not represent a company's intellectual capital. These assets only represent a company's *holdings* or *tenure* and hence intellectual assets but not its intellectual *property*, *capital*, or *ownership*.[49]

To point out the difference between intangible assets and property more clearly, we refer to the already above mentioned metal alloy. If a company solely holds the knowledge of how to produce the alloy, the company can appropriate the returns generated by the process-knowledge by means of trade-secrecy and internal use. Thus, the company does not own legal property rights on its knowledge and in the case of another company discovering the metallurgic know-how in a legal way, e.g., detailed re-engineering of the final-product or random discovery, the second company cannot be prevented to use this know-how. Consequently, intellectual property or capital can be defined as those assets of a company that are protected by legally enforceable rights which are respected by society and thus represent the company's private ownership.[50]

---

48 Cp. Parr, R. L. & Sullivan, P. H. (1996a).

49 For a detailed discussion of legal property rights and alternative forms of appropriation see chap. III.3.

50 Cp. Johanson, U. (1999).

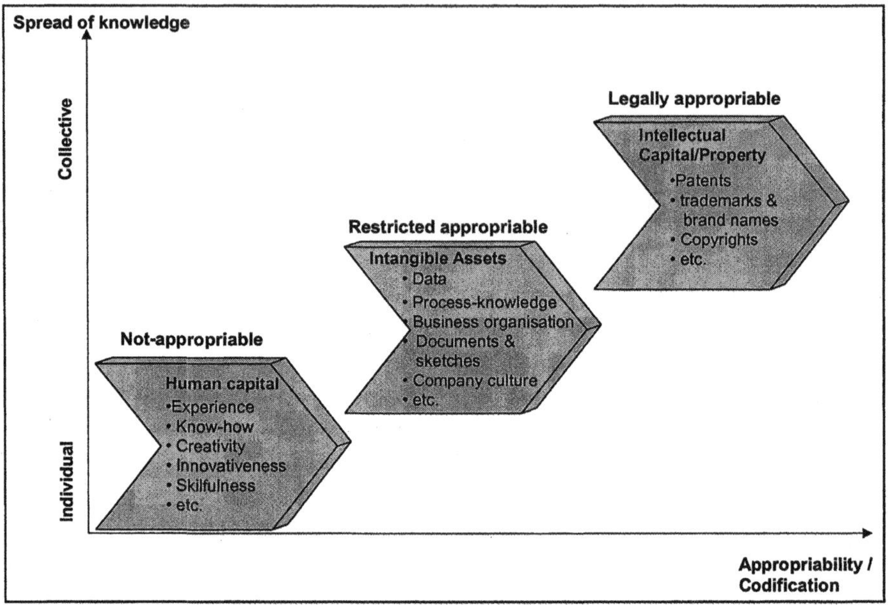

Figure III.3: Human capital, intangible assets, and intellectual capital or property

Figure III.3 visualises the coherence of human capital, immaterial assets, and intellectual capital. The human capital possesses inherent knowledge, e.g., know-how, experiences, skills, on which the company cannot assert any right of ownership or possession. If those human capital based immaterial asserts are extracted and codified in numbers, words, sketches, rituals, codes of conduct, or transferred to a large number of the company's employees, the immaterial valuables get bound to the organisation and thus represent the company's immaterial possession or intellectual assets. Intellectual capital or property, however, represents merely the part of a company's codified intellectual assets on which it holds legally enforceable property rights such as patents, trademarks, copyrights, etc., or which are bound to the company by another legal way. As can be seen in figure III.4, intellectual capital only represent a subset of the company's intellectual asset stock. This established classification coincides with the classification established by Sullivan (2000), who has classified intellectual valuables according to the degree of codification.[51]

[51] Cp. Sullivan, P. H. (2000), chap. 9.

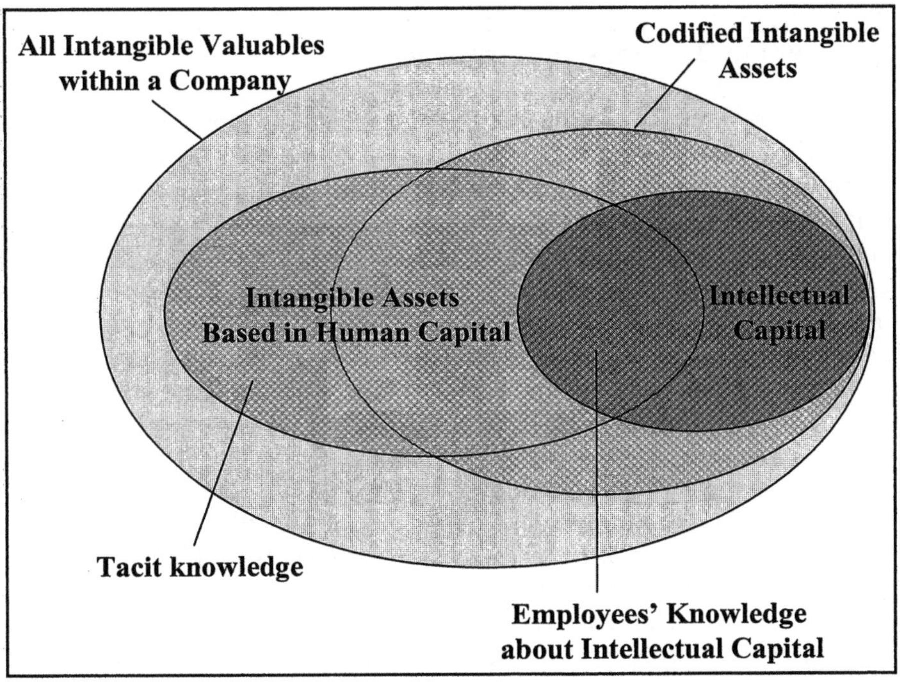

Figure III.4: Immaterial assets, human capital, and intellectual capital within companies

As shown in figure III.3, the legal appropriability of the assets and their codification increases from left to right. A company cannot assert any rights of possession or ownership on the immaterial assets located in its employees. Hence, the company cannot directly appropriate the intangibles inherent in its human capital. However, if these assets are extracted and codified, its possession rights subrogate to the company in question. The company can then increase the appropriation of these assets by several means, e.g., trade secrecy and internal utilisation of the assets. The maximum level of appropriation is attained if the company obtains legally enforceable intellectual property rights on its codified assets. The intellectual capital of a company is represented by its patent-, trademark-, copyright-, registered design-portfolios. However, by extracting and codifying the knowledge previously embodied in an employee, not only the level of appropriation and codification increases but also the spread of the knowledge. Human capital based assets, e.g., skills, experiences, etc., are located in only one person and thus represent assets held by the individual person. If the company extracts and codifies the knowledge and ideas, they will spread over a larger number of people and finally become collectively held assets.

III.1.3 Upshot I: Types and Characteristics of Intangible Assets within Business Enterprises

This section analyses the general characteristics of intangible assets and established definitions of the different types of intellectual assets prevailing in companies according to their legal connectedness to a company and thus its ability of appropriation. As discussed before, the *human capital* of a company represents all employee-based assets. The company cannot assert any rights of holding or ownership to the assets inherent to the company's workforce. In contrast, a company's *intellectual assets* are all codified knowledge and information that represent the company's holdings. These immaterial assets can be classified as *restricted appropriable* (see figure III.3). Intellectual assets turn into *intellectual capital* or *property* if the company gains legal property rights on these assets. Intangible assets of a company thus represent a subset of the company's overall immaterial valuables and intellectual capital again constitutes only a part of its intellectual assets (see figure III.4).

As pointed out, intangible assets can be characterised as public-goods and hence are marked with an appropriation problem. Under the appropriability problem we subsume the difficulties of companies investing in the generation of intangible assets in appropriating the current and future revenues created by these assets. Furthermore, the problem of appropriation entails the non-functioning of the market's 'invisible hand' and consequently the socially optimal provision of the economy with immaterial assets is not warranted. To minimise the problem of non functioning market mechanism regulatory interventions are required, the most important of which is the allocation of intellectual property rights. These intellectual property rights which are in part limited in their duration, bestow their owner with the exclusive user-rights which in turn guarantee, at least in theory, the owner the perfect appropriation of the revenues generated by his intellectual capital.

A further central characteristic of immaterial assets within business enterprises is their non-abrasion in use. In contrast to physical assets, the value of immaterial assets is not diminished, but rather increased by their use. At the beginning of the cycle of the corporate knowledge generation stands the human capital of a company. The company can, however, not assert any possession or ownership rights on this human capital, but only increase the contractual commitment of the employees towards the company. Hence, the aim of any business enterprise has to be the extraction and codification of the employees' know-how in order to be able to claim holding or even ownership rights on these intangible assets. The immaterial valuables on which a company can claim holding but no ownership rights are defined as a company's intangible assets. If the company attains legal protection of its intangible assets, the assets become its legal ownership and thus represent its intellectual capital or property. This leads to the thesis of chapter III.1.

Thesis I:
Human capital represents the source of any immaterial assets. Once these immaterial assets have been codified they show the characteristics of non-rivalry, non-excludability, and non-abrasion in use. To better account for the considerable differences between intangible assets a further specification of intangibles into three distinct types, according to the spread of knowledge and the degree of legal appropriation and codification, is necessary.

III.2 Generation and Acquisition of Immaterial Assets

As already pointed out in chapter I and III.1, intellectual assets and property take an ever-increasing role in the determination of the success of business enterprises. Companies have to selectively generate and acquire new intellectual assets in order to be able to survive in a knowledge-based economy. These new intellectual assets have to be embodied in new products and services which in turn generate a particular *customer benefit*. As Clark (1987) has pointed out, companies compete on the basis of differentiated products and services. Such distinctive features which give an individual company a competitive advantage, are the efficiency, reliability, simple usability, aesthetic appearance, cost , and a combination of those features which customers regard as valuable and which are superior with regard to competitors' products and services.[52]

Such distinctive features that can give a company an advantage on the market can be generated by scientific R&D activities amongst others.[53] Nelson (1959) has defined *scientific research* as a human activity directed towards the progression of knowledge.[54] The author differentiates in his discussion two sorts of knowledge: Facts and data which are observed in reproducible experiments, and theories and relationships between factors. The scientific research conducted in business enterprises is often associated with so called inventions, where the term *invention* is defined as the human activity aimed at generating new and improved products and services. In this context, however, the term *innovation* has to be delimited

[52] Cp. Clark, K. B. (1987).

[53] For a detailed illustration of the history of the economics of innovation see Graham, M. B. (1985); Freeman, C. (1994); Freeman, C. & Soete, L. (1997).

[54] Cp. Nelson, R. R. (1959), p. 299.

from the term *invention*. According to Freeman (1974) an innovation represents the first market introduction of an invention:

> *In this Schumpeterian distinction "[a]n 'invention' is an idea, a sketch or a model for a new or improved device, product, process or system. Such inventions ... do not necessarily lead to technical innovations .... An innovation in the economic sense is accomplished only with the first commercial transaction involving the new product, process, system or device ...."*[55]

Such innovations can be further distinguished and classified.[56] We do not discuss the different classes of innovation, since they only have a marginal influence on the appropriation of innovations and thus the analysis would go beyond the scope of this contribution. In the next paragraphs we analyse the different existing possibilities of companies to generate and acquire immaterial assets. As can be seen in figure III.5, there are several different potential founts of immaterial assets that can be generally distinguished in *company external* and *internal sources*.[57]

In figure III.6 we can identify two general sources of intellectual asset: The *company internal value chain*, and the *national or regional environment*. A company's environment is determined by the interaction with suppliers, competitors, clients, research institutes, universities, and national politics and regulations. The internal value chain can, on a very rough level, be subdivided into R&D, production, and marketing and distribution. As illustrated in figure III.6, the different functions mutually interact and interrelate which again influences a company's internal process of immaterial asset creation.

Once a company has identified the potential of an invention or innovation, the company faces the problem of how to enter the innovative market and how to acquire the required competencies and technologies for production and distribution most efficiently. Companies have a vast range of potential ways of market entry and competence acquisition.[58] In our discussion we concentrate on three basic organisational means of access to immaterial assets:

1. Company internal generation of intangible assets;

---

[55] Freeman, C. (1974), p. 22.

[56] For a discussion of the different types of innovation see, e.g., Abernathy, W. J. & Clark, K. B. (1987); Clark, K. B. (1987); Henderson, R. M. & Clark, K. B. (1990); Pisano, G. P. (1990); Powell, W. W. (1998); Christensen, C. M., Suárez, F. F. et al. (1998).

[57] Cp. Durand, T. (1998); Kogut, B. & Zander, U. (1992).

[58] Cp. Roberts, E. B. & Berry, C. A. (1985).

2. Acquisition of company external intangible assets on the market; and
3. Co-operative forms of creating intangible assets.[59]

<table>
<tr><th colspan="2" rowspan="3"></th><th>Internal</th><th colspan="3">External</th></tr>
<tr><th colspan="2">Development</th><th colspan="2">Acquisition</th></tr>
<tr><th>Make (R&D)</th><th>Let Make (R&D)</th><th>Acquisition of Technologies</th><th>Mergers and Acquisitions</th></tr>
<tr><td rowspan="4">State of corporate attitude</td><td>Exclusive competitive-ness and rather centrali-sation</td><td>• Cen-tralised R&D
• Decen-tralised internal R&D</td><td>• Subcon-tracted R&D; split up or exclusive</td><td>• Collection of information, following the current state of art
• Enticement of specialists from the competitors
• Technology acquisition (licensing)</td><td>• Take over control</td></tr>
<tr><td rowspan="3">Co-operative partnership and rather decentrali-sation (entrepre-neurial)</td><td>• Internal entrepre-neurs</td><td>• Co-sub-contracted R&D</td><td>• Barter trade</td><td rowspan="2">• Equity partici-pation
• Net-working</td></tr>
<tr><td colspan="3">• R&D collaboration</td></tr>
<tr><td colspan="4">• Joint venture</td></tr>
</table>

Source: Durand, T. (1988), p. 12.

Figure III.5: Sources of immaterial assets

In the following discussion, however, we do not consider *technology* as a given factor combination that generates a certain output. In this widespread approach, the technological advance is defined as an outward shift of the production possibility frontier.[60] In our discussion we adopt the definition established by Dosi (1982), who has defined a technology as a compilation of knowledge, methods, procedures, experiences, as well as physical devices:

> *"Let us define technology as a set of pieces of knowledge, both directly 'practical' (related to concrete problems and devices) and 'theoretical' (but practically applicable although not necessarily already applied) know-how, methods, procedures, experiences of*

[59] Cp. Liebeskind, J. P. & Oliver, A. L. et al. (1996).

[60] Cp. Krugman, P. R. & Obstfeld, M. (1994); p. 93-96; Sloman, J. (1991), p. 9-19.

success and failure and also of course, physical devices and equipment."[61]

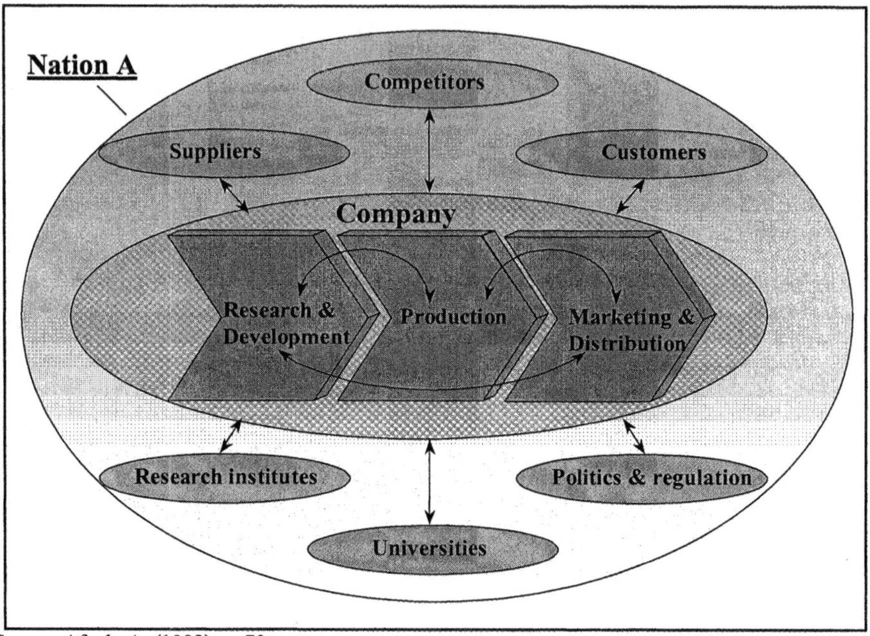

Source: Afuah, A. (1998), p. 70.

Figure III.6: National sources of intangible assets

In chapter III.2.1 we analyse a company's internal creation of intangible assets by distinguishing between two forms of internal intellectual asset creation: *R&D activities* and *learning-by-doing*. In this context we point out the advantages and limits of a company's internal creation of intangibles and reveal the central role of companies' R&D activities in the generation of immaterial assets. In the subsequent chapter III.2.2 we discuss the feasibility and relevance of acquisitions of externally created immaterial technological assets. Sections III.2.2.1 and III.2.2.2 discuss the means of acquiring intangible assets by licensing agreements and M&As. In paragraph III.2.2.3 we then analyse the role of companies' internal R&D in the acquisition of intangible assets. Due to the increasing role of co-operative forms of intellectual asset creation, we take up this subject in chapter III.2.3 and explain the main advantages, risks, and complications of this co-ordination form. The chapter closes with an upshot in chapter III.2.4.

[61] Dosi, G. (1982); p. 151-152.

III.2.1 Generation of Intangible Asset within Business Companies

This chapter analyses how companies can internally create new immaterial assets. In general all functions within a company can be a source of new knowledge and information and thus of intangible assets (cp. figure III.7).[62] Fundamentally, we can distinguish two principal forms of internal immaterial asset generation: Learning-by-doing without searching and searching without doing. In this context the term searching is synonymous to R&D activities.[63] In business enterprises these two forms are synchronous and closely interrelated and thus cannot be clearly distinguished. Nevertheless, for the purpose of analysing the various sources of intangible assets, we keep up this clear-cut distinction of R&D and learning activities in our discussion.

As shown in figure III.7, the value chain can be roughly subdivided into R&D, production, and marketing and distribution. In the following discussion we analyse the role of explicit search activities and learning-by-doing which cover the phases R&D and production (cf. figure III.7).

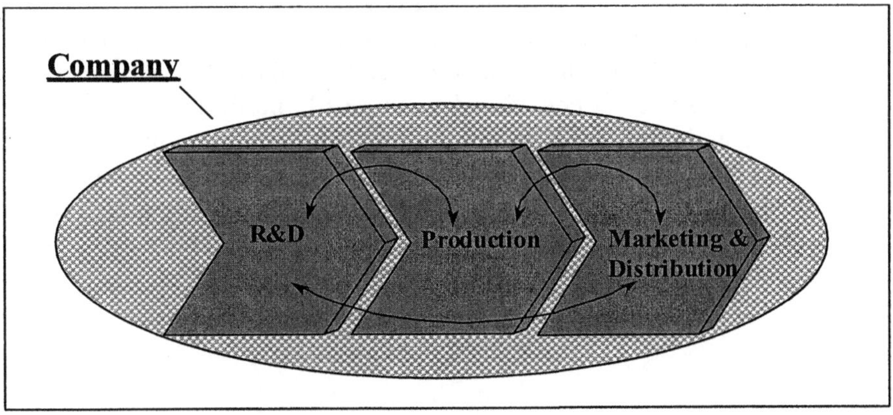

Figure III.7: Company internal sources of innovation

Section III.2.1.1 discusses the form of internal searching without doing and points out the central significance of such focused search activities in the creation of new intellectual assets. Furthermore, we describe the phenomenon of the increasing internationalisation of R&D activities within companies and show their influence on the generation of immaterial assets. The succeeding chapter III.2.1.2 then presents learning-by-doing as

[62] Cp. Afuah, A. (1998), p. 68-88.
[63] Cp. Saviotti, P. P. (1998).

a further distinct possibility of intangible asset generation within an organisation.

III.2.1.1 Research- and Development Activities

R&D is seen as an effective way of creating new technologies and products.[64] This important role is reflected in companies' R&D expenses (cp. figure III.8). The R&D expenditures of business enterprises in the USA, Japan, France, and Germany haven risen from 1983 to 1997 in average by 150 percent.[65]

In the theoretical literature the innovation process is often depicted as a linear process subdivided into *basic research, applied research, development and market introduction.*[66] These models usually see the task of basic research in the revelation of fundamental concepts which are necessary for understanding a technology field in general.[67] Thus, the focus of basic research is not a certain product or service but rather the advancing of the *scientific knowledge* and *understanding*. Although basic research is not directly aimed at the development of a particular product or service, nonetheless, it represents an extremely important source of new information and knowledge which provides the basis for new products and processes. However, due to the lacking ready applicability of the research results, basic research is considered to be mostly performed by public and private research institutes, and universities and not by companies themselves.[68] The task of applied research is then again seen in building on the results of basic research to find new products and processes which are finalised in a subsequent development phase. If a new product or process reaches a certain maturity it is introduced to the market.

---

[64] Cp. Graham, M. B. (1985); Teece, D. J. (1988).

[65] Cp. Kodama, F. (1995).

[66] See Nelson, R. R. (1959); Pavitt, K. (1991); Gambardella, A. (1992); Pearce, R. & Papanastassiou, M. (1999).

[67] Cp. van Reekum, A. H. (1999), p. 67; Saviotti, P. P. (1998), p. 846.

[68] Cp. Nelson, R. R. (1959).

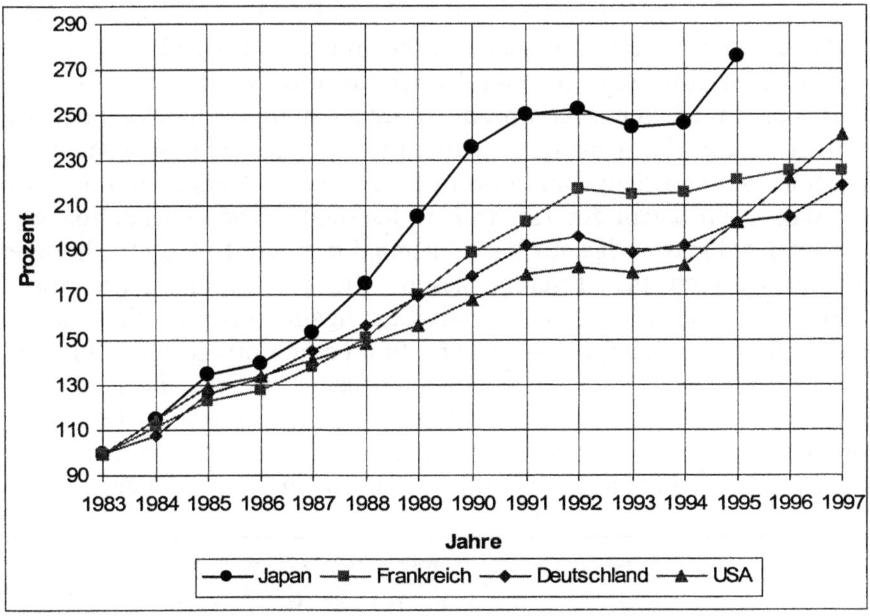

Data source: OECD (1999).

Figure III.8: Development of companies' R&D expenditures in France, Germany, Japan, and USA[69]

However, as Kuznets (1962) has pointed out, no clear distinction of basic and applied research on the one hand, and research and development activities on the other hand is possible in practice.[70] Furthermore, Kline & Rosenberg (1986) put the entire linear model with the distinction of the innovation process in basic and applied R&D, as well as development phase into question and developed a *chain-linked model of the innovation process* which better embraces the complex nature of innovation (cf. figure III.9).

According to Kline & Rosenberg (1986), the innovation process in not characterised by a single linear path of activity, but rather several different paths co-exist.[71] The main path is the *central-chain-of-innovation* which is label "C" in figure III.9. The path sets out with a design and continues through development and production to marketing. A second path which is marked "F," indicates the *feedback loops* which repeat the steps and also

[69] Figures in percent (1993=100%) calculated on the basis of 'million current purchasing power parity US$'.

[70] Cp. Kuznets, S. (1962); Mansfield, E. (1984).

[71] Cp. Kline, S. J. & Rosenberg, N. (1986); Gerybadze, A. (2004), chap. 1.3.2.

connect back from observed needs and requirements for improvement of product and service performance in the subsequent round of design. The authors also point out the central importance of *accumulated knowledge* that is consulted whenever a problem occurs along the innovation process. This illustrates the behavioural pattern to first call on known science and accumulated knowledge and information on several stages and only when all stages fail a call for *research* is justified.[72] The consultation of the accumulated knowledge stock is illustrated in figure III.9 by the horizontal arrows between the different design and production stages and the knowledge block. Research activities again increase the stock of accumulated knowledge and respond to a certain problem encountered in one of the stages of the innovation process. Thus, the linear models of innovation with its simple distinction between research, development, production, and marketing oversimplified the innovation process and totally neglected the influence of feedback and prior existent knowledge.

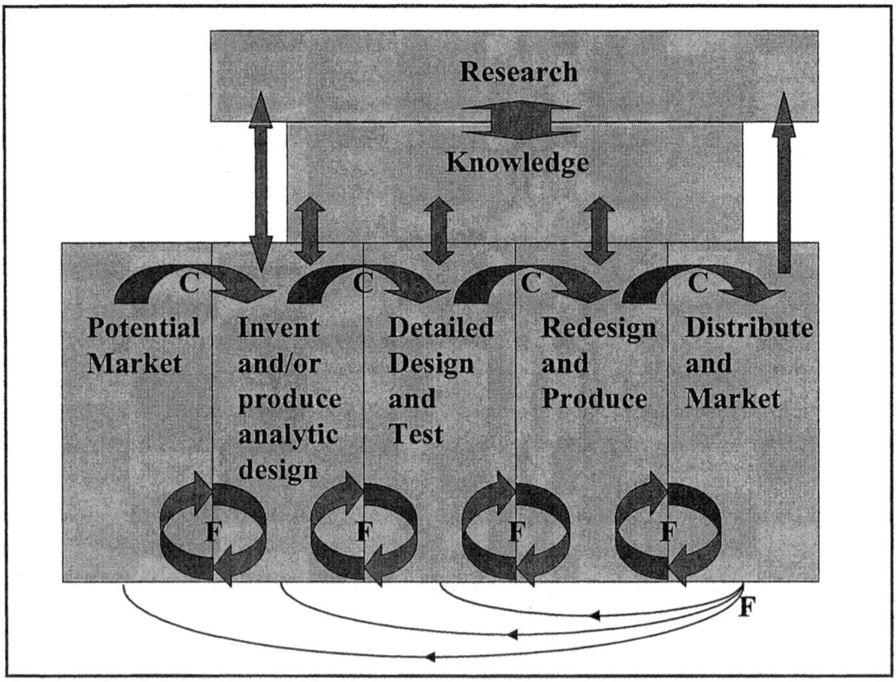

Source: Kline, S. J. & Rosenberg, N. (1986)

Figure III.9: The chain-linked model of innovation

[72] Cp. Kline, S. J. & Rosenberg, N. (1986).

R&D and the Generation of Immaterial Assets

Nowadays, the generation of immaterial assets is no longer seen as exogenously given as in the late 19th and the beginning 20th century.[73] A possibility to generate new knowledge and expertise and hence intangible assets within companies which contribute to the development of new products and processes and thus influence the current technological development and status quo, are R&D activities in company internal laboratories.[74] R&D activities are defined according by the OECD as:

> *"... creative work undertaken on a systematic basis in order to increase the stock of knowledge and the use of this stock of knowledge in order to devise new materials, products, devices, processes, systems or services, or improving substantially those already produced or installed."*[75]

Accordingly, companies invest in R&D to generate new ideas and knowledge that respond to specific problems encountered in the innovation process of new products, processes, or services and add to the current stock of accumulated knowledge. These new ideas and knowledge take, in the case of R&D, mostly the form of technologies or improved understanding of existing technologies and technical relationships and consequently represent immaterial assets.

The interplay of R&D expenditures and the creation of new technological knowledge has been subject of multiple investigations in the past.[76] In these studies the *analysis of patent data* took a considerable role in the measurement of the R&D output.[77] However, the use of patent statistics in the measurement of technological change has been severely criticised by researches. The critique concerned in particular the comparability of the quality of the patented inventions which can neither be assumed to be congruent between patents assigned in different industries or time periods within the same nation nor between different nations over the same period or in the same industry.[78] Several authors

[73] Cp.Freeman, C. (1994).

[74] Cp. Mossinghoff, G. J. (1984); Shapiro, C. (1985); Grindley, P. C. & Teece, D. J. (1997).

[75] Van Reekum, A. H. (1999), p. 58.

[76] Cp. Bound, J., Cummins, C. et al. (1984); Griliches, Z. (1984a, 1984b); Gambardella, A. (1992); Engelsmann, E. C. & van Raan, A. F. J. (1993).

[77] Cp. Kutznets, S. (1962); Scherer, F. M. (1965, 1984); Pakes, A. & Griliches, Z. (1984); Hall, B. H., Griliches, Z. et al. (1986); Basberg, B. L. (1987); Griliches, Z. (1984a, 1989, 1990); Arundel, A. & Kabla, I. (1998); Kortum, S. & Lerner, J.. (1999).

[78] Cp. Sanders, B. S. (1962); Patel, P. & Pavitt, K. (1995).

have tried to resolve this problem of diverging patent qualities by means of citation analyses.[79]

In spite of the critique, the assumption of a *positive correlation* between R&D expenditures and patent filings on the one hand, and innovations on the other hand has been asserted. This predominance of patent statistics in the measurement of innovations can be explained by the aesthesia of other units of measurement of the innovative output. As Schmookler (1962) has pointed out, an accurate measurement must always be preferred to an imprecise index. Unfortunately, however, researchers only have this approximate index in form of patent registrations at their disposal which is still better than no indication of measurement of the innovative output of business enterprises at all.[80] The *uniqueness* of patent figures and their *good availability* have provoked a strong concentration on these statistics in the measurement of companies' innovative output. Nevertheless, in general it has been widely acknowledged that these figures only represent an imprecise indicator.[81]

Before analysing the relationship between R&D investments and patent applications in detail, we indicate some important shortcomings of patent statistics in the quantification of the output of creative activities.

As figure III.10 visualises, investments in creative activities such as, for instance, R&D expenditures not only create legal property rights such as patents, trademarks, and copyrights, but also generate further immaterial and human capital based assets. These immaterial valuables which are not protected by legal property rights, are not observable by external analyses such as patent counts and even company internal quantification of these assets is practically impossible. Thus, the readily available patent figures neglect a significant part of a company's innovative output, since not all inventions and innovations are patented or are even patentable.[82]

As outlined in chapter I.4, the outstanding majority of empirical studies analyses the relationship between a company's R&D expenditures and patent applications. Most of these studies found a positive correlation between patent applications and R&D expenditures on the company level.[83] From the results of these studies we can conclude that investments

---

[79] Cp. Narin, F., Noma, E. et al. (1987); Alber, M. B., Avery, D. et al. (1991); Narin, F. & Olivastro, D. (1992); Harhoff, D., Narin, F. et al. (1997).

[80] Cp. Schmookler, J. (1962).

[81] Cp. Pakes, A. & Griliches, Z. (1984).

[82] For a detailed discussion see chap. III.3.1 and III.3.3 and cp. Kutznets, S. (1962); Pakes, A. & Griliches, Z. (1984).

[83] Cp. Bound, J. Cummins, C. et al. (1984); Pakes, A. & Griliches, Z. (1984); Griliches, Z. (1984a, 1984b); Hausman, J., Hall, B. H. et al. (1984).

in R&D generate intangible assets that are at least partially protected by intellectual property rights. However, none of these studies has revealed which percentage share of the overall R&D output is covered in a company's patent application. As stressed by numerous authors, process innovations and so-called incremental innovations, for example, are either not patentable or patents are not enforceable and hence ineffective.[84] Consequently, we can conclude that patent figures represent an imprecise and approximate measure of a company's innovative output which nevertheless found widespread use in the scientific community due to the ready availability of the data.

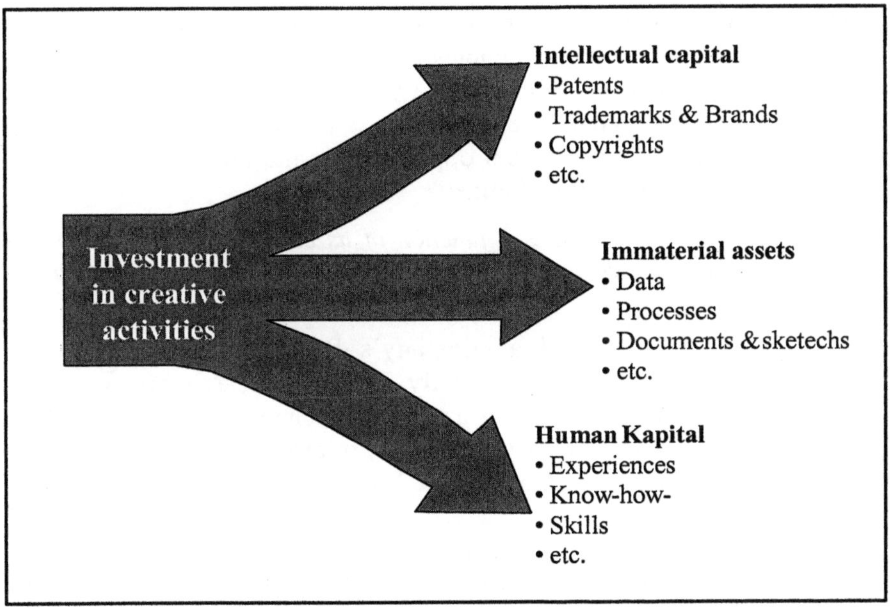

Figure III.10: Differentiation of creative output

Moreover, it has been recognised that R&D investments and the resulting immaterial assets do not only contribute to the current generation of new products, processes, and services, but also form the basis of future inventions and innovations.[85] In Nelson's model investments in R&D represent an enlargement of the company's knowledge base whereby the efficiency of search activities, as well as the company's sensibility to

[84] For a detailed discussion see chap. III.3.
[85] Cp. Rosenberg, N. (1974).

current and potential demands and needs is increased.[86] Accordingly, Nelson associates with an enlarged knowledge base a more rapid technological development by a given R&D budget or, alternatively, the costs of an envisaged research project are reduced by the already accumulated knowledge. The increased efficiency of the company's R&D activities due to the larger knowledge base is explained by the possibility to conduct better focused search activities due to the employees' accumulated experiences, skills, and know-how. These skills and know-how of the employees constitute together with the nature of a company's decision making processes, as well as the link between R&D, production, and marketing a company's *core capabilities*.[87]

Thus, a company's idiosyncratic R&D capabilities represent a *strategic resource* because these competencies are valuable, rare, and hard or even impossible to imitate or substitute.[88] On the other hand, the long-dated character of these capabilities limits the possible fields in which a company can seize technological opportunities and build up new abilities or as Teece (1997) has pointed out:[89]

> *"Where a firm can go is a function of its current position and the paths ahead. Its current position is often shaped by the paths it has travelled."*[90]

This *path-dependency* of a company's R&D activities results in a limitation of the number of currently feasible research projects that a company can carry out with a reasonable chance of success. These promising research projects are opposed by a large number of projects that the company in question cannot or at least not alone realise with a real chance of success.

Thus, we can summarise, a company's investments in R&D not only lead to new technologies and products which are protected by intellectual property rights, but also generate experiences, knowledge, and skills that are accumulated and expressed in a company's stock of intangible assets, e.g., data bases, documents, processes, and human capital (see figure III.10). The current technological know-how also represents the basis of development projects and feasible paths a company can go in the future. Consequently, there exists a certain path-dependency in R&D activities

---

[86] Cp. Nelson, R. R. (1982); Kline, S. J. & Rosenberg, N. (1986); Narin, F. & Olivastro, D. (1992).

[87] Cp. Nelson, R. R. (1991).

[88] Cp. chap. IV.1.

[89] Cp. Siegel, I. H. (1962); Grossman, G. M. & Helpman, E. (1990); Nelson, R. R. (1991); Patel, P. & Pavitt, K. (1997); Lei, D. T. (1997); Shane, S. (1998).

[90] Teece, D. J., Pisano, G. et al. (1997), p. 522.

which limits the feasible research options according to a company's previously performed R&D projects and activities.

International R&D Activities

Since the beginning of the 1980s, an increasing internationalisation of companies' innovative activities has been observed (see table III.1).[91] Companies no longer concentrate their R&D in their home countries and transfer their technological know-how to the respective peripheral nations, as assumed by Vernon (1966), but increasingly globalise their R&D activity. Gerybadze & Reger (1998) even allude to a paradigmatic change that has taken place in the organisation of innovative activities within companies:

> *"The new paradigm of transnational innovation builds on multiplicity and dispersion of competencies on a global scale, both research and technology-supply-related, as well as end-user- and demand-induced. Developments in science and technology have lead to the transition to a polycentric structure of national research and innovation systems."*[92]

Table III.1: Percentage of R&D performed outside the home-region

	1995	1998	2001e
Japan	4.6	6.9	10.4
Europe	26.8	31.4	34.9
North America	24.3	29.6	33.0

Source: Roberts, E. B. (1999), p. 15.

There exists a multitude of reasons for the internationalisation of companies' R&D activities. In general, it has been stated that companies with internationally organised R&D activities and thus generation of immaterial assets have advantages vis-à-vis companies that are only active on a national or regional level.[93] These advantages stem from the sheer size, the accumulation of technological knowledge, the possibility of a stronger risk-differentiation, access to different regional and national developments, and cheap input factors. However, not all ideas and

[91] Cp. Wortmann, M. (1990); Dunning, J. H. (1994); Patel, P. & Pavitt, K. (1996); Gerybadze, A. (1997a, 1997b, 1999); Gerybadze, A. & Reger, G. (1998).

[92] Gerybadze, A. & Reger, G. (1998), p. 5.

[93] Cp. Dunning, J. H. (1994); Gerybadze, A. (1997a, 1997b); Gerybadze, A., Meyer-Krahmer, F. et al. (1997); Tidd, J., Bessant, J. et al. (1997), pp. 137; Cantwell, J. & Piscidello, L. (1999); Patel, P. & Vega, M. (1999).

innovations which result in new products, processes, and services are, the outcome of focused R&D activities within companies. Further important internal sources of immaterial assets and thus of innovations are a company's value-adding activities such as production, marketing, and distribution.[94] The following chapter outlines how companies learn and hence generate new immaterial assets by performing so called routine activities within the organisation. Our discussion concentrates on the production of products and neglects the functions of marketing and distribution, as well as the administrative activities which, nevertheless, represent equally important sources of information and knowledge.

III.2.1.2 Learning-by-Doing

As already indicated, R&D activities do not represent the only source of intangible assets within business enterprises. In addition to the companies' R&D activities which have been profoundly discussed in the scientific literature, a few authors also mention routine activities as a principal source of information, knowledge, and technologies that have a significant cumulative influence on the quality, customer satisfaction, production cost, etc. of a product or service.[95]

The starting point of the discussion of the so called "*learning curve effects*" is demarcated by Arrow's (1962b) article which integrates the given technological level as an endogenous element within the growth theory. The author's discussion builds upon the observations of Wright & Lundberg who observed productivity gains in companies although no new investments took place and hence presumably no change in the method of production.[96] Solow (1997), building on Arrow's argumentation, puts these productivity increases in relation to discrete innovations which represent *continuous improvements* that can be consolidated under the term *learning-by-doing*.[97]

The term learning-by-doing consequently comprises product and process improvements which are not the result of focused search activities, but of routine activities that are located close to the factory floor. Cohen (1989) has defined routine activities as:

[94] Cp. von Hippel, E. (1986, 1988); Afuah, A. (1998).
[95] Cp. Pavitt, K. (1990); Solow, R. M. (1997), chap. 1 & 2.
[96] Cp. Arrow, K. J. (1962b); Solow, R. M. (1997), chap. 1.
[97] Cp. Solow, R. M. (1997).

> *"... the automatic process by which the firm becomes more practised and hence more effective at doing what it is already doing."*[98]

In the case of learning-by-doing nothing new is created per se which would increase a company's product or technological diversity. This process rather adds to the employees' knowledge base and thus enlarges the company's immaterial assets inherent to its human capital. On the basis of the cumulative nature of learning activities and the before mentioned phenomenon of non-abrasion in use of knowledge and information, a *circular model of knowledge accumulation* can be established.

The circular model illustrated in figure III.11 builds upon Nonaka's assumption that knowledge is formed by individuals out of information which are used for the accomplishment of duties within a company.[99] By actively using the existing knowledge new information is generated that in turn influences the employees know-how and hence the general knowledge prevailing in the company.[100] Arrow (1962a) has illustrated this process by means of the production of aeroplanes. According to the author, the number of man-hours needed for the production of an airframe (aeroplane without engines) is a decreasing function of the number of previously produced planes of the same sort.[101] Thus, employees gain experiences by performing routine activities and subsequently improve the production process and/or the product design whereby customer satisfaction is increased and/or production costs decreased.[102]

Central aspects of the presented circular model are the cumulative nature of learning activities and the fact that these activities are most efficient if the object of learning is closely linked to what is already known.[103] Moreover, it can be noted that learning only takes place during an activity and it does not occur by simple observation or memorisation.[104] The circular model presented in figure III.11 visualises the cycle of knowledge utilisation, generation of new information, and the creation of new knowledge. At the beginning of the production of a new product, for

[98] Cohen, W. M. & Levinthal, D. A. (1989), p. 570 and cp. Arrow, K. J. (1969), p. 30.

[99] Cp. Nonaka, I. (1994).

[100] "Every discoverer actually builds upon a foundation of 'old' knowledge that has become part of the cultural heritage … ." Siegel, I. H. (1962), p. 442.

[101] Cp. Arrow, K. J. (1962b).

[102] Cp. Solow, R. M. (1997).

[103] Cp. Cohen, W. M. & Levinthal, D. A. (1990); Solow, R. M. (1997).

[104] "Learning can only take place through the attempt to solve a problem and therefore only takes place during activity." Arrow, K. J. (1962b), p. 155; see also Stiglitz, J. E. (1999a).

instance, the individual employee already possesses a certain stock of know-how and codified knowledge which he uses in performing his job. By the routine use of his knowledge, the employee encounters new problems and challenges that he tries to solve and thereby increases his stock of accumulated know-how and experiences. In solving these unknown problems and new challenges the employee builds upon the experiences and knowledge previously accumulated. In this context, the underlying assumption of a cumulative knowledge stock is in accordance to the observations of Solow and Nilsson.[105]

Consequently, routine activities represent a significant source of human capital based immaterial assets. As Solow affirms in his study, learning-by-doing is one of the most important sources of productivity increases in mature industries.[106] On the other hand, learning activities also play a significant role in young and dynamic industries since knowledge becomes rapidly obsolete.[107] Subsequently, a company that wants to remain at the forefront of technological development in such dynamic markets has to be in an ongoing process of learning and unlearning. This process which comprises the learning of how to do new task, how to master unknown situations, and how to attain access to information and knowledge located outside the company borders, mostly takes place by solving the problems occurring in everyday life. Thus, learning-by-doing has an influential role on a company's competitiveness that has, however, been neglected in the past and is still shadowed by the discussion of the generation of independent innovations by company internal R&D activities.

In our discussion we have solely focused on the production process as the location of learning. However, the company's contacts to its environment including its customers, suppliers, competitors, etc. play an equally important role as a place of learning. In this respect marketing and distribution take a particularly important role, since they are in close contact with the company's environment and they subsequently transfer what they learned to other functions within the organisation, e.g., R&D and production (cf. figures III.6 and III.9).

In conclusion, we can define two central sources of intangible assets within companies: search activities without doing (R&D) and learning-by-doing without searching. These two sources are, in reality, closely interlinked and extremely difficult to differentiate. However, such internal sources of intangible assets represent but one side of the coin and have to be completed by sources of intangible assets located outside a company's

[105] Cp. Nilsson, E. A. (1995); Solow, R. M. (1997), chap. 2.
[106] Cp. Solow, R. M. (1997), chap. 2.
[107] Cp. Lundvall, B. A. (1998).

boundaries. In the following sections we focus on external sources of intangible assets and discuss in more depth the possibilities of acquisition and integration of intangibles, as well as co-operative forms of immaterial asset creation.

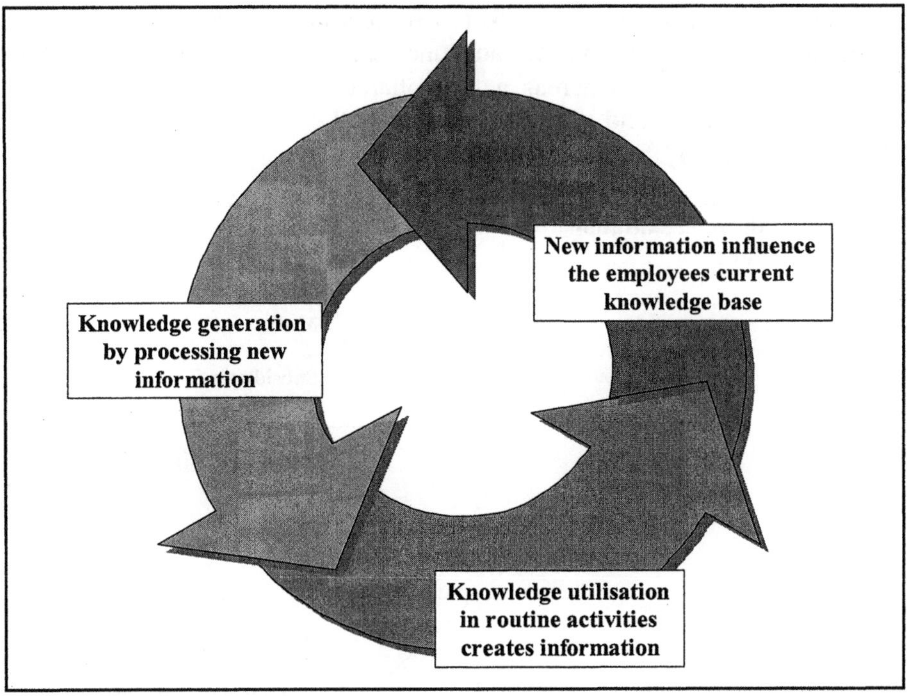

Figure III.11: Circular model of knowledge accumulation within companies

III.2.2 External Sources of Intangible Assets

Besides the generation of intellectual assets by activities of searching and learning within business enterprises, companies have the possibility to acquire immaterial assets on the free market. The companies have several alternative ways of acquiring intangibles, e.g., licensing, franchising, informal knowledge trading, co-operative forms of knowledge generation and/or utilisation, the integration of two formally independent organisations by merging or acquiring, as well as the enticement of specialised employees from other companies.

The choice of the *transaction mode* depends, according to Williamson (1979), on the cost generated by the transaction. Thus, a company has an advantage to buy a certain output on the market, if the costs of the market transaction are lower vis-à-vis a hierarchical solution.[108] Hence, the transaction mode is defined according to the nature of the task (specificity, uncertainty), the bearing of the involved parties (opportunism, bounded rationality), and the general conditions surrounding the transaction (e.g., frequency, infrastructure, market efficiency). Consequently, a high specificity, strategic relevance, and uncertainty of a task rather call for a hierarchical solution, whereas a task characterised by a low specificity, strategic relevance, and uncertainty is more the kind of a market solution (see figure III.12).[109]

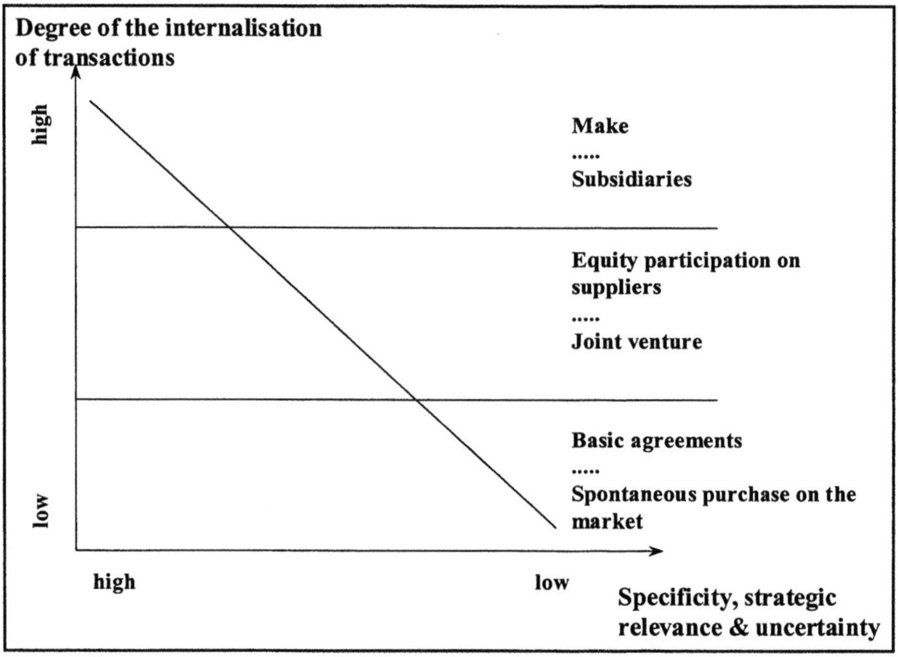

Figure III.12: Strategic choice of transaction mode

This transaction cost approach, however, reaches its limits in explaining strategic alliances and co-operations which have experienced a widespread increase in their use over the past few decades.[110] Thus, our discussion is based on the broader approach of Gerybadze (1995) which has recognised

[108] Cp. Williamson, O. E. (1979); Ouchi, W. G. (1980).

[109] Cp. Picot, A., Reichwald, R. et al. (1996), chap. 6.2.2; Pfaffmann, E. (2001), chap. 3-4 & 6.

[110] Cp. Freeman, C. (1994); Chesnais, F. (1996); Yamin, M. (1996).

co-operative forms of organisation as an independent form of co-ordination and not, as in the case of Williamson, as a badly defined transaction of an intermediate category.[111] In this model the author has defined in conformity with Williamson two extreme forms of co-ordination: Market co-ordination and organisational integration. However, these two co-ordination forms are complemented by an equivalent third, that of co-operation.

According to Gerybadze (1995), the integrated solution represents the superior transaction mode if a cost reduction can be realised by taking advantage of economies of scale and/or of synergies and by reducing the risks inherent to the transaction. If, however, the integration provokes diseconomies of scale or decreasing returns to scale and these cost increases are not compensated by a sufficiently high risk reduction, the integration mode does not represent the preferred mode of co-ordination. Moreover, in general the risk of a transaction is further increased by integration that induces a further increase in costs. This is in particular the case, if the future is not predictable and the integration decision may lock the company into a certain technology or institutional arrangement that later appears as burdensome or wrong. Hence, an integration decision is only advantageous if the integration generates economies of scale and/or risk reductions that are in sum positive.

Consequently, a co-operation is the superior co-ordination form if advantages of scale and flexibility can be combined. This is the case, for example, if the uncertainty surrounding an integration and the potential scale effects are high. Thus, by co-operating, the risk-costs can be kept reasonably low in comparison to an integrated solution by realising at the same time economies of scale advantages (which might be lower as under full integration, but still higher as under a market solution). Such advantages of co-operative forms over integration are of particular importance in industries that are characterised by frequent changes affecting the outcome of a particular institutional choice. Gerybadze has thus established a model that puts the co-operative solution on the same level as the integrated and market solution.[112]

Following the discussion of the optimal form of co-ordination, the following sections analyse the diverse options companies possess to acquire external intangible assets. We focus in particular on the acquisition (licensing) and the integration (M&A, employee recruitment) of intangible assets. Section III.2.2.3 then presents an excursion analysing the central

---

[111] Cp. Gerybadze, A. (1995), chap. 1.
[112] Cp. Gerybadze, A. (1995), chap. 1.

importance of a company's expertise and skills in the acquisition of immaterial assets.

III.2.2.1 Acquisition of Intangible Assets: Licensing

Licensing activities have three principal functions: (1) The acquisition of company external knowledge to economise on company internal research and/or development costs; (2) the prevention of two companies active in the same field mutually blocking each other; and (3) the reduction of the risk of infringing the property of other companies by using the company's own intellectual property. In the following we analyse the problems and limits of licensing agreements and point out their primary objectives.

A *licensing agreement* represents in general the acquisition of intangible assets which have not been created by a company itself but by another, external organisation. This definition does not only subsume *ex-post acquisitions* of intangibles under the term licensing, but also *ex-ante acquisitions* such as the outsourcing of R&D activities to universities, research institutes, or other companies. The most important and widespread form of licensing agreements represent ex-post acquisitions. By negotiating an ex-post licensing agreement, the legal owner of an intellectual property grants another person or organisation the right to use and/or exploit one or several of his intellectual property rights. The surrender of the user-rights that can be limited in time and geographic dispersion, can involve the exchange of physical, monetary, and/or further intellectual properties. Due to the existence of numerous *market imperfections*, legally enforceable intellectual property rights, e.g., patents, trademarks, copyrights, etc., play a crucial role.[113] The owner of the intangible assets, the potential licenser, possesses, for example, better knowledge about the quality and the value of the assets as the potential buyer, the licensee. If the owner of the intangible asset, however, provides the potential licensee with the asset for their evaluation, it is in general extremely difficult or even impossible to take it back or to prevent the potential licensee of using and/or spreading the transferred knowledge. Hence, the intangible asset has been transferred to the potential buyer without any reward.

Katz & Shapiro (1986) have presented a *partial solution* to the problem of asymmetric information and non-appropriability. The authors argue that the potential licenser can signal a high quality of his immaterial asset by negotiating a royalty-fee licensing agreement. Such an agreement,

[113] Cp. Arrow, K. J. (1962a); Shapiro, C. (1985); Baumol, W. J. (1993), chap. 8; Geroski, P. (1995).

however, is accompanied by high organisational costs of controlling the licensee. Moreover, the authors assume that intangible assets are generally protected by legally enforceable intellectual property rights. We can thus conclude that companies are only prepared to acquire or sell codified and legally protected intangible assets and refuse to transfer immaterial and human capital based intangible assets in ex-post licensing agreements.[114]

By acquiring external intangible assets, companies usually expect to lower the cost of creating these immaterial assets. It has been estimated that licensing costs represent approximately 2 to 10% of the company's internal development costs.[115] Furthermore, the licensee can out-source his R&D activities and the associated risks to the licenser. By doing so, the licensee cannot only reduce the risks of R&D, but also achieves a calculability of the costs since he only has to pay for the achieved successes and not for incurred failures. Finally, in industries where advanced products and processes predominantly determine the success of businesses, companies cannot build solely on technologies developed on their own. In many high-tech industries the scope of necessary technological knowledge is too large, so that one company cannot develop its entire needs internally, or as an IBM patent process manager has pointed out:

> *"Market driven quality demands that we shorten our cycle times. This means we have to speed up the process of innovation. And that means there is less time to invent everything we need. We can't do everything ourselves. IBM needs to have access to the inventions of others."*[116]

On the other hand, the advantages of the licenser lie in the possibility of generating extra income from their intellectual property through *fees* and *royalties*. Further reasons to out-license intellectual property are financial constraints which impede a company to exploit the R&D results or developed products on its own. As stated by Grindley & Teece (1997) and Grindley (1990; 1995, chap. 2), companies can increase the spread of their technology by generous out-licensing agreements or co-operating with companies active in the same field and consequently increase the probability of establishing a *de facto standard*.[117] Moreover, companies can prevent expensive R&D races by licensing contracts or just eliminate a technological mismatch within the company. An example of existing

[114] Cp. Winter, S. G. (1987); Arora, A. (1995); Bierly, P. & Chakrabarti, A. (1996); van Reekum, A. H. (1999), pp. 77-78.

[115] Cp. Atuahene-Gima, K. (1992).

[116] Grindley, P. C. & Teece, D. J. (1997), p. 14.

[117] Cp. Teece, D. J. (2000a), pp. 128-132; and see case study on Cisco Systems in chap. II.3.

financial constraints that force companies to out-license a technology present young biotech companies. The majority of these young companies cannot afford to develop marketable products, due to the long development phases, expensive clinical test phases, and the long and expensive regulatory market approval procedures which prevail in the live-science industry.[118] Therefore, most start-up companies in the biotech industry concentrate on research activities and license their results to large, established pharmaceutical companies which have their particular competencies in the clinical test and market approval stages, as well as in the international distribution of new products.

In this discussion of the in-licensing of external intellectual property we also have to mention the disadvantages associated with the strategy of acquiring externally created intellectual assets. Such shortcomings or threats represent for the licensee the possibility of becoming *technologically dependent* on external sources of intangible assets and the *frustration of the company's own R&D staff*.[119] On the other hand, the licenser faces the danger of losing its technological lead and hence its competitive advantage in the medium to long-term by out-licensing his latest technological attainments which are in turn further developed and improved by the licensee.

Often cited reasons that, however, justify the engagement in licensing agreements are the existence of mutually blocking patents and the risk of patent interference. This is of particular importance in industries that are characterised by cumulative technologies such as the electronics- or biotechnology industry in which new inventions built on previous innovations.[120] To attain these goals companies establish *cross-licensing agreements* that include a part or even the totality of the licensing partners' patented intellectual property rights.[121]

Grindley and Teece (1997) have analysed in detail the practice of cross-licensing agreements on the basis of the development in the radio- and computer industry.[122] Companies active in these industries try to attain cost-efficient access other companies' intellectual assets by building up a patent-portfolio that is of interest to these companies. In these industries,

---

118 Cp. Solt, M. E. (1993).

119 In respect to the frustration of a company's R&D employees authors often refer to the NIH or 'not-invented-here-syndrome'. Cp. Katz, R. & Allen, T. J. (1982); Atuahnene-Gima, K. (1992); Gupta, A. K. & Govindarajan, V. (2000).

120 Cp. Ordover, J. A. (1991); Galimberty, I. (1993), chap. 2. and 10; Grindley, P. C. & Teece, D. J. (1997).

121 Cp. Grindley, P. C. & Teece, D. J. (1997).

122 See also Teece, D. J. (2000a), pp. 193-224.

characterised by high propensities to protect innovations by patents, companies must have access to other companies' intellectual achievements in order to maintain their competitiveness by ensuring 'freedom-to-operate', 'design-freedom', and access to complementary technological developments by relatively low licensing payments or even generating a licensing income. This system of cross-licensing in industries with cumulative technologies has to be delimited from industries in which new developments are largely autonomous and consequently do not build upon previous innovations. Such industries are among others the pharmaceutical industry (based on organic chemistry) or the chemical industry. In these industries companies mainly try to obtain cost-effective access to certain technologies by means of licensing agreements.[123]

Thus, we can affirm that licensing agreements play an important role in today's economy by allowing companies rapid access to technologies and complementary intellectual properties and by ensuring frictionless R&D activities and use of existing intangible assets. Moreover, licensing agreements represent an increasingly important source of revenues as shown in figure I.1.[124] This rising importance has provoked companies to more and more integrate licensing agreements in their strategic considerations. As Grindley &Teece (1997) have affirmed, a strong patent portfolio of a company may represent the key lever in cheaply accessing other companies intellectual properties. This strong leverage of a company's portfolio of valuable intellectual property rights leads to a strategy of focusing in a company's R&D activities only on those technological fields where the company possesses particular strengths in order to establish a portfolio of valuable intellectual capital. This portfolio is not just of high value for internal exploitation but also for potential licensees. Consequently, the company can use its intellectual property portfolio for obtaining cost-effective access to interesting patents in fields where the company does not have strong R&D capabilities.

III.2.2.2 Integration of Intangible Assets: Merger & Acquisitions and Enticement of Employees

The above discussed licensing agreements represent just one of several possibilities of acquiring intangible assets. As mentioned above, these licensing agreements are in general limited to codified and legally protected immaterial assets. Hence, companies cannot acquire tacit, human capital based, or even codified but not legally protected intellectual assets

[123] Cp. Grindley, P. C. & Nickerson, J. A. (1996).

[124] Cp. Parr, R. L. & Sullivan, P. H. (1996); Grindley, P. C. & Teece, D. J. (1997).

by licensing contracts. In order to get hold of such assets located outside a company's boundaries, businesses usually follow an integration strategy and purchase the company that owns the desired immaterial assets such as specialised knowledge inherent in scientists, organisational structures, or even databases.[125] Another, and perhaps cheaper way of integrating human capital based intellectual assets is the selective enticement and recruitment of specialists. In this section we discuss these two ways of integrating intangible assets, as well as the acquisition of intellectual assets by the means of implicit knowledge trade.

Merger & Acquisition

Company acquisitions and mergers have continuously increased in value on a national but also international level over the past decades (see figure III.13). As Scherer (1988) has pointed out, these acquisitions cannot be explained satisfactorily by economies of scale and scope. A plausible explanation of the phenomenon could rather be the *circumvention of market imperfections* in the transaction of intangible assets, as well as the associated *rapid access* and *perfect control* over these assets.[126] Pisano (1990) ascertained in the pharmaceutical industry the acquisition of young, innovative biotech companies by established pharmaceutical companies. The aim of integrating the biotech companies by acquisition was the avoidance of market based transactions and the associated uncertainties and opportunistic actions and hence the enhancement of the appropriation of the acquired immaterial assets.

Famous examples of acquisitions where the purchase value of the company significantly surpassed the physical value of the company stated on the balance sheet are, for example, the acquisition of Kraft by Philip Morris, Perrier by Nestlé or of Rolls-Royce by BMW. In the case of Rolls-Royce, BMW has paid in 1998 just for the trademark US$ 60 million and has not acquired any physical assets such as machines, buildings, or premises.[127] These assets, not accounted for on companies' balance sheets but which can explain the considerable deviations between the book value of a company and its purchase value, represent the so-called '*goodwill*'. Thus, the goodwill represents the value of all intangible assets of the acquired company and which is expressed in the balance sheet of the

[125] Cp. case study on Cisco Systems in chap. II.3.

[126] Cp. Madhok, A. & Osegowitsch, T. (1998).

[127] Cp. Aaker, D. A. (1991), p. 23; Fellman, M. W. (1998); Wermelskirchen, S. (1999).

acquiring company. This asset item is then written off according to national legislation over several years.[128]

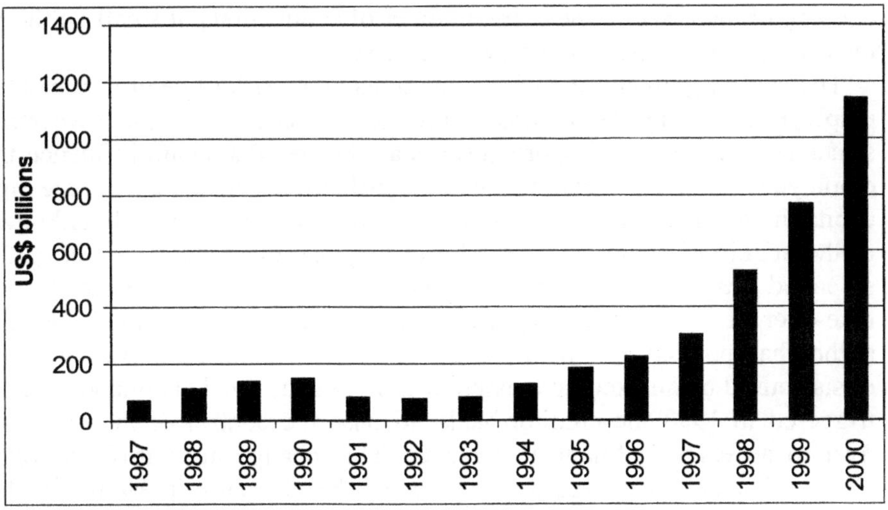

Data source: UNCTAT (2001).

Figure III.13: The value of cross-border M&As, 1987-2000

A particular emphasis has been put on the acquisition of complementary technologies, and in this respect, on the purchase of small innovative companies by large technology based enterprises. Granstrand & Sjölander (1990a) have conducted a study on Swedish and Japanese companies on their practices in the acquisition of small innovative companies. The authors assume that small companies possess comparative advantages in early stages of the innovation-process while large, established enterprises show advantages in later innovation-stages.[129] The results of the study allude that company acquisitions represent a from of *technology trade* whereby the technology is packaged in small firms. This form of technology trade is comparable to trading licenses and R&D resources. The main reason for the acquisition of a small firm was mostly the comparative nature of the technology and not the relatively higher growth rate of these companies.[130] Another important advantage represents the efficient access of companies to a nation's science and technology system by acquiring a company on the international level. In this respect small

[128] Cp. Cook, T. E. (1988); Granstrand, W. & Sjölander, S. (1990; 1990a); Edvinsson, M. S. & Malone, M. S. (1997).

[129] Cp. Granstrand, W. & Sjölander, S. (1990a).

[130] Cp. case study on Cisco Systems in chap. II.3.

technology based companies which stand in close contact to universities and national research institutes, seem to be of particular interest. In this context, Grandstrand & Sjölander (1990a) have pointed out the increasing concern of the USA by the rising number of acquisitions of small US high-tech companies by large Japanese enterprises.

The central problem of such acquisitions is the risk of central, specialist employees leaving the company due to the change in the ownership structure and the resulting organisational changes that again influence the employees' motivation and incentives. Further risks emanate from the high capital investments and by taking control over activities formerly unknown to the acquiring company.[131] Sveiby (1997) has illustrated the risk of the so-called *brain drain* and the associated loss of immaterial assets by the take-over of the British advertising agency *Saatchi & Saatchi*.[132] As the author has pointed out in his study, the agency entered into a financial crisis caused by an excessive external growth strategy. This financial crisis triggered in 1993 the creditor-banks to pass the control of the company over to an external financial manager. This change in control provoked Charles Saatchi, who was the founder of the company in 1970, and his brother Maurice Saatchi to leave the agency that later changed its name into *Cordiant*. The brothers established a new advertising agency under the name *M&C Saatchi* that caused a migration of Cordiant's customers to the newly found agency. The set up of the new agency by the Saatchi brothers caused an immediate decline in Coriant's overall budget volume by 6% or £40 million and the market value of the agency declined to 2% of its all-time-high.

This example shows that companies in which a majority of the intangible assets are inherent to its employees can react extremely sensitively to changes in its organisation and ownership structures. Moreover, this case illustrates that the assets responsible for the success and hence the value of the company can be located in only a few collaborators. Consequently, a company acquiring an entity in which most intangible assets are human capital based has to ensure the retention of the employees post-acquisition. This can be achieved by so called '*earn-outs,*' which do not anticipate the immediate payment of the negotiated purchase value but rather payments-on-account to the owners that are influenced by the company's profits after the acquisition.[133] Furthermore, the corporate

---

[131] Cp. Roberts, E. B. & Berry, C. A. (1985); Pisano, G. P. (1991); Haspeslagh, P. C. & Jemison, D. B. (1991), pp. 129-32; Quélin, B. (1997); Sveiby, K. E. (1997), pp. 145-46; Madhok, A. & Osegowitsch, T. (1998).

[132] See Sveiby, K. E. (1997), pp. 33-39.

[133] Cp. Sveiby, K. E. (1997), p. 34.

culture and structure plays a decisive role in attracting, holding, and stimulating highly talented employees to attain a high-performance in their creative activities.[134]

Employee Recruitment

A further possibility of business enterprises to acquire intangible assets represents the integration of specialised and/or talented employees. Companies that wish to acquire in particular human capital based assets can realise their intent by either acquiring a suitable company, as shown in the preceding section, or by selectively recruiting employees showing the desired skills. In the case of M&As, the acquiring company confronts the problem of the migration of key-workers due to changes in the incentive structures, corporate culture, and structure. Consequently, a focused enticement of highly qualified employees from other organisations can be advantageous, especially in industries characterised by a very limited number of so-called 'high-potentials'.

As Sveiby (1997) has indicated, companies can change their concept as well as increase or decrease their immaterial asset stock by well considered strategic recruitment of its employees. However, the recruitment of employees represents a growing challenge for business enterprises, since skilful employees are, even in periods of recession, in short supply.[135] Liebeskind, Oliver et al. (1996) have stated in their study that the number of star-scientists in biochemistry which have generated valuable inventions, has remained low over the past few decades in spite of the significant rise in the overall number of scientists active in this field. The recruitment of these scarce star-scientists is rendered extremely difficult by the particular criteria of these highly skilled employees in selecting a potential employer. As numerous authors have stated, star-scientists in biochemistry, for example, prefer employers that show a working culture comparable to a climate usually associated with universities.[136] Deutschman (1994) has alluded that the majority of these star-scientists do not strive for the highest possible monetary remuneration, but rather for a compensation by scientific recognition that is achieved by publications and/or presentations among other things. The possibility of rapid publication of research results, for example, has only been possible in the past in universities and research institutes or in small companies closely

[134] Cp. case study on Cisco Systems in chap. II.3.

[135] Cp. Liebeskind, J. P., Oliver, A. L. et al. (1996); Sveiby, K. E.. (1997); pp. 98-100.

[136] Cp. Pisano, G. P. (1991); Deutschman, A. (1994); Liebeskind, J. P., Oliver, A. L. et al. (1996); Powell, W. W. (1998); van Reekum, A. H. (1999), pp. 99-100.

interrelated with scientific development. According to Pisano (1991), young biotech companies have or had an advantage in recruiting highly qualified employees due to university like organisational structures and the freedom of their employees to freely publish scientific results.

The big established pharmaceutical companies, on the other hand, often encounter severe problems in recruiting highly qualified scientists in the biotechnology field. Furthermore, the integration strategy of many pharmaceutical companies which envisaged the acquisition of small biotechnology companies, appeared to be rather unsuccessful since many star-scientists feared a degradation of their working-environment post-acquisition and left the company. Due to these problems of large, established pharmaceutical companies in recruiting star-scientists, these companies also confront problems in accessing knowledge networks which scientists use to exchange experiences, knowledge, and information.[137] These networks are, however, of central importance for companies active in industries characterised by high technological uncertainties, technological diversity, and a rapid technological development to remain flexible and to minimise sunk-costs.

As shown in the discussion of the biotechnology industry, companies not only compete on the market for products and services, but also on the market for highly qualified employees. This does not only apply to the biotechnology industry, but to most knowledge based industries which possess a high share of human capital based intangible assets, e.g., the consultant or IT industry. In order to be able to survive in such a competitive market as the market for star-scientists, companies must provide their employees with an ideal working environment. As Deutschman (1994) has revealed, such a perfect work environment is mostly typified by an open, communicative, as well as co-operative corporate culture, a flexible organisation with a flat hierarchy, a culture characterised by team-work, and company principles that respect the employees' interests. Moreover, the recruitment process of highly qualified employees should not be the task of the personal management department only, but rather the top-management of a company has to be in charge of the recruitment process.[138]

A restriction to an extensive integration of intangible assets by recruiting highly qualified employees represents the low efficiency and high fluctuation of these new employees. Sveiby (1997), for example, has stated that the efficiency of a company with an excessive portion of new employees declines because of their unfamiliarity with the company's

---

[137] Cp. Liebeskind, J. P., Oliver, A. L. et al. (1996); Powell, W. W. (1998).

[138] Cp. Deutschman, A. (1994); Seeiby, K. E. (1997), pp. 98-100.

tradition and organisation. In addition, an excessive share of new employees risks to alter the corporate culture which may provoke long-standing employees to leave that again would decrease the efficiency and the stability of the organisation.

In summary, we can affirm that companies can integrate intangible assets in knowledge based industries on two distinct ways. Firstly, by acquiring a company which holds the desired intangible assets, and secondly, by a focused recruitment of employees that carry the looked-for immaterial assets. A strategy of integration thus reduces the shortcomings of market based transactions. Nonetheless, these strategies also show operational shortcomings. The acquisition and integration of a company, for example, has a high inherent risk because of the high capital investment. This risk is further increased by the jeopardy of a brain-drain released by the change in ownership and organisation. With respect to the recruitment of highly qualified employees, companies confront an extremely competitive market on which they can only transact if they fulfil certain prerequisites. Most high-potentials, for example, are only inclined to change employer, if this change is accompanied by an amelioration of their *working environment*. The nature of such a suitable working environment is usually a lean and flexible organisation, a motivating and open corporate culture, as well as the company's membership in the group of leading companies in the respective technology field. In generalising, we can assert that companies which want to access external sources of intangible technological assets, must possess internally generated technological knowledge and competencies in order to be able to access these external sources and to absorb the acquired assets. The central role of internally generated technological assets in the acquisition of external intangible assets is discussed in the succeeding excursion.

III.2.2.3 Excursion: Internal R&D and the Acquisition of External Immaterial Assets

As mentioned before, companies that want to fall back on external sources of intangible assets must possess a minimum of internal technological competencies and expertise in order to be able to select, evaluate, absorb, and effectively use these externally created intangible assets.[139] One of the principal possibilities to obtain such company internal technological competencies represents R&D activities within a company. Cohen & Levinthal (1989) have reasoned that companies not only invest in R&D

[139] Cp. Killing, P. (1980); Graham, M. B. (1985); Gambardella, A. (1992); Patel, P. & Pavitt, K. (1995).

activities in order to generate new innovations internally, but also to be able to identify, assimilate, and exploit externally generated immaterial assets. The authors have defined these competencies of recognising, absorbing, and efficiently using external intangible assets as a company's '*absorptive capacity*'.[140]

Thus, the extent of a company's R&D expenditures no longer depend solely on the probability and value of company internally generated innovations but are, in addition, influenced by the magnitude by which the company wants to access externally created intangible assets and to benefit from so called '*research spillover*". These research spillovers epitomise freely available technological externalities that are generated by the R&D activities of other organisations. These technological spillovers influence the success of a company's internally effected R&D or as Jaffe (1986) has asserted:

> *"...the existence of technological spillovers implies that a firm's R&D success is affected by the research activity of its neighbours in technology space."*[141]

Accordingly, companies not just invest in company internal R&D to directly generate new intangible technological assets, but also in order to be able to identify and integrate immaterial assets already prevailing in the company's surroundings.[142] Moreover, Nelson (1982) has identified the importance of internal R&D successes in recruiting new qualified employees and to tie these employees to the organisation in the long-term. By the means of good R&D attainments which result in scientific publications and patent registrations, a company can build up a positive reputation in a certain technological field. This reputation in turn facilitates the enticement of qualified employees for the company.

As could be shown, a company that wants to access external sources of intangible assets has to possess a minimum of *internal technological expertise* in order to be able to access these external sources, and absorb and use the acquired assets. This stands in clear contradiction to the opinion of Leonard-Barton (1995), who believes that companies can break free of their path-dependency by external acquisitions.[143] In conclusion we can hypothesise that companies must possess certain internal technological

---

[140] Cp. Cohen, W. M. & Levinthal, D. A. (1989; 1990).

[141] Jaffe, A. B. (1986), p. 986. Cp. Katz, M. L. (1986); Jaffe, A. B., Trajtenberg, M. et al. (1993).

[142] Thus, these spillovers are not available free of charge but in fact companies must invest in internal R&D to build up a certain 'absorptive capacity' in order to be able to benefit from the positive externalities. Cp. Levin, R. C. (1988).

[143] Cp. Leonard-Barton, D. (1995), chap. 6.

competencies in order to be able to access and efficiently use external sources of intangible assets. Consequently, company internal R&D activities and other alternative company internal sources of expertise do not only represent an important source of new intangible assets, but are also of critical magnitude in the acquisition and integration of externally generated immaterial assets. Thus, in general, these external sources have to be seen as complementing and not substituting for internal sources of intangible technological assets.[144]

III.2.3 Co-operative Forms of Intangible Asset Creation

Co-operative organisational forms have significantly increased in importance over the past decades. This development has been ascribed by Coombs, Richards et al. (1996a) to the escalating costs of R&D, the increasing risk of radical technological changes, the increasing competition in ever more globalised markets, and the importance of synergies, complementarities, and mutually interacting of various technological fields.[145] In this case the co-operative activities just represent the concealment of the attempt to absorb complementary abilities of partner companies. In addition to the classification of co-operations according to their aim, co-operative forms can also be distinguished on the basis of the number of participating parties. As shown in figure III.14, Gerybadze (2004) distinguished three principal forms of R&D co-operation: Bilateral, consortia, and network co-operations.

Bilateral co-operations, again, can be distinguished in a vertical and horizontal division of tasks. A horizontal co-operation connotes the collaboration of two competing companies in precisely defined fields. In vertical co-operation, in contrast, the participating companies stand in a supplier-buyer relationship. Another type of co-operation represents the consortia which is typified by one company standing in the centre of communication and all other partners communicating with each other only by means of this central company that is also responsible for co-ordination (cp. figure III.14). The third form identified by the author is the network relationship. In this rather loose form of co-operation the participating companies are in an open dialogue and knowledge exchange. A particular form of network co-operation represent the phenomenon of informal

[144] Cp. Bierly, P. & Chakrabarti, A. (1996).

[145] Cp. Katz, M. L. (1986); Ouchi, W. G. & Bolton, M. K. (1988); Lei, D. & Slocum, J. W. (1992); Hagedoorn, J. (1993); Geroski, P. (1995); Grant, R. M. (1996a, 1996b).

knowledge trading between competing business enterprises. This phenomenon will be analysed in the context of network co-operations.

Within these three main forms, co-operations can be further distinguished into different forms, e.g. strategic alliances or joint venture. In the following chapter we analyse the relevance of the two forms of R&D co-operation, strategic alliances and joint venture, in the generation of intellectual assets. Subsequently, we discuss the special form of knowledge trading within a techno-specific network and portray the ascertained behaviour of companies and individuals. The chapter ends with an upshot in section III.2.3.

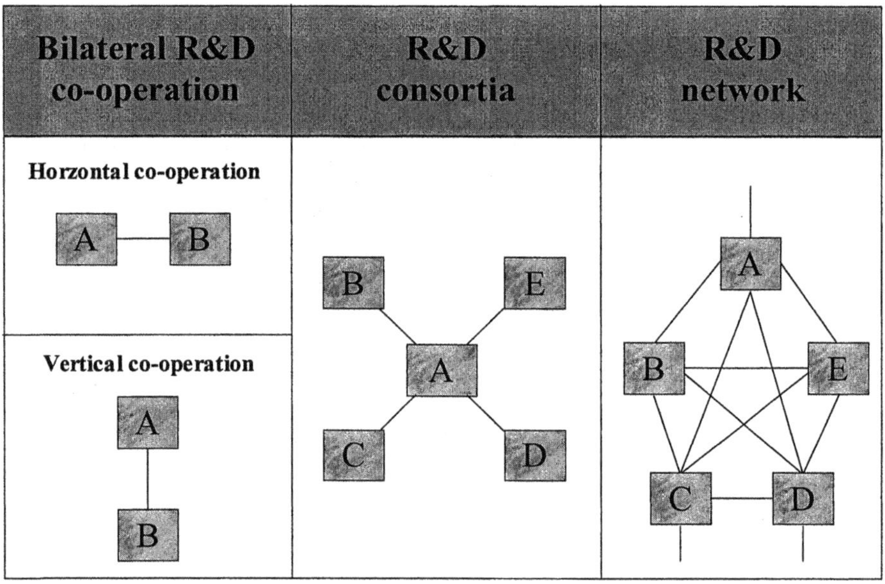

Source: Gerybadze, A. (2004), p. 408.

Figure III.14: Forms of co-operative R&D activities

III.2.3.1 Joint-Ventures, Strategic Alliances, and Networks

Co-operative forms of co-ordination of companies in general, and of innovative activities in particular are often cited as new forms of co-ordination which best suit the current economic environment. These 'new forms' of co-ordinating innovations which are commonly subsumed in the literature under the term of strategic alliances, are, however, not as new as believed by many studies. Co-operative forms, indeed, represented one of the main sources of innovation for companies before the Second World

War.[146] In our analysis of co-operative forms of the generation of intangible assets and innovations we focus in particular *on technological joint venture* and *strategic R&D agreements* and neglect the forms of company co-operations which are merely directed towards the collective use of production plants, the establishment of price-fixing agreements, and barriers to entry.

Under the term *joint venture* we understand a combination of the economic interests of at least two independent legal entities in a mutually administered and controlled company.[147] The most widespread form of such joint ventures is a jointly lead company or research institute. The revenues and losses of these companies are usually shared according to their equity participation. In general, the aim of these joint ventures is the combination of the participating company's idiosyncratic resources.[148] These resources can either be technological or market based, e.g., an established distribution system or an established brand. However, the participating companies usually do not contribute all their knowledge to the joint venture in order to avoid the *hollowing out* of their main business by other partners. The advantage of such a jointly owned venture lies in the availability of complementary resources that are resident in different companies which may again be localised in different nations or even regions. These resources are subsequently used in the production and/or development of products, processes, or services that one company on its own could not realise or at least not as fast as the joint venture. Moreover, intangible assets located in specific individuals can rapidly and at low transaction cost be transferred to the joint venture. Many companies also aspire the absorption of partner companies' knowledge by the means of participating in a joint venture. This attitude, however, leads inevitably to conflicts within the co-operation and commonly even provokes the failure of a joint venture.[149]

Such R&D co-operations in form of joint venture usually represent long-term commitments because of their high organisational, managerial, and financial complexity.[150] These long-term ventures show advantages in comparison to more short-term and looser forms of co-operation, such as the licensing of intellectual property. Key advantages are the unambiguous

---

[146] Cp. Graham, M. B. (1985); Freeman, C. & Soete, L. (1997), chap. 1.2-1.4.

[147] Cp. Harrigan, K. R. (1988); Hagedoorn, J. & Schakenraad, J. (1991), pp. 4-14.

[148] Cp. Buckley, P. J. & Casson, M. (1996).

[149] This practice of a partner's second objective that is kept secret from the other co-operation partners is defined by Gerybadze as a 'hidden agenda'. Cp. Gerybadze, A. (2004), pp. 423-426.

[150] Cp. Hagedoorn, J. & Narula, R. (1996); Hagedoorn, J. (1993).

ownership and holding rights of intangible property created by the joint venture. In general the jointly owned company represents the owner of the intellectual assets and controls and co-ordinates their use. Moreover, the drop-out of a partner does not inevitably lead to the failure of the entire venture since it is bestowed with all necessary organisational, financial, and managerial functions, as well as the necessary ownership and user rights of the intellectual assets. Thus, the leaving of a partner company is frequently only perceivable in the equity structure of the joint venture.

Joint ventures also show disadvantages, such as the high organisational and managerial complexity, the high capital investments required, the long-dated nature that entrenches a reduction of the flexibility, and the opportunistic behaviour of individual partner companies.[151] Due to the nature and problems of joint ventures, this co-operation form is usually favoured in industries or technological fields that show a predictable progress in a stable environment.[152]

A further variant of so called strategic alliances represent *strategic ex-ante R&D agreements*. Such ex-ante R&D contracts are defined as close co-operations of at least two independent legal entities which agree in advance on the attainment of mutually defined goals.[153] Such goals can, for example, be the development of a specific product module, a (product and/or process) technology, or a particular service. The main advantages of such joint developments are the prevention of R&D spillovers, and since the partner companies commit themselves ex-ante and thus before any R&D spillovers are created to a certain contribution towards the development, no participating company can free-ride on the efforts of the other partner companies.[154] Such contractual forms of R&D co-operation are mostly oriented towards short-term goals and hence focus on joint development projects and not on collaborative basic-research that is by definition of a more long-term nature.

The main motives of such ex-ante R&D agreements lie, just as in the case of the before discussed technology joint ventures, in the combination and absorption of complementary and idiosyncratic resources. However, problems arise in such agreements with regard to their contractual formulation. The literature has emphasised as the main reasons of failure of these R&D co-operations ownership right problems of the jointly

[151] Cp. Lei, D. & Slocum, J. M. (1996).

[152] Cp. Harrigan, K. R. (1988).

[153] Such ex-ante agreements are defined according to Buckley, P. J. as “an inter-firm collaboration over a given economic space and time for the attainment of mutually defined goals.” Cf. Jennewein, K. (1997), p. 14.

[154] Cp. Katz, M. L. (1986).

created intangible assets, the opportunistic behaviour of certain/all partner companies, the interface problems, as well as the disproportionate contribution of resources to the joint project.[155] Furthermore, companies are often engaged in several different ex-ante R&D co-operations at the same time which engenders a supplementary complexity by administering and continuously monitoring of advantages of the individual co-operation. The central key problem of these contractual ex-ante R&D co-operations is, however, the retention of resources by partner companies. This problem is provoked by companies that strive for the absorption of intangible technological assets by means of such co-operation agreements, and in turn endeavour to minimise the knowledge flows towards other partner companies. This opportunistic behaviour and mistrust of partner companies creates an atmosphere that endangers the attainment of the envisaged goals and often results in the complete failure of the ex-ante R&D arrangement.

Strategic technological alliances epitomise, in recapitulation, a rapid means of accessing already existing intangible assets. Moreover, such co-operative forms of co-ordination also allow for an efficient transfer of human capital based and implicit immaterial assets across company borders by a close interaction of the participating partners. These advantages of a rapid and economical access to intangible assets of partner companies and the effective creation of new immaterial valuables are opposed by numerous problems. The key problem of strategic alliances is the opportunistic behaviour of partners and the resulting mistrust of companies anxious about loosing strategic resources and hence being weakened by the strategic R&D alliance. The significance of these problems, however, varies considerably between the two types of strategic alliances: Joint venture (with equity participation) and contractual ex-ante R&D co-operation. In any case, the participation of companies in such strategic R&D co-operations represents an important option to generate and absorb new immaterial assets.

III.2.3.2 Networks and Informal Knowledge Trading

An additional means to obtain intellectual assets from external sources are networks of companies that are typified by a *reciprocal scheme* of trade and communication. Such networks which can be characterised as *deliberate* and *long-term arrangement* of independent companies that strive for a competitive advantage vis-à-vis companies not integrated in the

[155] Cp. Gerybadze, A. (2004), chap. 8.

network by loosely co-operating and communicating.[156] These network arrangements induce important *strategic implications* for the involved companies. This co-operation form enables the involved companies, on the one hand, to concentrate on those activities within the value-chain which are essential in sustaining their competitive advantages and, on the other hand, to dispose of a rapid access to reliable information and knowledge. Such *reliable* information and knowledge whose value is difficult to determine, are, as Powell (1990) has pointed out, usually not transferred over formal chains of command but rather over *informal channels* and persons who have appeared to be reliable in the past. Thus, reputation, friendship, mutual dependence, and altruism are integral elements of such networks.[157]

These above described networks are often found in industries characterised by a complex knowledge base, dispersed sources of expertise and/or a rapid technological development.[158] The biotechnology industry represents, among others, an example of an industry in which companies trade information and knowledge in a network build on common norms and trustworthy behaviour. The biotech-industry is typified by strict intellectual property rights on innovations, and moreover, establish and respected social norms that minimise the risks of misappropriation and unlawful replication of intangible proprietary assets.[159] If a scientist, nonetheless, violates these established norms he must reckon with his exclusion of the network and hence of the information flows which in turn severely impairs his future career opportunities. Moreover, companies violating or disrespecting the norms will be punished by the exclusion of the network, as well as by a *bad corporate reputation*. The reputation of the company, in turn, affects aversely the possibility to recruit leading scientists and qualified employees and to establish co-operative arrangements in general. Thus, we can affirm, such social norms in networks can provide better protection in trading immaterial assets within markets than intellectual property rights.[160]

Mansfield (1985) has ascertained in his empirical study of 100 manufacturing firms that company information concerning the nature and

---

[156] Cp. Jarillo, J. C. (1988); Powell, W. W. (1990).

[157] Cp. Jarillo, J. C. (1988); Powell, W. W., Koput, K. W. et al. (1996); Powell, W. W. (1990; 1998).

[158] Cp. Liebeskind, J. P., Oliver, A. L. et al. (1996); Powell, W. W., Koput, K. W. et al. (1996).

[159] Cp. Liebeskind, J. P., Oliver, A. L. et al. (1996).

[160] Cp. Arrow, K. J. (1962a); Levin, R. C., Klevorick, A. K. et al. (1987); Liebeskind, J. P., Oliver, A. L. et al. (1996).

operation of new products and processes are, within 12 months, in the hand of competitors. The so called '*leaking out*' of mostly secret and proprietary information and knowledge has been attributed by von Hippel (1987; 1988) and Schrader (1991) to *informal social networks* of companies' employees. In this informal trade, employees of different, legally independent companies exchange proprietary information and knowledge against other valuable intangible assets. However, the exchange does not necessarily occur simultaneously, but the employee demanding another company's employee about information feels a commitment to respond which does not have to be settled instantaneously.[161] Von Hippel (1988) has considered that a certain code of conduct exists which makes the colleague, who received help, understand that he has entered an obligation which he must reciprocate:

> *"The code of behaviour is similar to that described by the anthropologist Marcel Mauss in The Gift: Forms and Functions of Exchange in Archaic Societies: 'A gift always looks for recompense'."*[162]

In such a trade that is based on social norms, a company's employees usually prefer colleagues that again promise the most useful information in return. Possibilities to encounter and assess colleagues of other companies and thus establish contacts which are the foundation of any informal social network, are typically conferences and congresses. Moreover, employees do not reveal any information but assess the request according to two criteria:[163]

1. Is the requested information *competitively valuable* or even vital for his company? If this applies, the employee will not provide the demanded information.
2. Is the requester a potentially useful and *knowledgeable colleague* who is prospectively of future value to the company? If this is the case, he will answer the request.

These informal networks which have been ascertained in various different industries, e.g., aerospace, biotechnology, steel, or chemical industry, create, according to Schrader (1991), economic advantages for the participating companies.[164] Von Hippel (1987) has pointed out that this

---

[161] Cp. von Hippel, E. (1987; 1988); Schrader, S. (1991).

[162] Von Hippel, E. (1988), p. 60.

[163] Cp. von Hippel, E. (1987).

[164] Cp. von Hippel, E. (1987; 1988); Schrader, S. (1991); Powell, W. W., Koput, K. W. (1996); Liebeskind, J. P., Oliver, A. L. (1996); Powell, W. W. (1990; 1998).

form of informal co-operation is one of the most efficient mode of R&D cooperation if:

- The required knowledge already *exists* in another company of the network;
- The know-how is merely *proprietary* due to trade secret protection; and
- The *value* of the traded knowledge is too low in order to justify an explicit agreement to sell, licence, or exchange the intangible assets.[165]

Hence, we can summarise that the *leaking out of information*, as titled by Mansfield (1985), is an integral part in obtaining and using existing intangible assets, as well as in the company internal process of generating new immaterial assets. Thus, the informal knowledge trade has to be understood by companies as a process creating a competitive advantage.[166] The participation in such a network has, however, not only a direct influence on a company's competitiveness by allowing for a direct and rapid access to company external proprietary intangible assets, but also provokes an indirect effect expressed by the rise of employees motivation due to the ability to mark themselves as knowledgeable and competent colleagues. Moreover, such participation has a significant and positive impact on a firm's reputation which presents the company as a good and competent co-operation partner and employer. Consequently, the participation and a central position in such a network already qualifies as a *intangible asset* of a company since it represents a competitive advantage of the company in comparison to companies not participating or not as centrally integrated in the network.[167] Hence, company networks are in particular in dynamic industries not only an important source of intangible technological assets, but also contribute to a positive reputation of the company in general. Such a good company reputation in turn facilitates the recruitment of highly qualified employees and the access to further formal and informal company co-operations.

III.2.3.3 Co-operation Decision Process

As shown in the preceding paragraphs, companies are confronted with a choice between several different possible co-operation forms. Building on the previous discussion of the different co-operation modes and the illustration of Hagedoorn & Naurula (1996), we can develop a co-

[165] Cp. von Hippel, E. (1987), p. 300.

[166] Cp. von Hippel, E. (1987; 1988); Baumol, W. J. (1993), chap. 10; Madhok, A. & Osegowitsch, T. (1998).

[167] Cp. Ordover, J. A. (1991); Powell, W. W., Koput, K. W. et al. (1996).

operation decision process. As discussed before, companies in industries characterised by high uncertainties and technological intensities prefer rather flexible forms of co-operation. These characteristics usually apply to technologies that are in an early phase of the technology-life-cycle.[168] With increasing maturity of the technology the associated uncertainties diminish and companies increasingly use more stable and less flexible co-operation forms (cf. figure III.15).

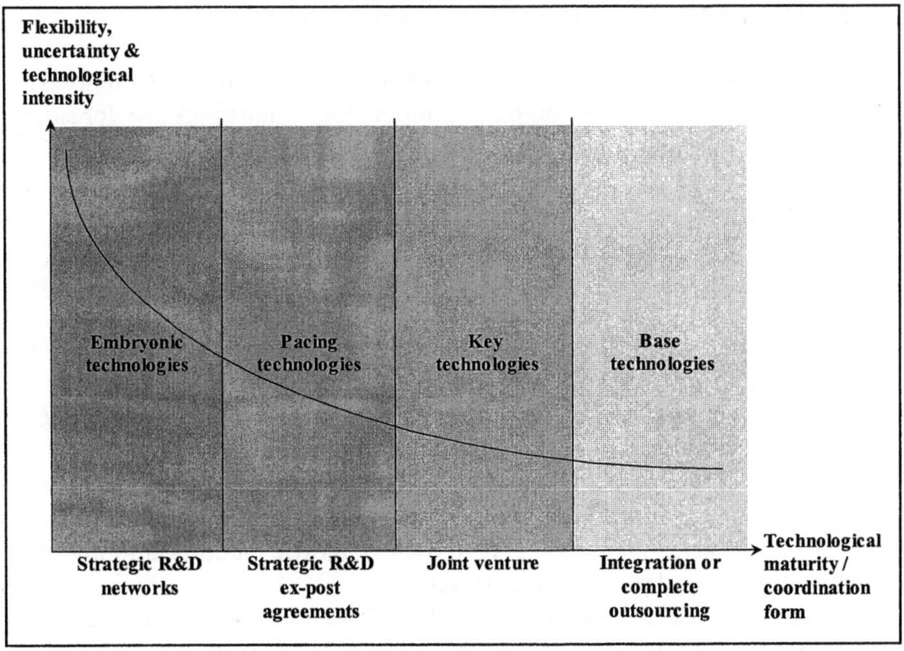

Figure III.15: Co-operation decision process

An example of a relatively young industry characterised by high technological uncertainties is the biotechnology industry. Companies try to preserve a high flexibility since they cannot identify with certainty the dominant technological path. Thus, if a company *A* establishes a long-term relationship, e.g., joint venture or integration, with company *B* for the development of a certain technology, and it later turns out that no longer company *B* but company *C* owns the superior technology, a change of the partner is accompanied by high costs. Therefore, we can ascertain, in industries based upon young technologies a preference of rather flexible arrangements such as strategic R&D networks. With increasing maturity of

[168] Cp. Gerybadze, A. (1995), chap. 1.

the technology companies increasingly use more stable forms. If the technology finally reaches maturity and merely represents a base technology for the companies active in a certain industry, companies chose between the two extreme options of full integration, or in the case of a low specificity and strategic relevance, the complete outsourcing of the technological competencies (cf. figure III.15)[169].

III.2.4 Upshot II: Sources of Intangible Assets

As discussed, companies dispose over several different sources of intangible assets whereof company internal R&D activities are considered to be the most important.[170] A further principal source of immaterial assets is learning-by-doing. A company's employees create in the process of using immaterial assets and/or the production of products and services new intangibles that improve the products and services per se, or their production process. These mostly incremental improvements which have a significant cumulative influence on the competitiveness of a company, can generally not be protected by patent rights. Furthermore, patent rights cannot protect all innovations directly attributable to R&D activities. As shown in our discussion, intellectual assets protected by intellectual property rights represent only a fraction of a company's overall immaterial holdings (cf. figures III.4 and III.10). In spite of these shortcomings of patent statistics as a measure of a company's output of intangible valuables numerous empirical analyses have shown a significant correlation between R&D activities and patent applications.

Company external immaterial asset sources such as licensing, integration of intangibles by M&As, employee recruitment, or company co-operations allow, in general, for a rapid access to technologies and complementary intellectual assets. These advantages are, however, accompanied by disadvantages such as the technological dependence on external sources, the risk of knowledge dissipation, the frustration and migration of central R&D employees, etc. In addition, a company must possess already some internal expertise in order to be able to absorb, integrate, and efficiently use external intangible assets.

Generally we can conclude that the different strategies to generate, acquire, and integrate intangible assets do not represent alternatives, but complementary sources of immaterial assets. In order to be able to fall

[169] For a discussion of the four maturity classes of technological competencies see Gerybadze, A. (1998).

[170] Cp. Teece, D. J. (1988); Ernst, H. (1998).

back on external sources a company must possess a minimum of internal expertise so as to be able to evaluate, absorb, and use these assets. On the other hand, a company should not merely concentrate on internally created assets since a company cannot master all required technologies sufficiently and consequently risks to miss out on important inventions and innovations. Subsequently, a company that wants to successfully operate in the era of immaterial asset cannot allow for the persistence of a *NIH syndrome* as stated by numerous authors.[171] In this respect a few authors, e.g., Albertini & Buttler, have even assigned the task of R&D activities to the preservation and improvement of a company's capacity to absorb and use externally created intangible assets.[172]

III.3 Protection Modes of Intangible Assets

As already stressed in the previous chapters, intangible assets show public good characteristics (cf. in particular chapter III.1.1). These implicate that new intangible assets created by a company can be transferred and at low costs easily replicated and imitated. Consequently, companies are not inclined to invest in activities to generate new immaterial assets such as those described in chapter III.2. The non-appropriability of intangible assets calls for legal protection of such assets at least over a limited period of time and geographic region.[173] This protection in turn should enable companies to appropriate the revenues generated by their intangible assets. If such a protection is not warranted, companies will not or at a much lower level invest in R&D and other creative activities which would endanger the company's competitiveness. Accordingly, Mansfield, Schwarz et al. (1981) have pointed out in their study on 48 product innovations, 50% of the considered innovations would not have been introduced on the market without an adequate protection.

The following sections present the various means companies can use to protect their intangible assets and will discuss their respective advantages and disadvantages. In particular we focus in chapter III.3.1 on legal

[171] The NIH syndrome is defined as "the tendency of a project group of stable composition to believe it possesses a monopoly of knowledge of its field which leads it to reject new ideas from outsiders to the likely detriment of its performance." Katz, R. & Allen, T. J. (1982), p. 7.

[172] Cp. van Reekum, A. H. (1999), p. 60.

[173] For a historical discussion of the mechanisms of protection of intangible assets see Kitch, E. W. (1977); Ouchi, W. G. & Bolton, M. K. (1988); Parr, R. L. & Sullivan, P. H. (1996a).

property rights such as patents, copyrights, and trademarks. Chapter III.3.2 analyses further possibilities of protecting immaterial assets, e.g., lead-time advantages and trade secrecy. Building on this discussion of the different protection modes a process of international intangible asset protection is developed in which the choice of protection mode is determined by the nature, the position in the technology life-cycle, and geographic dispersion of the use of the assets.

III.3.1 Legal Property Rights

In order to encourage the private sector to provide intangible assets, a certain protection of these assets has to be warranted. To a certain extend companies can fall back on established social norms and trade secrecy to protect their privately generated assets, however, these measures often show restrictive organisational limits. For this reason, most countries have established a *system of intellectual property rights* which is older than the capitalistic, industrial society.[174]

This system which includes patents, trademarks, copyrights, etc., had been neglected until the end of the 1970s and only since the 1980s intellectual property rights and in particular patent rights have experienced a substantial increase in significance.[175] This rise in importance of such intellectual property rights is in particular attributable to the reinforcement of the U.S. patent system in order to provide the U.S. industry with an efficient protection of its R&D investments with respect to the success of many Asian economies. This mounting importance of legal rights on immaterial assets is also expressed in legal disputes and infringement payments (cf. table III.2).

In contrast to physical property, intellectual property does not bestow the owner with the unique rights of material ownership and holding, but rather confers the owner the right to exclude other parties from the use of his intangible assets. This again implies that these rights have to be respected by society so that the owner can restrict the use of his immaterial property.[176] In the following sections we do, however, not present and discuss all sorts of intellectual property rights, but concentrate on three central forms: Patents, trademarks, and so called petty-patents.[177] In several nations, e.g., USA, trade secrets are recognised as intellectual property,

[174] Cp. Granstrand, O. (1999), chap. 1.

[175] Cp. David, P. A. (1993); Thurow, L. C. (1997); Granstrand, O. (1999), chap. 1.

[176] Cp. Demsetz, H. (1967); Grandstrand, O. (1999).

[177] Petty-patents (Gebrauchsmuster) are a particularity of the German intellectual patent right system.

however, in our discussion we take a rather European point of view and do not regard trade secrets as property per se, since the holder does not possess the exclusive rights to use or enjoy.[178]

Table III.2: The biggest patent infringements in the USA

Patent right holder (nationality, size)	Damages (US$ millions)	Infringer (nationality, size)	Year
Litton (US, large)	1200.0	Honeywell (US, large)	1995
Alpex (US, small)	253.0	Nintendo (Japan, large)	1994
Honeywell (US, large)	166.0	Minolta (Japan, large)	1994
Stac Electronics (US, small)	120.0	Microsoft (US, large)	1994
Hughes Aircraft (US, large)	114.0	USA	1994
Coyle, J. R. (US, individual)	43.0	Sega (Japan, large)	1992
Polaroid (US, large)	873.2	Eastman (US, large)	1991
3M (US, large)	106.0	J&J Corp. (US, large)	1991
B&H (US, medium)	36.5	Owens (US, large)	1991
Lubrizol I (US, large)	86.0	Exxon (US, large)	1988
Syntex (US, medium)	36.5	Paragon (US, medium)	1987
Smith Int. (US, medium)	204.0	Hughes Tool (US, large)	1986
Trans-World (US, medium)	31.3	Dura&Kiddie(US, small)	1986
Shiley (US, large)	44.8	Bentley Labs (US, large)	1985
Pfizer (US, large)	55.8	Int. Rectifier (US, large)	1983

Source: Grandstrand, O. (1999), p. 6.

III.3.1.1 Patent Rights

A patent bestows its holder with the right to exclude all other persons from producing, selling, or using the subject matter of his valid patent over a certain period of time (20 years after application within the EU and 20 years after application or 17 years after assignment in the U.S.) and geographic region.[179] This *monopoly right* allows the owner, at least in theory, to perfectly appropriate the revenues generated by his intellectual property. This protection of immaterial assets by patents is, however, limited to technological inventions which are:

[178] Cp. Friedman, D. D., Landes, W. M. et al. (1991).
[179] Cp. Besen, S. M. & Raskind, L. J. (1991).

1. *New* in the sense that they do not belong to the current state of the technique;
2. The result of a *creative, inventive activity* so that they cannot be developed by an expert in a routine manner; and
3. Economically valuable and useful.[180]

This legislation implies that companies cannot protect all their immaterial assets by patent rights and hence patents only represent a fraction of the company's intangible asset stock. Moreover, companies do not protect all inventions accomplishing the legal requirements by patent rights. And finally not all inventions, protected by patents or not, are used in innovative products, processes, or services (cf. figure III.16). There are several reasons explaining the reluctance of companies to protect their technological inventions by patent filings. On the one hand, a company has to reveal all relevant information concerning an invention in order to obtain patent protection.[181] This *disclosure* of the relevant information which obliges the complete codification, aims at the rapid spread of the invention so that other companies can realign their research activities and consequently increases the overall advance of the technological development.[182]

The disclosure of the information in relation to patent applications creates two principal problems for the inventing firms. First of all, the companies have to *codify* the information and knowledge regarding the invention which represents a difficult undertaking in respect to tacit knowledge. Furthermore, not all knowledge can principally be codified. Secondly, the cost of protection of intangible assets increases by codifying the underlying knowledge since codified knowledge can easily be transferred, verified, stored, and reproduced. Foray (1995) describes the relationship between codification and appropriation:

> *"The codification of knowledge which reduces the marginal cost of transfer and diffusion, narrows the gap between knowledge-information and non-excludability. In other words, it is always possible to prevent other agents from using knowledge, but the cost of*

---

[180] Cp. German patent law, §1 PatG and cp. de Pay, D. (1996); Xuyen, G. N. S. (1998).

[181] The very word 'patent' derives from the Latin word 'literae patentes' meaning open letter.

[182] For a discussion of the welfare effects of patents see, e.g., Kitch, E. W. (1977); Wright, B. D. (1983); Shapiro, C. (1985); Galllini, N. T. (1992).

exclusion will increase once the knowledge in question has been codified."[183]

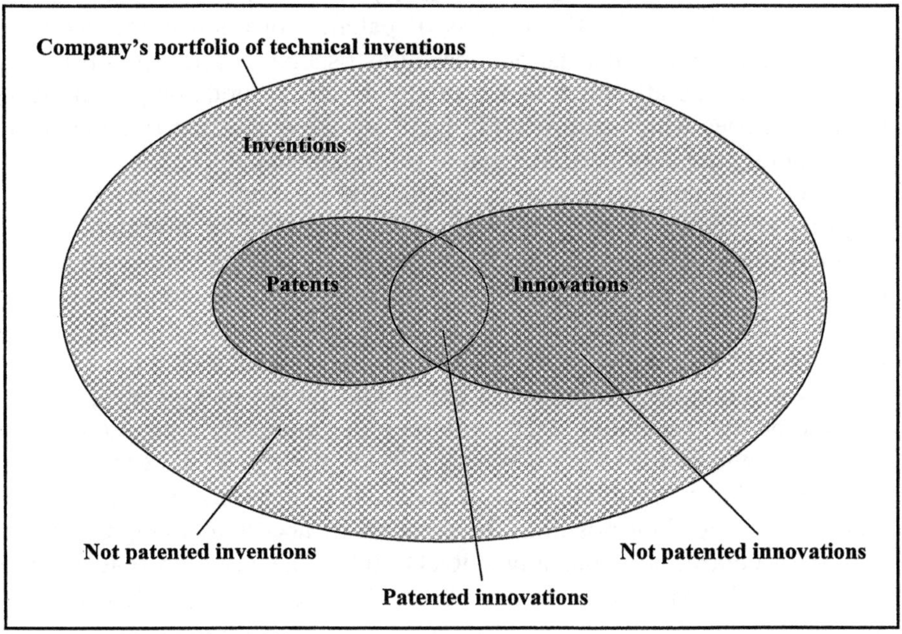

Source: Ernst, H. (1999), p. 1148.

Figure III.16: Technological inventions, patents, and innovations

Further motivations not to apply for patent protection for certain technological inventions are, according to a survey of the European Patent Office (EPO) including 1006 companies, the *high fixed costs* of such applications which a company always incurs even if the patented information appears to be of low value or if the patent protection emerges to be only of limited effectiveness (cf. figure III.17).[184] Mansfield, Schwartz et al. (1981), for example, have stated that 60% of the successfully patented innovations in the sample had been *imitated within 4 years* after their introduction. This rapid imitation of innovations can be explained by the bypassing of the patented information. The possibility of *inventing around* varies, however, considerably between different

[183] Foray, D. (1995), p. 81; cp. also Teece, D. J. (1981); Zander, U. & Kogut, B. (1995).

[184] Cp. Mansfield, E., Schwartz, M. et al. (1981); Levin, R. C., Klevorick, A. et al. (1987); Friedman, D. D., Landes, W. M. et al. (1991); EPO (1994), chap. 2.2.

industries, as well as between products and process patents.[185] As a result, the propensities to patent and effectiveness of patents differ according to the nature of the invention and the industry in question. An industry that is associated with a high effectiveness of patent protection is the chemical industry and in particular the pharmaceutical sector.[186] The high efficiency of patents can be attributed to the relatively clear standards prevailing in these industries which significantly facilitate the evaluation of patents and consequently the verification of patent infringements.

Which arguments do, however, support the patenting of information if a majority of these patented innovations are imitated or invented around within 4 years? The protection of innovations by patents must have further qualities beyond just keeping other companies from imitating the subject matter. Such further qualities of patents are, among others, the delaying of imitation, the increasing of imitation costs, the blocking of the innovation process of competing companies, the establishment of a patent portfolio and innovative reputation that reinforces the company's position in co-operations and in recruiting new specialised employees, the generation of income by licensing intellectual property, the signalling of a company's technological leading position, the creation of access to foreign markets, and/or to control the company's R&D staff. The last two reasons why company's file patents which have been identified by Levin, Klevorick et al. (1987), only have a marginal relevance in the appropriation of returns generated by R&D investments. Moreover, the significance of these motives in explaining why companies file patents has to be questioned.

As opposed to the control of a company's R&D employees and the creation of access to foreign markets, the arguments of delaying the imitation, increasing the cost of imitation, establishing a valuable patent portfolio, building up of an innovative corporate reputation, as well as blocking of competitors seem to better explain the patenting activities of business enterprises. Mansfield, Schwartz et al. (1981) have ascertained in their study that patents increase significantly the imitation costs. This is particularly true for product innovations, even though a majority of the innovations had been imitated years before the patent protection expired.[187] The influence of patents on imitation cost varies greatly between different industries which in turn can be an explanation of the inter-industry variations in the propensity to patent stated by Patel & Pavitt (1990).

---

[185] Cp. Mansfield, E., Schwartz, M. et al. (1981); Levin, R. C., Klevorick, A. K. et al. (1987).

[186] Cp. Mansfield, E., Schwartz, M. et al. (1981); Levin, R. C., Klevorick, A. K. et al. (1987); Narin, F., Noma, F. et al. (1987); Arundel, A. & Kabla, I. (1998).

[187] Cp. Geroski, P. (1995).

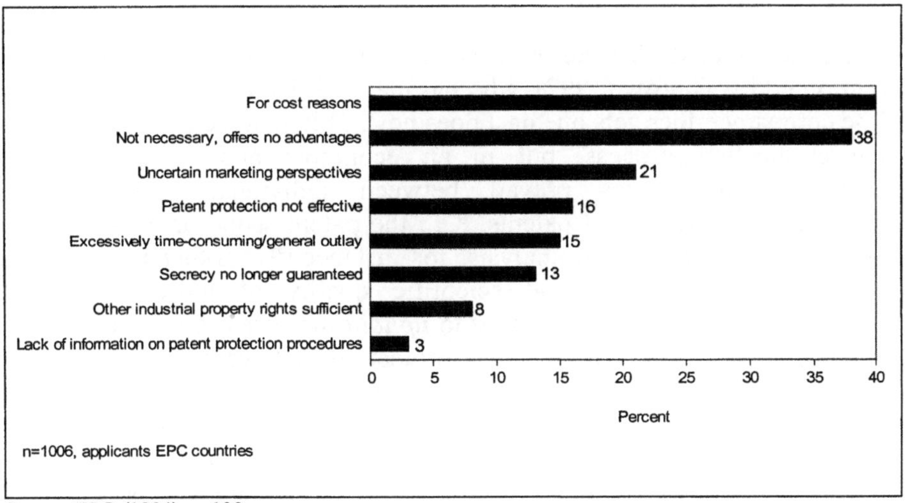

Source: EPO (1994), p. 109.

Figure III.17: Reasons not to apply for patent protection

Further key aspects that call for patent filings represent the increase in the reputation of a company as an innovator and the improved negotiation position due to its patent portfolio which is also of value to other companies. By possessing an innovative reputation a company's ability to recruit knowledgeable scientists, who bring their knowledge into the company, is improved and the company in general is regarded as a competent co-operation partner.[188] Moreover, von Hippel (1982) has discovered that companies in dynamic industries endowed with a rich patent portfolio show advantages in cross-licensing agreements.[189] The strategic advantage of a substantial and high-quality patent portfolio also applies to industries with a large number of non-expired patents with closely related contents. In such industries, e.g., electronics industry, a high probability exists to infringe on the patents of other companies while using a company's own intellectual property. In order not to hinder the technological advance, companies establish cross-licensing agreements in which companies with a large, valuable portfolio of patents that play a central role in the further development of the technology have a good stand in the licensing negotiations.[190]

---

[188] For a detailed discussion see chap. III.2.2 and cp. van Reekum, A. H. (1999), pp. 99-100.

[189] Cp. also Teece, D. J. (2000a), pp. 203-213.

[190] For a more detailed discussion see chap. III.2.2.1.

In this discussion of pros and cons of patent protection, the impression could be created that all patents are equal. This perception is even reinforced by Thurow (1997), who has claimed that all patents are equal – 'the company either gets one or it does not'. This statement may be true for the application process, but in an economic and scientific regard significant differences prevail between individual patents. These *qualitative differences* of patents, e.g., the patent scope or breadth,[191] can be revealed by a citation analysis, for instance.[192] Another possibility to evaluate the economic and scientific quality of individual patents represents the payments necessary to *uphold* the patent protection and the *geographic dispersion* of the patent protection. If a company, for example, does not effect these routine payments the patent protection will expire before the maximal possible patent duration which in turn can be valued as an indication of a low patent value.[193] On the other hand, *international patent applications* that are characterised by a parallel application at several different national patent offices or the filing of an application at a supra-national institution, e.g., WIPO or EPO, can be valued as an indication of high patent value because of the significantly higher application and maintenance costs.[194]

III.3.1.2 Trademarks and Brand Equity

The second most important intellectual property right represents trademarks and registered brands. According to the German brand and trademark legislation all characters and words, including names of persons, figures, letters, phonetic signs, and three-dimensional forms which are useful to distinguish products and services of a specific company of those of other companies, are legally protectable.[195] A trademark can be obtained either by officially registering the name or sign in the trademark register of the respective national patent office or by simply using the name or sign in

[191] "Scope [breadth] of the patent can be interpreted as the portion of an abstract product/technology space covered by the innovation ..." Ordover, J. A. (1991), p. 48; cp. also Engelsman, E. C. & van Raan, A. F. J. (1993); van Reekum, A. H. (1999).

[192] Cp. Narin, F., Norma, E. et al. (1987); Albert, M. B., Avery, D. et al. (1991); Narin, F. & Olivastro, D. (1992); Harhoff, D., Narin, F. et al. (1997).

[193] Cp. Griliches, Z. (1990); Katopis, C. (1997); Harhoff, D., Narin, F. et al. (1997).

[194] Cp. Schmoch, U., Grupp, H. et al. (1988); Harhoff, D., Narin, F. et al. (1997); Xuygen, G. N. (1998); Grupp, H. & Schmoch, U. (1999).

[195] Cp. German Trademark law, §3, sect. 1 MarkenG..

business activities. A registered trademark is then *infinitely valid* except the trademark is not used over a period of five years or the trademark turns into a *customary term* of a commodity or service.[196]

The initial function of a trademark to allocate products and services to a certain source is nowadays only one of many reasons why companies register trademarks and brands. Today, trademarks do not only matter before and during the process of purchase, but also continue to have an important effect on the buyer after the purchase took place. Trademarks and brands have in addition to their communication function an intangible, psychic, and social utility for the consumer. Four general functions of trademarks for the consumer can be identified which are to:

1. *Inform* the customers and structure the offer;
2. Represent a *guarantee* of quality and continuity;
3. Have a *signalling effect*; and/or
4. *Guarantee* the use of a particular recipe or procedure.[197]

A trademark enables a customer to orient himself on markets characterised by a large offer of differentiated products and to structure the different proposals. Thus, trademarks facilitate the allocation of products and services to particular price segments, types, forms, producers, etc. and hence reduce a customers *search costs*. Moreover, market transactions show an inherent risk concerning the quality of the service or product and the future existence of the company and consequently the possibility of indemnity, exchange, and/or maintenance of the product. Concerning the possibility of quality evaluation of products or services Kapferer (1999) distinguishes three generic groups of goods and services:

1. The quality can be assessed (by contact and/or sight) before purchase;
2. The quality can only be assessed by consumption (experience goods); and
3. The quality cannot be assessed even after consumption (credence goods).

In the case of a textile, for example, the quality can be assessed before the purchase by thoroughly looking at and touching the tissue. The quality of a service or a soda can, however, only be measured by consuming the product or service in question. The quality of other products and services

[196] The trademark 'Aspirin' has been eliminated from the trademark register by the USPto because the trademark had turned into a generic term for products containing acetylsalicylic-acid. Cf. chap. II.2.

[197] Cp. Allegrezza, S. & Guarda-Rauchs, A. (1999); Kapferer, J. N. & Thoenig, J. C. (1994); Kapferer, J. N. (1999), chap. 1; Güldenberg, H. G. (1999a).

again, cannot be objectively assessed even after consumption. In the case of such *credence goods* the perception of quality rests upon trust and belief which are more or less shared by society. In respect to products and services of the second and third category, trademarks have a function of guarantee concerning the quality and thus reduce the associated risks for the purchaser.[198]

Another function of trademarks is their signalling function. Hence, a purchaser can express an affiliation to a certain social class or a specific mood. Accordingly, purchasers *identify* themselves with a certain trademark or brand and their associated image. The last noteworthy function of a trademark or brand represents its guarantee concerning the utilisation of a certain recipe or production process. The brand Coca-Cola, for example, signals the use of special recipe that has been kept secret for more than 100 years, or trademarks such as Body-Shop or Weleda stands for a particularly environmentally friendly production which completely renounces the use of animal experiments. The consumer can, however, not verify the truthfulness of such assertions and judges a certain trademark or brand as more or less trustworthy.

Due to these functions of trademarks and brands and the high costs of establishing a new trademark or brand on the market, these intellectual assets show great economic value.[199] As can be seen in table III.3, the value of such brands and trademarks can take the order of magnitude of the GDP of small states. These brand values do, however, not result from mistakes in the brand valuation, but are rather the outcome of the five dimensions of brand equity (cf. figure IV.7).[200] These dimensions are in particular:

1. Brand loyalty;
2. Brand awareness;
3. Associated quality;
4. Other brand associations; and
5. Brand virtues (e.g., patents, distribution, etc.).

Hence, at the moment of registration the brand has no economic value besides the registration fee. The value is built up over time by continuous investments in marketing and communication, constant product and/or service quality, adaptations to new trends and technologies, customer proximity, and investments in R&D which in turn result in continuous

---

[198] Cp. Aaker, D., A. (1991) p. 87; Kapferer, J. N. (1999), pp. 23-24; Kapferer, J. N. & Thoenig, J. C. (1994), pp. 110-115.

[199] According to Demuth (1999) the costs of introducing a new trademark or brand in the market costs between DM 50 and DM 100 million.

[200] For a detailed discussion see chap. III.3.1.3 and IV.2.

innovations and improvements. Consequently, a brand or trademark is not just an attribute of distinction and assignment, but rather stands for the associated product, service, or even whole company. Thus, the value of a trademark or brand does not only comprise investments in marketing and communication, but also further intangible assets within the company such as particular technological capabilities, process technologies, and patents.[201]

In the registration process a trademark has to be assigned to a certain class. Hence, another company can register the same name for another product or service located in another trademark class if the responsible patent office does not perceive the risk of confusion, dilution, and/or exploitation of an existing reputation.[202] A significantly more important problem presents the enforceability of trademarks on international markets and in particular in the Internet. Companies frequently encounter problems of enforcing their trademark rights against the production of *counterfeits* and imitations in developing and newly industrialised countries. Moreover, the Internet represents a legal space where intellectual property rights cannot or are very difficult to enforce.[203] Companies thus cannot effectively control the use of their intellectual properties such as trademarks, brands, and copyrights in the Internet and thus prevent infringement.

Advantages of trademark protection are, on the other hand, the relatively simple registration process and perpetuation of trademarks and brands. The most important advantage of trademarks and brands is, however, vis-à-vis patent protection, their *infinite validity*. Once a company has registered a trademark, the trademark is valid as long as the company frequently uses the brand and settles the regularly upcoming renewal fees, as well as if the trademark does not turn into a common denotation for the product or service in question.[204] Thus, a trademark or brand usually accompanies a product or service over its entire lifetime and in certain circumstances outlives the product or service, such as in the case of the model 2CV from Citroën which was produced in the years 1949 to 1990 and still shows a high level of notoriety across all generations in France and other European countries.

---

[201] Cp. Kapferer, J. N. (1999), pp. 19-34.

[202] Cp. German trademark legislation, §9, sect. 2 MarkenG; Verlit, W. (1999), pp. 12-17.

[203] N.A. (1998a); N.A. (2000).

[204] For a detailed discussion see chap. II.2.

Table III.3: The worlds most valuable brands[205]

Brand Name	**Country of Origin**	**Industry**	**Brand Value** (US$ billion)	**Market Capitalisation of Parent Company** (US$ billion)	**Brand Value as a % of Market Capitalisation**
Coca-Cola	US	Beverages	83.845	142.164	59%
Microsoft	US	Software	56.654	271.854	21%
IBM	US	Computers	43.781	158.384	28%
General Electric	US	Diversified	33.502	327.996	10%
Ford	US	Automobile	33.197	57.387	58%
Disney	US	Entertainment	32.275	52.552	61%
Intel	US	Computers	31.021	144.060	21%
McDonald's	US	Food	26.231	40.862	64%
AT&T	US	Telecoms	24.181	102.480	24%
Marlboro	US	Tobacco	21.048	122.437	19%
Nokia	Fin	Telecoms	20.694	46.926	44%
Mercedes	D	Automobiles	17.781	48.326	37%
Nescafé	CH	Beverages	17.595	77.490	23%
Hewlett Packard	US	Computers	17.132	54.902	31%
Gilette	US	Personal care	15.894	42.951	37%

Source: Interbrand (1999).

Brand Equity vs. Trademark Rights

Hitherto, one can find the terms brand equity, trademark and brand name used interchangeably in the literature. However, this approach totally neglects the *reputational foundations* of brand equity and the rather *legal aspects* of brand names and trademarks that concentrate in particular on the distinguishing of products and services of a certain company from

205 The value of brands and trademarks can be determined on several different ways. The existence of these deviating methods can in part explain the significant disparities in the valuation of individual trademarks. Cp. Badenhausen, K. (1996); Interbrand (1999a).

those of other companies.[206] As pointed out above, a trademark or brand name starts to exist with the official registration of the name or symbol at the respective patent office. However, at the moment of registration a trademark or brand name has no economic value. The value that is associated with a certain established trademark or brand name is generally built up over a long time through *superior competence* vis-à-vis competitors.[207]

The economic value ascribed to a certain trademark results from the loyalty, acquaintance, associations, experiences, etc. of current and potential customers with a certain trademark or brand name that can be summed up under the terms *reputation* or *image*. Such a reputation of a product, service or even entire company which can be positive or negative, is build up by consumers through any direct and indirect contact with the company, product, and/or service, and is highly complex and always remains extremely ambiguous.[208] Such *direct influences* can, for example, be the use or consumption of a product or service, interaction with the company in form of its employees, but also marketing and promotion activities of the company about its offerings. *Indirect influences* are, on the other hand, all information which shape the opinion of the current or potential customer about a certain product, service, or company, that cannot be directly influenced by the company in question. Such indirect impacts are the opinion of good friends and/or respected third parties such as consumer organisations, expert opinions or specialised journals, etc. Hence, the factors building and influencing the image or reputation a consumer associates with a certain trademark is extremely complex and never fully understandable neither by the company holding the reputation nor by competitors or even consumers. Consequently, we can define the reputation or image of a company, product or service as an *intangible and highly tacit* asset.[209] Moreover, the image or reputation associated with a certain product, for example, is never uniform across several current and potential customers, but each individual has his own and particular image in mind which might be more or less identical to the image held by another person.

In summary, a trademark or brand name is the underlying *property right* with which current and potential customers associated a certain positive or

---

[206] Cp. German Trademark Law, §3, sect. 1 MarkenG..

[207] Cp. Jacobsen, R. (1988); Hall, R. (1992); Rutledge, J. (1998); Demuth, A. (1999); Majer, W. (2000); Teece, D. J. (2000).

[208] Cp. Bird, M., Channon, C. et al. (1970); Roeb, T. (1994); Aaker, D. A. (1991), pp. 85-128; Aaker, D. A. (1996), pp. 145-149; Pettis, C. (1995a), pp. 18-23.

[209] Cp. Hall, R. (1992); Porter, M. E. (1996).

negative reputation. Such a trademark or brand name can be readily sold or acquired on the market. The associated reputation and feelings, however, of a certain product, service, and/or company cannot be protected by legal property rights such as trademarks nor can it be readily bought or sold on the market for reputation. The image of a product, service or company has to be build over several years.[210] Consequently, reputation cannot be defined as an intellectual capital, but rather as a company's *intangible asset* with a high tacit component. Accordingly, Hall (1993) has pointed out:

> *"The intangible resource or reputation may also be classified as an asset due to its characteristic of 'belongingness', and whilst it may be defendable to attack with respect to libel, it cannot be said to have the property rights of say, a trademark which can be bought and sold."*[211]

Thus, trademarks and brand names represent the intellectual property of a company which can be bought and sold on a free market. Reputation, however, also often closely interlinked and hard or even impossible to separate from a trademark or brand name is not protectable by legal rights and cannot be bought or sold on the market. Thus, a reputation has to be created by a company and its offerings over a relatively long period of time. However, what do we precisely understand under the term brand equity?

The term *brand equity* combines the *legal aspects* of trademarks and brand names and the highly *tacit* reputational aspects associated with a certain product, service, or company (see figure IV.7).[212] Henceforth, we will use the definition of brand equity established by Farquhar (1989) who defined a brand as:

> *"... a name, symbol, design, or mark that enhances the value of a product beyond its functional purpose. Depending on which perspective is considered, the brand can have added value to the firm, the trade, or the consumer."*[213]

This definition of brand equity, amalgamating the legal aspects of trademarks and brand names with reputational aspects, is of central importance in understanding the strategic importance and the value associated with brand equity.

---

[210] Cp. Mascarenhas, B. & Aaker, D. A. (1989); Dierickx, I. & Cool, K. (1989); Hall, R. (1992; 1993).

[211] Hall, R. (1993), p. 608.

[212] Cp. Richards, I., Foster, D. et al. (1998).

[213] Farquhar, P. H. (1989), p. 25.

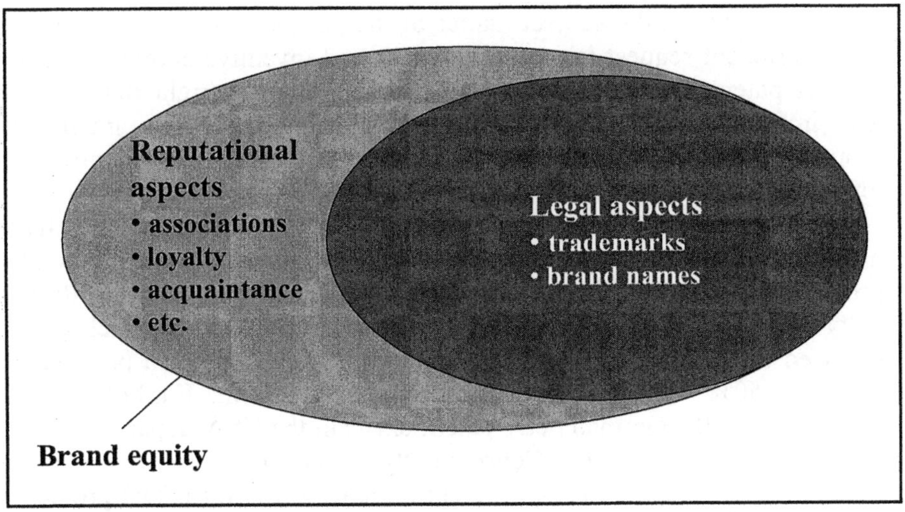

Figure III.18: Legal and reputational aspects of brand equity

A further specification of the term brand equity and a description of the different dimensions of brand equity is given in chapter IV.2. Moreover, chapter IV will discuss in detail the strategic role of brand equity in the protection of intangible technological assets and thus in enabling a company to appropriate efficiently the returns generated by these assets in the long-term.

III.3.1.3 Petty-Patents[214]

The last type of intellectual property we are going to discuss are petty-patents. This intellectual property right does only exist in this form in Germany and it is often compared to *patent rights*. The petty-patent indeed shows some similarities to patents but also some significant differences.

A petty-patent can, just as a patent, be applied for *technological inventions*, e.g., chemical substances and technical installations. In contrast to patents, a petty-patent becomes assigned already after a few weeks and not, as in the case of patent applications, only after one or two years. The rapid processing of petty-patent applications is attributable to the examination process which only takes form aspects, e.g., general possibility of protection, into consideration. Only in the case of a request of deletion the patent office examines if the petty-patent accomplishes the required criteria. The criteria demands for newness, creative activity, and

[214] "Gebrauchsmuster" in German.

economic value of the subject matter of the petty-patent, where, however, a less stringent request is put on newness and inventive activity as in the case of patent applications. This intellectual property right thus permits less important inventions with a lower economic value intellectual property protection due to the less stringent demands and significantly lower registration and renewal fees vis-à-vis patent protection.[215]

These advantages of petty-patents in comparison to patents have, however, to be contrasted with the disadvantages of a generally weaker protection, a shorter lifetime, and an even more limited applicability. A petty-patent has a duration of three years after registration which can be renewed three times up to a maximum of ten years. Thus, a petty-patent shows a 50% shorter maximal lifetime of a patent. Furthermore, no equivalent for the German petty-patent exists in the USA, Japan, as well as on an European level. Consequently, companies seeking for an international protection of their invention have to file for patent protection outside Germany. Lastly, companies cannot protect process inventions and scientific theories by petty-patent rights.[216]

This nationally applicable, but nevertheless important property right provides smaller, less important inventions with intellectual property right protection which would not justify the costs of patent application. It is usually employed by small and medium sized companies as well as individual persons that envisage to protect inventions with a low economic value on a national level.

III.3.2 Further Possibilities of Protection

Besides the above discussed intellectual property rights which bestow their owners with internationally, legally enforceable rights on their inventions and intangible assets, companies possess further mechanisms of protection. These mostly *organisational means* of protection show important advantages, but also shortcomings in comparison to intellectual property rights. Such organisational measures are, for example, the protection of intangible assets by secrecy and internalisation of their use, the acquisition or creation of idiosyncratic specialised assets complementing the immaterial assets, the non-codification of knowledge, the tying-up of employees to the organisation in question by long-lasting contracts, or the exploitation of lead-time-advantages. Several empirical studies have shown that intellectual property rights only represent one and often not the

[215] Cp. Deutsches Patent- und Markenamt (2000).

[216] Cp. De Pay, D. (1996); Deutsches Patent- und Markenamt (2000).

preferred mode of protecting intellectual assets.[217] These analyses show in addition that business enterprises consider trade secrecy, lead-time-advantages, as well as complexity as more important modes of protecting their innovations than patents or any other intellectual property right. In the following discussion we analyse the three modes of intellectual asset protection considered as the most important besides intellectual property rights which are: trade secrecy, complementary resources, and lead-time-advantages.

III.3.2.1 Trade Secrecy

The trade secret protection of innovations is considered as an effective measure of protection which allows companies to appropriate the returns generated by their intangible assets. In particular with *process innovations* companies regard secrecy as a more effective protection mode than patents.[218] The preference of trade secrets in association with the protection of process know-how is, according to Ransley & Gaffney (1997) and Arundel & Kabla (1998), due to the problems of detecting and proving intellectual property right infringements. Moreover, many companies want to avoid the obligatory publication of their innovation by applying for a patent, and try to appropriate the returns of an innovation by secrecy and company internal use of the knowledge. Such trade secrets are in general defined as:

> *"...any formula, pattern, device or compilation of information which is used in one's business, and which gives him an opportunity to obtain an advantage over competitors who do not know or use it. ... It differs form other secret information in a business ... in that it is not simply information as to single or ephemeral events in the conduct of the business. ... A trade secret is a process or device for continuous use in the operation of the business."*[219]

Consequently, trade secrets are characterised as economically valuable know-how or information that bestow the company, possessing these intangible assets, an advantage on the market vis-à-vis companies not possessing these assets. However, a trade secret protection of intangible assets is only possible if the company can publicly offer the product or process and still keep the underlying product or process innovation secret.

[217] Cp. Levin, R. C., Klevorick, A. K. et al. (1987); EPO (1994); Tibesar, A. (1997; 1998); Arundel, A. & Kabla, I. (1998).

[218] Cp. Levin, R. C., Klevorick, A. K. et al. (1987); Aaker, D. A. (1989); Tibesar, A. (1998).

[219] Cheung, S. N. S. (1982), p. 42 and cp. Besen, S. M. & Raskind, L. J. (1991).

Trade secret protection of intangible assets for their appropriation shows some central advantages in comparison to intellectual property right protection. These advantages which do not only comprise the circumvention of the *disclosure* of the inventions, are the prevention of the *codification* of the underlying know-how, the *infinite lifetime* of a trade secret, and the avoidance of the *fixed costs* associated with a patent application. If a company desires to protect a technological invention by a patent, the company has to codify the underlying knowledge and hand-in a written application to the patent office. This codification substantially reduces the cost of intra- and inter-company information transfers that provokes a more rapid diffusion of the innovation. According to Foray (1995), the codification of knowledge significantly increases the appropriation costs by controlling the compliance of the intellectual property rights and the juridical prosecution of infringements. This codification of knowledge can be avoided by a strategy of trade secrecy and the risk of unintentional diffusion of the innovation can be further reduced by the *dispersion* of the relevant knowledge over several employees within the company.[220] Moreover, by following a strategy of trade secret protection, a company avoids the cost of codification and patent application which a company always incurs even if the innovation appears to have low economic value. In contrast, a company only incurs the cost of trade secret protection if the innovation appears to be economically valuable.[221] However, in the case of a valuable invention the cost of trade secret protection will rapidly increase due to the efforts of competing companies to reveal the underlying information by re-engineering, enticement of employees, or even espionage, in order to imitate and replicate the innovation. If the other companies do, however, not succeed in revealing the innovation, the inventing company can appropriate the revenues generated by its trade secret over an infinite period of time. Thus, a company, confident that other companies will need more time to independently develop the innovation than the lifetime of a patent, will not patent the invention, but protect the intangible assets by trade secret protection. Accordingly, Friedman, Landes et al. (1991) have stated:

> *"By [keeping an invention secret] he will in effect be contending that the social value of the invention is greater than the patent law assumes – and he is offering to demonstrate it through the failure of*

[220] Cp. Winter, S. G. (1987).
[221] Cp. Friedman, D. D., Landes, W. M. et al. (1991).

other inventors to duplicate the invention though legally free to do so."[222]

However, as Katopis (1997) has emphasised, the period needed by companies to independently develop or reveal the underlying information by reverse engineering is in general substantially shorter than the general patent duration. This is attributable to the fact that second-innovators do possess information because of the simple existence of the product and its characteristics which the first-innovator had to uncover by his own research.[223] Moreover, the cost of trade secret protection increase disproportionately with the value of the intangible asset in question compared to patent protection. This cost increase can be traced back to the control costs for supervising employees, higher wages to impede the migration of knowledgeable employees, measures against espionage, etc. (cf. figure III.18).[224] Furthermore, the possibility of the company to co-operate with suppliers, customers, but also competitors is severely restricted by the existence of trade secrets. A co-operation could evoke the diffusion of information and knowledge protected by trade secrecy and hence endanger the company's competitiveness. Besides, a company cannot protect product and process innovations by trade secret protection that are observable on the final product or service, e.g., chemical and pharmaceutical innovations, or innovations which are intended to be recognised by customers and/or competitors, such as an innovation in the field of marketing or distribution.

Consequently, we can hypothesise that companies effectively protect intangible assets by trade secrecy only if the innovation cannot be discerned by means of the product and/or service. A strategy of trade secret protection is preferable, too, if a technological invention shows a low economic value and hence does not justify the cost of patent protection.

As can be seen in figure III.19, the cost of patent protection transcends the cost of trade secrecy up to an economic value of EV_1 of the intangible assets. If the value of the intangible assets surpasses EV_1, the costs of trade secret protection increase disproportionately vis-à-vis the costs of patent protection. Thus, the patent protection of highly valuable intangible assets is advantageous for business companies in general. In addition, trade

222 Friedman, D. D., Landes, W. M. et al. (1991), p. 62.

223 Cp. Mansfield, E., Schwartz, M. et al. (1981).

224 Employees of different companies do trade information under each other (cp. chap. III.2.3.2). According to von Hippel (1988), the official prohibition of these practices will not stop the information trade but rather drives the employees' activity into illegality.

secrets do not represent intellectual property that guarantees a company a legally enforceable duration.[225] Consequently, if another company makes the same invention or reveals the relevant information on another legal way, e.g., re-engineering, enticement of employees, luck, etc. the first-inventor cannot prevent the second inventor from using and exploiting the intellectual assets.

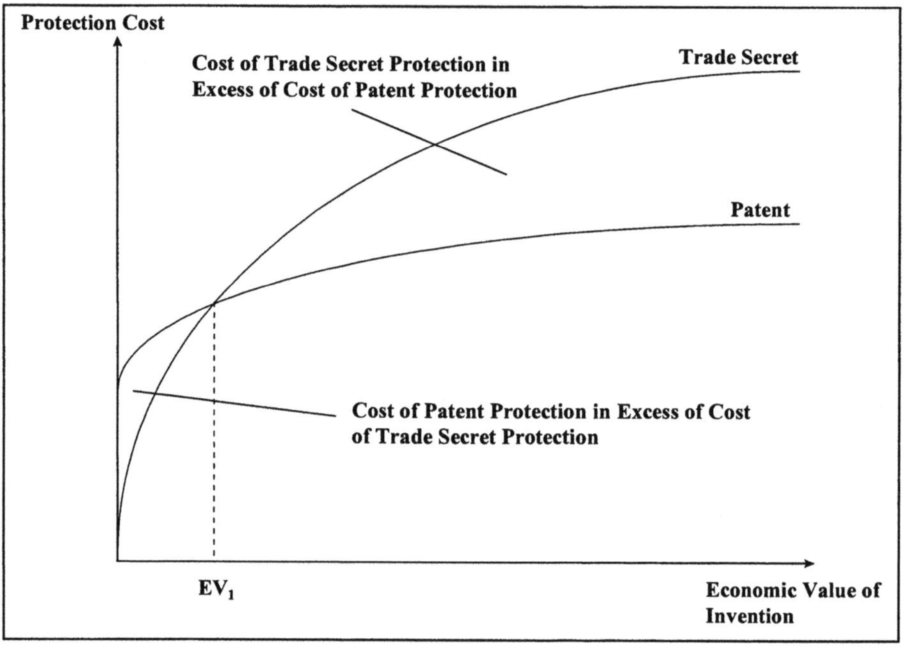

Figure III.19: Cost of trade secret protection in relation to the invention's economic value

III.3.2.2 Lead-Time-Advantages

Another possibility to protect innovations which European companies perceive as central, are so called lead-time-advantages. According to Eurostat, more than 65% of the questioned companies rate lead-time-advantages as a very important means of protection whereas only 32% and

[225] Cp. Cheung, S. N. S. (1982); Friedman, D. D., Landes, W. M. et al. (1991); Besen, S. M. & Raskind, L. J. (1991).

27%, respectively, regard trade secrecy and patent protection as more import protection modes.[226]

Such lead-time-advantages represent *time advantages* of the innovator in respect to technologically following companies or imitators. Innovative companies in dynamic industries which are characterised by short product and technology life cycles, can use their temporary monopoly position in order to recuperate their investments, earn sufficient interests, as well as develop the next product or technology generation before the following companies have successfully duplicated or replicated the innovation.[227] The standard example of such an industry in which innovating companies usually completely abstain from legally protecting their innovations and thus only appropriate the returns of their innovations over a relatively short time period, is the semiconductor industry. Intel, the leading company in the market, brought its new technology on the market and benefited from its temporary monopoly position which was sufficiently long to recover its investments made, and to develop the new technology generation. At the stage when competitors finally succeeded in imitating Intel's technology, the company was already about to introduce the new product or technology generation.[228] In such *fast-cycle industries* patents are inapt to protect innovations due to the long processing and approval periods of patent offices and the relatively short average technology live time. In the semiconductor industry, for example, the next technology generation would be already on the market before the patent office would have decided about the preceding technology's protection.

Further benefits that result from the time advantage of the innovator are, on the one hand, that he can acquire assets in advance to the market introduction whose value will increase due to the new technology. On the other hand, the innovator can generate and/or acquire assets in advance which complement the innovation and create market entry barriers for succeeding companies.[229] Such complementary assets that are analysed in detail in the following section, can be created by the innovating company at relatively low cost due to its temporary monopoly position. Succeeding

[226] Cp. Tibesar, A. (1998).

[227] Cp. Winter, S. G. (1987); Allegrezza, S. (1998).

[228] Cp. Mirow, M. (2000); Pettis, C. R. (1995a), pp. 70-76; Pettis, C. R. (1995b); Aaker, D. A. (1996), pp. 12-13.

[229] Cp. Hirschleifer, J. (1971); Kitch, E. W. (1977); Teece, D. J. (1986); Ghemawat, P. (1986); Rumelt, R. P. (1987); Amit, R. & Schoemaker, P. J. H. (1993); Geroski, P. (1995); Edvinsson, L. & Sullivan, P. H. (1996).

companies, however, have to invest significant financial resources and time in the attainment of these complementary assets.[230]

III.3.2.3 Complementary Resources

As previously mentioned, complementary assets are closely interlinked with lead-time-advantages since these resources can be established at low costs by the leading company. Succeeding companies, however, have to invest considerable resources in their establishment or cannot at all acquire or create such assets. Thus, such complementary resources constitute considerable market entry barriers. We can distinguish two principle types:

1. Generic complementary assets; and
2. Innovation specific or specialised complementary assets.[231]

Companies can acquire *generic complementary assets* on the free market or gain access to such assets by contractual agreements. Moreover, these generic complementary assets are used in the commercialisation of several different technological applications. Consequently, the economic value of such an assets is only marginally affected by the introduction of a new innovation. In addition, it can be presumed that such generic complementary assets are supplied under almost perfect market conditions. On the other hand, we have to distinguish *specialised* or *innovation specific complementary assets* that can be used strategically. As Teece (1986) has pointed out, such specialised complementary assets have to be specifically developed or at least adapted with respect to an innovation. Thus, such innovation specific complementary assets are not available on the market and hence represent a strategic resource in the sense of the definition given in chapter I.2.[232]

Examples of such innovation specific complementary resources are the access to scarce natural resources, complementary process know-how, or market based assets such as an established customer list, distribution, or

[230] Bayer AG was the first company able to establish a strong brand in the market for analgesic which has enabled the company to appropriate revenues from its innovation 'acetylsalicylic acid' far beyond the maximum official duration of the patent right (see for a detailed discussion chap. II.2).

[231] Cp. Teece, D. J. (1986); Geroski, P. (1995); Sullivan, P. H. & Edvinsson, L. (1996).

[232] A strategic resource is defined by its economic value, scarcity, and difficulty to imitate and/or substitute (cf. chap. IV.1).

brand name.[233] These complementary resources generate, in addition to the innovation, economic value that can be skimmed off by higher margins. In fact, the owner of such specialised complementary resources can tap the totality of the innovation-rent, or as Sullivan & Edvinsson (1996) have stressed:

> "... *controlling the specific complementary assets is equivalent to controlling the underlying intellectual asset and the ultimate commercial value of an intellectual assets. This has the advantage of protecting a technology without having to reveal the technology itself.*"[234]

The control over such innovation specific complementary assets enables a company to appropriate the revenues generated by its innovation far beyond the official length of the patent rights. One of the best known examples is Coca-Cola which has achieved a long-lasting appropriation of the revenues generated by its innovation, the 'original mixture', by trade secret protection and a strong complementary brand name which represents a specialised complementary resource. Moreover, the established distribution channels of large business enterprises in the pharmaceutical industry represent specialised complementary assets. Companies newly entering such a market have to invest considerable financial resources and time in the establishment of distribution channels so that a direct access to the pharmaceutical market is generally foiled.[235]

III.3.3 Choice of Efficient Protection Mode for Technological Assets

As shown in the preceding chapters, companies have a multitude of alternative protection mechanisms to protect their immaterial assets and hence to appropriate the generated revenues. The problem of the companies is, however, to *determine the most efficient protection mode* with regard to the intangible asset's economic value, the observability of the innovation on the product or service, the speed of technological obsolescence, the way of envisaged utilisation of the asset, and the geographic dissemination, as well as the position of the invention in the technology life-cycle.

---

[233] See for a more detailed discussion of the role of complementary brands and distribution channels chap. IV.

[234] Sullivan, P. H. & Edvinsson, L. (1996), p. 258.

[235] Cp. Liebeskind, J. P., Oliver, A. L. et al. (1996).

The following section first analyses the optimal protection of intangibles in respect to the nature of the asset. Subsequently, we outline the role of the technology life-cycle, as well as the increasing globalisation of markets and thus the need to ensure an international protection and international transferability of immaterial assets.

Efficient Protection of Intangible Assets in Respect to Their Nature

As analysed before, patents do not always present the optimal and/or preferred mode of safeguarding technological innovations. Companies often regard lead-time-advantages and trade secrecy as more efficient protection mechanisms than intellectual property rights. However, the efficiency of the alternative modes of protection is not constant across industries and innovation types. According to the survey of Levin, Klevorick et al. (1987) companies in the pharmaceutical, chemical, steel, as well as petroleum refining industries rate patents as efficient protection of their inventions (cf. Table III.4).[236] Yet, we have to distinguish between product and process inventions within the same industry. Producers of steel mill products, for example, rate product patents as an effective protection method, process patents, however, as rather deficient method of safeguarding process inventions. Although the study of Levin, Klevorick et al. (1987) represents to date the most extensive investigation on different appropriation methods in various industries, one has to bear in mind the general shortcomings of survey based investigation. Thus, even though the study included a total of 803 companies the sample companies still only presents a sub-sample of the total population and more importantly, the results may be subject to personal bias of the persons having completed the survey.

As table III.4 clearly shows, patents are rated across all industries as a more efficient means of protecting *product innovations* than *process innovations*. This is attributable to the fact that product innovations can be easily ascertained by analysing the product. Process innovations, on the other hand, are often not detectable on the final product and can, in general, be protected against imitation by keeping them secret behind the company walls.[237] Moreover, a process patent is rather difficult to enforce since the owner can often not detect infringements of his property. Thus, in the case of process innovations, trade secrecy often represents the most efficient protection mode which can be enforced at low costs. In this

[236] Cp. Arundel, A. & Kabla, I. (1998), who have conducted a more recent but less extensive study on European companies.

[237] Cp. Winter, S. G. (1987); Levin, R. C., Klevorick, A. K. (1987); EPO (1994); Pisano, G. P. & Wheelwright, S. C. (1995); Arundel, A. & Kabla, I. (1998).

respect, however, we have to mark-off innovations that can be readily detected on the product. In the case of such innovations that can be imitated by competitors by simple reproduction, intellectual property rights, e.g., patents, represent the most effective protection mode against misappropriation and imitation.

Table III.4: Effectiveness of process- and product patents in industries

	Process patents		**Product patents**	
Industry	**Mean[a)]**	**Standard error**	**Mean[a)]**	**Standard error**
Pulp, paper, and paperboard	2.6	0.3	3.3	0.4
Cosmetics	2.9	0.3	4.1	0.4
Inorganic chemicals	4.6	0.4	5.2	0.3
Organic chemicals	4.1	0.3	6.1	0.2
Drugs	4.9	0.3	6.5	0.1
Plastic materials	4.6	0.3	5.4	0.3
Plastic products	3.2	0.3	4.9	0.3
Petroleum refining	4.9	0.4	4.3	0.4
Steel mill products	3.5	0.7	5.1	0.6
Pumps and pumping equipment	3.2	0.4	4.4	0.5
Motors, generators, and controls	2.7	0.3	3.5	0.5
Computers	3.3	0.4	3.4	0.4
Communications equipment	3.1	0.3	3.6	0.3
Semiconductors	3.2	0.4	4.5	0.4
Motor vehicle parts	3.7	0.4	4.5	0.4
Aircraft and parts	3.1	0.5	3.8	0.4
Measuring devices	3.6	0.3	3.9	0.3
Medical instruments	3.2	0.4	4.7	0.4
Full sample	3.5	0.06	4.3	0.07

Source: Levin, R. C., Klevorick, A. K. et al. (1987), p. 797.
a) Range: 1=not at all effective; 7=very effective

The *rule of thumb*, to protect observable innovations by intellectual property rights and non-observable innovations, e.g., process innovations, by trade secrecy and internal use, also applies to non-technological innovations. An innovation in the distribution process, for example, can be protected efficiently by secrecy and the internalisation of its use. In contrast, an innovation in the realm of marketing which has the aim to be recognised on the market, can be safeguarded by the registration of a trademark or slogan.

Efficient Protection of Intangible Assets in Respect to Their Position in the Technology Life-cycle

Any technology goes through a certain life-cycle just as a product. The *technology life-cycle* starts with the first invention of a particular product- or process technology which is brought to market in the second, so called innovation phase. In the third and last phase of the technology life-cycle, the standardisation phase, the technology represents merely basic knowledge which is mastered by the majority of the companies active in the specific market (cf. figure III.20). In the final phase the technology does no longer generate any competitive advantage.

As Magee (1977) has pointed out, the *position of a technology in the life-cycle* has a considerable influence on the appropriability of the returns generated by the technology, as well as the possibility to effectively protect the technology against imitation. The choice of protection mode is thus not a constant, but rather a *dynamic process* that has to be determined in accordance to the technology's position in the life-cycle. As can be seen in figure III.20, the technology life-cycle is split up in the three phases: Invention, innovation, and standardisation. The appropriation of revenues is decreasing along the technology life-cycle and hence is characterised by a decreasing function in respect to the technology's maturity.[238]

Magee (1977) assumed that a company can perfectly protect an invention by trade secrecy, patents, and further intellectual property rights and hence an invention can be traded on an open market. In the second phase which is defined by the first market introduction of the invention, the effectiveness of patents and trade secrets starts already to diminish. This reduction in the appropriability is due to the expiration of patents and the autonomous discovery of the invention by competitors. In the standardisation phase, all companies active in the market are knowledgeable about the innovation and the inventing company can no longer appropriate the revenues generated by the technology in question.

Building on these assumptions a *sequence of action* for inventing companies can be derived which maximises the period of time over which the company can appropriate the returns generated by its invention. In the invention phase a company can efficiently appropriate the revenues generated by the invention by means of *intellectual property rights* and alternative modes of protection. However, in the innovation phase the effectiveness of these measures is deteriorating and companies have to fall back on the use of other means, e.g., the *internalisation* of the utilisation of the information. In order to be able to benefit from its technological

[238] Cp. Magee, S. P. (1977).

invention even in the standardisation phase, however, the company has to build up and/or internalise *innovation specific complementary assets* in advance or at least in an early stage of its market introduction.

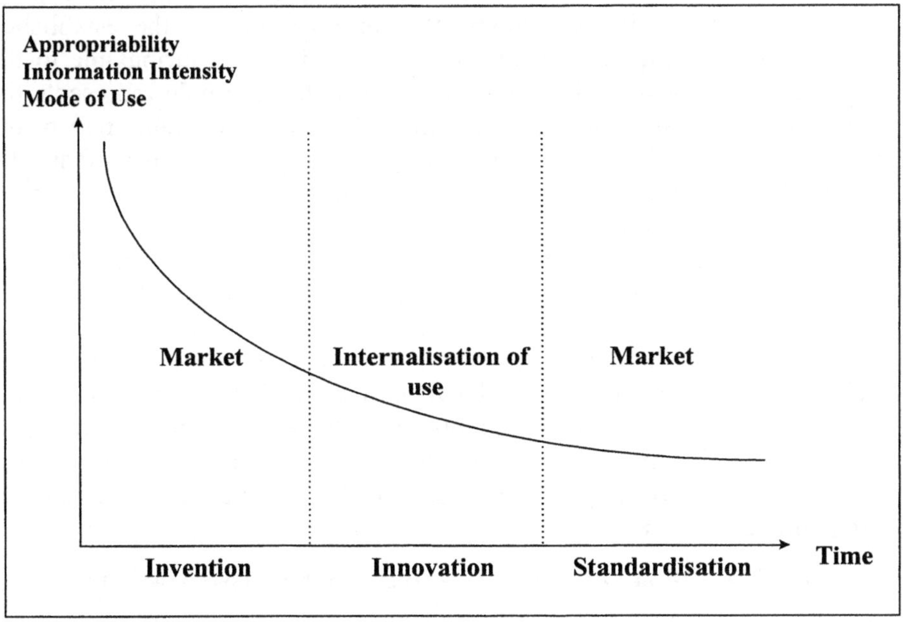

Figure III.20: Technology-life-cycle according to Magee (1977)

These specialised complementary resources which represent a *bottleneck* in the particular industry, enable a company to appropriate revenues generated by its invention in the long-term and thus even in the standardisation phase. The company can use its information advantage which it possesses in advance to the market introduction of its invention, to acquire or build up specialised complementary assets at low cost. These innovation specific complementary assets constitute significant market entry barriers and thus represent a key success factor for companies facing weak or expiring intellectual property rights.[239] Such specialised complementary assets are among others scarce natural resources needed for the production of the innovative product, process technologies bestowing the company with a cost advantage vis-à-vis its competitors, knowledge in other technology fields which competitors still have to be build up in tedious learning processes, but also other intangible assets such

[239] Cp. Hirschleifer, J. (1971); Teece, D. J. (1986); Rumelt, R. P. (1987); Lawless, M. W. & Fisher, R. J. (1990); Sullivan, P. H. & Edvinsson, L. (1996).

as established customer relationships, distribution channels, brand names, and image.[240]

The company Borden, for example, which was the first to sell processed lemon juice, could realise even after the arriving of competitors a price premium of 50% vis-à-vis comparable products due to the established brand name and the high customer loyalty which was attributable to the high risk-averseness of the consumers.[241] Another example represents the company Bayer AG which can still appropriate a considerable part of the revenues generated by its innovation *acetylsalicylic acid* more than 100 years after the initial market introduction due to the possession of a strong complementary brand.[242]

Thus, we can establish the thesis that the choice of the most effective protection mode is not solely influenced by the nature of the intangible asset (product or process) in question, but also by the position of the immaterial asset in the technology life-cycle. The choice of the most effective protection mode to achieve a sustainable appropriation of the revenues of an innovation is not a one-time decision, but rather a dynamic process. This dynamic process calls for the adaptation of the appropriation mode according to the particular phase of the life-cycle of the intangible technological assets.

Efficient Protection of Intangible Assets in Globalised Markets

Another factor which has to be taken into consideration while determining the optimal method of protection of a certain intangible asset, is the intended *degree of global diversification* in commercialisation and utilisation. This represents in particular in relation to process innovations an extremely critical factor. If a company wishes to exploit a certain process innovation uniquely in one production site it will choose a diverging protection strategy than if it plans to utilise the process in various locations situated in different nations. In addition, in the case of a product innovation that a company plans to commercialise in international markets, it has to respect certain principles in order to achieve an effective protection for its innovation.

In order to be able to obtain patent protection, companies must completely codify the underlying intangible assets. This codification of knowledge increases the inter- and intra-company transferability and decreases the transfer costs of these immaterial assets considerably.[243] In

[240] For a detailed discussion see chap. III.3.2 as well as chap. II.2 and II.3.
[241] Cp. Ghemawat, P. (1986).
[242] Cp. chap. II.2.
[243] Cp. Foray, D. (1995).

the case of *product innovations* which the company wishes to utilise at different internationally dispersed production sites and which can be efficiently protected by intellectual property rights, at least for a limited period of time, the codification of the knowledge has some important advantages. By codifying the knowledge and information the company can rapidly and at low costs transfer the intangible assets to the different international production sites.

However, in the case of *process innovations* the codification of the knowledge and their protection by intellectual property rights is usually not the preferred mode, since the detection of property right infringements appears to be extremely difficult.[244] Consequently, companies usually follow a strategy of the internalisation of the use and trade secret protection of their process innovations. A specific problem of the international exploitation of process innovations presents, however, their *transfer* and use in different subsidiaries. On the one hand, knowledge protected by secrecy is usually not codified and hence its transfer is associated with high costs. On the other hand, the cost of trade secret protection which mainly represents control cost, increases disproportionately with the rising diffusion of the knowledge across several subsidiaries and thus increasing number of people initiated into the secret. In this respect it has to be reconsidered that foreign subsidiaries frequently cover a smaller part of the value-chain and consequently show a closer collaboration with external suppliers. This co-operation with external partners necessitates a more intense communication and integration of the latter which again increases the risk of unravelling and diffusing the knowledge protected by trade secrecy. Subsequently, the utilisation of process knowledge protected by secrecy should be centralised at one location with a minimum of persons involved. This again does not imply that the final-products cannot be commercialised on international markets, but rather the centralisation of the utilisation of the intangible assets and the implementation of an export strategy.

In the case of intangible assets protected by intellectual property rights, companies have to make sure to attain legal protection in the *most important national markets*. Furthermore, companies face a multitude of different possible ways and methods of application of which they have to chose the least expensive and most advantageous for their particular case (cf. figure III.21). A company can, for example, file for patent protection of its innovation at various national patent offices independently which is, however, associated with relatively high administrative efforts. Moreover, this approach necessitates the filing of individual patent applications in the

[244] Cp. Winter, S. G. (1987); Arundel, A. & Kabla, I. (1998).

respective national language, as well as a separate examination of the patentability of its innovation at each individual national patent office. On the other hand, in the case of cumulative applications, application costs are considerably higher as in the case of an application at a supranational patent office which allows for patent protection in several national markets at the same time, e.g., the EPO. Then again, in the case of patent application or trademark registration at the EPO, companies have the choice between three different, alternative ways: Initial national, PCT, or direct EPO application (cf. figure III.21).

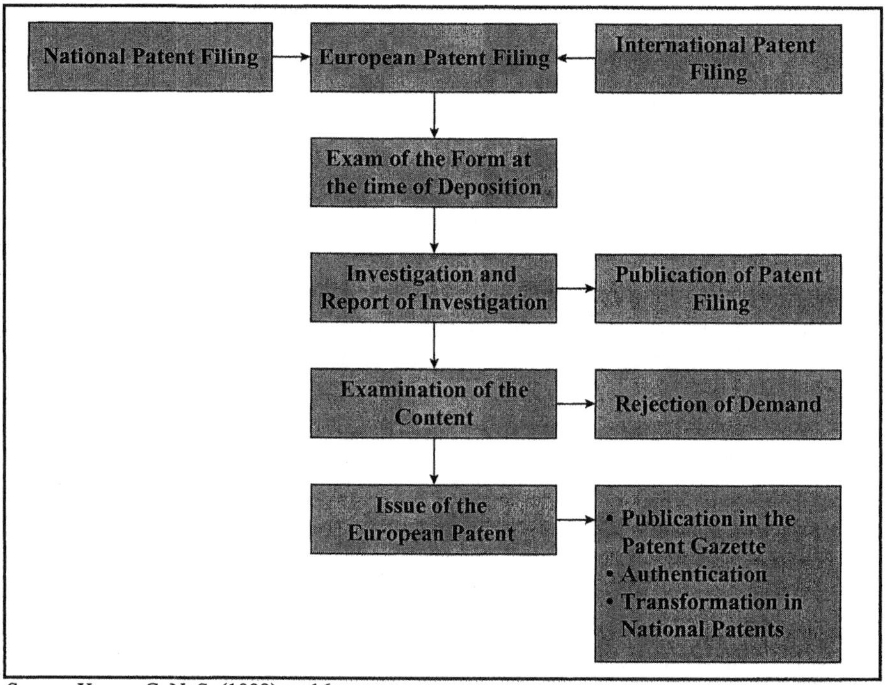

Source: Xuyen, G. N. S. (1998), p. 16.

Figure III.21: Possible ways to apply for a European patent

In the case of a *direct application* for patent protection of a certain intangible asset at the EPO, a company can file an application for a patent in one of the three official languages which can cover up to 15 national markets within the EU. However, since the EPO does not substitute for the different national patent offices, a company can also follow the way of a first national application within the EU and, by keeping the term of 12 months, apply subsequently for an European patent which will expand the property right to other EU countries. A last possible way, according to the *'Patent Co-operation Treaty' (PCT)*, is the international patent application at a national patent office. Such an international application can result in the protection of the innovation in up to 43 countries, e.g., USA, Japan, and all EU countries.[245]

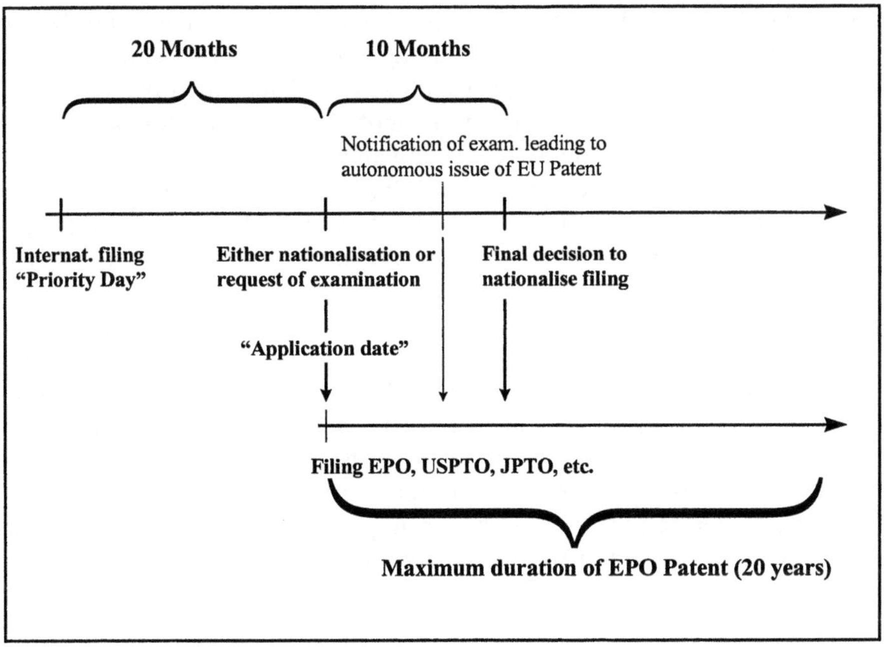

Figure III.22: Process of PCT application

The European patent has a maximum duration of 20 years which starts with the submission of the patent application at either the national or supranational patent office. In the past years, PCT applications have considerably increased in popularity. The rising number of PCT applications can be attributed to delayed company decisions into which particular national markets to apply for patent protection (cf. figure III.22). These subsequent national applications, however, are accompanied by significant application costs.[246]

As figure III.22 visualises, the respective national patent office allows a company a period of 20 months to decide between the *nationalisation* and the *request of examination* of its international patent application. In the case of nationalisation, a company has to decide at which national patent offices to apply for patent protection and to translate the document into the

[245] Cp. Schmoch, U. (1990), pp. 23; Xuyen, G. N. S. (1998).

[246] According to Maser the translation cost already accumulate to several DM 10.000 for one national application. Cp. Sahl, C., Xuyen, G. N. S. et al. (1998).

respective national languages. If a company decides after the period of 20 month to request an examination of its application, it will be allowed another 10 months for deciding where to file for patent protection. If a PCT application is submitted to the EPO, the company will be notified about the success chances of its patent application and this notification may already lead to an autonomous assignation of an European patent. The expiration date of the European patent will be determined on the basis of the *priority day* so that a company cannot provoke a prolongation of the overall protection duration by requesting an examination of its application.

As seen in this section, companies have to take multiple factors into consideration in order to achieve an effective protection of their intangible assets. The most important factors are the *nature of the immaterial asset*, its *position in the technology-life-cycle*, as well as the *geographic dispersion of the exploitation and utilisation* of the asset in question. Nowadays, in a world characterised by increasingly globalised markets and shortening product and technology life-cycles, a rapid exploitation of intangible assets on a global scale and hence their global protection becomes increasingly important. In this respect Mossinghoff (1994) has pointed out the role of intellectual property rights in entering new national markets. Nevertheless, in view of the important role intellectual property rights play in the international protection of immaterial assets and the numerous agreements established on a multilateral level, such as the Madrid agreements, TRIPS, or the establishment of the WIPO,[247] one should not forget the problems associated with the laxity of many nations in enforcing these rights. This constitutes not only a severe problem with regard to trademarks and brand names, but equally concerns patents and copyrights.

III.3.4 Upshot III: Intangible Assets and Their Effective Protection in Globalised Markets

This chapter has illustrated the numerous possibilities innovating companies have to protect their intangible assets from imitation or replication. The most important and widespread means is the filing of intellectual property rights, e.g., patents, trademarks, copyrights, petty-patents. These intellectual ownership rights are opposed by further possibilities of protection, such as trade secrecy, lead-time-advantages, and

[247] The WIPO has been established to improve the protection of intellectual property in the world by co-operating with numerous nations and to administration of multilateral agreements which focus on legal and administrative issues of intellectual property rights (www.wipo.org [05.2000])

complementary assets, to name but a few. The efficiency of the general applicability of the individual measures is heavily influenced by the characteristics of the individual immaterial asset. A company can, for example, only protect technological inventions by patent rights that show the characteristic of newness, economic value, and are revealed in an innovative activity. Assets not fulfilling the criteria have to be protected by alternative methods.

The costs of protection also play a decisive role in the company's choice of appropriation mode. If a company protects its intangible assets by trade secrecy and internal use, the costs of protection only arise if the asset appears to have an economic value. In contrast, in the case of intellectual property right protection a company already incurs costs by applying for protection and hence before even knowing the value of the asset or its general possibility of protection. The argument of cost-value relation in trade secret protection has, however, to be put into perspective by the disproportional increase in protection cost by rising value of the intellectual asset and the insecure length of protection duration. Patent rights, on the other hand, show further advantages in the international protection of immaterial assets, since these rights are internationally enforceable. Last but not least, the filing of a patent forces the company to codify the underlying information and knowledge which in turn significantly decrease the transfer costs of the knowledge.

The efficiency of the different protection modes is again influenced by the nature of the intangible asset in question. Studies have shown that companies perceive trade secret protection and lead-time-advantages as superior protection modes for process inventions compared to patent rights. This inefficiency of process patents which can be traced back to the difficulties in recognising property right infringements, forces companies to protect such innovations by trade secrecy, complementary resources, and/or the exploitation of lead-time-advantages.

In general we can assert that the choice of the effective protection mode is a dynamic process and not a one-time decision. Along the technology life-cycle which can be distinguished in three principal phases, the effectiveness as well as the possibility to protect intangible assets with a certain mode changes. In the invention and early innovation phase, companies can effectively protect their immaterial assets by intellectual property rights or trade secrecy. However, in the innovation phase patents start to expire and the risk of revelation of the innovation protected by trade secrecy increases. Thus, in order to guarantee a long lasting protection of an innovation, a company has to establish specialised complementary resources during early stages of a technology's life-cycle. Such innovation specific complementary resources allow a company to appropriate the revenues of its innovation in the long-term, and sometimes even in the standardisation phase.

A last factor which has experienced an important rise in magnitude, is the protection of intangible assets in international markets. In this respect a company has to distinguish, in particular regarding process innovations, between the international commercialisation and the international use of its assets. If a company intends to use its process know-how at different national production sites it is considered to be advantageous to file for intellectual property right protection. Conversely, if the company has the objective to concentrate the use of the process knowledge at one location only, a strategy of trade secret protection appears superior. With respect to product innovations that are usually easily observable on the final product, intellectual property rights protection shows substantial advantages.

As shown in the preceding discussion, the choice of the efficient and long lasting protection mechanism for its immaterial assets is influenced by the nature of the asset, its position in the technology life-cycle, and the degree of the planned international diversification in use and commercialisation of the intangible asset. This leads to the thesis of chapter III.3.

Thesis II:
The selection of the efficient protection mode for a particular intangible asset is determined by its nature, its position in the technology life-cycle, as well as, the intended international diversification in use and commercialisation of the asset. The effectiveness of a particular protection modes is not constant along the technology life-cycle and thus the choice of protection mechanism represents a dynamic process.

IV Strategic Management of Intangible Assets

IV.1 Intangible Technological Assets as a Strategic Resource

The discussion of the economic role of intangible assets and the problem of appropriation of revenues created by these assets, outlined in chapter III, dates back to Arrow (1962a). The purpose of chapter III has been to point out the distinctive characteristics of intangible assets, as well as to establish a clear and coherent classification of immaterial assets which clarifies and facilitates the further discussion. Moreover, we have revealed the most important sources and discussed the central protection modes of immaterial assets within business enterprises. Of key importance for our further discussion are the public good characteristics of immaterial assets and the efficient protection mode decision process which is characterised by a dynamic process.[1] Although patent rights are an effective protection mode of intangible technological innovations in early phases of the technological invention, companies can only achieve a sustainable appropriation of an innovation's returns by establishing specific complementary assets.

Building on the framework established in the preceding chapter, we point out the strategic role of immaterial technological assets in business enterprises and in this respect examine the central significance of *sustainability*, turning such an intangible asset into a persistent competitive advantage. The following discussion focuses on the strategic relevance of intangible technical assets, examines the role of complementary brand equity in the appropriation of intangible technological assets, and develops a model of complementary brand equity which allows for a sustainable competitive advantage. In this context we adopt the widely accepted definition of a competitive strategy established by Chandler who has defined a company's strategy as:

> *"... the determination of long-term goals and objective of an enterprise, and the adoption of courses of action and the allocation of resources necessary for carrying out these goals."*[2]

Thus, a strategy represents a set of competencies and the provision of resources employed in the attainment of long-term goals. As has been pointed out by various authors, such goals are the establishment of

---

[1] Cf. thesis I and II of chap. III.

[2] Stopford, J. M. & Wells, L. T. (1972), p. 26.

competitive advantages that are sustainable in the long-term and create returns that can be appropriated by the company in question.[3] Consequently, the foundation of a company's competitive position is the set of existing resources and competencies which can be employed to build product features that appeal to customers.[4] According to Porter, such competitive advantages can be divided into two essential types: *lower cost* than rivals, or the capability to *differentiate* one's products and services and thereby command a premium price that exceeds the extra cost incurred by differentiation.[5] Any superior performance of a company can be attributed to the achievement of one or both advantages. However, as widely accepted, a certain strategy must be *sustainable* vis-à-vis competitors, this implies that there exist barriers that make the imitation of a company's advantage difficult.[6] The distinctive characteristics of such strategic resources and/or capabilities which create sustainable competitive advantage and explain persistent firm heterogeneity, are their *economic value* (generation of consumer benefit), their *non-imitability* and *substitutability*, as well as *rareness* among a company's actual and potential competitors.[7] Consequently, a certain innovation that does not show these distinctive characteristics may generate a financial return, but it does not create a defendable advantage and hence does not influence the company's competitive position.[8]

Sustainability

So far we have identified the characteristics of company resources and competencies that have the potential to create a sustainable competitive advantage, however, at that point the question arises of how long is sustainable? Reed & DeFilippi (1990) have argued that the *duration* of sustainability is linked to the *planning horizon* of a firm and consequently the question of how long is sustainable rests specific to each individual

---

[3] Cp. Coyne, K. P. (1986); Aaker, D. A. (1989); Porter, M. E. (1991); Grant, R. M. (1998), chap. 9; Grant, R. M (1997).

[4] Cp. Hauser, J. R. & Simme, P. (1981); Porter, M. E. (1985), chap. 1; Coyne, K. P. (1986); Clark, K. (1987); Hall, R. (1992; 1993).

[5] Cp. Kline, S. J. & Rosenberg, N. (1986); Aaker, D. A. (1989); Porter, M. E. (1991; 1996).

[6] Cp. Barney, J. B. (1986; 1991); Clark, K. (1987); Dierickx, I. & Cool, K. (1989); Lawless, M. W. & Fisher, R. J. (1990).

[7] Cp. Wernerfelt, B. (1984); Coyne, K. P. (1986); Prahalad, C. K. & Hamel, G. (1990); Aaker, D. A. (1989); Reed, R. & DeFilippi, J. R. (1990); Barney, J. B. (1991); Amit, R. & Schoemaker, P. J. H. (1993); Henderson, R. & Cockburn, I. (1994); Teece, D. J., Pisano, G. et al. (1997); Durand, T. (1998; 2000).

[8] Cp. Clark, K. (1987).

company. According to Porter (1985), sustainability is achieved when *barriers of imitation* exist:

> *"The sustainability of a generic strategy requires that a firm possesses some barriers that make imitation of the strategy difficult."*[9]

Lippman & Rumelt (1982), among others, have stressed the key importance of *causal ambiguity* encompassing a company's activities and outcomes that create a substantial imitation barrier by making it extremely difficult for competitors to emulate a certain strategy.[10] Reed & DeFilippi (1990) have identified three characteristics of resources or competencies that can generate causal ambiguity individually or in combination which are: *Tacitness*, *complexity*, and *specificity*.

An important enigma initially stated by Polanyi is, that individuals know more than they can actually explain.[11] Thus, crucial to *tacitness* is the lack of ability of even specialised and skilled players to codify the rules and practices underlying performance. Consequently, tacitness creates ambiguity due to the unawareness of the underlying actions that create an advantage and hence the relationship between actions and outcomes is not obvious and rests incomprehensible to rivals.[12] Subsequently, tacitness provokes causal ambiguity and factor immobility resulting in imitation barriers.

Complexity, on the other hand, arises from the combination of a large number of different technologies, routines, and experiences. As Nelson & Winter (1982) have pointed out, the scale and complexity of competencies make it impossible for any one person to have a sufficient understanding of the individual parts in order to understand the entire relationship between inputs and the performance of a company. Consequently, a company's competitive advantage is not put in jeopardy when individual employees are enticed by competitors, or, as MacMillan, McCaffery et al. (1985) have stressed:

> *"If a new product requires extensive reorganization of interdependent procedures and/or the co-ordination of many skills and multiple departments, the product is considered to be complex. We argue here that the more complex the product, the greater the logistic problem of*

[9] Porter, M. E. (1985), p. 20; and cp. Jacobsen, R. (1988).

[10] Cp. Lippman, S. A. & Rumelt, R. P. (1982); Nelson, R. R. & Winter, S. G. (1982), chap. 5; Dierickx, I. & Cool, K. (1989); Reed, R. & DeFilippi, J. R. (1990); Lei, D. T. (1997).

[11] Cp. Winter, S. G. (1987); Kogut, B. & Zander, U. (1992); Nonaka, I. (1994); Senker, J. (1995).

[12] Cp. Nelson, R. R. & Winter, S. G. (1982), chap. 5; Reed, R. & DeFilippi, R. J. (1990); Chesbrough, H. W. & Teece, D. J. (1996).

revising existing procedure, policies and programmes to incorporate the required activities. Therefore, response time will be longer the greater the complexity."[13]

Subsequently, we can affirm, a company's superior performance is difficult to imitate by competitors if the advantage is the outcome of the fusion of various technologies and/or scientific fields which creates complexity and in consequence ambiguity. Hence, *complexity can be defined as a factor creating ambiguity* and thus barriers to imitation.

The last factor generating ambiguity and consequently barriers to imitation is *specificity*. By means of continuous transactions companies invest in their relationships with its stakeholders, e.g., suppliers, customers, and thereby establish transaction specific relations with these parties. Consequently, the *relationships* a company establishes and maintains with its transaction partners by means of its resources and competencies are highly specific and interdependent with the individual internal or external partner.[14] Thus, such company specific relationships are highly ambiguous and represent significant imitation barriers for competitors.

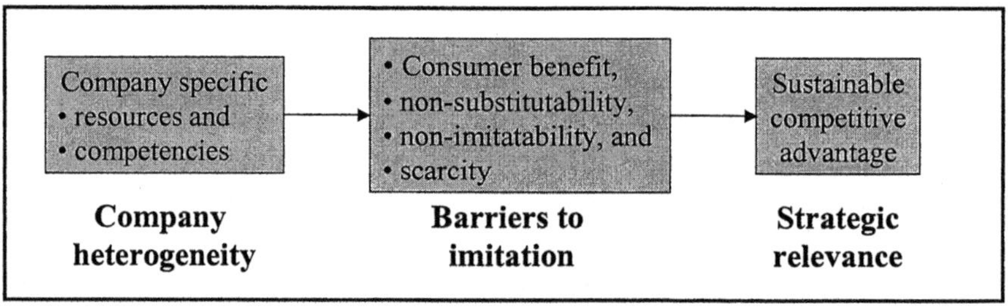

Figure IV.1: Resources, capabilities, and competitive advantage

Another factor that has often been neglected in the strategic discussion of sustainability are *legal barriers* to imitation. Such regulatory arrangements, e.g., patents, copyrights, trademarks, can constitute important barriers to imitation thwarting any attempt of competitors to directly imitate a certain successful company strategy. This specific imitation barrier and its strategic relevance are discussed in more detail in chapter IV.1.

---

[13] MacMillan, I., McCaffery, M. L. et al. (1985), p.77.

[14] Cp. Reed, R. & De Filippi, R. J. (1990); Dyer, J. H. (1997).

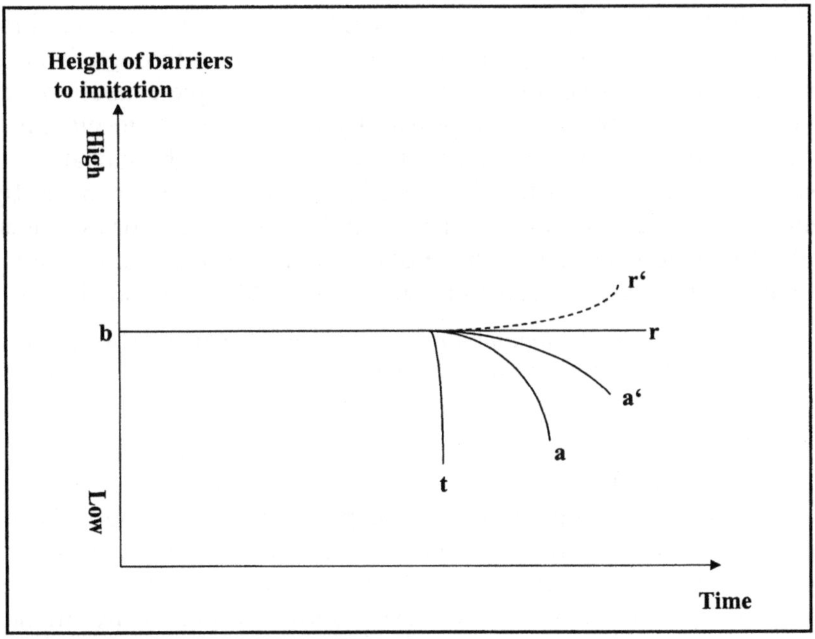

Source: Reed, R. & DeFilippi, R. J. (1990), p.97.

Figure IV.2: Decay in barriers to imitation

As presented in Figure IV.1, companies are endowed with specific resources and competencies that explain prevailing *company heterogeneity*.[15] These company specific resources and competencies create a sustainable competitive advantage if barriers prevail which render the imitation and/or substitution of these resources and competencies and thus the consumer benefit difficult for competitors. In consequence, we can define idiosyncratic company resources and competencies protected by barriers to imitation as sustainable competitive advantages. The imitation barriers protecting these advantages, no matter how pronounced they are, are, however, never insurmountable and subject to decay.[16] Reed & DeFilippi (1990) have argued that ambiguity and competition are the key variables which influence the height and decay of barriers to imitation. In order to achieve sustainability decay must be overcome by *reinvesting* in the factors creating ambiguity and consequently to up-hold barriers to imitation.

---

[15] Cp. Barney, J. (1991); Amit, R. & Schoemaker, P. J. H. (1993); Lei, D. T. (1997); Pearce, R. & Papanastassiou, M. (1999).

[16] Cp. Porter, M. E. (1985; 1991) chap. 1; Ghemawat, P. (1986); Reed, R. & DeFilippi, R. J. (1990); Markides, C. C. (1999).

As illustrated in figure IV.2, the heights and decay rates of different imitation barriers vary significantly. A certain breakthrough innovation, for example, can lead to the immediate and complete abolition of an imitation barrier, or opens the possibility to competitors to circumvent a certain barrier. The case of a technological breakthrough innovation which instantly overcomes existing barriers, is shown by line b-t in the figure. However, companies also have the possibility to maintain or even increase imitation barriers and thus resist erosion by reinvesting in ambiguity (line b-r and b-r' respectively). Accordingly, Porter (1985) has stated:

> *"Since barriers to imitation are never insurmountable, however, it is usually necessary for a firm to offer a moving target to its competitors by investing in order to continually improve its position."*[17]

Building on the systematic of company resources and competencies and sustainable competitive advantage chapter IV.1 analyses the strategic role of technological intangible assets and points out the importance of the appropriation of the economic returns generated by strategic resources and competencies. Chapter IV.2 investigates the role of complementary brand equity in the appropriation of the returns generated by immaterial technological assets. In this context we develop a definition of the term 'complementary brand equity' and analyse how such complementary assets can be build by companies. Chapters IV.1 and IV.2 constitute the cornerstones of our discussions in chapter IV which lead to the development of the model of complementary brand equity for the sustainable appropriation of intangible technological assets presented in chapter IV.3. This model discusses the relationship between technological inventions, patent protection, and market based assets. As is pointed out, the close interrelation between technological inventions, patents, and market based assets and the particular characteristics of brand equity give these assets an important strategic role in the appropriation of technological improvements in the long-term. Finally, chapter IV.4 discusses the organisational implications of the developed model and presents general management tools of how business companies can integrate brand equity and technology strategies at the process level so as to allow for an efficient appropriation of the returns of technological innovations in the long-run.

[17] Porter, M. E. (1985), p. 20.

IV.1.1 Strategic Role of Intangible Technological Assets in the Competitiveness of Business Enterprises

As shown above, a company's competencies and resources can be sources of sustainable competitive advantage and thus are of strategic relevance if the company uses these resources and competencies to build product features and services that appeal to the marketplace and if these resources and competencies are rare, not substitutable, as well as if barriers to imitation exist. These criteria do equally apply to tangible, as well as to intangible company assets. However, as Durand (1998) has pointed out:

> *"...any tangible resource can be identified, described and thus imitated, if not acquired. The imitability criteria put forward by Prahalad & Hamel requires intangibility ...."*[18]

Thus, intangible assets have some characteristics that make these assets, from a strategic viewpoint, particularly important. But, what are these characteristics and how do they influence the strategic significance of immaterial company strengths?

In the past, authors have particularly stressed the importance of the ambiguity surrounding intangible assets, as well as the complementary nature of company strengths forming a competitive advantage. In the following sections we analyse the ambiguity surrounding intangible assets and its influence on existing barriers to imitation. Building on the ambiguity argument, we then enlarge the discussion to the field of complementary firm strengths constituting a competitive advantage and the ability of competing companies imitating or substituting and thus offsetting an advantage. Last but not least, we take up the point of regulatory barriers to imitation and their strategic importance in respect to codified intellectual technological capital. In the last section of chapter IV.1.1 we then analyse company strategies that up-hold or even enhance existing imitation barriers and hence warrant persistent entry deterrence.

IV.1.1.1 Intangible Asset Ambiguity and Barriers to Imitation

An argument brought forward by numerous authors is that company advantages based on tangible assets can be scrutinised, illustrated and thus copied or even bought on the market. Consequently, such advantages can be easily imitated or substituted by competitors. In contrast, intangible resources are generally never entirely understood nor can they be easily identified and examined and therefore, imitation or substitution of such

[18] Durand, T. (1998), p.309.

advantages by competitors is extremely difficult. The argument presented is that physical assets are mostly explicit and contain codified information that can be easily revealed by meticulous observation or reengineering. Thus, tangible assets show a lower level of ambiguity. Intangible assets, on the other hand, are more difficult to observe than physical assets and, more importantly, any form of intangible asset, tacit or explicit, contains always a certain *tacit dimension*.[19] Accordingly, Polanyi has stressed:

> *"...these two [tacit and explicit knowledge] are not sharply divided. While tacit knowledge can be possessed by itself, explicit knowledge must rely on being tacitly understood and applied. Hence all knowledge is either tacit or rooted in tacit knowledge."*[20]

Any immaterial asset can thus be located on a scale of tacitness ranging from low to high degrees of tacitness, but never being entirely explicit. Therefore, the less codified and thus the more *tacit* the intangible asset in question, the more ambiguous and consequently more difficult to imitate is the advantage for competitors.[21]

Moreover, the imitation of a company's intangible assets, e.g., knowledge, know-how, competencies, brand names, etc., which can constitute a strategic advantage, requires the imitation and/or undergoing of irreversible investments, learning, and sometimes even the replication of the entire development path of the company holding the desired advantage. Hence, the perfect imitation of an advantage built on immaterial assets is almost never feasible or at least extremely difficult.[22] Even in the case of intangible assets being reconsidered as codified and/or explicit by a certain individual or group, the underlying codified knowledge in question may not be comprehensible and thus of any value to other persons. This is due to the *cumulative nature* of most technological knowledge and the *specific code* used in codification. So, people and groups of people not knowing the code are excluded from using the knowledge or at least have to incur considerable costs and time in order to become skilled in reading the code and using the knowledge.[23] Or, as Saviotti (1998) has stated:

> *"... even a completely codified piece of knowledge could not be used at zero cost by everyone. Only agents who know the 'code' can use the piece of knowledge at zero (imitation) cost."*[24]

---

[19] Cp. Quintas, P., Lefrere, P. et al. (1997); Saviotti, P. P. (1998).
[20] Cp. Senker. J. (1995).
[21] Cp. Teece, D. J. Pisano, G. et al. (1997).
[22] Cp. Barney, J. (1991); Lei, D., Hitt, M. A. et al. (1996).
[23] For a more detailed discussion see chap. III.2.
[24] Saviotti, P. P. (1998), p. 848.

Furthermore, as already pointed out above, a person always knows more than he or she can explain. Codified knowledge never contains all information and know-how of the person but is subject to *abstraction*.[25] Consequently, knowledge is associated with high ambiguity and thus imitation barriers due to the existence of a specific code which has to be known in order to be able to understand and utilise the codified knowledge, and the systematic incompleteness of even codified knowledge.

An example of the difficulty to imitate codified knowledge even with existing manufacturing facilities is presented in the case study on Bayer Aspirin in chapter II.2. The company Sterling Inc. acquired all intellectual property rights, as well as any other intangible and tangible holdings and ownership of the Bayer AG in the USA from the Alien Property Custodian which had confiscated most German holdings in the USA by virtue of German warship during the 1st World War. Sterling Inc., however, was not able to use the intellectual property rights, knowledge, and production facilities efficiently and thus was dependent on the aid of the Bayer AG in producing Aspirin. Although Bayer AG gave some advice and help (although not by altruism) how to produce Aspirin and use its facilities in Rensselaer, Sterling Inc. was never able to produce Aspirin as efficiently as Bayer AG did before the war.[26] This was primarily due to the lack of process knowledge acquired over years of experience by German supervisors of Bayer who had been jailed or deported, and the inability of Sterling employees to decode the subject matter of Bayer's patents. These patents which were supposed to specify the manufacturing processes used by Bayer, were according to Sterling 'marvels of obfuscation'.[27]

Therefore, we can allege that intangible assets show a high level of ambiguity which can in general be appraised to be superior to the level of ambiguity surrounding physical assets. Consequently, intangible assets are protected by higher imitation barriers than physical assets. This may explain why many authors ascertain intangible assets as a key source of competitive advantage and some, e.g., Drucker, even claim that knowledge represents the *only meaningful* economic resource.[28]

---

[25] Cp. Kogut, B. & Zander, U. (1992), Saviotti, P. P. (1998);

[26] For a more detailed discussion see chap. II.2.2.2 and cp. Mann, C. C. & Plummer, M. L. (1991), chap. 3.

[27] Cp. Mann, C. C. & Plummer, M. L. (1991), chap. 3.

[28] Cp. Quintas, P., Lefrere, P. et al. (1997); Teece, D. J. (2000); Gupta, A. K. & Govindarajan, V. (2000).

IV.1.1.2 The Complementarity of Strengths

Besides the barrier to imitation established by the ambiguity surrounding a certain competitive advantage, imitation of a company's competitive advantage is usually reinforced by the multiplicity of individual *competitive strength* adding up to one significant competitive advantage. As Porter (1996) has clearly pointed out, a firm's competitive advantage grows out of the combination of *several complementary strengths* and can, therefore, not be explained by means of one specific individual strength, i.e., tangible or intangible. For a competitor it is much harder or even impossible to imitate a certain competitive advantage that is based on a whole array of interrelated and highly ambiguous resources and competencies than to imitate an advantage building on only one isolated strength.[29]

We can thus argue that barriers to imitation and the strategic relevance of a competitive advantage rise with increasing interrelatedness of complementary strengths. The total ambiguity surrounding a competitive advantage is hence not the sum, but rather the *product* of the ambiguity surrounding each individual strength which contributes to the overall advantage.[30] Subsequently, as illustrated in figure IV.3, the imitation barrier and hence the strategic relevance is not a linear, but rather an *exponential function* of the number of the complementary strengths and their ambiguity constituting a certain competitive advantage.

The presented argument of rising ambiguity by combining different strengths applies equally to physical, as well as immaterial resources. However, as already pointed out before, intangible resources and capabilities in general show higher levels of ambiguity than tangible resources. Moreover, intangible assets and competencies can, in contrast to most physical assets, not be bought on the market, but *have to be built internally* by a company.[31]

[29] Cp. Ghemawat, P. (1986); Teece, D. J. (1986); Kogut, B. & Zander, U. (1992); Teece, D. J., Pisano, G. et al. (1997).

[30] Cp. Porter, M. E. (1996).

[31] Cp. Teece, D. J., Pisano, G. et al. (1997); Durand, T. (1998).

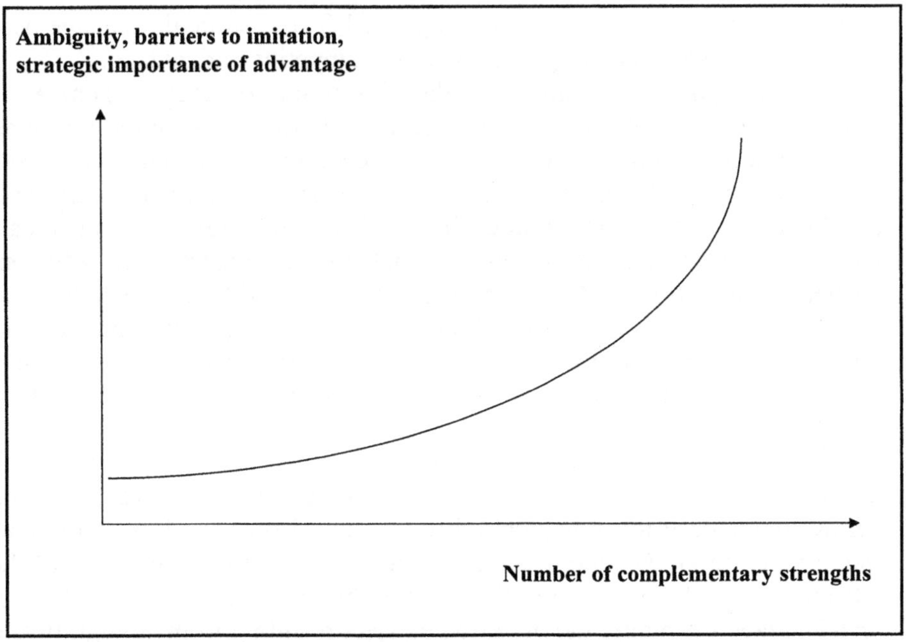

Figure IV.3: Number of competitive strengths, ambiguity and strategic importance of competitive advantage

Subsequently, competitive advantage stemming from multiple and interrelated intangible resources and competencies is surrounded by *maximum ambiguity* and therefore highest barriers to imitation with the greatest potential of sustainability since these immaterial strengths *combine* tacitness, complexity, and specificity.[32] Because of the relatively higher level of ambiguity of intangible assets vis-à-vis tangible resources, we can claim that intangible assets represent a central economic resource playing a key role in the establishment of companies' sustainable competitive advantage.

IV.1.1.3 Legal Barriers to Imitation

Imitation barriers of intangible assets do not only result from ambiguity and complementarity as discussed before, but also from legal barriers, e.g., patents, copyrights, trademarks.[33] Legal barriers to imitation, although profoundly discussed in the innovation and technological management

[32] Cp. Reed, R. & DeFilippi, R. J. (1990).
[33] Cp. Coyne, K. P. (1986); Hall, R. (1992).

literature have, so far, often been neglected in the strategic management literature as barriers creating a sustainable competitive advantage.

This lack of consideration in the discussion of factors generating sustainability may be due to the fast imitation or inventing around ascertained in relation to patent rights.[34] However, patent rights constitute not the only type of legal barriers, and furthermore, not all patents are easy to obviate by inventing around. In specific industries, e.g., chemicals industry, process and even product patents are regarded as efficient barriers to imitation.[35] Moreover, in the case of codified knowledge that can be readily observed on the final product, patents represent the only means to efficiently protect innovations. Companies thus face a trade-off between ambiguity and legal protection in the case of patents. If a company wants to protect its technological innovation representing a competitive advantage by patent rights, it has to codify the underlying knowledge and thus reduce ambiguity. Consequently, the more codified a certain immaterial technological advantage and hence the less ambiguous the underlying knowledge, the more efficient is the legal protection of the advantage. On the other hand, the more ambiguous and consequently tacit an advantage the higher the imitation barriers resulting from ambiguity and the more difficult it is to impose legal barriers to imitation.

Building on the classification of intangible valuables established in chapter III.1.2, we can now determine the imitation barriers surrounding the different types of intangible technological assets. As shown in figure IV.4, imitation barriers stemming from ambiguity decrease with increasing codification and spreading of knowledge over several different individuals and groups of individuals. On the other hand, the possibility of legal protection increases at the same measure as ambiguity barriers decrease. The know-how embedded in a certain employee, for example, shows a high level of ambiguity and might thus be difficult to imitate by a competitor. Alternatively, codified knowledge dispersed over several employees or even groups of specialists within the company, such as a certain product feature or production process, may be easily patented or protected on another, legally enforceable way.

---

[34] Cp. Mansfield, E., Schwartz, M. (1981); Mansfield, E. (1985); Teece, D. J. (1986); Levin, R. C., Klevorick, A. K. et al. (1987).

[35] For a more detailed discussion see chap. III.3 and cp. Levin, R. C., Klevorick, A. K. et al. (1987); Arundel, A. & Kabla, I. (1998).

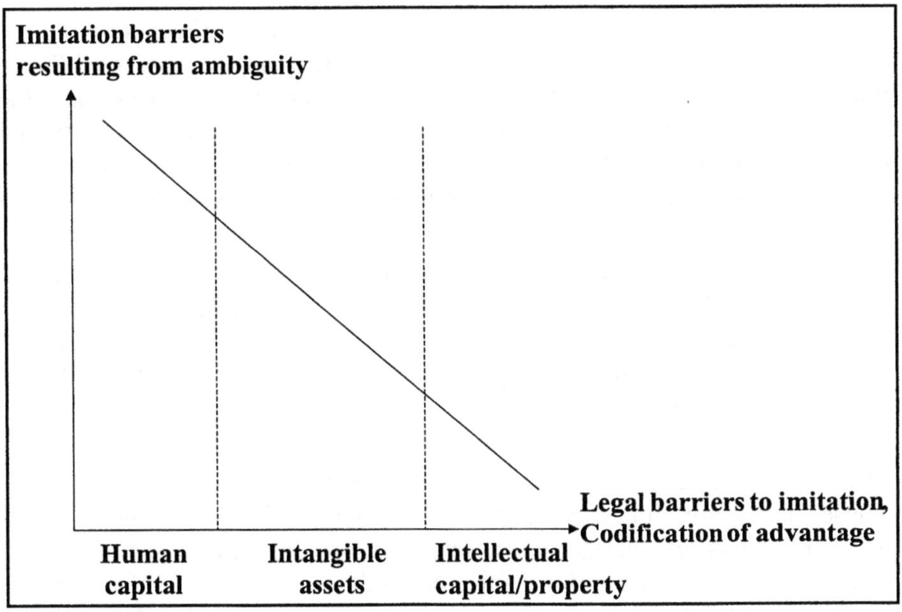

Figure IV.4: Imitation barriers of intangible technological assets: patent rights versus ambiguity

In addition, the protection of a specific competitive advantage is mostly not based on one singular patent right but rather on the combination of several different intangible assets located in different classes.[36] This combination of several different complementary intangible assets adding up to one competitive advantage not only increases the ambiguity surrounding the strategic advantage by multiplying the ambiguity inherent to each individual strength, but also by the different observability of the individual strengths. A certain company strength that is, for example, protected by trade secrecy may not easily be noticed by competitors and thus competitors trying to imitate a certain competitive advantage may only concentrate on the imitation or substitution of easily perceivable strengths which are, for example, protected by patent rights. Consequently, competing companies may try to imitate a certain competitive advantage which they do not fully understand due to the existence of complementary strength '*hidden*' within the company.

Furthermore, not all intellectual property rights show this rather patent specific problem related to the simplicity to obviate an established right by inventing around. Other intellectual property rights, such as brand names or trademarks, for example, are extremely difficult to imitate or

[36] For a more detailed discussion see chap. IV.1.2.2.

circumvent. This is in particular due to their high tacit dimension and the easy observation of any trademark infringement on the market.[37] Thus, brands can be allocated in the upper-right corner of figure VI.4 showing high legal, as well as ambiguity barriers to imitation. In particular trademark protection has been identified as an important barrier to imitation with a high strategic dimension. Accordingly, Hall (1992) has stressed:

> *"In an age when the brand name can represent the essence of the ideas and feelings associated with a product, the protection afforded by the trade mark can be crucial to the well being of a company so that it may avoid unfair competition and the 'borrowing' of its reputation by rivals."*[38]

Consequently, we can affirm by building on our discussion in previous chapters that inherent limits to legal protection of immaterial assets exist. These limits are, however, not uniform across different industries, or different types of immaterial assets nor are all kinds of intellectual property rights equally enforceable. As outlined elsewhere, infringements of process patents are difficult to perceive, on the other hand, trademark infringements can be easily observed on the market and the legal rights efficiently enforced. Nevertheless, intellectual property rights in general represent a significant imitation barrier and thus can be the source of sustainable competitive advantage.[39]

VI.1.1.4 Up-holding Imitation Barriers

So far, we have presented different barriers to imitation that can turn a competitive advantage into a sustainable and thus strategically relevant advantage. However, irrespective of the nature of the barrier and its height, an imitation barrier is never insurmountable and always subject to decay. Consequently, firms must invest in the upholding of existing barriers or generate new barriers that deter current and potential competitors from imitating a specific advantage.[40] As Reed & DeFilippi (1990) have pointed out, companies do have the possibility to invest in imitation barriers in order to uphold or even increase these barriers over time which coincides

---

[37] For a more detailed discussion of the strategic importance of trademarks and brand names see chap. IV.2 and IV.3.

[38] Hall, R. (1992), p. 137.

[39] Cp. Hall, R. (1992; 1993); Aaker, D. A. (1989); van Reekum, A. H. (1999), p. 55.

[40] Cp. Dierickx, I. & Cool, K. (1989); Reed, R. & DeFilippi, R. J. (1990).

with Porter's (1985) idea of presenting a 'moving target' by continuously reinvesting in the company's competitive position.[41]

By upholding or even increasing imitation barriers of a certain advantage, companies can antagonise or at least slow down the decay of existing imitation barriers and thus sustain a strategic advantage. In consequence, we can argue the longer the sustainability of a company's competitive advantage and the higher the competitive advantage, i.e., the product's or service's value perceived by the customer, the higher the potential returns a company can reap of its advantage and thus the higher its profitability vis-à-vis competitors not possessing the specific advantage. Hence, by following a strategy of upholding and reinforcing deterrence of imitation and consequently slowing down or even reversing the convergence process of profits, the company can benefit of a higher return in each period in which the barrier is held up.[42] Furthermore, the longer an existing imitation barrier is held up, the more opportunities exist to build up new imitation barriers or at least reinvest in existing ones.[43]

However, which kind of investment can be considered as a reinvestment in imitation barriers? In any case, an investment in barriers to imitation must have one or more of the following aims:

1. Increasing *ambiguity* surrounding a certain competitive advantage;
2. Adding a *complementary strength* to the already existing competitive advantage; and
3. Establishing, upholding, and/or reinforcing *legal protection* of a particular advantage.

By investing in one or more of the above factors a company can in effect uphold or even increase imitation barriers and thus warrant a persistent deterrence of imitation. Such investments are, for example, R&D expenditures to generate new and/or improve existent technologies, products, or services. Such R&D expenditures thus lead to new intangible assets that reinforce and/or complement an existent competitive advantage or even generate an entirely new and so far unknown competitive lead.[44]

---

[41] Cp. Porter, M. E. (1985), chap. 1; Reed, R. & DeFilippi, R. J. (1990).

[42] Cp. Jacobsen, R. (1988); Barney, J. B. (1986; 1991); Mascarenhas, B. & Aaker, D. A. (1989); Aaker, D. A. (1989); Lawless, M. W. & Fisher, R. J. (1990).

[43] Cp. Ghemawat, P. (1986).

[44] For a more detailed discussion of the generation of intangible assets see chap. III.2.

These new competitive strengths are then again protected from imitation by high ambiguity or legal rights at least over a certain period of time.[45]

Building on the lore of how to uphold imitation barriers by continuously investing in ambiguity, complementarity, and legal protection rights, the question arises of how much a company should invest in the barriers protecting a certain competitive advantage. Reed & DeFilippi (1990) have suggested that the volume of reinvestments in existing imitation barriers should be determined by the *initial height* of the imitation barriers and by its *rate of decay*. Moreover, the amount of reinvestments in upholding imitation barriers should also reflect the *returns* the company anticipates from the concerning competitive advantage over the planning horizon. Consequently, the lower the existing imitation barriers, the higher the rate of decay, and the higher the expected returns of the competitive advantage in question, the higher the reinvestments in upholding the barriers to imitation and vice versa.[46]

We can thus conclude, management can follow strategies to uphold and reinforce existing imitation barriers that in turn add to the sustainability of a certain competitive advantage or may even entirely prevent other companies from entering a specific market. Such strategies consequently slow down the decay of abnormal returns and result in a higher return in each period in which competitors are deterred from entering in direct competition. This prolonged period of above normal returns generated by the competitive advantage not only influences the financial well-being of the company, but may also justify higher expenditures for activities generating new competitive advantages, e.g., R&D.[47] Moreover, the height of reinvestments into barriers of imitation of a certain exiting competitive advantage is determined by the heights of existing imitation barriers, the rate of decay of the barriers, and the anticipated returns of the concerning competitive advantage.

IV.1.2 Central Problems of Intangible Technological Assets in the Generation of Sustainable Competitive Advantage

As we have seen in the previous section, intangible assets occupy a special role in the competitiveness of companies. Because of the high level of ambiguity surrounding intangible assets, their complementary nature, and

---

[45] Cp. Ghemawat, P. (1986); Jacobsen, R. (1988); Senker, J. (1995); Johanson, U. (1999).

[46] Cp. Reed, R. & DeFilippi, R. J. (1990).

[47] For a more detailed discussion of the relationship between the appropriation of returns and R&D spending see chap. III.1.

possible legal barriers to imitation, competitive advantage based on immaterial assets is perceived to be particularly sustainable and thus of high strategic relevance. However, companies possessing a competitive advantage based on immaterial assets face problems resulting from the special characteristics of intangible assets.[48] As already pointed out in chapter III, intangible assets are accompanied by the central problem of appropriation that results from their public good characteristics. In this section we discuss the key importance of the *appropriation of economic returns* stemming from competitive advantage, i.e., intangible technical assets, in a company's strategic reasoning. This discussion leads us to a more *holistic view of the term appropriation* and points out the key significance of the discussion of appropriation in the management of technology. Building on this discussion, we point out the shortcomings and limits of patent rights in appropriating the returns of competitive advantage based on intangible technological assets. The last section then discusses the specific problems companies face in appropriating the returns of their intangible assets in international markets and points out the virtues of enterprises active in various different national and regional markets.

IV.1.2.1 The Key Importance of the Appropriation of Economic Returns of Intangible Resources

As pointed out above, company specific resources and/or competencies must be protected by imitation barriers in order to be of *strategic importance* for a company.[49] Such a strategic advantage that is appreciated by customers and sustainable vis-à-vis competitors can represent a significant source of revenue for the company in question. However, the final *economic rent* a company can generate with a certain competitive advantage depends on the possibility to *appropriate the returns* generated by the advantage in question.[50] It is often mistakenly assumed that the possession of a strategic advantage inevitably leads to an economic return for its holder which lies above the level currently assumed to be normal for a certain industry or branch. There are, however, four main factors that influence the appropriation of the returns generated by a certain sustainable competitive advantage:

---

[48] For a more detailed discussion of the characteristics of intangible assets see chap. III.1.

[49] Cp. Clark, K. (1987).

[50] Cp. Grant, R. M. (1998), chap. 5.

1. Ownership rights and embeddedness of resources and capabilities;
2. Relative bargaining power;
3. Existence of complementary assets; and
4. Regulatory influences.[51]

As discussed in chapter III.1, immaterial assets show public good characteristics and hence *ownership and/or possession rights* of such assets are often rather ambiguous. Moreover, a certain intangible asset which classifies as a sustainable competitive advantage, can often not be owned by the concerning company and thus the company cannot, for example, prevent the advantage to leave the organisation. A prominent example is *human capital* based skills and know-how. Such know-how and experiences classify as sustainable competitive advantage since they are valuable, rare, and often difficult or impossible to substitute and/or imitate. However, the individual employee is the owner and holder of the asset and thus the company can usually not prevent the employee from leaving the company. Of course, a company can try to tie its human capital to the organisation by long-lasting labour contracts, financial and non-financial incentives and compensations, etc., however, this will not completely thwart the possibility of central employees leaving the company. Furthermore, such arrangements result in a reduction of the returns the company can appropriate form its competitive advantage in favour of the employee.[52] As outlined in chapter III.1.2.1 different types of immaterial assets within business companies can be identified which are classified according to their appropriability and codification on the one hand, and regarding the spread of knowledge with in the organisation, on the other hand (cf. figure III.3). Thus, we can say that the appropriation of the returns of a certain immaterial asset is influenced by the type of intangible asset, i.e., human capital, intangible asset, or intellectual capital, and the embeddedness of the resource or capability. Consequently, the ownership and/or possession rights a company can claim on its intangible assets which build competitive advantage significantly influences the height of revenues the company can appropriate.

The second factor which has been identified to crucially influence the appropriation of the returns generated by a certain competitive advantage, is the *relative bargaining power* of the holder and/or owner of the competitive advantage. If a certain competitive advantage can be clearly attributed to one single employee, the employee can reap off a substantial

---

[51] Cp. Grant, R. M. (1998), pp. 128-133.

[52] For a more detailed discussion of the appropriation of human capital bound assets see in particular chap. III.1.2 and III.2.2.2.

part or even the totality of the revenues. The bargaining power and thus the extent of the revenue stream which the individual can appropriated, depends on his *mobility* and if the skills offer the same *productivity* in another company.[53] An example of an industry where the advantage of a company can be clearly allocated to one single person represents the formula-one industry. Since the technical specifications and requirements are extremely tightly set, the success of a certain team is almost entirely dependent on the fortune and aptitude of the driver. The drivers are thus able to appropriate the bulk of the benefits generated by a successful participation in the industry. The high bargaining power of the drivers in the formula-one industry may be an explanation of the extremely high salaries of the top drivers and the extremely low or even negative profitability of the racing teams.

The existence of *specific complementary assets* outside the company holding the competitive advantage represents another factor which can significantly influence the appropriation of the returns generated by a certain sustainable competitive advantage. The company holding the specific complementary asset has the power to appropriate a better part of the returns generated by an advantage, although the advantage itself is owned by another company.[54] A prominent industry in which companies, even though bestowed with resources and competencies showing the characteristics of strategic advantage, are, however, unable to appropriate the returns generated by their advantages due to established firms holding specialised complementary assets, represents the Internet Service Provider (ISP) industry. Companies offering all-inclusive services (also referred to as 'flat-rate'), such as AOL, T-Online, Wannadoo, etc., which offer clients a portal to access the Internet via established telephone lines, may possess a strategic advantage in terms of a high commitment of the customer to a certain ISP due to high switching costs, the distinctive service offerings provided on the portal, but also because of the extremely high set up costs of such a service (server capacity, global presence, software development, etc.). However, these companies cannot fully appropriate the returns generated by their strategic advantage due to the existence of the complementary assets of the 'telephone connection'. Anyone who wants to access the service of one of the ISPs has to use the already established telephone infrastructure of large telecommunication operators, e.g., France Télécom, Deutsche Telekom, British Telecom. These operators can, in turn, appropriate a better part of the returns generated by the ISPs'

[53] Cp. Grant, R. M. (1998), pp. 132-133.

[54] Cp. Teece, D. J. (1986); Teece, D. J., Pisano, G. et al. (1997); Madhok, A. & Osegowitsch, T. (1998).

advantage because of the connection-fees the ISPs have to pay for their customers which have to use the infrastructure provided by the operators in order to access the provided service. Thus, a company has to control all specific complementary assets and activities in order to be able to appropriate the returns of its strategic advantage.[55]

The last factor identified as having a significant influence on a firm's possibility to appropriate the returns of a sustainable competitive advantage are *regulatory influences* on the use and commercialisation of a certain strategic advantage. Such regulatory influences can have various different forms, such as a certain price ceiling, minimum provision of a certain service or product at a fixed price, establishment of a dejure standard or the prohibition of the commercialisation of a certain product or service. A recent example of the significant influence of regulatory forces on the appropriation of the returns of a competitive advantage represents the biotechnology industry in the EU. A biotech company that has developed a bio-engineered seed (e.g., a certain sweet-corn seed particularly resistant against a particular varmint) owns a sustainable competitive advantage since the knowledge to produce the seed is company specific, economically valuable, non-substitutable, hard to imitate, and the final seed generates consumer benefit (less expenditures for pesticides). However, the EU currently follows a policy that bans the mass-cultivation of genetically modified organisms due to unknown risk stemming from the uncontrolled spreading of such modified plants in nature. Consequently, although the knowledge is strategically relevant, the company cannot appropriate the returns its strategic advantage would generate on the market. Accordingly, regulatory authorities can significantly influence the appropriation of the returns of a strategic advantage by implementing certain policies.

Figure IV.5 illustrates the relationship between company specific resources and/or competencies and the economic rent these idiosyncratic assets generate. Such a company specific resource or competency is often born in an invention or a technological advancement and thus investments in the generation of new inventions.[56] Such new company specific intangible assets often result in innovations that, if they meet the criteria for strategic relevance (see figure IV.5), can be a source of sustainable competitive advantage and hence are of strategic relevance.[57] The strategic relevance, however, does not necessarily determine the profit earning

[55] Cp. Teece, D. J. (1986); Nelson, R. R. (1991).

[56] For a more detailed discussion of the generation of intangible assets see chap. III.2.

[57] Cp. Güldenberg, H. G. (1999a).

potential of the company holding the advantage. The possibility and the extent to which a company can extract a financial return from its sustainable competitive advantage depends on the possibility to appropriate the economic rent generated by the advantage in question. Consequently, the appropriation of the returns of a certain advantage considerably influences a company's *willingness to invest* in certain technologies and markets. As shown above, the appropriation is determined by the four factors: (1) the ownership rights and the embeddedness of the resource or competence, (2) the relative bargaining power of the agent holding the resource and/or competence, (3) existent complementary assets not owned by the company holding the strategic advantage, and (4) existing and potential regulatory influences.

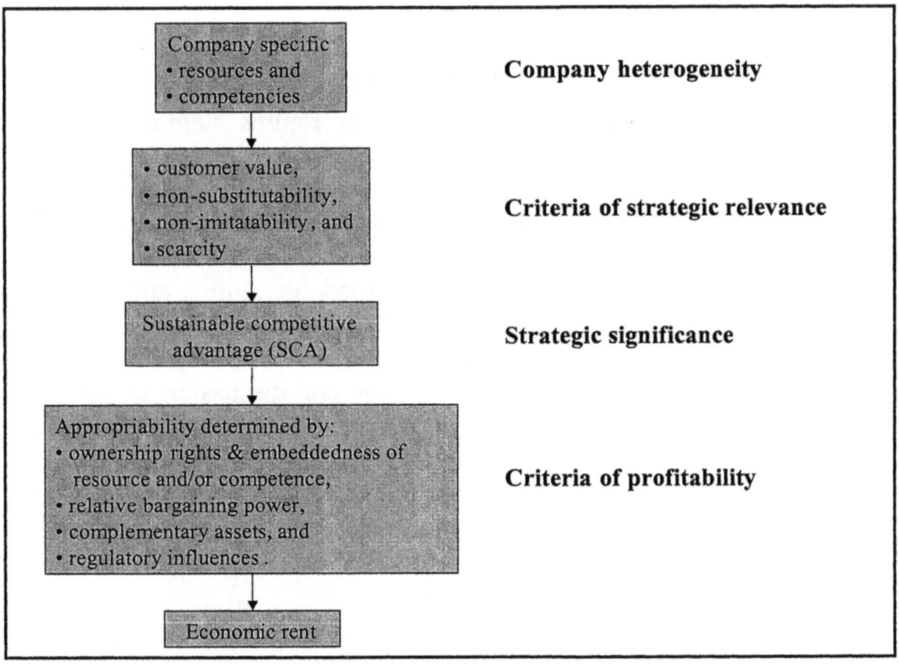

Figure IV.5: The role of appropriation in generating economic rent

A general conclusion which can be formulated on the basis of the discussion of the factors determining the appropriation of returns of a certain advantage, is that companies have to increase the *embeddedness* of the resource and/or obtain *ownership rights* on the resource or competency, *reduce the bargaining power* of the agent holding the resource, and try to integrate or generate the necessary specialised complementary assets. A company can, for example, *reduce the mobility* of employees by long-lasting contracts or equity participation and thus increase the embeddedness of the resource. Another, perhaps more efficient method, is to *extract the knowledge* constituting a competitive advantage from the individual employee by codification and/or spreading of the knowledge over several different employees within the firm and consequently increase the *connectivity* of the intangible asset to the company and reduce the bargaining power of the individual agent.

Our discussion has so far merely considered the appropriation of the returns generated by an existing competitive advantage. This point of view does, however, not account for future strategic assets and completely neglects the central importance of appropriation in the management of technology. The next section therefore expands our contemplation and presents the appropriation of technology as a key component in the technology management system.

A Holistic View of the Appropriation of Intangible Assets

As pointed out above, the appropriation of returns stemming from an existing company specific advantage considerably determines the profit earning potential of the business enterprise. However, in order to fully account for the strategic role of the appropriation of intangible assets in the field of *technology management*, we have to enlarge our understanding of the term appropriation. Because of the broad literature available on the general subject of technology management, we have to concentrate our discussion and do merely present the model developed by Morin (1988). The particular relevance of the model for our discussion is due to its explicitness about the centrality of appropriation in the management of technology.

Morin (1988) has identified six central functions of technology management. These functions are in particular:

1. Optimisation;
2. Enrichment;
3. Safeguarding;
4. Stocktaking;
5. Evaluation; and
6. *Surveillance*

of a company's technological patrimony (cf. figure IV.6).[58] The author subsumes under the term *optimisation* the verification if all resources and capabilities are efficiently employed. In order to be able to confirm if all resources and capabilities are used to their best potential a company has to

[58] Cp. Morin, J. (1988), p. 79.

access and evaluate its current stock of technological assets and this *stocktaking* might reveal 'hidden treasures' so far neglected by the company. This stock of resources and competencies has to be *enriched* and *upheld* in order to oppose depreciation and to avert obsolescence of these resources and competencies due to the fast progression of technological development. The management, however, has to *evaluate* the individual resources and competencies in order to be able to efficiently manage the assets and enhance their value. According to Morin (1988), the *safeguarding* and *supervision* functions represent the central axes which link the different key functions of the technology management system. The basic model and the interrelation of the different functions of technology management are visualised in figure IV.6.

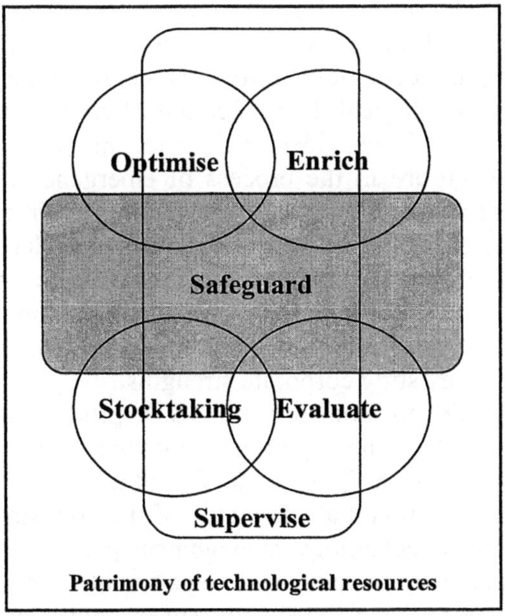

Cp. Morin, J. (1988), p. 80.

Figure IV.6: The six functions of technology management

These six functions can again be distinguished in three *active functions* (optimisation, enrichment, and safeguarding) and three *supporting functions* (stocktaking, evaluation, and supervision). As the author has clearly pointed out, the six functions have to be managed in accordance and the efficiency of the entire system of technology management would be endangered by the negligence of any one function.[59] In this system of technology management the function of *safeguarding* technological resources and competencies corresponds to what commonly is understood under securing assets and associated returns and thus substitutes for the term *appropriation*. However, appropriation must not only concern the safeguarding of a company's existing technological patrimony and its returns, but also of potential future technological resources and competencies that may be a source of competitive advantage tomorrow.

Consequently, the system of technological management established by Morin clearly points out the central importance of safeguarding and hence of appropriation of technological resources and competencies in the management of technology. However, the management of technological resources does not only concentrate on currently existing resources and competencies but has to include *future resources and competencies* which can be generated with the existing set of company assets. In respect to the importance of future technological resources and competencies, Morin has referred to the technological diversification of companies and pointed out that companies have to consider in their technology management future technologies, which are in the process of emergence and evolution, and cannot only bear in mind established technologies already existing in the company.[60] Therefore, a company has to consider in the strategic management of technology, and hence in the appropriation of its intangible technological assets, not only currently existing resources and competencies, but also future resources and competencies that can be generated with the existing corporate strengths.

Moreover, we do not consider the R&D, production, and intellectual property departments as the key divisions within the system of technology management presented in figure IV.6. We rather include *any function* of a company in the system and all functions of the company have to perform the six functions of technology management presented above. So is, for example, the personal management department extremely important in recruiting employees that fit to the current or envisaged corporate culture and add to the current stock of human capital. Thus, a company must be able to attract not only employees with the needed technical skills and know-how but which also show the required social characteristics and needs. Consequently, the personal management has to work in close interrelation with the marketing, R&D, production, and any other functions

---

[59] Cp. Morin, J. (1988), pp.77-81.

[60] For a detailed investigation of the field of technological diversification of companies see Stephan, M. (2003) and cp. Morin, J. (1988), chap. II.1; Quintas, P., Lefrere, P. et al. (1997).

within the company. Hence, we can affirm, a company that wants to efficiently manage its current and potential future stock of intangible technical assets, and thus appropriate its technological assets, has to integrate any function of the company in its technology management system and a flaw in any one function results in the weakening of the whole system.

We can hence summarise, the appropriation of the immaterial technological assets which is encapsulated in the notion of 'safeguarding' in Morin's technology management system, represents a central aspect of technology management interfering with any of the other five functions. Moreover, the management of technology does not only concern existing technological resources and competencies, but includes future assets, which might not currently exist or are even considered as unrealisable. Last but not least, the technology management with its six principal functions has to be implemented and considered in any acting of the company reaching from top management to the individual employee on the production floor.

IV.1.2.2 Strategic Limitations and Shortcomings of Patent Protection

As seen in the discussion above, companies have to take a more holistic view of the appropriation of the returns generated by current and future intangible technological assets which is determined by four principal factors: ownership rights & embeddedness, relative bargaining power, complementary assets, and regulatory influences. So far authors have concentrated their discussion of the protection of technological assets principally on the aspects of patents and trade secrets. Such an approach, however, only covers two factors and entirely neglects the important role of specific complementary assets. Furthermore, a sustainable competitive advantage generally results from the combination of several complementary strengths. As shown above, the total ambiguity surrounding a specific competitive advantage increases by the number of individual strengths and the tacitness of the assets underlying each individual strength. Patent protection, however, considerably reduces tacitness, and hence the sustainability of a competitive advantage is reduced to the remaining maximum duration of the patent right.

The limited lifetime of patent rights, the low ambiguity surrounding intangible assets protected by patent rights, the ready observability of patents by competitors, and the mostly rapid circumvention of patents are just a few of the most *important shortcomings of patent rights* in protecting a competitive advantage.[61] Another weakness of most patent rights which significantly endangers the appropriation of the returns generated by a certain technological invention, are the mostly *juridical-technical language and focus* used in the formulation of patent documents.[62] The writing of a patent in such a juridical-technical language makes the resulting property right vulnerable to *colliding patents* with a more social-economic language and focus and thus market based approach in their formulation, placed subsequently by competitors. Moulin and Rocher instanced the case of the patent filed by Jean Moulin on the memory-chip placed on a plastic card which is nowadays commonly used on telephone-cards, credit-cards, etc. As Moulin pointed out, he was able to file a patent on the *chip-card* even though IBM, Matsushita and other companies had already filed patents on the memory-chip beforehand. The subsequent patent placement was feasible because the existing patents on the memory-chip were written in a juridical-technical language which has neglected the expectations of the market. Consequently, Moulin has been successful in filing a patent on the chip-card 20-30 years after the invention of the memory-chip which was long since expected by the market, and in doing so to dodge the existing patents and appropriate a hefty stake of the economic returns of the initial invention of the memory-chip.

Another problem of patent rights stressed by the interviewees is that a system established upon certain patent rights can be easily destabilised which in turn forces the company owning the patents to negotiate with the company infringing its property right. Such a *destabilisation of an established system* can be attained by filing a patent on almost the same content matter of another, already existing patent right. As soon as the patent is placed, the patent is valuable until the responsible patent office decides that the patent application does not correspond to the criteria of patentability. However, due to budget constraints of most patent offices, as well as time constraints of individual examiners in investigating a patent application, such an examination can take several years. Moreover, if the potential infringer's patent document mentions some new, deviating characteristics the probability of the examiner to find an already existing patent document covering exactly the same invention is close to zero. Consequently, the company can enforce its rights until the application has

[61] Cp. Kitch, E. W. (1977); Mansfield, E., Schwartz, M. et al. (1981); Mansfield, E. (1985); Horstmann, I., MacDonald, G. M. et al. (1985); Levin, R. C., Klevorick, A. K. (1987); Glass, B. (1990); Geroski, P. (1995); Thurow, L. C. (1997); Arundel, A. & Kabla, I. (1998).

[62] Cp. Morin, J. (1988), pp. 147-161.

been officially refused by the patent office. This again can most efficiently be done by writing warning letters not to the actual holder of the colliding patent and/or system integrator, but rather to the suppliers and distributors accusing them for *complicity of fraudulent infringement*. This will release a 'domino effect' which forces the companies involved in the existing system to react and thus to *negotiate*. Moulin clearly pointed out that any company, infringing or legally owning the intellectual property right, has to avoid fighting the problem out in court because of the exorbitant costs associated with legal action and the relatively long time lag until a final decision is reached. As the interviewees stressed, a solution is almost never found in the courtroom, but at the negotiation table.

A partial solution to the problems analysed above represents the reconsideration of the company's strategy in writing a patent. As Moulin & Rocher pointed out, a company first has to know what it exactly wants to do with a certain invention in order to be able to choose the most adequate protection mode. If the preferred protection mode represents a patent right, the company has to write a patent document not only bearing in mind technical and legal aspects but also economical and social factors. Of course, companies often do not know what is feasible with a certain invention and may even not be familiar or aware of the market that might present the most interesting opportunities for its innovation. Thus, companies are often not fully aware of all opportunities and consequently tend to file broad patents which largely focus on technical and legal aspects. Another possibility to increase appropriation is to follow certain *patent strategies* such as to protect a certain valuable patent by several different less important patents or to block a whole technology field by multiple, minor patents which represent a considerable nuisance to competitors by slowing down their development.[63] Although such patent strategies increase the difficulty of current and potential competitors to attack a certain competitive advantage or to invent around the subject matter of a certain patent, it is always possible to destabilise established systems or to be blocked by patent rights established by competitors in order to force the company to negotiate.

We can affirm, in accordance with Moulin & Rocher, that the filing of patent rights does not represent an end in itself. A patent bestows its holder with ownership rights on the subject matter of a valid patent and thus enables him, at least in theory, to appropriate the returns of its intellectual capital over the patent's lifetime. However, in the real world patents generally do not function that perfectly and hence the appropriation of the returns by the legal owner is put in jeopardy by following a singular patent

[63] Cp. Granstrand, O. (1999), chap. 7.4.

strategy in protecting competitive advantage. Consequently, to achieve a sustainable appropriation of returns, companies do not only have to assure efficient patent protection and enforcement of the rights. An efficient and sustainable appropriation of the returns necessitates, moreover, the establishment of strengths that complement resources and/or competencies currently generating a competitive advantage which again show the criteria of strategic relevance and are protected by imitation barriers.

IV.1.2.3 The Advantage of Multinational Enterprises in the Appropriation of Intangible Technological Assets

As already pointed out in chapter III.2.1, multinational companies have an advantage vis-à-vis national companies in the generation of immaterial assets. However, these advantages of multinational enterprises in generating and accumulating intangible assets are supplemented by advantages in the *international appropriation* of the returns generated by these assets. Various authors have ascribed the existence of multinational enterprises to the fact that these companies have substantial advantages in transferring and appropriating the returns of their competitive advantages which mostly build upon intangible technical assets.[64] There are two distinct explanations, one centres on the *transaction costs approach* pointing out the difficulties and costs of transferring knowledge assets over an open market. The other concentrates on the risks associated with the *diffusion* of knowledge bestowing a company with a strategic advantage and the associated problems in *appropriating* the returns generated by the intangible asset. Most authors agree that companies maximise the returns of their intangible assets by exploiting them simultaneously in a variety of markets and applications due to the characteristics of non-rivalry and non-excludability, as well as the need for a fast global exploitation of the assets due to the rapid technological progress and the technological assets becoming obsolete.[65] Intangible assets are in general associated with *high sunk cost* but once the assets exist, the *marginal cost of using* and *replication* are negligible or even equal to zero.[66]

---

[64] Cp. Teece, D. J. (1976), chap. 1; Teece, D. J. (1977; 1998; 2000); Magee, S. P. (1977); Hymer, S. H. (1990); Buckley, P. J. & Carter, M. J. (2000); Gupta, A. K. & Govindarajan, V. (2000).

[65] Cp. Caves, R. E. (1971); Teece, D. J. (2000); Buckley, P. J. & Carter, M. J. (2000).

[66] For a more detailed discussion of the characteristics of intangible assets see chap. III.1.

The argument of *high costs of transferring intangible* assets over open markets is based on the transaction cost approach of Coase (1937) which has been further developed by Williamson (1979). Building on these foundations and the special characteristics of intangible assets, Teece has pointed out that the multinational enterprise is an *organisational mode* that allows for an efficient and effective internal transfer of such asset among its various business units.[67] The ineffectiveness and inefficiency of transferring immaterial assets over the market results from the high tacit nature and the public good characteristics of know-how and knowledge assets. Moreover, the more recent a certain technological item, often referred to as leading-edge technology, the less codified the asset and the less familiar is the receiving company with the technology.[68] Consequently, the transfer of a highly tacit immaterial asset may necessitate additional training of the transferee's staff, subsequent transfer of people, etc., which not only increases costs but also the time needed to effect such a transfer. Thus, multinational enterprises are able to more effectively and efficiently transfer intangible assets internally and hence avoid the high costs of market transaction which are due to prevailing market inefficiencies, and furthermore, reduce the time needed to transfer intangible assets internationally.

Besides avoiding the high costs of transferring intangible assets over the market place, Magee (1977) pointed out that *multinational enterprises* are an efficient mode to *appropriate the returns* of intangible assets on an international level. Building on Vernon's (1966) product life-cycle, Magee developed a technology life-cycle according to which the knowledge intensity and appropriability are declining with the progress of time (cf. figure III.20).[69] The author has assumed that in the early invention phase a company can perfectly protect and appropriate the returns of its R&D investments by patent rights and consequently can trade the invention over the market. However, once the invention has turned into an *innovation* by its first commercialisation, although the information content of the innovation and the R&D investments are still high, the protection and the appropriation due to patent rights is diminishing. This reduction in the appropriability is attributable to expiring patent rights and to the problems of protecting the returns on information and knowledge by intellectual property rights. In the *standardisation* stage, finally all companies do possess the same information and knowledge about the basic technology

[67] Cp. Magee, S. P. (1977); Teece, D. J. (1981).

[68] Cp. Teece, D. J. (1977; 1981; 1998); Teece, D. J., Pisano, G. et al. (1997).

[69] For a more detailed discussion of Magee's technology life-cycle see chap. III.3.3.

and investments in R&D are almost equal to zero. Consequently, companies can use the market for transaction.

We can thus summarise, *multinational enterprises* have a distinct advantage in particular in the innovation phase by internally transferring information as well as knowledge and thereby ensure *appropriation* by keeping them within the hierarchy. Furthermore, by using the hierarchy to transfer intangible assets, a company can evade the *costs of market transaction* attributable to market inefficiencies. A last point in favour of multinational firms is the possibility to transfer intangible assets rapidly over national boundaries. This is an important advantage in a world characterised by ever increasing technological progress and thus declining technology life-times. Consequently, we can underpin the assertion that multinational enterprises enjoy advantages in transferring intangible assets and appropriating the returns of the assets in international markets vis-à-vis companies with a predominantly domestic focus.

IV.1.3 Upshot IV: Strategic Role and Importance of the Protection of Intangible Assets in the Generation of Sustainable Competitive Advantage

This chapter has pointed out the strategic importance of company specific resources and competencies which are rare and create a certain consumer benefit. Such a company specific advantage creates a *sustainable competitive advantage* if substantial barriers to imitation exist and if the advantage is not substitutable. As discussed, the sustainability of a strategic intangible advantage is significantly influenced by the *ambiguity* surrounding the asset and the existence of *legal barriers*. Moreover, the multiplicity of *complementary strengths* adding up to a certain competitive advantage increases the ambiguity and thus the sustainability of the overall competitive advantage. Such barriers to imitation are, however, never insurmountable and subject to decay. Thus, in order to *uphold or even increase imitation barriers* of a specific strategic advantage, a company has to invest in order to increase ambiguity, adding a supplementary strength, and/or establish, uphold, or reinforce intellectual property rights.

Intangible technological assets in general meet the criteria of strategic significance, however, such a strategic advantage does not necessarily result in an economic return for the company owning the advantage. The possibility to *appropriate the returns* of a certain competitive advantage is determined by the criteria of profitability. In this context we have to broaden our understanding of the term appropriation. As Morin (1988) pointed out, technology management embraces six principal functions whereof appropriation represents just one. However, appropriation is one of the most central functions in the *technology management system* since it interferes with any other function of the system and enables the company to extract an economic return from its established advantage. In order to function efficiently, the technology management system has to be implemented in any function of the company, i.e., from R&D to marketing and distribution. Furthermore, a company has not only to consider currently existing intangible technological assets in the technology management but also future resources and competencies which can be generated with the existing set of company assets.

In the past, the discussion of the appropriation of intangible technological assets has predominantly concentrated on the analysis of *patent and trade secret protection.* However, as broadly recognised, these protection modes show significant shortcomings and limits which put their importance in safeguarding the competitive advantage in question. In addition, the current language and focus used in writing patent documents has to be thought over and companies have to take their strategy into consideration in determining the most adequate protection mode and in formulating the patent document.

The last section has analysed the advantage of multinational enterprises in the international appropriation of the returns of intangible assets. As pointed out, multinational companies can transfer immaterial assets effectively and efficiently within their hierarchy and thereby avoid *market inefficiencies* inherent to the market of immaterial assets. Moreover, multinational companies show advantages in *appropriating the returns* of intangible assets. This leads to the thesis of chapter IV.1:

Thesis III:
Intangible company specific assets show a high strategic importance. To fully account for the strategic meaning of intangible assets and to warrant an economic return, companies have to put the appropriation of current and future intangible technological assets in the centre of their technology management and assure the accomplishment of the profitability criteria. The mere assurance of singular patent right protection is, however, inadequate.

IV.2 Brand Equity in the Protection of Technological Assets

As seen in the preceding chapter VI.1, intangible and in particular intangible technological assets occupy an important strategic role, where appropriability determines the economic return a company can generate with its strategic resources and capabilities. In relation to the appropriation of returns generated by a certain sustainable competitive advantage complementary strengths take a key strategic role. So far, however, authors have predominantly considered complementary technological resources and competencies in the protection and appropriation of intangible technological assets. The strategic role of *complementary market based assets*, such as trademarks, distribution, customer loyalty, etc., have hitherto been largely neglected in the theoretical discussion of securing competitive advantage stemming from intangible technological assets. Some authors have even claimed that market based assets are not related to a company's knowledge resources and competencies, but merely result from marketing activities.[70] Over the last years, however, a discussion has evolved largely independent of the technology management domain which has stressed the key importance of market based resources and in particular brand equity in strategic management.[71]

In many technology based companies the belief still prevails that a certain company specific technological advantage will without failure attract customers which will explicitly ask for the product or service. This attitude corresponds to Emerson's point of view, who has once illustrated:

> *"If a man ... make a better mouse-trap than his neighbour, tho' he build his house in the woods, the world will make a beaten path to his door."*[72]

However, this is, and perhaps never was, unanimously true for all technical innovations. First of all, if a company does not inform its potential customers about his new improved 'mouse-trap' the customers might not even know that they have to search. Consequently, it may happen that customers do not realise that there is a certain product or service which delivers a certain utility and consequently before the customers have made 'a beaten path' to the company's door, there will already be a new, even better 'mouse-trap' offered by another company. Certainly there still exist innovations, such as a new drug which have such a magnitude that the information about their existence will spread almost by itself and customers will make their way to the company to be able to benefit of the new product or service. However, most markets are so complex, with products and services only showing marginal differences,

[70] Cp. Van Reekum, A. H. (1999), p. 99.

[71] See in particular Aaker, D. A. (1991); Hall, R. (1992); Aaker, D. A. & Jacobson, R. (1994); Güldenberg, G. H. (1999; 1999a); Interbrand (1999); Majer, W. (2000).

[72] Ghemawat, P. (1986), p. 53; Bennett, P. D. (1988), p. 13.

that customers cannot readily identify the product or service offering maximum utility. Thus, the *consumers' decision making process* is often extremely complex and cannot be assumed to be a fully rational process.[73] Moreover, due to the acceleration of technological development, competitive advantage resulting from technological assets is nowadays of very limited duration. Consequently, in order to maximise the returns of a technological lead, a company has to rapidly commercialise its technical innovation on a global scale, use its technological lead to establish new advantages to up-hold or increase its current lead, and/or create market entry barriers that efficiently deter competitors from entering the market. Such an asset which can be created by means of a technological lead and that subsequently improves the initial innovator's ability to develop and efficiently commercialise successive product or service improvements, and in addition constitutes a significant market entry barrier for following companies, represents *complementary brand equity*.

However, before analysing the strategic role of complementary brand equity in protecting and appropriating intangible technological assets constituting a competitive advantage in section IV.2.2 and how companies can establish such complementary market based assets with the aid of a technological lead in section IV.2.3, we clarify in the upcoming section what complementary brand equity is. Section IV.2.1 outlines the dimensions of brand equity which leads to a discussion of the strategic relevance of brand equity within business companies.

IV.2.1 What is Brand Equity?

Although, brand equity is nowadays recognised as an important asset that often accounts for more than 50% of a company's market value, no clear and uniform definition has yet been established of what authors understand under the term brand equity (cf. figure I.1 and table III.3).[74] Moreover, little has been said about how the extremely high values which are attributed to individual brands, come about. Interbrand (1999) estimated, for example, the brand equity value of Coca-Cola on more than US$ 83 billions which represented almost 60% of the companies entire market value in 1998.

This high value of individual brands is, on the one hand, attributable to the extremely *high uncertainty* and long time periods associated with the

[73] Cp. Bettman, J. R., Johnson, E. J., et al. (1991).

[74] Cp. Pettis, C. R. (1995); Graves, L. (1998); Kerin, R. A. & Sethuraman, R. (1998); Interbrand (1999); Sattler, H. (1999); Schrage, M. (1999).

process of establishing a brand,[75] as well as the *uniqueness* of an established brand due to its *specific history*.[76] In general, the *value of the brand equity* is measured by the additional amount of money the consumer is willing to pay to get the same product or service attached to a certain brand. Accordingly, Pettis (1995a) has defined the term brand value as:

> *"... the financial advantage of a brand over a generic or less worthy brand. The financial value of the difference between the brand and product value is measured financially as the incremental cash flow that accrues from the linking of the brand with the product."*[77]

However, the incremental cash flow which can be generated by linking a brand with a product or service, is not the result of mere luck or purely arbitrary but attributable to the dimensions of brand equity. The analysis of these dimensions and their characteristics in the upcoming section leads to the clarification of the strategic relevance of brand equity in business enterprises outlined in section IV.2.1.3.

IV.2.1.1 Dimensions of Brand Equity

The considerable economic value of brand equity attributes Aaker to *five principal dimensions* which are in particular: (1) Brand loyalty; (2) brand awareness; (3) perceived quality; (4) brand associations; and (5) further brand advantages (cf. figure IV.8).[78] To clarify the contribution of each dimension to the overall value of brand equity we analyse the characteristics of each individual dimension.

Brand Loyalty

The *relatedness* of a certain consumer with a trademark or brand name is defined as customer loyalty. The brand loyalty of the consumer is significantly influenced by the *satisfaction* of the customer, the *switching costs*, but also by other, more complex and *individual associations*, e.g., a souvenir of the 'good-old-times'. Thus, it is often hard to understand why a certain customer or even customer group keeps its fidelity with a certain brand. Moreover, customers can be classified according to the relatedness of the individual person to a certain brand. For instance, the most brand

[75] Cp. Erickson, G. & Jacobson, R. (1992).

[76] For a more detailed discussion of the uniqueness of brands see chapter IV.2.1.2.

[77] Pettis, C. R. (1995a), p. 205.

[78] Cp. Aaker, D. A. (1991; 1992; 1996); Keller, K. L. (1993); Dimitriadis, S. (1994), pp. 59-61; Kapferer, J. N. & Thoening, J. C. (1994), pp. 110-115; Ellsworth, R. K. (1998); Kapferer, J. N. (1999); pp. 24-27.

loyal may be a consumer who wants to persuade his friend that Aspirin from Bayer is much better than any other generic brand of acetylsalicylic acid. On the other end of the scale we can place the consumer who is not attached to any particular brand and only seeks for the cheapest offer.[79]

Brand loyalty thus expresses the probability of the customer to change the brand if the product or service experiences a change in its performance characteristics or price. A high brand loyalty of the customer consequently reduces the susceptibility of the brand to competitor actions and hence a large loyal customer base reduces significantly a company's *marketing costs* since it is much easier to hold his current customers than to attract new ones. In addition, a high customer loyalty gives the company *time to react* if it has to adjust to competitive threats.[80] This is due to the nature of human beings, who are creatures of habit and thus reluctant to any kind of change. Moreover, why should a satisfied consumer change its habitual brand if he does not know if the new brand really offers the same or superior utility and thus incur the risk of being disappointed. Consequently, brand loyalty enables a company to reduce its marketing costs vis-à-vis competitors with a smaller or less loyal customer base and moreover it bestows the company with a certain time lag to respond to a competitive threat.

Brand Awareness

The level of awareness of a brand is the capability of a potential buyer to recognise or remember that a certain brand belongs to a certain product class. The backbone of the consumers notoriety with a certain trademark or brand names is the marketing and communication activities of a company. Brand awareness is usually taken as an indicator of the *solidity* and *commitment* of a company which is of vital importance in the purchase decision process of *long-lived investments*. This indicator function of well known brands can be ascribed to one or more of the following factors: (1) The company can afford to invest in extensive advertisement campaigns; (2) the company is already in the market for a long time; (3) the products and/or services of the company are available almost everywhere; and/or (4) the brand is used and thus is successful.[81]

A high brand awareness among potential customers represents an advantage with regard to competitors with less recognised brands since

---

[79] Cp. Aaker, D. A. (1991), pp.57-65.

[80] Cp. Zeithaml, V. A. (1988); Porter, M. E. (1991); Lane, V. & Lacobson, R. (1995); Pettis, C. R. (1995).

[81] Cp. Allegrezza, S. & Guarda-Rauchs, A. (1999); Aaker, D. A. (1991), pp. 83-91; Pettis, C. R. (1995a), pp. 136-141.

customers usually do not take unfamiliar brands into consideration in their purchasing decision. Nevertheless, the awareness of potential customers about a certain brand does not represent a guarantee for high sales figures by itself. As Bettman, Johnson et al. (1991) have shown, the customers' purchasing decision is a highly complex process that takes various different information into account. Nevertheless, the notoriety of a brand represents an extremely valuable asset due to the high *set-up costs* of brand names. The estimated costs of establishing a new brand ranges up to US$ 100 million p.a. for some products. Thus, an established brand with a high level of awareness can represent an important barrier to imitation.[82] These extremely high set-up costs accrue because the company has to acquire a *stake in customers' brain* and thus it has to invest high amounts of money over a long period of time in marketing and communication, and continuously justify customers' expectations about the product or service marketed under the brand.[83]

Perceived Quality

The quality a current or potential customer perceives of a product and service can significantly diverge from the *actual* or *objective quality* of the offering.[84] Perceived quality expresses the *subjective appraisal* of the quality of a certain product or service that is associated with a certain brand.[85] Rao & Monroe (1989) have claimed that consumers use diverse indicators to deduce the quality of a product or service. These indicators can be classified in '*extrinsic*' and '*intrinsic cues*' where extrinsic indicators are not directly related to performance (e.g., brand name, price, distribution channel), and intrinsic indicators are directly related to physical attributes of the product or scale of the service. A consumer, for example, intending to buy a computer might judge the quality of the individual offering by the brand name of the whole system or of individual components, the price, the notoriety and trustworthiness of the dealer (extrinsic indicators), as well as the capacity of the computer (e.g., processor capacity in MHz and/or memory capacity in MB), included software and the compatibility of the system with other components

[82] Cp. Jacobsen, R. (1988); Porter, M. E., Koput, K. W. et al. (1996); Demuth, A. (1999).

[83] Cp. Pettis, C. R. (1995b).

[84] "'Objective quality' refers to measurable and verifiable superiority on some predetermined ideal standard or standards. Published quality rating from sources such as Consumer Reports are used to operationalize the construct of objective quality in research studies." Zeithaml, V. A. (1988), p. 4.

[85] Cp. Zeithaml, V. A. (1988); Roa, A. R. & Monroe, K. B. (1989); Aaker, D. A. (1991), pp. 108-127.

(intrinsic cues). Empirical analyses have shown that brand names represent an important indicator of the product or service quality followed by other indicators such as the product's comparative price.[86]

The quality customers perceive in relation to a product or service associated with a certain brand is an important aspects of differentiation. Moreover, it represents a key argument why to buy or not to buy a certain branded product or service and determines the preparedness of the consumer to pay a price which lies above the price of comparable offers sold without or under another brand.[87] Perceived quality is a highly *personal* and *idiosyncratic* brand characteristic that is extremely difficult to seize.[88] Nevertheless, customers evaluate the quality by means of underlying dimensions and thus a company cannot convince customers of the high quality of the offerings sold under a certain brand in the long-run, if the products and services do not fulfil these promises in reality. A strategy of not fulfilling the promises given by a brand can destroy the trustworthiness of the company and hence render a certain brand worthless. The *underlying dimensions* that determine the perceived quality are, however, highly context and consumer dependent. Consequently, a company has to continuously collect information on consumers' expectations and desires which are subsequently used by the consumers to evaluate the quality of the offering. Moreover, a mere improvement of the objective quality, does not instantaneously lead to an increase in the perceived quality but these quality improvements have to be communicated and confirmed in every-day life over a certain period of time. Aaker (1991), for example, has affirmed that it takes about 5 years until an objective quality improvement in an automobile translates into an improvement in the perceived quality associated with the automobile brand.

Brand Associations

Brand associations represent the totality of associations that a consumer connects with a certain brand and which influence the effect he expects from the purchase of the product or service which carry the trademark or brand name.[89] Such associations generally base on *immaterial attributes*, e.g., role of technological leadership, innovativeness, or particular environmental-friendly characteristics of a product or service which is sold

---

[86] Cp. Zeithaml, V. A. (1988); Rao, R. A. & Monroe, K. B. (1989).
[87] Cp. Buzzell, R. D. & Gale, B. T. (1987), pp. 91-96; Aaker; D. A. (1991), pp. 109-113.
[88] Cp. Zeithaml. V. A. (1988).
[89] Cp. Roeb, T. (1994), p. 163.

under a certain trademark or brand name. These associations represent assumptions that do not necessarily have to accord to reality and which are built up over time through direct and indirect contact. The associations towards a certain brand are claimed to be the more solid and pronounced the more often it has been encountered and used.[90]

Such brand associations can generate value since they can be of influential importance in the purchasing decision by delivering information, differentiating a certain product or service from competing offers, generating positive attitude or feelings, and thus represent a reason to purchase or not to purchase a certain product or service sold with a certain brand. These brand associations are highly complex and related to the *distinctive history of the product or service* marketed under the brand and consequently cannot easily be imitated nor substituted by competitors.

Further Brand Advantages

The last dimension of brand equity summarises all brand related proprietary advantages not dealt with in the preceding sections. Such advantages are, for example, a specific distribution channel, the packaging of the products, but also the exclusive ownership or permission to use the subject matter of a valid patent.[91] Such assets can reinforce an existing brand, as well as significantly reduce the costs of establishing a new brand in the marketplace and thus contribute to the overall value of brand equity.[92] Moreover, such other proprietary assets, e.g., a particular product patent that bestows its owner with a legal monopoly can be the source of a company's initial competitive advantage which enables a company to efficiently build initial brand equity.

---

[90] Cp. Aaker, D. A. (1991), chap. 5.

[91] Cp. Aaker, D. A. (1992).

[92] For a more detailed discussion of the role of complementary technological advantages in the establishment of brand equity see chap. IV.3.

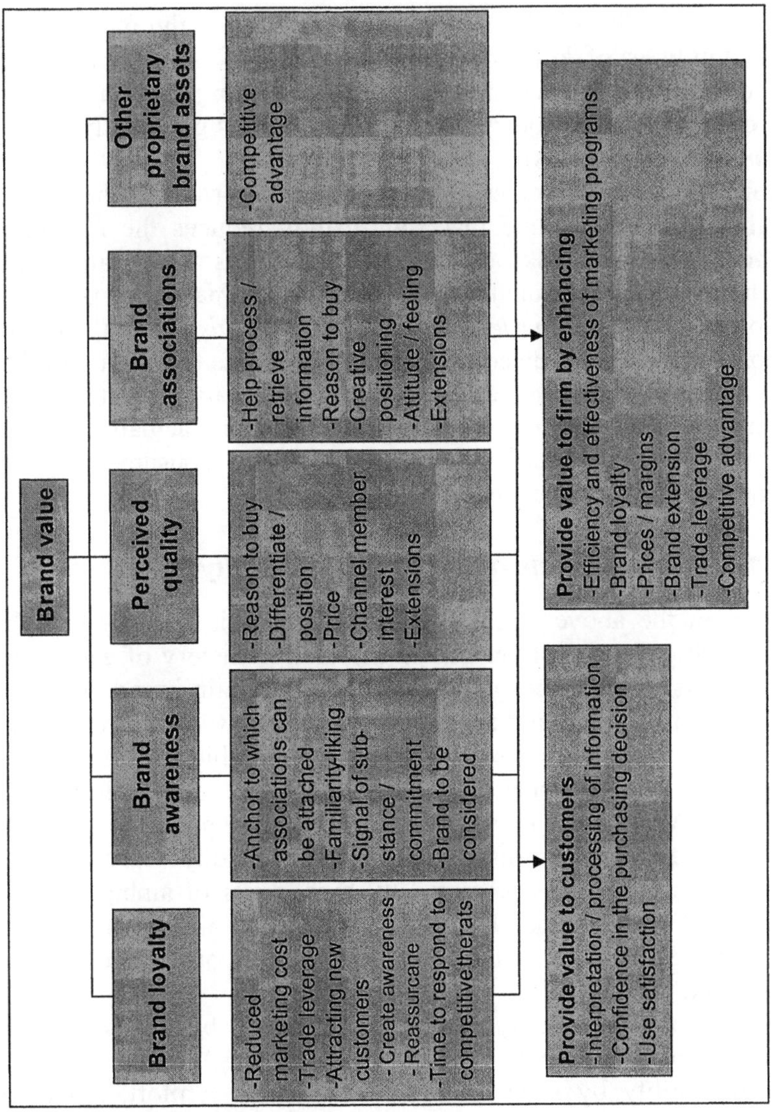

Source: Aaker, D. A. (1991), p. 312.

Figure IV.7: Five dimensions of brand equity

Recapitulating, we can affirm that brand equity represents a bundle of information, associations, and knowledge that consumers hold about the associated product, service, or even entire company. These information and associations of a brand can be assigned to the different dimensions of brand equity and, accordingly, brand equity can be defined as a '*complex quality*' where the whole is more than the sum of the individual parts.[93] Brand equity is of key importance in enabling consumers to *orientate* themselves in the market and to choose the offering that *maximises utility*. This orientation function of brand equity thus significantly reduces the *consumers' search costs*.

Moreover, consumers can draw further information from a certain trademark or brand name that significantly reduces the *risk* of market transaction.[94] These risks of market transactions which are due to the uncertainty about the quality of the offering, are particular pronounced in relation to so called *experience* and *credence goods* where the customer is not able, or only after the consumption, to evaluate the quality of the offer. Thus, brands represent a bundle of information that reduces the consumers' *uncertainty* about the offering before actually effecting the purchase, and may increase satisfaction of the consumer once he has bought the product or service (cf. figure IV.7).

IV.2.1.2 Strategic Relevance of Brand Equity

As seen in the above discussion, brand equity is a rather complex and highly ambiguous construct due to the unique history of each brand and the products and services associated with a certain brand. Thus, we can affirm that a certain brand represents a *company specific* and *unique asset* that creates a consumer benefit associated with a high *economic value* that exceeds the value of most other assets, physical or intangible, within the company. Moreover, brand equity is never perfectly *imitable* nor *substitutable* and thus we can affirm brand equity represents a *highly strategic asset* which is protected by high levels of ambiguity and legal protection.[95] Last but not least, a certain brand allows the consumer to affirm and express his personality and feelings on a *psychological and social level*.[96]

We can illustrate these qualities of brand equity by means of an example of an automobile brand. The brand 'Mercedes,' for instance, creates consumer utility by signalling high reliability, comfort, longevity, etc. before the consumer can actually evaluate these qualities. Moreover, the brand 'Mercedes' is unique due to its idiosyncratic history so that certain isolated attributes of other brands, e.g., BMW, Jaguar, or Rolls-Royce,

---

93 Cp. Güldenberg, H. G. (2000).

94 Cp. Aaker, D. A. (1992); Kapferer, J. N. & Thoenig, J. C. (1994), pp. 217-228; Kapferer, J. N. (1999), pp. 23-27.

95 Cp. Lei, D. T. (1997); Goebbels, R. (1997); Majer, W. (2000).

96 See for a more detailed discussion chap. III.3.1.

may coincide, however, the totality of the associations a certain consumer holds towards the individual brands do considerably diverge. In addition, established brand equity is not only impossible to imitate or substitute but moreover the establishment of a new brand is associated with extremely high set-up costs. A trusted brand, such as 'Mercedes,' for example, cannot be easily substituted for by 'guarantees,' as claimed by Barney (1991). This is because the customer has to belief that the company will still exist when problems occur and he may claim for mending and/or damages. However, the consumer's belief of solidity is closely linked to the brand of the product, service, and/or company and thus even the assurance of high guarantees cannot substitute for a brand associated with high quality, substance, solidity, etc. Moreover, the promotion of far-reaching warranties may even result in a signal of low quality for the customer. Last but not least, brands do have an important social-physiological function. A consumer can, for example, signal his affiliation to a certain social class or his personal success by owning a high priced premium brand.

Thus, brand equity is an important strategic asset associated with high ambiguity and legal barriers which makes imitation for competitors extremely difficult if not impossible. Moreover, the unlawful utilisation of a registered trademark or brand name is, in contrast to other intellectual property rights, immediately ascertainable in the marketplace. So, Daimler-Chrysler will instantaneously recognise, for example, the appearance of a car manufactured by another company but sold under its trademark 'Mercedes'. Finally, trademarks and brand names have in contrast to patent rights an unlimited lifetime.[97] However, one has to bear in mind that brand equity is not the result of mere luck or simple registration, but has to be earned, usually over a long period of time, through continuous *superior product and/or service competence* vis-à-vis competitors, or as Pettis (1995a) has pointed out:

> *"The basic building block is a strong product; branding won't help if the product is a bad one. But if you want to build a business, you've got to get somebody to pick up your product, and then you've got to build a good relationship with the customer."*[98]

Accordingly, Young & Feigin (1975) have established a '*customer value chain*' that integrates functional, practical, as well as psychological benefits consumers derive of a certain product and/or service offering. As illustrated in figure IV.8, the product and/or service that offers some

[97] For a more detailed discussion of the legal aspects of trademarks and brand names see chap. III.3.1.

[98] Pettis, C. R. (1995a), p. 61.

unique functional benefits represents the starting point of any customer benefit. Building on these functional benefits, customers can reap some practical benefits which again generate an emotional or psychological pay-off which is closely related to the customers' perception of the associated brand.

To build on the above cited example of an automobile sold under the brand Mercedes, the product may deliver certain specific functional benefits such as high reliability and passenger safety. These functional benefits translate in the practical benefits of lower maintenance costs and reduced risks for the passengers. The emotional pay-off of the consumer may be the feeling to be a diligent and successful person who cares about the safety of the passengers and who has the means to buy such a high priced quality product.

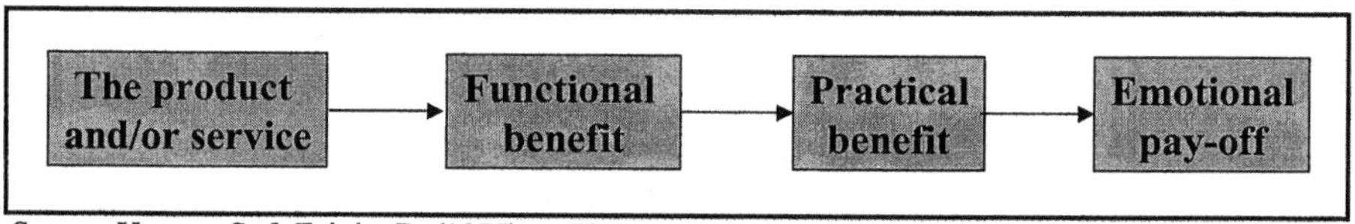

Source: Young , S. & Feigin, B. (1975), p. 73.

Figure IV.8: Consumer benefit chain

However, not only the consumers can reap a benefit from established brand equity but also the company owning the underlying trademarks and brand names and holding the associated reputation. Advantages of established brand equity for the firm arise, for instance, from the increase of effectiveness of marketing activities, the loyalty of customers that lowers the volatility and vulnerability of cash-flows, the increase in time to react to a competitive threat, and most importantly, the possibility to differentiate its products and services of those of competitors and thereby allow for relatively higher prices and profit margins.[99] As discussed before, to *sustain* a competitive advantage a company has to invest in the upholding of these assets. Such investments do, however, not only imply marketing expenses in the case of brand equity, but also investments to improve the products and services so as to better meet the customers' expectations.[100]

[99] Cp. Dimitriadis, S. (1994), pp. 34-39; Kapferer, J. N. (1999), pp. 28-30.
[100] See for a more detailed discussion chap. IV.3.2.1.

IV.2.2 Generation of Brand Equity and the Advantage of Being First

As pointed out in section IV.2.1 above, brand equity represents a competitive advantage that is protected by high imitation barriers due to the combination of high ambiguity and legal property rights. However, as Porter (1991) has pointed out, a competitive advantage building on brand equity is not a cause but rather an *outcome*. Moreover, *marketing expenditures*, also often quoted as investments in brand equity, are insufficient in building a strategic advantage since such marketing expenditures are easily imitated.[101] Companies can, nevertheless, *differentiate* their products and service from the offerings of competing companies through marketing activities by building subjective attributes. However, as stressed above, if the product or service does not hold its promises the advantage generated through marketing expenditures will be very short-lived.

As argued in section IV.2.1.3, the starting point of any positive reputation or image associated with a certain trademark or brand name is the underlying superior product and/or service offering. Thus, the starting point of any superior brand recognition is a *technological advantage* the company holds in relation to competitors. This advantage generates by offering customers an objectively superior product and/or service a positive image on the market.[102] Firms that own such a technological lead and thus are able to enter a market ahead of competitors with a new or improved product or service are called *first-mover firms*.[103] Such a first-mover position is either gained through luck or through the systematic generation of new immaterial technological assets.[104] These original innovators have three significant advantages besides the possibility to appropriate the returns of investments in R&D due to their *temporary monopoly position*, as discussed in chapter III.2.3. These three advantages that emerge from technological innovation, are the possibility (1) To move down the *experience curve* ahead of competitors; (2) to acquire *scarce complementary resources* and thus pre-empt competitors; and (3) to *lock-*

---

[101] Cp. Erickson, G. & Jacobson, R. (1992).

[102] Cp. Lieberman, M. B. & Montgomery, D. B. (1988); Teece, D. J. (2000).

[103] No consistent definition of the term 'first-mover' has been established in the literature so far. Thus, the fundamental question arises of whether a first-mover is defined according to market entry or innovation, or rather to the initiation of preliminary work, e.g., R&D.

[104] For a more detailed discussion of the generation and acquisition of immaterial technological assets see chap. III.2.

in customers through high switching costs.[105] As will be presented, all three first-mover advantages can be used by the original innovator to efficiently establish brand equity which in turn represents a considerable and extremely long-lasting market entry barrier for companies envisaging to subsequently enter the market. The following section investigates in particular how established brand equity influences the *switching cost* of customers, as well as which particular circumstances enable innovating companies to most efficiently build brand equity.

IV.2.2.1 Pioneering Brands and Customer Switching Costs

As discussed previously, customers can often not evaluate the objective quality of a certain offering ex-ante consumption. By assuming that consumers are in general *risk averse*, they stick to the brand on which they possess the most information about its quality (in particular if they had been satisfied in the past) even if the established brand is more expensive than unknown 'me-too' brands.[106] Schmalensee (1982) has cited the example of prescription drugs, where following companies cannot overcome the disadvantage vis-à-vis pioneering brands by merely offering the same pharmaceutical at a lower price, but they have to offer distinct therapeutic benefits. Thus, consumers can be expected to face considerable switching costs if they have to change to a brand whose quality they do not know in advance. This phenomenon is particularly pronounced in industries that are characterised by high cost of acquiring information, a low frequency of purchase, and relatively stable technology and consumer requirements. On the other hand, also an information overflow can be assumed to increase consumers' brand awareness because of the extremely high costs of information processing.[107]

But why do first-mover have an advantage in building brand equity? Psychological literature argues that customers pay *disproportionate attention* to innovations. Consequently, pioneering brands will occupy a relatively large *mind share*. Moreover, a first-mover firm occupies a *temporary monopoly* so that customers do not have the choice between several different product offerings sold under different brands and consequently customers acquire significant information about the pioneering brand. In addition, the initial innovator is able to define the product or service attributes which customers will subsequently consider

---

[105] Cp. Clark, K. (1987); Lieberman, M. B. & Montgomery, D. B. (1988); Barney, J. B. (1991); Lawless, M. W. & Fisher, R. J. (1990).

[106] Cp. Schmalensee, R. (1982); Conrad, C. A. (1983).

[107] Cp. Grandstrand, O. (1999), chap. 7.

as important within a particular product or service category.[108] Thus, successive entrants have to invest considerable amounts in advertising, offer their products and/or services at considerably lower prices, and/or have a *significantly superior offering* in order to attract customer attention and create purchasing incentives.[109]

These advantages of first-movers in establishing brand equity – the mostly risk averse nature of consumers – and the high costs of collecting and processing information about new brands – explains why first-movers often occupy a better part of the market and can charge higher prices than followers. Previous studies have shown that market pioneers have much larger market shares than followers in consumer goods markets, as well as industrial markets. Furthermore, the association between the order of market entry and market share is almost as pronounced as that between market share and the achieved return on investment (ROI), although the phenomenon is stronger in consumer goods markets than in industrial markets.[110]

Thus, established brand equity can be assumed to be an important market entry barrier for late movers that cannot be overcome by offering the same product and simply charging a lower price than the established firm. It follows, that established brand equity presents an important strategic advantage which puts in particular 'me-too' brands at a disadvantage and thus effectively deters potential market entry. However, how can firms possessing a certain invention establish most effectively brand equity that builds a significant market entry barrier for subsequent entrants in the market?

IV.2.2.2 Brand Equity and First-Mover Advantages

As pointed out in the preceding discussion, companies that are first on the market with a certain innovation which creates a perceivable consumer benefit, have advantages in building brand equity vis-à-vis late-movers. Moreover, such established brand equity which combines legal and reputational aspects, represents an important strategic resource due to asymmetric information prevailing on most markets about the objective quality and characteristics of the various offerings and the risk-aversion of customers. Thus, established brand equity increases customers' switching costs and in turn augments customer loyalty. However, which factors do

---

[108] Cp. Lieberman, M. B. & Montgomery, D. B. (1988).

[109] Cp. Davidson, J. H. (1976); Schnaars, S. P. (1986); Lieberman, M. B. & Montgomery, D. B. (1988).

[110] Cp. Robinson, W. T. & Fornell, C. (1985); Robinson, W. T. (1988).

lead to such first-mover advantages that result in a persisting strategic advantage? The following sections analyses in particular the two factors of *pre-emptive market entry* and *patenting* which are crucial in the establishment of brand equity.

Pre-emptive Market Entry

Innovating firms are, by definition, the first to offer a certain product or service on a specific product, service, and/or national market. Advantages of pre-emptive market entry that result in a favourable brand equity position emanate from four main effects:

1. Fast establishment of loyal customer-base;
2. Opportunity to gain broad distribution;
3. Benefit of learning-curve and economy of scale effects; and
4. Standard building prospect.[111]

As already discussed above, customers pay more attention to innovations as to subsequent 'me-too' products and gain information about the quality of the innovating brand since they cannot choose between different comparable offers. Thus, first-mover firms can benefit from a rapid formation of their customer-base which will show a high brand loyalty. This is due to the *temporary monopoly position* of the innovator and the customers' *accumulated information* about the quality of the products and/or services sold under the specific brand. Moreover, innovators can, by simply being a pioneer, profit from a *favourable product image*. Hence, pioneering firms have to spend less on marketing and promotion activities to inform customers about their offerings and simultaneously profit from a positive image of being the 'innovator.'

Another point in favour of being first is that innovators can in general more easily establish a broad distribution and obtain advantageous shelf- or store-space locations.[112] This represents a significant advantage since customers' contact with the brand is improved so that brand awareness will be increased. Moreover, in industries where retailers have a decisive influence on customer purchasing behaviour and represent an important source of information about the product quality (so called '*shopping goods*') a broad distribution can lead to favourable sales figures. However, in industries where retailers can reliably evaluate product quality and endanger their reputation in the case of inaccuracy of the evaluation, the

---

[111] Cp. Robinson, W. T. & Fornell, C. (1985); Fornell, C., Robinson, W. T. et al. (1985); Robinson, W. T. (1988).

[112] Cp. Robinson, W. T. & Fornell, C. (1985); Lieberman, M. B. & Montgomery, D. B. (1988).

positive effect of a broad distribution gained by the innovator may be relatively unimportant and/or short-lived.[113]

In industries where learning curve and economy of scale effects prevail, first-mover firms can *build rapid brand recognition* which in turn increases the quantity sold and thus drives again economy of scale and learning curve effects. Consequently, the innovating firm will, by following a target costing strategy, efficiently deter imitation and market entry in the long-run due to the impossibility of subsequent market entrants to *eliminate the innovator's cost advantages*.[114] As can be seen in figure IV.9, the demand curve D1 shifts out to D2 due to the increased appeal of the good through the innovation. By lowering the prices from P1 to P2 the innovator increases the quantity sold from Q1 to Q2. Consequently, the innovating firm benefits from a reduction in the long-run average cost (shift from LAC1 to LAC2) because of economies of scale (EoS) and learning curve effects due to the increase in quantity sold. Thus, late-mover firms which are expected to sell lower quantities because of the lack of established brand equity, will be effectively deterred from entering the market by the innovator's predatory pricing strategy.[115]

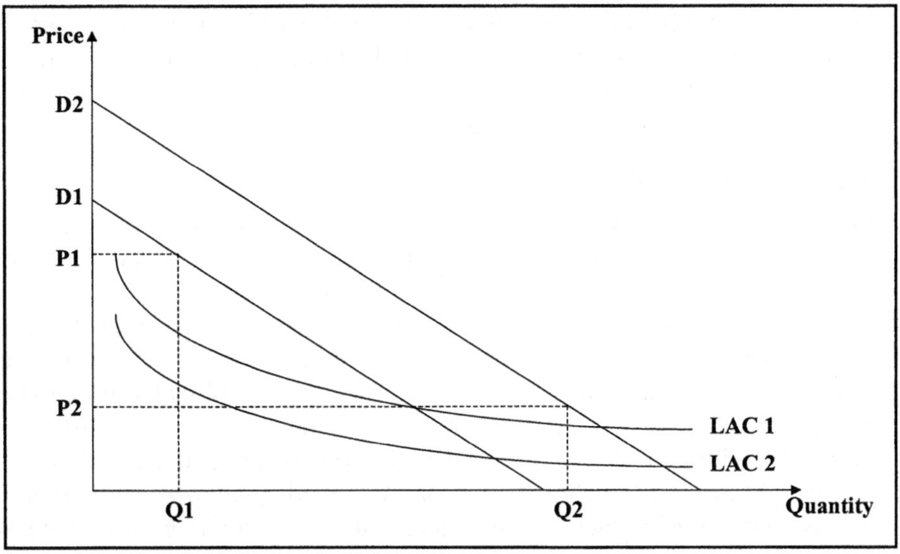

Source: Kim, W. C. & Mauborgne, R. (1999), p. 48.

Figure IV.9: Market dynamics of innovation

---

[113] Cp. Schmalensee, R. (1982).

[114] Cp. Lieberman, M. B. (1989); Kim, W. C. & Mauborgne, R. (1999).

[115] See also case study on Cisco Systems in chap. III.3.

Another advantage of innovating companies is their ability to establish a product or even technology standard. Once consumers are used to the qualities of the leading brand subsequent entrants have to *fulfil the same qualities* and they have to invest in informing the customers about the specific qualities of their offering.[116] Although, late-movers may be able to offer the same product or service with some new features and/or at a lower price, customers may stick to the established, innovating brand because of the acquired information about its quality and the risk-aversion of customers. Moreover, if a brand that customers rather perceive as a late-mover, offering comparable products at a lower price, tries to sell a high priced, innovative product, customers may just get confused since the *product may not fit the brand's image or reputation*.[117] Consequently, the company has to invest in intense customer information and still faces an extremely high risk that the market launch of the innovation may result in a complete failure.

A well documented example represents the company Intel which has successfully build considerable brand equity due to its technological leadership position. The company's image of innovativeness and technology leadership and the broad brand awareness generated by Intel subsequently enabled the company to gain and guard a substantial share of the market for microprocessors. Although, Intel's technological lead has significantly decreased, the company still owns a considerable strategic advantage vis-à-vis competitors due to established brand equity.[118]

Brand Equity and Pre-emptive Patenting

Another advantage of first-mover firms and in particular firms that generate *patentable inventions* is that they can deter immediate imitation of its invention by legal prosecution of patent infringes. However, as broadly discussed, patents do not bestow its holder with perfect protection and thus appropriation of the returns of the innovation. In most industries patents are invented around within a few years or are obviated on another legally feasible way years before the actual patent right officially expires.[119] Although, the temporary monopoly position delivered by the patent right may be too short to appropriate an adequate part of the returns of the innovation, it may be sufficiently long to *establish market based*

[116] Cp. Schmalensee, R. (1982).
[117] Cp. Porter, M. E. (1996).
[118] For a detailed discussion see Mirow, M. (2000); Cp. Pettis, C. R. (1995a), pp. 70-76; Pettis, C. R. (1995b); Aaker, D. A. (1996), pp. 12-13; Interbrand (1999).
[119] For a more detailed discussion of the shortcomings of patent rights see chapter III.3.1.

brand equity. Moreover, as Maser, a patent attorney, pointed out, patents do represent an important 'image-object' since the company can efficiently communicate competitors, potential co-operation partners, as well as customers its inventive capacity and the leading technological position of its products and services by filing patents.[120] Thus, we can argue that companies can, by filing for patent protection on their technological innovations, benefit from a temporary monopoly not only to *appropriate a sufficient part of the returns* of the innovation to justify the investments in their generation, but also to *establish market based assets* such as strong brand equity.[121] Thus, innovative companies bestowed with patent protection of their invention may be able to benefit of a longer duration of its monopoly position and thus to more effectively establish considerable brand equity vis-à-vis innovators not owning patent right protection and hence a legal monopoly over their technological invention.

Brand equity is, in contrast to patent rights and technology in general, extremely long-lasting and hard or even impossible to obviate by competitors. Once the innovating company has successfully established a favourable brand equity position with regard to later entrants by means of its temporary monopoly position established by patent right protection, the company benefits of the advantages of a company that followed a pre-emptive market entry strategy, as described above. These *market based advantages will persist* even if competing companies succeed in inventing around the subject matter of the patent or if the patent right expires. Thus, patent protection bestows the innovating company with a legal monopoly that subsequently enables it to effectively build complementary brand equity. The established brand equity will then substitute for the loss of patent protection once the patent has expired or competitors have successfully invented around the subject matter of a valid patent right. Accordingly, Schmalensee (1982) has stressed:

> *"By granting pioneering brands exclusive use of their trademarks forever, society grants something like a patent with infinite life."*[122]

Consequently, brand equity can be classified as an important strategic resource that may enable an inventing company to efficiently uphold market entry deterrence or at least bestows the innovator with a long-

[120] Cp. van Reekum, A. H. (1999), p. 100.

[121] In the pharmaceutical industry not only patents may deter imitation, but also the existence of extensive and expensive regulatory approval procedures that may even proof to be a more efficient protection mode than patent right protection. Cp. Lieberman, M. B. & Montgomery, D. B. (1988).

[122] Schmalensee, R. (1982), p. 361.

lasting advantage which enables him to appropriate a significant part of the revenues generated by his innovation. A prominent example of a company that successfully used its monopoly position due to patent right protection to establish brand equity represents the case of G. D. Searle & Co., the innovator of NutraSweet.[123]

Consequently, first-mover firms benefit from lasting advantages vis-à-vis later entrants. This is in particular true in industries characterised by *durable, irreversible, market-specific assets*, such as brand equity, and that are not subject to frequent changes in the underlying technology. Moreover, established market-specific assets are of particular strategic importance in markets where *information about product quality* is difficult or even impossible to obtain ex-ante purchase (e.g., in the case of experience and credence goods), and/or if the perceived risk of the purchaser is relatively high. This is in particular the case if the product or service is *infrequently purchased* and thus private information are incomplete, if the *unit price is high*, and if the *consequences of a bad choice* are significant. These factors create a *high importance of brand equity* in conveying information about a product's quality and create a high awareness of the consumer about the pioneering brand. In addition, first-movers benefit from the consumers' information advantage in relation to subsequent 'me-too' brands due to previously accumulated experiences. These accumulated information create a significant customer lock-in due to apparent brand switching-costs. In these circumstances pioneers have an advantage in developing brand equity with regard to later entrants. The established brand equity, in turn, represents an important sustainable strategic advantage which may enable the innovator to effectively deter market entry. This assumption is substantiated by the findings of Booz, Allen and Hamilton, who found that almost 80% of the leading brands in 1923 were still leaders some 65 years later.[124]

Nevertheless, one has to keep in mind that technological innovation does not unreservedly entail success. Various authors have stressed the immanent disadvantages of being first since fast-followers may be able to enter a market more efficiently due to the opportunity to learn from the original innovator's experience.[125] This is in particular the case in industries that are confronted with *frequent changes in the underlying*

---

[123] For more information see www.nutrasweet.com/.../his_story.html (10.09. 1999); Nalebuff, B. & Brandenburger, A. (1996), pp. 84-88, 166-167, 278-280; Teece, D. J. (1986); Aaker, D. A. (1991), p. 36; Smit, M. (1999), p. 73.

[124] Cp. Jacobsen, R. (1988).

[125] Cp. Teece, D. J. (1986); Lawless, M. W. & Fisher, R. J. (1990).

technology or where *no dominant design* has been established, yet.[126] Moreover, in markets where *no uncertainty* and thus no risk for the purchaser exists, brand equity does not have a significant economic value.[127] In such circumstances pioneering firms cannot rely on establish brand equity as a sustainable strategic advantage and consequently followers may be able to *leapfrog* market-leaders.

IV.2.3 Strategic Role of Complementary Brand Equity in Protecting Intangible Technological Assets

The preceding section has shown that pioneering brand equity is of particular strategic relevance in markets where customers do not possess perfect information about the quality of the product sold under a certain brand and where the consequences of a bad purchasing decision are important. Thus, brand equity can be said to be of particular strategic importance in industries with a high perceived risk of the purchaser.[128] However, as already shown above, a company's first-mover advantage and established brand equity are not causes, but rather *outcomes*. Thus, the question arises which factors do enable a company to pre-empt competitors and use its temporary monopoly position to establish brand equity which consequently translates in a strategic advantage vis-à-vis competitors subsequently entering the market?

In this section we investigate the relationship between technological assets and brand equity and point out their complementary nature. In particular we stress the importance of proprietary technological assets in building brand equity and the importance of established brand equity in the long-term protection of these technological assets and the appropriation of their returns. Section IV.2.3.3 then points out the importance of an integrated approach of technology and brand equity management in order to attain sustainable competitive advantage and thus appropriability of the returns of technological assets.

---

[126] For a discussion of the concept of dominant design see in particular Abernathy, W. J. & Clark, K. B. (1985); Anderson, P. & Tushman, M. L. (1990); Henderson, R. M. & Clark, K. B. (1990); Suárez, F. F. & Utterback, J. M. (1995).

[127] «Fondamentalement, il y a marque quand il y a risque. A contrario, lorsque le risque perçu par l'acheteur disparaît, la marque perd de son utilité, elle n'est plus qu'un nom sur le produit : elle cesse d'être repère, guide et source de valeur ajoutée.» Kapferer, J. N. (1999), p. 23.

[128] Cp. Kapferer, J. N. (1999), chap. 1.

IV.2.3.1 The Role of Intangible Technical Assets in Establishing Brand Equity

As shown in section IV.2.2, brand equity is most efficiently built by market-leaders by simply being the first to offer a certain product and/or service presenting advanced customer utility. Thus, brand equity can be built by means of an already existing strategic advantage which may be more or less durable. Such an advantage that enables a company to establish pioneering brand equity must have the characteristics of generating an *objective or real* and *perceptible advantage* that translates into a significant customer benefit. Such advantages are, in general, of *technical nature* since only technical advances can bring about a real product improvement or permanently reduce production cost. Accordingly, Teece (2000) has stressed:

> *"While brands are likely to be important, competitive advantage is built in the old fashioned way (by keeping customers happy)."*[129]

Thus, we can say that an important source of brand equity represents a company's *superior technological knowledge* which translates in superior product offerings and/or cheaper production costs. Through communicating the offering's advantages to consumers which often necessitates considerable investments in marketing and communication, the company can use its superior technological knowledge to establish brand equity that reflects the positive associations the consumers hold about the company's offering.

The company Bayer AG, for example, was in a position to rapidly build strong brand equity around it's trademark 'Aspirin' due to the unique advantages of the active molecule acetylsalicylic acid (ASA) with regard to competing substances. Aspirin's advantage over competing substances in fighting fever and pain was so evident that, although Bayer did initially not advertise its drug directly to the public, the trademark was immediately known among patients and the medical community, and Aspirin became within a few years the world's most widely used drug. The positive characteristics of ASA became so strongly attached to the brand that in many countries Aspirin was used as a synonym for products containing ASA and even physicians became uncertain if products sold under Bayer's trademark Aspirin and other products containing ASA, but sold under a generic brand, are the same thing.[130]

---

[129] Teece, D. J. (2000), p. 48 and cp. Porter, M. E. (1991).

[130] For a more detailed discussion of the case Bayer Aspirin see chapter II.2.

Of course, companies can also try to build brand equity by advertising and promotion. However, if the products or services do not keep these promises, customers will associate negative experiences with the brand in question. Consequently, if a company has been truthful once, customers may choose to believe it a second time, however, customers may categorical judge the assertions of companies that have lied once as false pretences be they true or false.[131] Thus, superior product perception build by subjective claims and advertising and which are not substantiated by the actual product or service offer, are extremely short lived and may turn into persisting disadvantages.

IV.2.3.2 The Complementary Nature of Brand Equity in Protecting Intangible Technical Assets

As outlined above, innovative companies can, by offering products and/or services with a real advantage vis-à-vis competing offerings, effectively establish brand equity. This brand equity represents an important resource that *complements the technological strengths* of the company. As outlined in chapter III.1, intangible assets show the characteristics of public goods and by applying for legal property rights, inventing firms are able to appropriate, at least in theory, the returns generated by the subsequent innovations. However, these legally enforceable property rights show significant shortcomings, in particular with regard to technical inventions and innovations.[132] Consequently, a strategic advantage build on a technical strength which is merely protected by patent rights or trade-secrecy, may be very short-lived. In comparison to technological resources, market based asset appear to be much more persistent (cf. table IV.1). In a national survey of chief executives in the UK designed to unveil the relative contribution of different intangible resources to the overall success of business firms, Hall (1992) has clearly identified reputation as the intangible resource with the longest replacement period.

Moreover, in addition to brand equity's relatively durable nature, it appears to be of *complementary nature* to a company's technological resources. As pointed out before, brand equity has an important strategic dimension in markets where the purchaser is confronted with *high risks*. Markets of technology products and services are inherently risky since the purchaser does not have perfect information about the offerings' quality and/or may even lack the basic technological knowledge necessary in

[131] "Fool me once, shame on you; fool me twice, shame on me."

[132] For a more detailed discussion of the shortcomings of legal property rights see chap. III.3 and IV.1.2.

order to be able to evaluate the different offers. Furthermore, the purchasing decision of many technology products is rather of infrequent nature so that the purchaser cannot rely on personally accumulated experience and, in addition, the consequences of bad choice in the purchasing decision are significant. This is in particular the case if the product is *expensive*, *long-lived*, and/or the purchasing choice determines a *technological lock in* that may later turn out to be mischievous. Moreover, in the case of durable and extremely expensive investments, such as the set-up of a mobile-telecommunication network,[133] the purchaser also faces the risk that the *supplier company may cease to exist* and thus may not be able to maintain and upgrade the product, or in the case of defects covered by guarantee to call for recompense.

Table IV.1: Replacement periods of different intangible resources

Intangible resource	Average replacement Period (years)
Company reputation	10.8
Product reputation	6.0
Employee know-how	4.6
Networks	3.4
Supplier know-how	3.1
Data bases	2.1
Distributor know-how	1.6

Source: Hall, R. (1992), p. 142.

Thus, the purchase of technology products is often accompanied by high risks not only about the product's quality and if it presents state-of-the-art technology, but also about technological lock-in, the company's continuity of service to meet a contract of guarantee, or ensure compatibility with other systems and components. Moreover, the purchasers' understanding of the technology may not suffice to evaluate the individual offers and, in addition, information is often not available ex-ante nor immediately ex-post acquisition, e.g., the compatibility with a new technology that may not even exist at the time of purchase or the continuity of the existence of the company. Consequently, in such circumstances customers may rely on established brand equity which signals state-of-the-art technology, innovativeness, good product or service quality, or just indicates a substantial financial backup that warrants the continuity of the company.

[133] E.g., Mobilcom assigned Ericsson to establish an UMTS mobile telephone network in Germany in the order of magnitude of some US$ 1.5 billions. See also case study on Cisco Systems in chap. II.3.

Accordingly, various authors have stressed the importance of the brand equity behind the letters IBM complementing the company's technological strengths. So that a product or service sold under the name IBM may be perceived as superior by customers due to the company's history of high quality and standard-setting nature of its products and the high compatibility to a large array of complementary products, the certainty of the customer that the products will be serviced in the company's tradition, and last but not least, that the company will most certainly continue to exist.[134] Consequently, if an employee is charged to decide about the acquisition of a company's new computer equipment he may be reluctant to buy a cheaper or apparently better solution with an unknown brand, since he may be made responsible for problems occurring in the future. Thus, by choosing a brand broadly perceived as a trustworthy and offering state-of-the-art, high quality products he may avoid the risk of being claimed guilty for unpredictable problems. Furthermore, in the case of actual problems he can assure to have chosen the best brand on the market so that any other solution may have been even worse.[135]

However, there are different kinds of risks purchasers are confronted with in the buying decision of technical products. We can distinguish *two principal types of risk* for the decision maker: (1) The *technology risk* which is particularly pronounced in the selection of a certain technology before a dominant design has emerged or different standards coexist; and (2) the *quality risk*, that emerges from the choice between different products within the same technology standard that offer different qualities and specifications. Technology risks thus represent worries of being locked into the wrong design/standard which may cease to exist after the establishment of a dominant design and the related problems of incompatibility and ability to up-grade. In contrast, quality risks represent uncertainties about the objective quality of the product, if it represents a high quality, state-of-the-art technological solution, as well as about the quality of the associated company, such as the availability of complementary service offerings for the product in question, if the continuity of the existence of the producer is guaranteed and consequently the availability of support/indemnification in the case of potential problems, etc. In our discussion we assume that the two types of risk are equally weighted by the decision maker, so that the *level of perceived risk* of the purchaser can be defined as the sum of the two risk types (cf. figure IV.10).

---

[134] Cp. Teece, D. J. (1986); Lawless, M. W. & Fisher, R. J. (1990).

[135] For a more detailed discussion of the role of brand equity in the purchasing decision see the case Cisco Systems in chap. II.3.

As illustrated in figure IV.10, the two different types of risk presented above do, however, not evolve in parallel along the *technology-life-cycle*. The technology risk associated with the purchasing decision will fall along the life-cycle since a dominant design will emerge and the number of competing standards will gradually decline. However, contrary to the technology risk, the quality risk will increase with the rising number of alternative offers within the same technology regime. In consequence, the purchaser is confronted with an increasing number of competing offerings that differ in objective and subjective attributes and hence the possibility to collect information about each individual offer declines. Thus, with increasing complexity of the market, and consequently reduced information of the purchaser about each individual offer, the risk associated with the buying decision increases. The decision maker's overall level of perceived risk, however, will remain virtually constant since the opposed developments of the two risk types will offset each other (cf. figure IV.10).

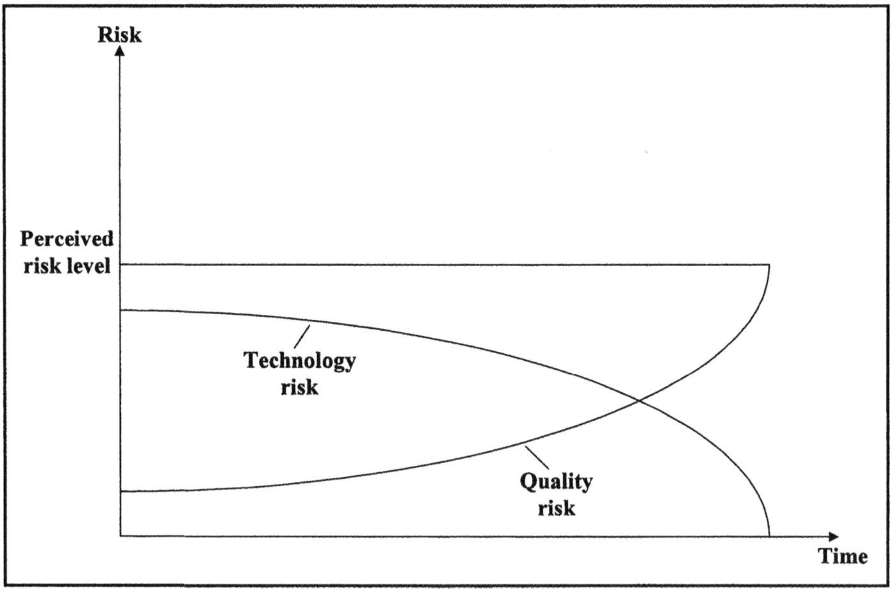

Figure IV.10: Development of perceived risk of purchaser along the technology-life cycle

As a result, purchasers of technical products can be assumed to face high risks at any moment in the technology-life-cycle and accordingly brand equity can be claimed to be of significant strategic importance in markets with a high technological intensity because of the persistence of incomplete information of customers and the resulting high levels of perceived risk. In such risk intense situations brand equity presents an *important source of information* that has a decisive influence on the outcome of consumers' decision making process. Hence, established brand equity is claimed to be an important strategic asset complementing a company's strengths in the technological field. In the long-run, established brand equity may even be a more important strategic advantage than the initial technological innovation due to its extremely long replacement periods with respect to the sustainability of technical protection modes, and its high importance in the purchaser's decision making process. Thus, brand equity can, if efficiently managed, effectively lock-in customers and thereby deter potential market entrants and consequently increases the length of time the company can *appropriate the returns* of its intangible technological assets. Nevertheless, a company should always keep in mind that brand equity represents a *quality promise* which it can only keep by owning specific technological advantages with regard to competing offers. Thus, technological advances, no matter if human capital based, intangible asset or intellectual property, are imperative in building and sustaining brand equity in the long-run.

IV.2.3.3 Integration of Technology Management and the Management of Brand Equity

As put forward above, technological assets and brand equity are of highly complementary nature. Thus, companies have, in order to efficiently build sustainable competitive advantage, to integrate the management of technology and brand equity management. However, many technologically based companies still put their main management focus on the technological aspects and completely neglect the management of the complementary market based assets. Although, *technological assets are of key importance* in generating competitive advantage and building complementary brand equity, companies solely focusing on technological advances and neglecting market based assets may be confronted with *insufficient appropriation* of the returns generated by its technological innovations because of the often short-lived nature of technological protection modes. On the other hand, once a company has succeeded in translating its technological advance into strong brand equity, the company cannot solely build on its market based strengths. A brand presents a *quality assurance* for customers in markets with high risk. If the actual product does not hold the promise given by the brand, the established brand equity deteriorates and customers may even relate negative associations with the brand. Consequently, in order to uphold brand equity a company has to maintain technological competencies. Thus, a company's technology and brand management functions have to be integrated and cannot be regarded as separate and independent corporate functions.

Moreover, the technological competencies should be used to generate *incremental innovations* which gradually improve the product or service and adapt it to the changes in customer needs. Such *incremental improvements* thus contribute to the ability of the product to keep the promise inherent to the associated brand and thereby sustain or even reinforce the customers' perception.[136] Such incremental technological improvements do, however, not only sustain or reinforce the associated brand, but may even increase the customers' satisfaction with the current prevailing technological standard associated with a certain brand and hence rise their reluctance to adopt a new technology sold under an unknown brand which has the potential to put the established technological standard in peril. Of course, the consumers' initial reluctance to abandon a certain brand may not prevent the implementation of the new technological standard, but it may permit the company possessing considerable brand equity to coexist at least over a certain time period with the new technology and consequently increases the *response-time* of the company to react to a competitive threat. Accordingly, Kline & Rosenberg (1986) have pointed out:

> *"... there is no necessary reason why new technologies should replace old ones merely by virtue of their newness. Newness is not, by itself, an economic advantage. Old technologies will often persist, even in the face of new technologies that appear to offer decisive advantages... "*[137]

Or, in the case of an incremental technological lead of the competitor, the consumer may not even realise that the company has lost its technology or quality leadership position due to incomplete information and established brand equity that customers associate with high quality, innovativeness, and state-of-the-art technology solutions.[138] However, the time period a company can build on its established brand equity is limited since consumers will sooner or later perceive the objective leeway which then will adversely alter the opinion consumers hold about the brand. The factors influencing the length of the time period consumers need to realise that perceived characteristics of the branded product diverge from the objective characteristics are identical to those determining the strategic

---

[136] Cp. Güldenberg, H. G. (1999a; 2000); Kunisch, R. (2000).

[137] Kline, S. J. & Rosenberg, N. (1986), pp. 284-285.

[138] See, e.g., the case example Intel-Inside in chap. IV.2.2.2.

importance of brand equity in a particular market, outlined in chapter IV.2.2.1.

In any case, in order to be able to benefit of these positive favourable qualities of brand equity, a company has to efficiently manage its intangible technological and market based assets which necessitates an integration of the functions of technology management and brand equity management. Principally, however, no company active in any technology market, no matter how excellent its technological competencies, can any longer afford to neglect the management of brand equity in an era where the *value of brands* can account for more than 50% of a company's market value and where brand equity represents the *quintessence of the information and feelings* consumers associated with products and services.[139] Thus, companies ignoring the importance of brand equity may accept a lower market value and hence stock prices which are in an economy dominated by *shareholder value maximisation* of key importance in the survival of the company.[140] Accordingly, Rappaport has stated:

> *"... managers who ignore the important signals from stock price – particularly in today's environment of corporate take-overs and restructuring – do so at their peril."*[141]

Another question that is often raised in relation to brand management issues is, if companies should either follow a strategy of concentrating on one *single corporate brand* or rather build up a *portfolio of independent product related brands*. Both strategies do have certain advantages, as well as shortcomings. The concentration on one single corporate brand surely *reduces the expenses for communication* and may enable the company to transfer a part of the brand equity build up by virtue of one dominant product or service to other products and services. However, such a one-brand strategy entails a *high risk* that one single product or service sold under the company brand not meeting customers' expectations causes considerable detriment across all products and services offered under the same brand. This is because of consumers' inability to differentiate

---

[139] According to company estimations, the value of brands represents in average 56% of a company's overall value. See Sattler, H. (1999) and cp. Kerin, R. A. & Sethuraman, R. (1998).

[140] For a discussion of the dangers of management adopting a dominant focus on short-term profit figures, immanent in the shareholder value approach, and the resulting under-investment in long-term strategies and assets not directly appearing on the company's balance sheet, e.g., investments in intangible assets such as technology and brand equity, see in particular Aaker, D. A. (1991), chap. 1; Aaker, D. A. & Jacobson, R. (1994).

[141] Erickson, G. & Jacobson, R. (1992), p. 1265.

between the different products associated with the same brand. On the other hand, a strategy of strong brands associated with individual products or even product generations may *increase the cost of brand management*, but definitely *limits the magnitude of damage* an isolated product or service not meeting customers' expectations can have on the company's overall brand equity and therefore significantly reduces the company's risk.

However, the above outlined discussion of corporate versus product brands does not take into consideration the *distinctive functions* of the different brands. In our view corporate and product brands do not represent substitutes, but rather complement each other. The primary functions of corporate brands is to convey information about the *overall quality and reliability* of the company's offerings, the likelihood that the company will *continue in its existence*, and *facilitate the establishment of new product brands* under the umbrella of the established corporate brand. The functions of product brands are, on the other hand, to carry product or service specific information (e.g., product's state-of-the-art, technological standard, etc.), ensure a better fit between the actual product or service and associated brand equity, permit to differentiate between different national markets and/or consumer segments that may be more or less brand aware,[142] and limit the potential damage a product group or generation that is afflicted with faults can have on the corporate brand. Therefore, we see a strong need of companies to cultivate their corporate, as well as individual product brands since they do not convey the same information to customers and hence product brands accomplish significantly different tasks than a company brand.[143]

IV.2.4 Upshot V: Strategic Significance of Complementary Brand Equity and Immaterial Technological Assets

This chapter has investigated the nature of brand equity and pointed out its importance as a strategic resource complementing a company's technological strength. As has been shown in chapter III.3, brand equity combines legal and reputational aspects and thus merges *legal property*

---

[142] Intel, for example, introduced in addition to its product brand 'Pentium' which is associated with leading edge technology, high capacity and high price, the brand 'Celeron' which is positioned so as to appeal to customers not seeking latest technology, but rather less expensive and nevertheless high quality products. Both products, however, do always appear in connection with the company name and the 'Intel-Inside' symbol.

[143] Cp. case studies on Bayer Aspirin and Cisco Systems in chap. II.

rights with *high ambiguity* which gives brand equity an important strategic dimension. This significant strategic relevance of brand equity is reflected in the high economic values attributed to individual brands. Moreover, our discussion has revealed that brand equity can be decomposed into five principal dimensions: (1) Brand loyalty; (2) brand awareness; (3) perceived quality; (4) brand associations; and (5) further brand advantages.

The establishment of such brand equity cannot, as broadly believed, be accomplished by mere marketing expenditures, but has to be built upon an objective technological advantage that translates into a superior product and/or service offer that appeals to customers. Companies owning such a technological advance over competitors are in a favourable position to establish brand equity which in turn generates a certain customer lock-in due to high switching cost. Nevertheless, a company holding such a technological advantage has to efficiently communicate the advantages of its offerings vis-à-vis competing offerings, and the product and/or service has to hold the promises made by the company in order to establish brand equity that will have a crucial role in repeated sales.

The customers' cost of switching from a well-known to an unknown brand is particularly pronounced in markets where high perceived risk for purchasers exist due to information asymmetries and bad choice leading to important consequences. Consequently, brand equity is of particular strategic importance in markets characterised by high perceived risks for customers in their purchasing decision. Markets of technology products and services are in general such markets where purchasers are confronted with high risks. Thus, established brand equity is of pronounced importance in the purchaser's decision making process of technology products and services. Moreover, brand equity appears to be extremely long-lived if managed appropriately so that it can be used to balance out the relatively short life-times ascribed to protection modes of intangible technical assets, e.g., patent rights and trade secrecy. The complementarity of technological strengths and brand equity is further increased by the necessity of a technological advantage in comparison with competitors in building and sustaining reputational assets. This leads to the thesis of chapter IV.2:

Thesis IV:
Brand equity represents an important strategic resource in markets characterised by a high technological intensity because consumers are confronted with high risks in their purchasing decision. In such an environment first-mover firms have considerable advantages in building a reputation for innovation and high quality combined with broad customer awareness. The established brand equity in turn extends the company's strategic advantage beyond the initial temporary exclusion and pre-emption time period created by proprietary technological knowledge.

IV.3 Model of Complementary Brand Equity

In the preceding chapters IV.1 and IV.2 we have discussed the strategic importance of intangible assets in business enterprises and analysed in particular the role of technological resources and brand equity. As we have seen, brand equity and technological resources are of strong complementary nature and supplement each other in particular with respect to sustainability and observability.

Building on the findings of chapter IV.1 and IV.2, as well as the analysis in chapter III we develop a model of efficient appropriation of the returns of intangible technological assets with the help of established complementary brand equity. As will be discussed in the upcoming section IV.3.1, brand equity does not only increase the appropriability of the returns of currently existing technological strengths but moreover contributes to the possibility to develop new technological assets and reduces the risk of the market introduction of subsequent, incremental technological product and service improvements. However, in order to be able to fully exploit the opportunities offered by idiosyncratic technological strengths and complementary brand equity, companies have to take the changing strategic roles of brand equity and technological assets along the technology-life-cycle into account in the management of technological assets and brand equity. The chapter closes in section IV.3.3 with an upshot of our findings analysed in chapter IV.3.

IV.3.1 Intangible Technological Assets, Complementary Brand Equity and the Effective Appropriation of Returns

As has been brought forward in the preceding chapters, intangible technological assets are, due to their global public good characteristics, subject to an important appropriation problem. Moreover, the intellectual property rights provided by regulatory authorities to protect intangible technological assets do only protect one category of intangible assets.[144] In addition, these legal property rights do not bestow their owner with perfect appropriation in the real world, as broadly assumed in theoretical discussions.[145] Thus, companies investing the significant resources necessary to generate new intangible technological assets are often confronted with the *problem of insufficient protection* of their immaterial

[144] For a more detailed discussion see chap. III.1 and in particular figure III.3.
[145] For a detailed discussion of the shortcomings of patent rights see chap. III.3 and IV.1.2.

assets which results in a rapid imitation of their innovations or even the poaching of the central employees who carry the intangible assets bestowing the company with an advantage. Consequently, companies encounter the problem of *imperfect appropriation* of the returns of their technological assets which not only reduces the companies' current profits, but also its ability, as well as readiness to invest current company resources in the generation of future intangible technological assets. Such an under-investment in technological innovation, however, endangers a company's competitiveness and thereby puts the company's future existence in jeopardy.

As pointed out in chapter IV.2, brand equity is an important market based asset with a significant strategic dimension which complements intangible technological assets. Furthermore, as stressed before, brand equity is most efficiently set up if the company in question benefits of an objective advantage as a result of a technological lead. However, how can companies utilise their established complementary brand equity to increase appropriation of the returns of their intangible technological assets? The upcoming sections discuss the importance of *brand equity in the appropriation of returns* of intangible technological assets and thus, as stressed in section IV.1.2.1, not only in safeguarding a company's currently *existing* intangible technological patrimony but also in building and protecting *potential* technological resources and competencies that might be a source of competitive advantage in the future.

IV.3.1.1 The Importance of Brand Equity in Appropriating the Returns of Technological Assets

Although numerous studies have pointed out the inadequacy of patent rights and trade secrecy in securing a company's strategic advantage built on an intangible technical asset, only a few authors have analysed the role of complementarity market based assets in appropriating the returns of intangible technological assets.[146] Moreover, the studies dedicated to the use of trademarks in protecting technological assets have dealt with the problem on a legal basis without pointing out the strategic relevance of brand equity in appropriating the returns of intangible technological assets and the resulting managerial implications. In this section we discuss how companies can use established brand equity as a complementary resource which bestows its owner with an extremely *sustainable strategic advantage* with regard to potential and actual competitors and thus may even *deter market entry* in the long-term. In addition, as will be stressed,

[146] Cp. chap. I.2.1.

brand equity has nowadays an important global dimension that facilitates the *international appropriation* of returns.

As analysed in chapter III.3, brand equity is of high strategic importance since it combines legal and reputational aspects. The reputation associated with a certain trademark or brand name is, as discussed in chapter IV.2, an extremely complex construct, closely linked to the idiosyncratic history of the company and its products. Thus, it is impossible for competitors to perfectly imitate a company's established brand equity and although trademarks can be acquired on the market, the underlying reputational aspects of loyalty, acquaintance, perceived quality, etc. has to be build by a company internally. Accordingly, Arrow has pointed out:

> *Trust " ... is not a commodity which can be bought very easily. If you have to buy it, you already have some doubts about what you've bought. Trust and similar values, loyalty or truth telling, are examples of what the economist would call 'externalities'. They are goods, they are commodities, they have real, practical value; ... but they are not commodities for which trade on the open market is technically possibly or even meaningful."*[147]

Furthermore, once brand equity has been established, it represents an important complementary resource to technological assets in the face of the *high intrinsic risks* of the technology product and service markets.[148] In order to reduce the perceived risk, consumers build on accumulated information in their purchasing decision and consequently *prefer well-known brands* which they relate to positive associations, e.g., high perceived quality, innovativeness, long track-record.

Brand Equity as Market Entry Barrier

Accordingly, we can affirm, that brand equity cannot be acquired but has to be built by the company itself through continuous superiority in its offerings. Besides, such brand equity is most efficiently built by the first-mover due to its temporary monopoly position and the particular attention paid by consumers to innovative products and services. Hence, innovating firms can, with the help of their proprietary technological assets, establish brand equity by attracting consumers' attention and build awareness of the brand by committing relatively few resources to marketing and communication. Later entrants, however, have to invest considerable resources in order to obtain a share in the consumer's mind. Even though it may be possible to achieve consumers' awareness about the new brand, late-movers still face the disadvantage that consumers have already

[147] Dierickx, I. & Cool, I. (1989), p. 1506.

[148] For a detailed discussion see chap. IV.2.3.

acquired information about the pioneering brand and thus are reluctant to change brands.

Thus, we can claim that pioneering brand equity combines two strategic advantages. On the one hand, first-movers face *lower cost* in establishing and maintaining brand equity than subsequent market entrants and, on the other hand, the established brand equity enables the innovator to *differentiate* its products from those of subsequent market entrants and hence enables him to command premium prices. Consequently, although potential competitors may be able to readily imitate the pioneering company's technological innovation and economise on the cost of technological invention, they face considerable strategic disadvantages because of the lack of established brand equity. Moreover, since the pioneer's investments in brand equity cannot be recuperated by, e.g., selling brand equity on the market, investments in brand equity represent *sunk costs* and thus market entrants can be prepared to encounter fierce price competition by entering the market.

Then again, authors have claimed in the past that subsequent 'me-too' brands are able to *free-ride* on the demand created by the innovator and enter the market without having to incur the expenses necessary to inform consumers about the advantages of new products and services.[149] This argument might be true at first sight since the innovator has to inform the consumers about a certain innovation not being pulled by the market. Nevertheless, subsequent entrants still have to inform consumers about their existence and create a certain awareness of their brand, what may appear extremely difficult since the first-mover has established broad brand awareness due to its information campaign. Most importantly, however, subsequent entrants have to convince the consumers to buy their brand although they have already gained familiarity and acquired information about the pioneering brand. Thus, consumers can be expected to be *unwilling to switch brands* and in particular to 'me-too' brands which do not offer further advantages except a lower price. Consequently, 'me-too' brands may be able to free-ride on the demand created by the innovator, however, they have to convince the consumers that they offer the same product or service with additional advantages although the consumers do not hold any information about the offerings' objective quality and the truthfulness of the company's claims. This can take the extent that consumers do not recognise or believe a company's effectively

[149] Cp. Kitch, E. W. (1977).

superior offer just because the product or service is not sold under the brand consumers associate with superiority.[150]

We can thus affirm that innovating firms can establish by means of their momentary technologically superior offering and their temporary monopoly position strong brand awareness and loyalty that in turn puts imitating firms at a *considerable strategic disadvantage*. Hence, pioneering brand equity represents a substantial market entry barrier that may even entirely deter imitation of the initial technological advantage and thus potential market entry. In addition, strong brand awareness generally translates into higher unit sales which again trigger economy of scale effects, and the innovator's early market entry generates learning curve effects which in combination bestow the first-mover with a *persistent advantage in average production costs*. Brand equity can consequently be claimed to be a strategic resource that complements a company's technological strengths and thereby enables the company to appropriate the returns of its intangible technological asset. Or, in Teece's (1986) terms, brand equity is a complementary asset needed in order to be able to effectively appropriate the returns of technological assets in the long-term.

Brand Equity and the International Appropriation of Economic Returns

As has been discussed above, complementary brand equity bestows the innovating firm with a sustainable competitive advantage which enables it to efficiently appropriate the returns of its complementary technological assets in the long-run. However, established brand equity is not only of strategic relevance in national or regional markets but also on a global scale. As argued in chapter IV.1.2.3, multinational enterprises possess advantages in the exploitation of intangible assets on international markets. Moreover, due to the mostly, relatively short product and technology-life-cycles and global technology standardisation, companies in technology markets are generally forced to market their products immediately on a global scale.

Thus, technology markets are usually characterised by a *global uniformity* where innovating companies are required to almost simultaneously launch their new product or service offerings at least within the Triad zone. This uniformity of markets is further increased by the emergence of the *Internet* as a truly global market place, where consumers can gather easily and at low cost information about the market

[150] This is, for example, the case in the microprocessor industry, where consumers associate the brand 'Intel' with technological leadership although AMD may currently offer the superior product. Cf. case Intel-Inside in chap. IV.2.2.2.

offerings and products' market positioning in various national markets. In such a global environment brands do play a particularly important role, since they often represent the only readily observable and reliable *orientation guide*, providing consumers with considerable information about the individual offer.

Moreover, established brand equity can be an *important leverage in the distribution channel* since channel members face less risk in dealing with well-known and proven brands.[151] Just like customers, channel members have accumulated information about the pioneering brand that they can use in subsequent decisions and, in addition, the customers' demand for products and services sold under a well-known and respected brand is high and less subject to general fluctuations in demand. Last but not least, products sold under a high quality brand are usually premium priced so that distributors can reap off higher absolute margins per product sold by benefiting at the same time from higher absolute quantities sold.[152] These effects are reinforced on a global scale and hence the requirement of global brand equity further increases *market entry barriers* due to the outrageously high costs of establishing global brand recognition and building a broad distribution in already established markets.

As already stated above, the appearance of the *Internet as a global market place* significantly increases the pressure for global integration and consequently the need of global brand equity. On the other hand, however, the Internet reduces the amount of information available for the consumer about a certain product offering. If a consumer seeks for information about a certain tissue in a specialised store, for example, he may be able to evaluate the quality by simply touching the tissue and/or gather further information by questioning the dealer about the differences between seemingly identical products. In the Internet, however, the consumer cannot evaluate the quality by touching or even trial-use of the different offerings and moreover no direct contact person is available to deliver specialised information. Consequently, products whose quality consumers have generally been able to evaluate before purchase in the store, turn into experience goods whose quality only becomes apparent after purchase in the Internet. Thus, the perceived risk of consumers has increased with the appearance of the Internet. Hence, the role of brands as an easily observable signal conveying important information about the product's quality is reinforced. Consequently, the Internet not only strengthens the role of global brands as vehicle of recognition and orientation but also as a

[151] Cp. Aaker, D. A. (1992); Richards, I, Foster, D. et al. (1998).
[152] Cp. case study on Bayer Aspirin in chap. II.2.

means to minimise the risk of consumers in a world of reduced information.

The advantages of a global brand strategy are opposed by arguments such as the company's unawareness of cultural differences, local peculiarities, or the non-recognition of attractive national market niches. However, many companies circumvent these problems of global integration and local adaptation by building a strong *global umbrella brand* which is complemented by *local product or service brands*. Such a strategy allows for local adaptations by profiting at the same time from the advantages of global integration. A prominent example of such a 'double-track' brand strategy represents Volkswagen which has built a strong umbrella brand around its corporate name and symbol 'VW'. The names of the individual models, however, differ across different cultural regions although the actual models remain the same. The company promotes, for example, the model which is known in continental Europe under the name 'Bora' in countries with a strong Anglo-Saxon influence, e.g., UK and USA, under the name 'Jetta.'

In conclusion, we can affirm that the establishment of brand equity by the innovator is a *pre-emptive strategic move*, since it creates a sustainable strategic advantage that competitors cannot imitate or substitute for. Thus, because of the innovators' established brand equity, subsequent entrants are confronted with a persistent disadvantage vis-à-vis first-movers. Moreover, the cost of establishing brand equity in existing markets is increasing due to the need of *global brand recognition*. Consequently, brand equity represents an important market entry barrier which bestows the first-mover with a sustainable strategic advantage and thereby enables him to effectively appropriate the returns of the initial technological innovation.

IV.3.1.2 The Role of Complementary Brand Equity in Generating New Intangible Technological Assets

The discussion of the preceding chapters has outlined the complementary nature of technological resources and brand equity, as well as the key role of established brand equity in the appropriation of the returns of existing intangible technological assets. However, established brand equity is not only of strategic importance in securing the returns of already existing intangible technological assets, but also plays an important role in the generation of new intangible technological assets, and in particular in the acquisition of external intangible assets.

Building on our discussion of the different company internal and external sources of intangible technological assets in chapter III.2, we now analyse the influence of established brand equity on the generation of new intangible technological assets in business enterprises. In the case of internal sources, where our discussion has primarily focused on R&D activities and learning-by-doing, brand equity can be considered to be of negligible importance. This is because of the strong influence of prevailing internal resources and capabilities on the creative outcome of the firm. In the case of *external acquisition of intangible assets*, however, market based assets and in particular brand equity can be expected to have a strong influence on the outcome of the company's undertakings. We concentrate our analysis in particular on the acquisition of human capital based assets and the access to intangible technological assets via co-operative agreements, since prevailing information asymmetries and the consequences of bad choice are considered to be significant.

Acquisition of Human Capital Based Intangible Assets

Labour markets can be considered as *inherently risky* since employees cannot objectively evaluate the quality of a potential employer before having signed the contract of employment and having spent a certain amount of time within the company. Moreover, almost no objective information about the potential employer's qualities such as good working climate or corporate culture are available ex-ante. Consequently, in order to minimise the risks associated with bad choice, employees use certain *criteria* in their decision of where to apply to and to work for. First of all, they can be expected to apply first to those companies which they know from direct or indirect personal contact, and here again employees will prefer those companies which they associate with a positive reputation. This *positive reputation* does not necessarily have to be based on the reputation as 'good' employer per se, but can also be based on the general success of the company or its reputation as a particularly innovative, stable, and/or international company.[153]

Thus, the employee may use information which he has acquired about the products and services offered by the company, and transfers these on the company's qualities as an employer. In Germany, for example, Daimler-Chrysler, BMW, or Porsche may be known as brands for prestigious, high quality products or successful companies active on an global scale. These associations are, in the absence of more objective

[153] JMC, an affiliated company of Thomas Cook in the leisure travel industry, has experienced an increase in job applications from the usual average of 200 to 300 per season to 6,000 by the market launch of its innovative services and the establishment of a brand standing for an innovative company fully dedicated to customers' needs. See Allen, D. (2000).

information, equated to the company's qualities as a potential employer. As can be seen in table IV.2, the majority of the fifteen companies ranked as the most favoured employers in West Europe are also present on the list of the world's most valuable brands. Consequently, this comparison of data from different sources supports the assumption that companies which are associated with well-known brands benefit of a large number of employees eager to work for them and thus can *chose the most qualified and apt* employees and thereby enrich the company's stock of human capital based intangible asset. Moreover, these companies may even be able to entice highly qualified and specialised employees or even whole groups of employees working for competitors and thereby acquire know-how from competing companies.[154] In this context, a company reputation of innovativeness, technology- or market-leadership may be of particular advantage since the potential employees may equate such established brand equity with a corporate culture fostering innovation and change and thus optimal conditions for creative work.[155]

Thus, companies owning significant brand equity are perceived as *attractive employers*. Such a reputation does, however, not only represent an advantage in attracting new potential employees but also in the *retention of current employees*. An employee not satisfied with his current employer may be reluctant to change to another company lacking a broad recognition and a positive reputation. This reluctance of employees to change employer due to a company's established brand equity may be of particular importance with respect to the perceived *brain-drain* in relation to M&As.[156] A company holding considerable brand equity, and in particular a reputation for innovativeness, market and/or technology leadership may have a better stand in preserving creative and highly qualified specialists since they expect a company holding such a reputation to offer good working conditions.

---

[154] For a more detailed discussion of the role of employee enticement in the enrichment of a company's portfolio of human capital based intangible asset see chap. III.2.2.2.

[155] Cp. case study on Cisco Systems in chap. II.3.

[156] For a detailed discussion of the risk of employees leaving the company as a consequence of M&As see chap. III.2.2.2.

Table IV.2: Employer attractiveness and brand equity

Company	Employer Ranking (West-Europe)[1]	Brand Value Ranking[2]
Anderson Consulting	1	NA
Coca-Cola	2	1
Sony	3	18
BMW	4	22
Nokia	5	11
Nestlé	6	13
Siemens	7	NA
Ericsson	8	17
Philips	9	NA
Procter & Gamble	10	33
IBM	11	3
Volkswagen	12	31
The Boston Consulting Group	13	NA
Shell	14	49
Hewlett-Packard	15	14

Data sources: Interbrand (1999); EMDS Group (1999).
Ranking of the most favoured employers in west Europe according to the statements of 12,000 employees. Our listing excludes the public sector.
Ranking of the world's most valuable product or corporate brands according to the Interbrand (1999) ranking.

However, brand equity does, just as in the case of consumer expectations, represent a *promise* given by the company to its potential and actual employees. Consequently, if the company is not keeping its pledges, no matter if towards consumers or employees, the neglect will result in the detriment of established brand equity. Accordingly, Hall (1997) has stressed:

> *"It is appropriate to suggest that companies should strive to make employees the custodians and promoters or their employer's reputation – if employees do not hold the company in high regard why should anyone else?"*[157]

Access to Intangible Technological Assets via Co-operative Agreements

As we have seen, brand equity appears to have a significant influence on a company's ability to attract new employees and thus acquire human capital based assets. Another market which is associated with considerable risks for the participating partners represents the market for corporate co-

[157] Hall, R. (1997), p. 44.

operation agreements. Moreover, the *risks* of such co-operation agreements are, because of the inability to evaluate ex-ante the effective technological and market based abilities of potential co-operation partners, extremely apparent and pronounced. Established brand equity can play in such environments of high asymmetric information an important role as an indicator for a firm's proficiency in a particular market or technology field. As we have seen in the discussion above, brand equity is built by a company through *superior performance* which translates into enhanced consumer utility. Moreover, since brand equity is primarily influenced by the final performance of the product/service it combines all strengths of the company regardless of their form, human capital based, intangible assets, or intellectual property. Consequently, established brand equity can be claimed to represent a *reliable indicator* of a company's current strength in a particular market and/or technology field. Furthermore, established brand equity used as an indicator of corporate strengths has the advantage, with respect to the analysis of a company's patent portfolio, to take all intangible assets held by a certain company into consideration and not merely legally protected technological innovations fulfilling the requirements of the relevant patent offices.

Thus, established brand equity can be used as an indicator of a potential co-operation partners' high capabilities in a particular field. In consequence, established brand equity can be expected to be a *key-factor* in accessing certain technology co-operation or knowledge networks, that may remain remote for companies not owning complementary brand equity. A close integration of the company in co-operation arrangements and knowledge networks, in turn, enable it to access new and/or complementary intangible assets and thus to expand and uphold its competitive lead with regard to competitors not having access to such co-operative networks.[158] However, the reputation as a good and valuable co-operation partner has to be proven in real terms otherwise the company endangers its stock of established brand equity and not only puts its reputation as a reliable and important co-operation partner in peril but also its image as a technological competent producer of products and services.

A co-operation agreement of a less renown company with an enterprise holding strong brand equity in a certain technology field is often already perceived as an *appreciation of the company's strategic positioning* which again is reflected in the company's market value. This is because consumers, competitors, as well as potential future co-operation partner take notice of the afore unknown company and thus the general awareness

[158] For a detailed discussion of the role of co-operative forms in accessing external sources of intangible assets see chap. III.2.3.

about the existence of the company, its product and/or service offerings. Furthermore, the co-operation partner lacking established brand equity will build, by co-operating with a company renown for its technology competencies and innovative offerings, a *reputation of technological competence* since he will be perceived as a 'dignified' co-operation partner of a renown company.[159] Thus, an unknown or less famous company can build brand equity by co-operating with companies holding considerable established brand equity. However, not only the less renown company can benefit from such co-operation agreements but also the company holding established brand equity since it benefits of a good stand in the *co-operation negotiations*. Accordingly, a company endowed wit considerable brand equity may be able to reduce its financial and/or technology contribution to the joint undertaking and/or may be able to impropriate the better part of the achievements of the co-operative arrangement.

A company holding established brand equity may thus be considered by potential co-operation partners as competent and thus a coveted partner which in turn facilitates the company's access to knowledge networks and co-operative arrangements and improves its stand in negotiations. However, just as before, we have to stress that brand equity advantages can be extremely short-lived if the company is not keeping the promises made by its brand and may even result in a negative reputation and thus will make future co-operation difficult if not impossible.

Thus, established brand equity confers a company an advantage in attracting and retaining employees and related human capital based assets, as well as in accessing external intangible assets via co-operative arrangements and knowledge networks. In turn, established brand equity can also be claimed to protect a company from competitors' attacks to *entice central employees* or to thwart an attempt of a *hostile take-over* because of the considerable economic value of established brand equity. Consequently, companies disregarding the importance of brand equity may not only miss out on beneficial co-operation which may have increased the company's technological competencies and thus improved its competitive positioning, but also endanger the company's currently existing stock of immaterial valuables, as well as the existence of the entire company.

---

159 This 'upgrading' of a company can even trigger an effect of increased demand for co-operation: "if even company X co-operates with them we have to do so, too!"

IV.3.2 Efficient Management of Established Brand Equity

As we have seen above, brand equity is an important strategic asset bestowing a company with sustainable advantages. However, brand equity has to be build by objective product and/or service advantages which translate into improved consumer utility, and does not fall from heaven just like manna. Moreover, established brand equity is an *extremely fragile strategic resource* that will not grow on its own over time, but has to be continuously cultivated and nurtured. However, if a company accurately manages its brand equity it represents an extremely persistent and important strategic advantage that enables a company to keep potential and actual competitors under control and appropriate an important part of the returns of its investments in technological assets.

So far, we have analysed the complementary nature of brand equity and technological assets and the strategic importance of established brand equity in efficiently appropriating the returns of technological resources in the long-term. This chapter now focuses on how companies can *invest in the uphold or even reinforce established brand equity which strategic role* brand equity occupies in the different stages of the *technology-life-cycle*, how it can efficiently be used in the market launch of *subsequent innovations*, and finally how management responsibility for brand equity should be *allocated* within business enterprises.

IV.3.2.1 The Role of Subsequent Technological Innovations in the Upholding of Established Brand Equity and the Advantage of the Innovator

As chapter IV.2.2 has clearly pointed out, innovating companies do have advantages in building brand equity. However, established pioneering brand equity is extremely fragile and can seriously be damaged or even permanently erased by not keeping the promises made by the brand or by bad communication of the company. This section outlines the possibilities companies have to nurture and grow their existing brand equity and thus to reinforce entry barriers for subsequent market entrants.

As has been described above, brand equity can be broadly defined as all associations consumers, partners and competitors hold about a company and its offerings. These associations are of particular importance in markets with high uncertainty since they convey important information that the actors cannot gather, or only in association with high cost. Thus, brand equity represents a guarantee of the company that, when it is kept, reinforces the associations of the actors. If, however, the company is not keeping brand equity's promises, the accumulated stock of brand equity will deteriorate and actors will no longer believe the guarantees given by the company's brand. In order to avoid the deterioration of existing brand equity or even enhance established brand equity companies have thus to make sure that the company's offerings *always keep the promises* other parties derive from the brand. On the other hand, a company can influence the expectations of consumers about the products sold under a certain name by clearly *communicating* the products' characteristics, for example, which subsequently have to be fulfilled by the product.

However, how can a company that has acquired considerable brand equity due to a successful product or service innovation fulfil the consumers' expectations of innovative offerings, showing a technological lead vis-à-vis competitors products in the long-term? It seems, that it becomes even harder to satisfy these expectations if competitors are able to easily imitate the technological innovation and thus avoid a large part of the initial research and development cost. Then again, it has to be ascertained that in most markets consumers and even companies themselves are *not able to perfectly compare* the offerings of competing companies because of the embarked strategies of product and service differentiation and consumers' lack of technological knowledge. In addition, in a market where consumers can evaluate the objective quality of an offering only by personal experience, the innovating company has a considerable advantage in comparison with simple imitators since consumers are extremely brand loyal due to existing *switching costs*. Consequently, consumers are reluctant to change brands if they do not expect significant advantages that outweigh the cost associated with switching brands. Thus, simple imitation or replication does not represent a real threat for the first-mover who is endowed with considerable brand equity.

Nevertheless, it will not suffice for a company to generate just one important innovation delivering considerable consumer utility that translates into brand equity and subsequently rely on consumers' loyalty. Since consumers expect from a company holding pioneering brand equity that it offers leading technological solutions and thus if the company wants to ensure the perpetuation of its established brand equity it has to *continuously improve* its offerings. In such continuous product and service improvements *incremental innovations* do play a central role and have significant cumulative influence on the products overall performance and/or production costs. As already analysed in chapter III.2, such incremental innovations are not the outcome of large scale investments in R&D but can rather be attributed to so called effects of learning-by-doing.[160] Thus, the innovating firm has a *head start* with respect to imitators which it can use to move down the learning curve. Moreover, since the innovator is in a position to establish rapidly and at low costs brand equity that in turn will allow for relatively high unit sales with respect to late entrants, it generates more easily incremental innovation due to *learning-by-doing* and benefits from larger *economies of scale*.[161]

Accordingly, innovating firms start earlier to learn about the exact requirements of consumers and the potential improvements in the product's design and the production process which bestow the first-mover with an *advance in the generation of incremental innovation*. In addition, due to the higher unit sales of products sold under a broadly known and respected brand, a company holding pioneering brand equity can use its established *brand equity as a leverage* in the generation of economies of scale and learning curve effects. These *continuous incremental innovations* in turn enable the company to better satisfy consumer expectations and to embrace its innovative and leadership reputation. Consequently, incremental product and service innovations represent continuous improvements in consumer utility and, if introduced in advance to competitors, are an important instrument to *uphold or even reinforce an innovative reputation* and thus a first-mover company's stock of brand equity.[162] Furthermore, the more satisfied current clients are with a brand, the less likely they are to switch to new and unknown brands although they may be less expensive, and in turn the lower the probability that imitators will actually enter the market or that existing competitors will be able to catch up on economy of scale and learning curve effects.

However, companies should not overestimate the stir caused by incremental innovations themselves moreover, the ready observability of such minor improvements in the offering by consumers is not always given. Thus, in order to fully benefit from incremental innovations and maximise its impact on brand equity a company has to *communicate improvements* in its offers and create awareness about the improved consumer utility. Again, a company cannot expect that the consumers will 'make a beaten path to its door' just because it is offering a 'mouse-trap' that is marginally superior to competing bids. Thus, a company has to communicate its improvements where again first-mover firms have advantages just because of being first. In addition, established brand equity which corresponds to the new improvement, facilitates and reduces the

---

[160] For a detailed discussion of learning-by-doing and the generation of incremental improvements see in particular chap. III.2.1.2.

[161] See also chap. IV.2.3.2 and figure IV.11.

[162] Cp. Srivastava, R. K., Shervani, T. A. et al. (1998).

costs of communication since the company can build on the *exiting awareness* and *information* of consumers about the brand. We can thus claim that brand equity represents an important barrier to imitation of technological assets that can be *upheld and even reinforced* by continuously and *incrementally improving* the actual product and/or service offering. However, in order to fully leverage the affects of these improvements the company has to *effectively communicate* its advances and advantages vis-à-vis competitors.

Moreover, such incremental innovation and their effective communication enable a company to *adapt its offerings* and the *consumers' perceptions* about its brand to the current needs and market trends. However, companies have to be aware that a strategy to satisfy the needs of *current clients* and thus to keep them loyal has to be preferred due to lower costs to hold clients already familiar with the company's brand and its offerings, and the influence of loyal clients on the acquisition of new customers by word-of-mouth information. Therefore, a company should follow a stable strategy of responding to the needs of current clients and not frequently adjust to new, short-lived trends, and consequently build a growing base of *loyal customers*. Repeated and frequent changes in a company's positioning of its brands and numerous adaptations to ephemeral trends may just blur the established brand perception and thereby *confuse consumers*.[163] Moreover, clients that can easily be attracted by such short-lived trends or simple marketing activities are, by their nature, not very *brand loyal* and easily change the brand with the new, upcoming trend. Nevertheless, a company has to regularly improve and, in doing so, adjust its offerings and brand perceptions to current customer needs and expectations. It is, however, important that these adjustments correspond to the established brand and thus follow a *long-term oriented strategy*, such as a technology, quality or price leadership strategy, for instance.

An often cited problem of companies, however, presents their reluctance to innovate since they fear that the new product generation will *deplete the demand* for the own, currently existing products. So, it is quite obvious that the demand for Intel's Pentium II processors declined substantially by the market launch of the Pentium III chip. Accordingly, Lieberman & Montgomery (1988) have pointed out:

> *"Arrow was the first to lay out the theoretical argument that an incumbent monopolist is less likely to innovate than a new entrant, since innovation destroys rents on the firm's existing products."*[164]

---

[163] Cp. Aaker, D. A. (1997).
[164] Lieberman, M. B. & Montgomery, D. B. (1988), p. 48.

Innovators, however, have to realise that initial success and established brand equity does not involuntarily grant a license for eternal competitive advantage but rather that they benefit of unique opportunities to build idiosyncratic complementary resources and get a head start on the learning curve. However, these *opportunities* and the *subsequent strategic advantages* of the pioneering company are extremely short lived if they are not fostered.[165] Thus, first-movers have to continuously innovate to meet changing technologies and customer requirements and to communicate their leadership position and thereby reinforce current technological, as well as brand equity advantages. By doing so, innovators become formidable rivals that are extremely difficult to defeat and consequently are able to sustain their strategic advantages and to appropriate the returns generated by their intangible assets. Or, as Deutschman (1994) has pointed out:

> *"What high-tech types have realized is that the real money isn't in making a one-time sale of computer hardware or software, but in maintaining a long-term relationship with the customer, who will keep coming back for service, support, and new, incremental improvements in the product. Most businesses based on such relationships are gloriously resistant to commoditization or price wars."*[166]

Another important problem is that companies only consider brand equity as an important strategic resource when market conditions become rougher and/or the company has apparent problems to meet market needs or customer requirements. Brand equity can, however, only be built by a company in a *position of relative strength* and the failure of the company to do so may not even be immediately noticed. Yet, as soon as competition becomes fiercer and the innovator's products are imitated, the neglect of brand equity will become apparent by the easy market entry of imitators and their ability to attract large numbers of consumers which again translates into *fierce price competition* and *rapidly declining profit margins* for the innovator. In such an advanced stage, however, when imitators already make the innovator's life difficult, it is extremely hard if not impossible to build significant brand equity. Thus, brand equity has to be *build in good times* so that the company can rely on it when times are getting tougher.

---

[165] Cp. Lieberman, M. B. & Montgomery, D. B. (1988).
[166] Deutschman, A. (1994), p. 102.

IV.3.2.2 The Management of Complementary Brand Equity and Intangible Technological Assets along the Technology Life-cycle

So far we have discussed the importance of brand equity and its efficient management in order to uphold or even reinforce barriers to imitation which in turn enable a company to appropriate the returns of intangible technological assets in the long-run. We have revealed that the innovator can effectively establish brand equity due to its temporary monopoly position and the considerable attention consumers pay to innovations in comparison to subsequent market entrants. However, the *strategic role of established brand equity* cannot be considered to be stable along the *technology's life-cycle*, but rather evolves with time and the increasing spread of the technology, as well as the number of competitors.[167]

As already discussed in chapter IV.2.3.2 the consumers' perceived level of risk can be assumed to remain almost constant along the technology-life-cycle since the reductions in technology risk is compensated for by the increase in quality risk (cf. figure IV.10). Thus, brand equity permanently plays an important role in the consumers' decision making process. However, from the point of view of the innovating company, brand equity's strategic importance will *increase along the technology-life-cycle.* At the beginning the company owns a competitive advantage due to its idiosyncratic technological assets that bestow it with a real advantage in its offerings vis-à-vis competing companies and does not yet, or only marginally, hold brand equity. However, as pointed out before, the innovating company can efficiently *establish complementary brand equity* and thereby balance out the *loss of its technological advantage* due to the relatively rapid imitation of its intangible technological assets. Thus, the more advanced the position in the technology-life-cycle the more important the strategic role of complementary brand equity.

As illustrated in figure IV.11, at the beginning of the technology-life-cycle the technological assets are of key importance in building a company's strategic advantage. In the *innovation phase* the accumulated stock of brand equity is low and thus adds only marginally to the company's strategic advantage. However, the more advanced the technology-life-cycle the more competitors appear on the market having successfully imitated the innovator's initial technological advantage and/or invented around established patents. Consequently, the innovator's technological advantage, although still important, starts to decline towards the end of the innovation and in the *early growth phase*, whereas brand

[167] See also chap. III.3.3.

equity's strategic importance continually increases in importance. The rise of brand equity's meaning as a strategic resource is due to the increase in competing offers and consequently the perceived quality risk of consumers. Moreover, the innovator is granted an advance with respect to me-too brands in building brand equity which bestows him a permanent advantage if managed appropriately. Towards the end of the growth phase and with the *beginning of the maturity phase* the basic technology is available to all companies in the market and thus the innovator no longer has a strategic advantage due to basic technological knowledge. However, the pioneering firm may still hold a technological lead in specific fields due to its advance on the learning curve and incremental innovations. In contrast, brand equity's strategic importance is continuously increasing due to the increasing number of competitors and thus complexity of the market which increases consumers' perceived risk.

Finally, towards the *end of the maturity phase*, the competitors show almost identical technological competencies or out-source the production of certain components that are of low strategic importance and specificity. Moreover, the currently established technology system is increasingly threatened by new technological generations which we call in accordance to Henderson & Clark (1990) architectural innovation. In the *phase of architectural innovation*, when the current technological standard coexists with the new technological improvements in the product architecture, however, no 'new' technological standard has been established, yet, the sales of the companies selling the 'old' technology can be attributed to the high technological risks of the new technology and the high brand equity of the established firms. Technological assets only play a marginal role to differentiate one's product from competing offers and merely applies to specific and isolated product features. Then again, as soon as the new technology standard has been established, sales of products based on the old technology standard will rapidly decline.

Thus, the *strategic role of technological assets* and *complementary brand equity* cannot be defined as stable but rather technological assets can be expected to gradually decline whereas brand equity will continually appreciate in strategic value along the technology's life-cycle. This is because of the inefficiencies and limited lifetime of the protection modes of immaterial technological assets and the increasing importance of a loyal consumer base, repeated sales, and protection of ruinous price warship and thus the maintenance of profit margins. Brand equity that enables the company to effectively *differentiate* its offers from competing bids is at the centre of any loyal customer base and the resistance to price competition.

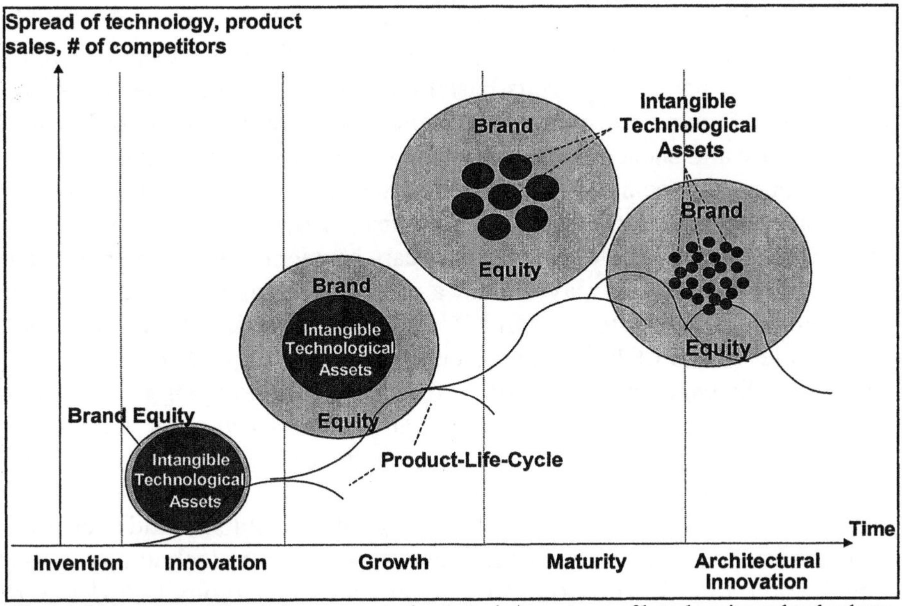

The (visible) surface of the circles represents the strategic importance of brand equity and technology assets, respectively.

Figure IV.11: The development of the strategic role of technological assets and brand equity in the technology-life-cycle

An example of the evolution of the strategic roles of technological assets and brand equity in the technology-life-cycle represents Bayer Aspirin. As was pointed out in chapter II.2, Bayer was able to establish considerable brand equity due to the apparent advantages with regard to competing offers in the market for analgesics and its temporary monopoly position because of the existence of patent right protection and the inability of competitors to readily imitate the underlying technology. In the course of time, however, the strategic importance of brand equity increased and became so dominant that new market entry was negligible, although potential competitors could readily imitate the underlying technology. Thus, Bayer was able to appropriate a major share of the returns generated by its invention of the synthetic production process of the molecule of acetylsalicylic acid due to the brand equity attached to its trademark Bayer Aspirin. The pronounced strategic importance of brand equity in establishing a competitive advantage became particularly apparent by Bayer's loss of its trademark and thus brand equity in specific national markets, e.g., Great Britain, France and associated colonies, where Bayer had completely left the market. On the other hand, in markets where Bayer was able to perpetuate its trademark and brand equity, e.g., Germany,

Argentine, the company has been able to defend its supremacy on the market of products based on acetylsalicylic acid for more than 100 years. Although new competing drugs based on different active substances have appeared that have shown distinct advantages, Bayer was able to defeat its market share and successfully co-exist with the new technologies.[168]

Of course, any technology standard may sooner or later be threatened by substituting and improved technologies. However, by incremental innovations the technology-life-cycle can be significantly extended and moreover brand equity may enable a company to increase the period of technological co-existence and thus increases its time to react. Nevertheless, it is of key importance to strike the *right balance* between *incrementally improving* the existing technology and keeping an eye on the *development of substituting, architectural innovation.* As stressed in chapter IV.3.1.2, companies endowed with considerable brand equity benefit from *advantages in accessing externally existing intangible technological assets*. Thus, by enticing star-scientists and accessing external knowledge, companies dominating the current technology system may be able to efficiently build know-how and technology knowledge on the new technological generation and hence to *transfer* at least a part of their *competitive lead* in form of brand equity on the next technological-life-cycle.

Consequently, the strategic importance of complementary brand equity increases along the technology-life-cycle. Nevertheless, technological resources remain important in incrementally improving and in differentiating the company's offers although their overall strategic role declines over time. Then again, innovating companies have to keep in mind that brand equity is build most easily in the early innovation phase of the technology-life-cycle, however, it becomes increasingly difficult and expensive to establish brand equity in advanced phases of the technology-life-cycle. Hence, innovators have to build brand equity when its strategic importance for the company may be negligible in particular with regard to its idiosyncratic intangible technological resources. However, if the innovator fails to establish considerable brand equity during the early phase of the technological-life-cycle, or it does not appropriately manage established brand equity, the company endangers its future strategic advantage and perhaps even the continued existence of the entire company.

[168] For a detailed description of the case Bayer Aspirin see chapter II.2.

IV.3.2.3 The Role of Established Brand Equity in the Market Introduction of Subsequent Product Generations

As the preceding discussion has shown, the strategic importance of brand equity increases along the technology-life-cycle which again will have considerable influence on the *introduction of the different product generations* within the same technology-life-cycle. During one technology-life-cycle several product-life-cycles can be identified (cf. figure IV.11). This is not surprising if one bears in mind the extreme length of certain technology-life-cycles which can easily persist over 100 years and more. If we take the examples of acetylsalicylic acid, the combustion engine and the automobile as we know it, MS-DOS based PCs, the analogue telephone technology, or just ordinary light bulbs, it becomes apparent that a certain technological standard can easily last over several decades or even a century. However, the underlying technology cannot be defined as stable over the whole technology-life-cycle, but is rather continuously improved by *incremental innovations* in the product and production process. These minor improvements in the existing technology nevertheless have a considerable cumulative influence on product qualities, as well as on unit production cost.

These cumulative incremental improvements do necessitate from time to time the adaptation of the company's product offer to efficiently integrate the improvements in the product's characteristics. In more or less regular time intervals the product's qualities are significantly improved and/or attributes considerably changed so that different *product generations* can be identified. As figure IV.12 illustrates, each product-life-cycle can again be subdivided in the four distinct periods: (1) Introduction; (2) growth; (3) maturity; and (4) decline. In the introduction phase the growth of sales figures is still relatively low, since consumers are not familiar with the new product. However, with increasing familiarity and information about the new product growth in sales significantly increases until the maturity phase when sales figures stagnate on a high level. In the subsequent level, when already the new and improved product generation is introduced on the market, sales of the old product will decline.

As can be seen in figure IV.12, initial product sales are low because of the consumers' *unfamiliarity* with the product and *lack of information* about the product's quality. However, as soon as consumers' knowledge about the product offer increases, growth of product sales picks up. To avoid the low initial product sales at the beginning of each product generation, a company may be able to transfer previously *established brand equity* on the new product generation and by doing so significantly increase consumers' *information* about the product attributes and create a *feeling of trust.*[169] Thus, the company can build on the existing *loyal customer base* established by earlier product generations and can thereby economise on marketing and communication expenses required to familiarise and inform consumers about the improved product and its basic qualities. Established companies that have already built up considerable brand equity in preceding product generations, consequently benefit of an *advantage* in the market introduction of the subsequent product generation.[170]

Figure IV.13 illustrates the progression of product sales within the technology-life-cycle. Accordingly, a company can build on the loyal customer base established by the preceding product generations by passing on established brand equity to the new product generation. This transfer of established brand equity in turn bestows consumers with information about the product's characteristics and qualities and thereby reduces uncertainty and thus perceived risk. Moreover, since the brand is already endowed with considerable consumer awareness, a company that succeeds in transferring established brand equity to the new product generation can *economise on costs of marketing and communication* with respect to companies not owning brand equity or not able to transfer established brand equity to the new product generation.

Companies owning established brand equity have, however, to *respect certain rules* in order to be able to effectively use existing brand equity in the market launch of the subsequent product generation and to further grow brand equity. First of all, the company has to make sure that the new product generation *fits the established 'picture'* consumers hold about the established brand. If this is not warranted, the benefit of using the established brand in the market introduction of the new product will only be short-lived because customer expectations will not be fulfilled. Consequently, the use of the existing brand in combination with the new product may only confuse consumers and thus endangers the company's existing customer base and established stock of brand equity.[171] Hence, a *balance of continuity and creativity* is extremely important in the use of established brand equity in the market launch of subsequent product generations.[172] In this respect continuity has to be understood as the fulfilment of the customers' established brand associations and basic

[169] Cp. Lane, V. & Lacobson, R. (1995); Pettis, C. R. (1995); Allen, D. (2000).

[170] Cp. Yip, G. S. (1995); Güldenberg, H. G. (2000).

[171] Aaker, D. A. (1989); chap. 9; Farquhar, P. H. (1989); Aaker, D. A. (1990); Lane, V. & Lacobson, R. (1995); Aaker, D. A. (1996), chap. 9.

[172] Cp. Güldenberg, H. G. (2000), for a more detailed discussion see also chap. IV.4.3.

expectations about the product's qualities. Creativity, on the other hand, has to be considered as a means to surpass the guarantees given by the brand, as well as an opportunity to respond to competitive threats and to adapt the product to the changing demands of the marketplace. Thus, creativity represents a chance for the company to uphold and increase its current stock of brand equity.

The second factor crucially influencing the success of succeeding product generation and the established brand equity's leverage is the *exact timing of the market introduction*. If the established company holding considerable brand equity launches its new product generation *too late*, i.e., maturity phase, it may give competitors leeway to introduce its new and/or improved product with a timely advantage and thereby attract new clients, as well as build brand equity. On the other hand, if the company introduces the new generation of its products *too early*, i.e., end of growth or beginning maturity phase, it may not use the full potential of the actual product to generate returns and build brand equity. Moreover, the company enables competitors by introducing their products with a delay to integrate the latest advances in technology and thus to offer superior products. These advanced products of competitors in turn will reduce the product's lifetime by forcing the company to react. Hence, the exact timing of the market launch of the subsequent product generations in dependence on the position of the actual product in its product-life-cycle, overall advance in the underlying technology, and competitors' product offers is of crucial importance for the success of the succeeding product generation and in using the full potential of established brand equity's leverage.

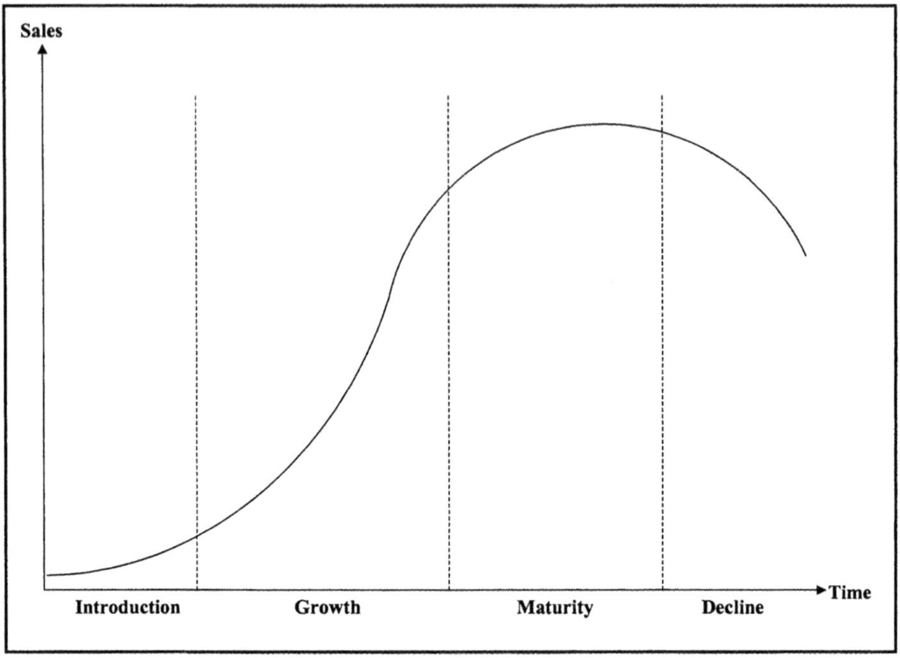

Figure IV.12: Product-life-cycle

In conclusion, each product generation represents for any company an opportunity to defeat and/or further strengthen the actual competitive position and to nurture and grow brand equity. However, in order to fully benefit of existing brand equity, companies have to insure that the new product generation corresponds to the established brand associations and exactly schedule the time of market introduction. By doing so, a company can transfer the better part of the established brand equity and build on the existing loyal customer base. This is of particular importance for companies having established considerable *pioneering brand equity* in the innovation phase of the technology-life-cycle since they can transfer their strategic advantage in brand equity from one product generation to the other. This cumulative nature and the inability of competitors to imitate or substitute brand equity, as well as its infinite life time bestows an innovating company with a sustainable competitive advantage of great magnitude. Moreover, the importance of brand equity increases along the technology-life-cycle and appears to be the *single most important strategic resource* of the company in advanced phases of the life-cycle.

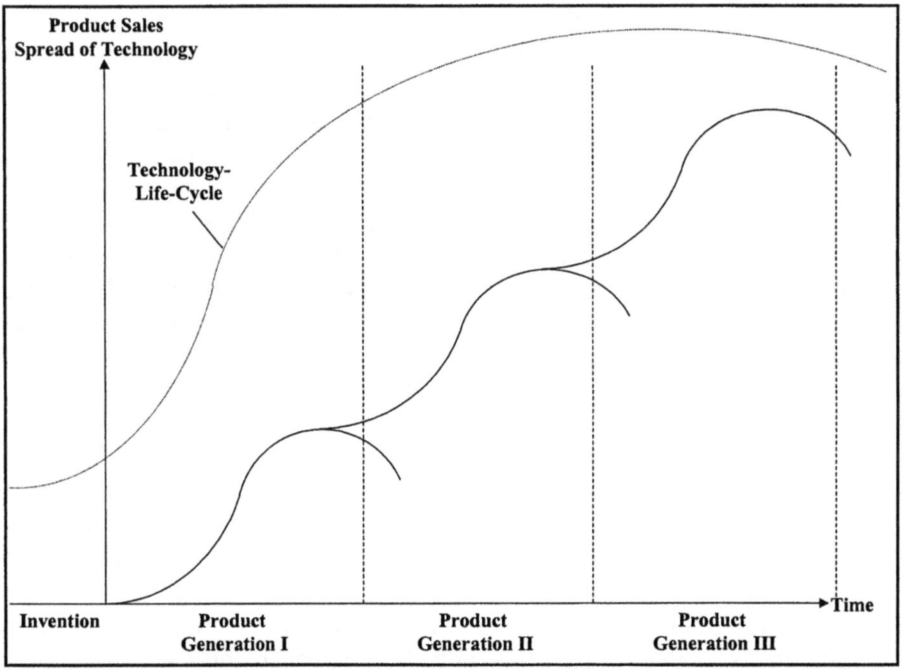

Figure IV.13: Subsequent product generations within the technology-life-cycle

IV.3.3 Upshot VI: The Strategic Role of Complementary Brand Equity in the Appropriation of Intangible Technical Assets

By building on the findings of chapters IV.1. and IV.2, as well as chapter III, we have developed a model that points out the strategic importance of brand equity in the efficient appropriation of the returns of innovative intangible technological assets delivering the company an initial, although generally short-lived, competitive advantage. Moreover, chapter IV.3 revealed basic management guidelines which enable a first-mover firm to effectively build and sustain brand equity, that in turn puts current and potential competitors at a persistent disadvantage.

As has been shown, brand equity classifies as a strategic resource complementing a company's technological strengths. In addition, a certain level of company specific technological assets generating an observable benefit for customers is needed for the effective establishing of brand equity as well as for nurturing and maintaining established brand equity and hence technological and market based advantages can be said to mutually complement each other. Moreover, once brand equity has been established it represents an important strategic resource setting current competitors at a significant disadvantage and generating formidable entry barriers for potential market entrants. Established brand equity not only enables a company to appropriate the returns of existing intangible technological resources but also gives the company an advantage in entering co-operation agreements and attracting skilled labour and thus to sustain or even enlarge its stock of intangible technological valuables.

In order to be able to benefit of the advantages of established brand equity, companies have to efficiently manage their market based resources. Brand equity basically represents a promise or guarantee given to customers, employees, co-operators, etc., which will have a significant influence on the outcome of the decision making process in particular if the decision maker is confronted with high risks and uncertainty. Thus, in order to build confidence and hence brand equity a company has to fulfil or even surpass the partners' expectations that they associate with the products and services sold under a certain brand. In this process of satisfying and/or exceeding expectations in order to uphold and reinforce brand equity incremental technological innovations and their effective communication are of key relevance. Moreover, in the case of apparent problems in the offerings a company has to immediately and appropriately react so as not to put its credibility in jeopardy and thus to avoid major and long-lasting damages to its established brand equity.

A company has, in addition, to reconsider the changing strategic roles of intangible technological resources and brand equity in its management. If a company does not account for the variations in the strategic importance of technological assets and brand equity, it may miss an opportunity to build a persistent competitive advantage in early phases of the technology-life-cycle that will reduce or even completely thwart the appropriation of the returns of the initial innovation. Thus, companies have to use periods of technological strength to build brand equity which in turn will balance out the loss of strategic advantage due to the rapid imitation of technological assets and inventing around of the subject matters of valid patents. Moreover, the general strategic role of technology can be expected to decline along the technology-life-cycle whereas brand equity will become increasingly important due to the increasing risks of purchasers concerning the quality of the offering. Thus, by efficiently transferring established brand equity from one product generation to the other the initial innovator benefits of a substantial leverage in the introduction of subsequent product generations and is able to continuously grow brand equity and consequently strategic advantage throughout the technology-life-cycle. This leads to the thesis of chapter IV.3:

Thesis V:
Brand equity which represents a strategic resource that complements a company's technological assets, is most efficiently build by a company's existing technological strengths. If the so established complementary brand equity is managed appropriately and fostered through continuous technological amelioration it puts current and potential competitors at a persistent strategic disadvantage and thus enables the initial innovator to effectively appropriate the returns of his original technological advantage in the long-run. Furthermore, an established brand enables a company to efficiently maintain and foster its technological capabilities and in turn to foster and further grow its market based advantage.

IV.4 Organising and Implementing Efficient Brand Equity Management

Chapter IV.3 has analysed the role of complementary brand equity in the appropriation of returns stemming from technological assets, as well as the role of the efficient management of brand equity in building a sustained competitive advantage. So far, however, we have not touched upon the topic of how companies can *allocate responsibilities* for brand equity and technological assets in order to ensure its efficient management. This section points out the principal organisational forms of how companies can allocate responsibility for intellectual property management and hence for brand equity and technological assets, as well as reveals the advantages of the different organisational forms. Moreover chapter IV.4.2.2 investigates the roles of corporate, business unit, and product divisions in the management of existing and potential future brand equity and consequently, the associated intangible technological assets. The analysis builds upon the model of complementary brand equity and shows how companies can assure, on the one hand, an efficient management of *existing brand equity* and in this respect not only sufficient investments in marketing and distribution but also in R&D. On the other hand, companies have to ensure at the same time sufficient investments in new technological competencies and market opportunities that have the potential to *create new brand equity* in diverse fields in the future. Subsequently, section IV.4.3 discusses the apparent problems companies face by integrating brand equity and technology management strategies. Finally, subchapter IV.4.4 develops on the possibility of enlarging the balanced scorecard concept to allow for the integration of brand equity and technology management strategies not at the organisational but at the process level. The chapter closes in section IV.4.5 with an upshot of the discussion of chapter IV.4.

The preceding discussion has revealed that the fulfilment of consumers' expectations about a certain brand and pledges given by the brand about the product's actual characteristics is of crucial importance in building and sustaining brand equity and thus strategic advantage. In order to best satisfy these expectations and guarantees and thus to generate maximum benefit for the company in form of appropriable profits, responsibility about brand equity should be concentrated where a *profound knowledge about the product's qualities*, as well as intense knowledge about the *consumers' expectations* and *general market trends and demands* exists. Consequently, for a company structured in global product division this would imply that brand equity is managed by the individual product division. Conversely, the discussion has revealed that brand equity plays a key role in determining the competitiveness of a company and thus is of considerable corporate interest. From a point of view of strategic relevance, brand equity management should thus rather be a *corporate task with top-management involvement*. Moreover, different responsibilities concerning the control of brand equity can be identified. There are, on the one hand, duties concerning the legal aspects of brand equity, e.g., the registration and enforcement of trademark rights which can usually be separated from more managerial duties such as marketing, product support, etc., on the other. The following sections investigate the exact tasks of the legal and managerial functions and how these functions should be organised.

IV.4.1 Legal vs. Managerial Responsibilities

As already mentioned above, one can differentiate between legal and managerial brand equity responsibility which is of crucial importance in the allocation of responsibility within the organisation. Under *legal responsibilities* of brand equity management any task concerning the legal aspects of brand equity is subsumed (cf. figure III.18). Such legal responsibilities thus include the registration of new trademarks, the enforcement and consequently any necessary legal action to prosecute infringement, as well as contractual questions concerning the in- and out-licensing of existing trademarks and brand names and associated legal functions. From these legal aspects of brand equity *managerial functions* have to be differentiated. The managerial responsibilities embrace any function influencing the reputational aspects of brand equity, e.g., brand associations, loyalty and acquaintance. These managerial responsibilities are generally administered by the marketing departments and general management in conjunction with corporate functions such as R&D and intellectual property management.

As pointed out in section IV.2.3.3, we can broadly differentiate *corporate or umbrella brands* and *individual product brands* which do not, as often mistakenly assumed, substitute but rather complement each other.[173] Thus, if we take a multinational company with an organisational structure of global product divisions,[174] for instance, we can assign *legal responsibility* for a company's brands to the *corporate function* of intellectual property management. Consequently, the enforcement of a company's intellectual property rights, the registration of new property rights, as well as contractual decisions concerning the in- and out-licensing of individual rights are usually handled by the corporate intellectual property management department (IPM).[175] On the other hand, functions concerned about brand equity management on the product division level, e.g., product marketing and sales people, are closer to the market place and thus detect more easily potential or actual trademark and patent infringements than the corporate IPM function. Consequently, to guarantee an efficient enforcement of existing intellectual property rights, a company has to warrant close collaboration of corporate IPM functions, e.g., legal department, with individual divisional IPM functions, e.g., marketing and sales.[176]

Conversely to the legal responsibilities, *managerial responsibility* for brand equity is usually concentrated at the level of product divisions and here in particular in the marketing and communication department. This applies in particular for product specific brands that are only used by one singular product division. Nevertheless, the influence individual product brands can have on the corporate brand, and vice versa, should not be undermined and thus has to be reflected in a *close integration* of the divisional level brand management in the overall corporate brand management. Hence, in order to maximise overall brand equity within the

---

[173] Multinational companies use, for instance, a global corporate brand and individual national product or service brands and so manage to combine advantages of global integration and local adaptation. See chap. IV.3.1.1.

[174] We assume a global structure, e.g., global product divisions, to best fit the environment of technological product markets. Cp. Stopford, J. M & Wells, L. T. (1972); Goshal, S. & Nohria, N. (1993).

[175] For a discussion of where to allocate control about technology licensing see Parr, R. L. (1996b).

[176] For a detailed discussion of the organisation of the management of intangible technological properties see chap. IV.4.2 and cp. Steward, T. A. (1997), chap. 7.

corporation, a company has to ensure a close integration of the brand management functions situated at the level of the individual product divisions and the corporate level. By integrating corporate and individual divisional brand management functions the company ensures the pursuit of the identical strategic goals and thus increases the overall efficacy of its brand equity management.[177] It may, for example, not be very wise to follow a strategy on the division level to position a certain product brand in a low price medium quality segment whereas the associated corporate brand is discerned by consumers as a premium brand positioned in the high price, high quality segment. Such a policy of combining diverging brand perceptions may cause consumer confusion and lead to the downgrading of the superior brand.

In the following subchapter IV.4.2 the principal organisational forms are presented of how responsibility for brand equity and technology management can be allocated within companies. Moreover, three principal models of how companies can integrate technology and/or brand equity management at the organisational level across different business units and product divisions are pointed out. Section IV.4.2.2 then examines how companies can ensure sufficient investments in brand equity. Although, the general discussion primarily focuses on multinational companies with a relatively strong technological diversification,[178] the discussion can be easily transferred to single product and/or single technology companies.

IV.4.2 Principal Organisational Forms of Brand Equity and Technological Management

Confronted with the rising importance of technological assets and brand equity, companies have developed different organisational forms in order to align brand equity and/or technology strategies across the various business unit levels. Moreover, due to the escalating costs of technological research and development many companies have seen a need to integrate these activities at the corporate level in order to avoid expensive parallel R&D projects in various business units or even product divisions. A similar integration development can nowadays be observed with respect to brand management. Over the past few years companies in general have considerably *reduced the number of brands* used by the company within the different business units and product divisions. An important number of

[177] For a detailed discussion see subsequent chap. IV.4.2.

[178] For a comprehensive investigation in the field of technological diversification see Stephan M. (2003).

companies has even completely consolidated its activities under *one single corporate brand*. The consolidation of the overall number of brands managed by the company is primarily driven by the already *high and still increasing costs of establishing and maintaining brand equity* with a global dimension. The cost of establishing and maintaining brand equity has continuously increased due to the rising number of brands with which consumers are nowadays confronted and the limited number of brands and associations that can be recognised and remembered by the human being. Thus, through concentrating marketing and communication activities on one single corporate brand, companies try to increase overall notoriety and associations held by customers, as well as sharpen the profile of the brand. On the other hand, companies generally underestimate the *risks associated with the use of one single umbrella brand*. These risks are generally born in the inability of the consumers to differentiate between the different product offers of the company all using an identical brand and thus the detriment of the overall brand equity across all business units and product divisions through problems in isolated product or technology fields.[179]

As already pointed out in section IV.4.1, different tasks concerning the management of technological assets and brand equity, as well as different levels within the company can be identified. Companies usually divide their activities with respect to the respective market and technology in different business units. Within these business units again several product division can be identified. Consequently, we have to differentiate between three principal levels within companies: The corporate, the business unit and the product division level. On the other hand, with respect to the organisation of intellectual property management one has not only to distinguish between brand equity and technology management tasks but also between managerial and legal responsibilities. The upcoming section IV.4.2.1 discusses the different responsibilities of brand equity and technology management functions at the respective levels and points out different models for an integrated brand equity and/or technology management organisation.

IV.4.2.1 Models of Organisational Integration of Technology and Brand Equity Management in Diversified Companies

Intellectual property management is generally divided into brand equity and technology management functions. Whereas technology management concerns the general technology strategy, co-ordinates the research and

[179] For a detailed discussion see chap. IV.3.2.2.

development activities, and decides about the measures to be taken to best protect the intangible technological assets, brand equity management generally concentrates on the three fields of marketing, communication and sales. Moreover, legal aspects, e.g., the registration of intellectual property rights or the taking of legal action against infringement, are usually administered at the corporate level either within the brand equity and technology management functions or are concentrated in one legal division. This is due to the generic characteristics of the encountered legal problems across the various business units and product divisions and often even with respect to questions concerning brand equity and technological assets.

On the other hand, the various hierarchical levels, i.e., corporate, business unit and product divisional level, within the company perform different tasks concerning the management of brand equity and technological assets. Whereas the corporate strategy and the general measures to be taken for the attainment of the envisaged goals, as well as the control of the implementation of the directives at lower levels are carried out at the corporate level, business units and product divisions generally are responsible for implementing and realising the brand equity and technology strategies decided at the corporate level. Thus, business units are generally responsible for marketing, communication, as well as research and development activities in their respective market and technology field and have to follow thereby the guidelines set at the corporate level.

Consequently, we can broadly distinguish between brand equity and technology management functions in companies. On the other hand the three hierarchical levels, corporate, business unit and product division, can be identified which do have specific responsibilities with regard to brand equity and technology management. In this respect two principal integration movements within companies can be recognised: A) an integrated brand equity management due to the increasing concentration of companies on a limited number of brands and symbols used in its various business activities; and (B) an integrated technology management in order to ensure a sufficient provision of the different business units and product divisions with new technological assets by at the same time avoiding expensive parallel R&D activities (cp. figure IV.14). A third possibility of integration which companies have largely neglected so far, is the organisational integration of brand equity and technology management functions. As pointed out in figure IV.14, such an integration can generally take place at three different levels: The corporate level (C); the business unit level (C_2); and at the mixed corporate – business unit level (C_1).

The next paragraphs point out the characteristics and the principal reasons of the three integration strategies pointed out above and discusses their advantages. Section IV.4.2.2 then discusses how companies can ensure sufficient investments in brand equity and technological assets before chapter IV.4.3 analyses the principal problems companies encounter by integrating brand equity and technology management and indicates how companies can align brand equity and technology strategies at the process level.

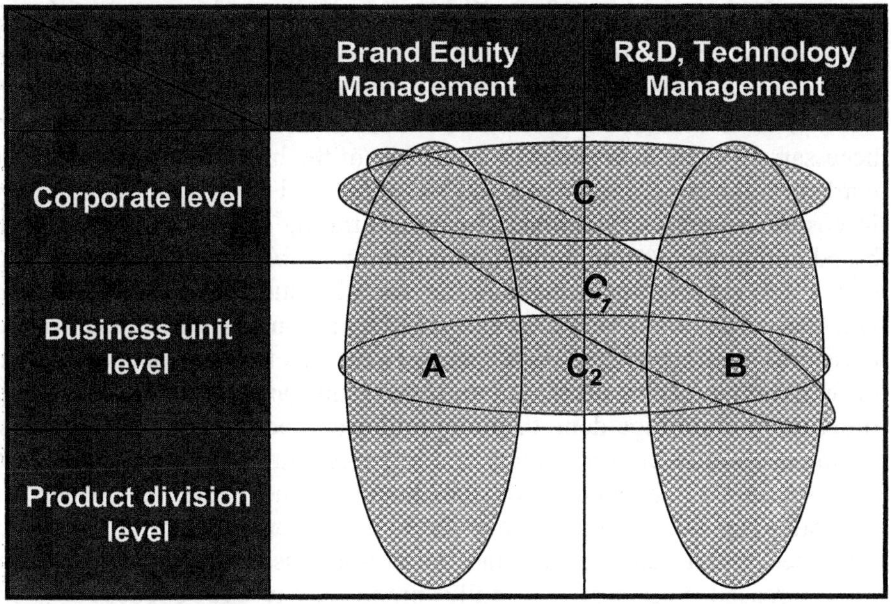

Figure IV.14: Integration of brand equity and/or technology management

Integrated Brand Equity Management (A)

Due to the existing trend of consolidating most or even all corporate activities in the various product and national markets under one corporate umbrella brand, companies have experienced the need to better ensure a coherent use of the corporate brand, symbols and slogans. To allow for such a coherent utilisation of the brand across the different business units and product divisions companies have increasingly established central marketing and communication departments responsible for the establishing of precise guidelines as well as controlling for their implementation at the different hierarchical levels. Moreover, many companies provide legal services for trademark registration and enforcement at the corporate level, such as the search of new product names, their registration and if needed take legal action in the case of infringement.

The advertisement, publication and communication activities are, however, implemented and administered by the different business units and/or product divisions which have the best knowledge about the respective market and their customers. Nevertheless, every advertisement or corporate publication has to be validated by the corporate level brand equity management department verifying if the layout, content, etc. corresponds to the set general guidelines. These corporate identity and corporate design (CICD) guidelines are often extremely detailed defining, for example, which fond to use, how the page has to be set up, the colours to be displayed, the minimum information content, etc.

Such close-knit CICD guidelines about the use of umbrella brands are necessary in order to ensure a coherent use of the brand across the different markets and business segments and hence to build an uniform brand image in customers minds. Moreover, by concentrating on one global umbrella brand companies confront the risk of quality problems in isolated product and/or service offerings damaging the overall brand image of the company and thus of all products and services sold by all business units and product divisions. Thus, corporate brand management has to ensure a coherent and clear communication across all business units and product divisions in order to limit damage done to the overall brand equity and not to confuse customers and create uncertainty about the general quality of the products and services associated with the brand. Hence, the advantages of consolidating all corporate activities under one umbrella brand of increased brand notoriety through the uniform use of the brand and thus the increased possibility to build brand equity are opposed by the disadvantages of an increased risk of the detriment of brand equity across all business units and the higher administrative costs.

Integrated Technology Management (B)

With regard to technology management three principal organisational forms can be distinguished: (1) *One central R&D laboratory* at the corporate level at the disposition of all business units and product divisions; (2) No central R&D laboratory but *various R&D laboratories at the business unit level*; and (3) one *central R&D laboratory* at the corporate level *supplemented by R&D laboratories at the respective business unit level.*[180] Whereas the form of one single centralised R&D unit can generally be found in single product or technology companies, companies with a diversified portfolio of different technologies and/or

[180] For a more detailed discussion see Gerybadze, A. (2004), chap. 5.

products either completely concentrate R&D activities at the business unit level or supplement the central R&D laboratory with R&D laboratories within the various business units.

Thus, diversified companies generally possess dispersed R&D activities at different hierarchical levels and/or within the different business units. However, in order to avoid expensive double and parallel research work across the different business units, responsibility for technology management at the corporate level has been allocated. The responsibility of the technology management department at the corporate level is to set the principal technology strategy and initiatives, keep an overview of the different research and development projects in order to avoid double and parallel research and development work, allow for a transfer of technological innovation in one isolated business unit to other units within the company in order to best exploit the technological asset, as well as initiate and control for joint research projects at the cross-business unit level. Furthermore, most companies possess a central R&D laboratory at the corporate level. These central R&D laboratories in general concentrate on more basic research projects which are too far from market launch as to be carried out within the respective business unit, research projects that transcend the resources and technological capabilities of the single business unit, and/or research and development projects in new fields of technological expertise.

The advantages of an integrated management of technology are the avoidance of expensive double and parallel research and development work across the different business units, to exploit technological innovations generated within one business unit in various units of the company, and to provide for research and development projects that surpass the resources and competencies of individual business units.[181] However, in order to avoid disagreement between the business units due to one business unit investing own resources in the generation of new technological assets that are subsequently used by various other business units which have not invested resources in the generation of the assets. So as to avoid under-investments in new technological assets by the various business units, the technology management department at the corporate level has to clearly define who owns the technological developments paid for and/or carried out by individual business unit.

With regard to the *ownership of technological assets within companies* two principal forms can be distinguished: A) Either the company defines all technological assets as *corporate ownership* and thus are freely available to all different business units interested in the asset, or (B) the

[181] For a detailed discussion see section IV.4.2.2.

respective business unit which has provided the resources necessary for the development of the technological asset and/or carried out the principal research work is the *exclusive owner* of the respective asset. In case A, however, the company has to provide for sufficient incentives in order not to discourage business units from investing the necessary resources into technological development which subsequently can be used by every business unit within the company having invested or not in the generation of the new asset. On the other hand, in case B, the company has to provide for an internal market for technological assets that allows the broad use of technological development generated by a specific business unit or product division across all units and divisions interested in the exploitation of the asset.

Integrated Technology and Brand Equity Management (C)

The third possibility of integration pointed out in figure IV.14 presents the *integration of brand equity and technology management functions*. This integration option that has been largely neglected by companies, so far, necessitates a certain integrated technology and brand equity management. As pointed out in figure IV.14, three principal forms have been identified: C) An integration of brand equity and technology management at the corporate level; (C1) an integration of brand equity management at the corporate and technology management at the business unit level; and (C2) an integration of brand equity and technology management at the business unit level. The choice of integration strategy thereby depends upon the integration strategy pursued at the individual level of brand equity management (A) and technology management (B).[182]

As pointed out above, companies can tie technology and brand equity management responsibility together at either the company or the business unit level. With regard to brand equity management, decisions concerning the management of an umbrella brand are principally taken at the corporate level and their pursuit at the business unit and product division level are closely monitored. In contrast, decisions about business unit and product brands not showing any connection to the general corporate brand are in general taken at the respective business unit level.[183] Thus, given the allocation of decision taking power with regard to brand equity technology

[182] Cp. figure IV.14.

[183] Although a general trend towards concentration on one single corporate brand can be identified, a few companies continue to exclusively promote and foster business unit and product brands. Unilever, for example, exclusively concentrates on product and business unit brands which in addition often vary across different national or regional markets.

management it can be put forward that the integration of technology and brand equity management functions has to be organised correspondingly. If decision making power concerning the management of brand equity as well as technological assets is located at the corporate or business unit level, the integration of the two has to take place at the corporate or business unit level, respectively. If, however, the technological strategy is developed at the business unit level and decision making responsibility regarding brand equity is located at the corporate level, integration has to take place at the cross business unit to corporate level. The fourth possibility of brand equity responsibility concentrated at the business level and technology management located at the corporate level appears extremely improbable due to the increasing concentration of companies on umbrella brands. In addition, no company following such integration strategy has been observed in the course of our research and has hence not been taken into consideration.

The advantages of such a strategy of integrating brand equity and technology management functions stem from the complementary nature of technological and market based assets. As put forward in the preceding chapters, leading edge technological competencies and in particular continuous technological innovation are necessary in order to successfully build and sustain brand equity in the long-run. On the other hand, established brand equity bestows the company with advantages with respect to acquiring new human capital based intangible assets, as well as improves the company's stand in co-operation negotiations. Thus, by integrating the management of market based and technological assets, and consequently aligning brand equity and technology strategies, companies can ensure a sufficient generation of technological innovation so as to generate new or foster already existing brand equity. However, such an alignment of brand equity and technology strategies and a close integration of the management of market based and technological assets is generally perceived by companies as extremely difficult and presenting a considerable source of conflict and hence has been largely neglected so far.[184]

The upcoming section will discuss how companies can ensure sufficient investments in brand equity and technological assets and point out the problems companies encounter by integrating brand equity and technology management in section IV.3. Finally, we will present some tools companies can use to better integrate their technology and brand equity strategies in section IV.4.4.

---

[184] For a detailed discussion of the apparent problems by integrating brand equity and technology management see chap. IV.4.3.

IV.4.2.2 Ensuring Sufficient Investments in Brand Equity and Technological Assets

As has been discussed in chapters IV.2.2 and IV.3.2, a company's superior technological competence in a certain field plays a key role in establishing new and upholding existing brand equity. Thus, a company has not only to assure the efficient allocation of managerial and legal responsibility for brand equity within the organisation, but moreover, has to ensure sufficient investments in creative activities, e.g., R&D, or the accessing of alternative sources of intangible technological assets in order to foster existing and generate new brand equity. The upcoming discussion, however, focuses primarily on internal sources of technological expertise and here again on R&D activities.

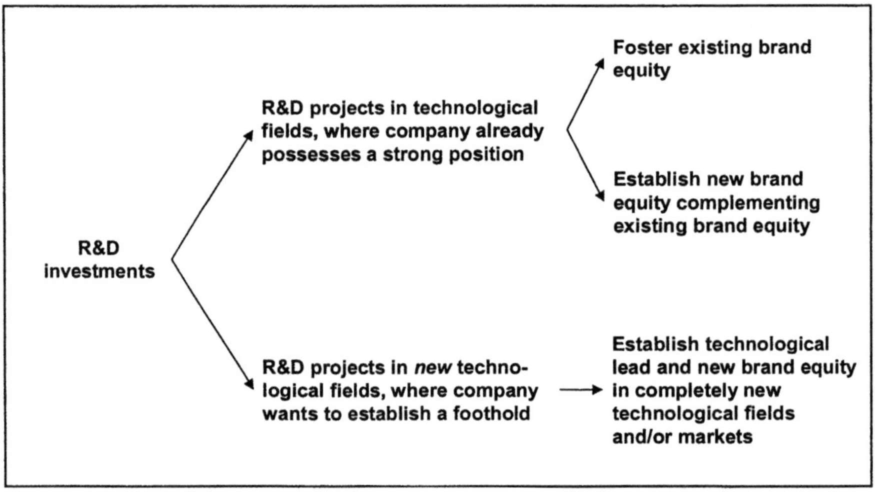

Figure IV.15: Differentiation of R&D investments

Consequently, a company can distinguish between investments aiming at the improvement of existing offerings in order to maintain *existing brand equity* and investments in *new fields of activity* to establish new trademarks and build up new brand equity. As figure IV.15 illustrates, investments in existing brand equity can have two principal forms. A company can either market the improved offering under the identical trademark associated with a certain brand equity, or to establish new brands complementing existing brand equity, e.g., new product generations launched under new trademark, that are, however, clearly associated with the already established trademark and existing brand equity.

These investments, building upon an established technological expertise are aimed at generating incremental innovations in order to improve existing products and consequently foster established brand equity by better satisfying or even surpassing consumers' current expectations.[185] Thus, such investments in product and process improvements aspire to *sustain existing brand equity* by improving technological expertise and hence, these investments can clearly be classified as expenditures in 'applied research.'[186] In addition to investments in the improvement of established products which have the aim to uphold existing brand equity, a company has also to assure sufficient *investments in completely new fields* that may have the potential to create considerable new brand equity in new fields of corporate activity. By such investments a company can ensure its ability to substitute for activities and associated brand equity which have reached the end of the technological life-cycle (cf. figure IV.11). As a result, these projects that rather show the characteristics of 'basic research,' may not be related to existing products or even the company's current fields of activity and can thus be seen as an *attempt to diversify*. Or, alternatively, existing business units may perceive these R&D projects as potential company internal competitors and may fight against the pursuit of these projects.[187]

Moreover, as Gerybadze (2004) has clearly pointed out, responsibility about R&D projects should be located where the best knowledge about the concerning project is available.[188] As we have seen above, this knowledge can either be located at the divisional and sub-divisional level, i.e., in the case of incremental improvements with the aim to maintain established brand equity, or at the corporate level, i.e., projects aiming at the development of new technological competencies and thus rather have the characteristics of 'basic research.' In the case of projects aiming at incremental innovations in fields where the company already possesses a relatively strong position in order to uphold established brand equity, managerial responsibility about the projects should be located at the

---

185 For a more detailed discussion of the role of incremental innovations in fostering existing brand equity see chap. IV.3.2.1.

186 For a distinction between 'applied' and 'basic research' see chap. III.2.1.1.

187 An example could be, for instance, the development of a new pharmaceutical based on a new active molecule aiming at an identical field of indication as an existing product using a different active molecule (e.g., acetylsalicylic acid vs. paracetamol).

188 "Entscheidungen über die Auswahl von Projekten, die Ressourcenzuteilung und die Budgetierung sollten möglichst dort getroffen werden, wo die jeweils besten und verlässlichsten Informationen vorliegen." Gerybadze, A. (2004), p. 328.

divisional level. Conversely, projects with rather 'basic research' character, e.g., long-term, high risk R&D projects, in new and/or competing fields of technological expertise with regard to the company's current areas of activity, should be managed at the corporate level.

In this regard, *management responsibility* about R&D projects should not only concern decisions about which projects to pursue but also how much to invest in the individual projects, as well as responsibility about the success of the projects. On the other hand, not only decision taking power and responsibility have to be clearly allocated but also the *financial resources of the projects* have to be assured. According to 3rd generation R&D finance model described by Gerybadze (2004), a company should use a combination of five financial elements in order to ensure an efficient allocation of resources:

1. R&D at the divisional level, financed by the division's cash-flow;
2. Centrally financed R&D projects in the field of pre-market and basic research;
3. R&D projects of the divisions carried out at the corporate R&D unit;
4. Pooling of financial sources of several divisions and establishment of lateral projects and programmes under the administration and moderation of the corporation;
5. Supply of seed-money from the corporation for the transfer of corporate R&D projects on the divisional level.[189]

By taking both arguments about the allocation of managerial responsibility and the source of finance of the respective R&D projects one can conclude that the large majority of the rather small and short-term projects aiming at the incremental improvement of existing offerings should be financed and carried out by the respective product division. The divisions have, however, the possibility to order the central R&D unit to carry out certain projects which surpass the competencies of the individual division. Yet, the respective division has to finance these divisional projects carried out by the central R&D unit. On the other hand, projects that rather show the characteristics of more basic research, aiming at the development of completely new activities and thus to increase the diversification of a company's activities, should rather be under corporate control and responsibility. Consequently, these projects should be centrally financed and carried out by the corporate R&D unit. Nevertheless, as Gerybadze (2004) has put forward, a company has to provide financial aid in order to assure an effective transfer and realisation of the R&D projects that are transferred from the corporate to the divisional level.

[189] Gerybadze, A. (2004), p. 329.

As can be seen in figure IV.16, besides the two extremes of R&D projects completely carried out and administered at the divisional and corporate level, respectively, a third important possibility present projects that may pool know-how of several different divisions and/or are of interest for several divisions of a company. By providing for such *cross-divisional projects*, a company can avoid projects carried out in parallel in several divisions and/or enable divisions to pursue projects that surpass the financial possibilities of one single division.[190]

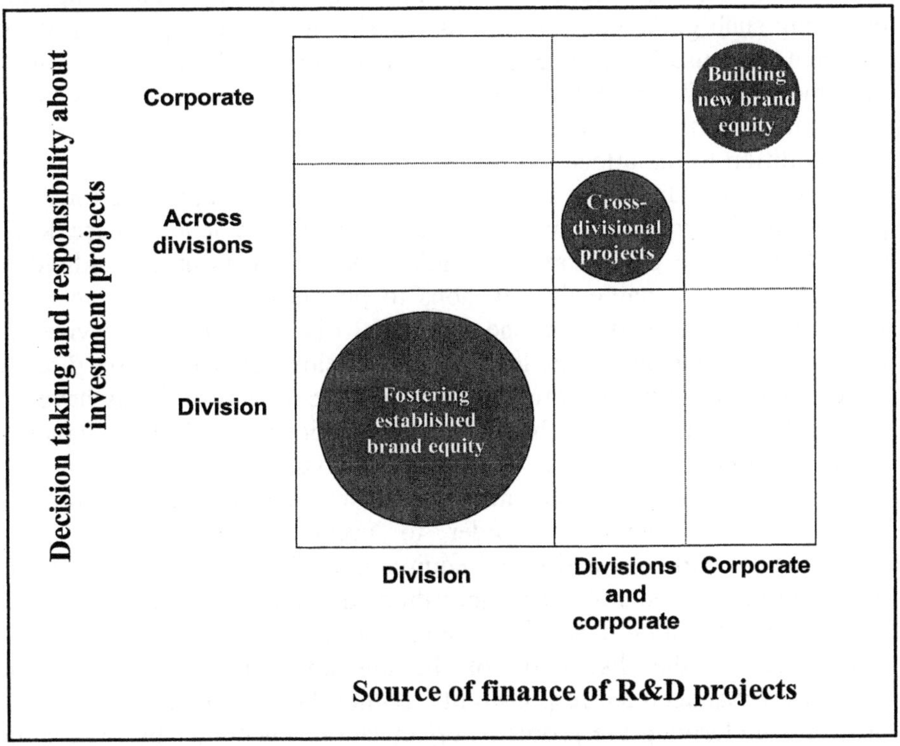

Figure IV.16: Corporate vs. decentralised R&D

In conclusion, companies have to make sure to allocate managerial and legal responsibility, as well as decision making power concerning investments in technological development projects and associated brand equity at the respective organisational levels where the *best knowledge* about the individual concerns exists. Furthermore, not only the decision about which projects to pursue and the allocation of resources but also the

[190] For a thorough discussion of models of resource allocation and the financing of innovation and R&D see Gerybadze, A. (2004), chap. 6.

provision of the budget should be made where best and most reliable information is available.[191] Thus, responsibility about brand equity and R&D projects merely concerning products of one single division should be located at the respective divisional level. Moreover, the division not only makes the decision where to invest and has full responsibility for the success of the project, but also has to provide the necessary financial resources. Nevertheless, these projects at the individual divisional level have to *follow the general guidelines* set by the corporate functions in accordance with the general corporate strategy. By establishing and enforcing such guidelines, as well as assuring a close co-operation of the different organisational levels, a company can avoid the confusing of customers by diverging brand signals and thereby maximises its brand equity at the corporate level.

In addition to the allocation of responsibility concerning R&D projects at the individual divisional level, companies should also provide for R&D projects at the cross-divisional, as well as corporate level. These R&D projects have the aim to avoid parallel R&D projects at the individual divisional levels, enable the divisions to pursue combined projects that would be too expensive for one individual division, and to provide for more radical innovations in technological fields that cannot be directly allocated to any of the existing divisions of the company and may have the potential to establish new brand equity independent of the company's existing market based assets. Thus, by effectively organising technology and brand equity management a company can achieve an optimal allocation of resources in order to uphold and expand existing technological expertise and brand equity, as well as ensure the sufficient provision of new technological innovations that may have the potential to generate brand equity in new fields of corporate activity.

Building on the discussion of the allocation of brand equity and technology management responsibility, section IV.4.3 points out the major problems underlying the problems organisations encounter by integrating the management of brand equity and technology competencies. These integration problems often present the principal causes of the failure of new product developments and/or of the deterioration of established brand equity. After the analysis of the principal causes of the apparent problems, managerial tools allowing for a better integration of brand equity and technology management at the process level are presented in section IV.4.4.

---

[191] Cp. Gerybadze, A. (2004), pp.327-330.

IV.4.3 Apparent Problems in the Integration of Brand Equity and Technology Management

A crucial point that has not been addressed so far in our discussion and which has largely been neglected by the general discussion of technology and brand management are the *problems organisations encounter by aligning and integrating market based knowledge and technological competencies*. So far, most companies active in technology intensive industries have put their main emphasis on the role of *technological innovation and the management of technological assets* and have often neglected the strategic role market based assets play. This extreme focus on technological assets and the widespread neglect of market based assets is often due to the companies' managerial structure. Managers do often have an engineering education and have grown in their position by a certain technological innovation and continue to overemphasise technology management even in advanced phases of the technology-life-cycle. *Marketing and sales efforts* are often only perceived as the final step in the product development process which have to *successfully launch and market the technological marvels*.[192]

The often radical change in the strategic importance of technology competencies and market based assets along the technology-life-cycle frequently causes considerable managerial problems. Whereas companies usually have to follow a technology-push strategy during early stages of the technology-life-cycle, during later phases of the technology-life-cycle, when the technology is in widespread use and the product has almost turned into a *commodity*, the focus shifts from the specific needs of isolated users to the broad needs of the mass market. Moreover, along the technology-life-cycle the increasing number of competitors offering products and services with comparable functional characteristics and minimal physical and/or physical-aesthetic variations, as well as the rising number of actual and potential customers turn the company's attention to *problems of communication and information* that are of mounting importance. Once a product approaches the state of a commodity, differentiation as well as communicating the advantages of the company's offer to those of competitors, and hence brand equity, becomes of central importance.

As has already been shown in the case study on Cisco Systems in chapter II.3, as long as the company was only targeting the market of service providers, telecommunication companies, and large enterprises it

[192] For a detailed discussion of the product development process see Gassmann, O. & von Zedtwitz, M. (1996), chap. 5; Cooper, R. G. (2001), chap. 2.

could rely on mouth-to-mouth propaganda of its products and could maintain a direct relationship with actual and potential customers. However, by entering the market of small and medium sized companies Cisco Systems was no longer able to directly contact and inform all potential clients but had to fall back on mass-media, e.g., television advertisement, in order to inform potential customers about the company's offer. Besides advertisement campaigns to inform potential clients, Cisco's considerable brand equity established over the years through its innovative products and services, extreme focus on customer needs, and high customer satisfaction plays an increasing role to convey detailed information about the characteristics of the products and services sold under the brand Cisco Systems, as well as to differentiate its offers from those of competitors.[193]

Although brand equity in general only appears to be of extreme importance in later phases of the technology-life-cycle, i.e., maturity and standardisation, the company *has to built brand equity well in advance* in order to be able to fall back on it once it actually needs it. Brand equity is not only difficult and lengthy to built but is also *extremely fragile* and hence hard to maintain and grow. Consequently, a company has to constantly satisfy or even surpass the expectations of actual and potential customers which they associate with products and services offered under a certain brand in order to maintain and grow brand equity. Of central importance for companies in the process of building and maintaining brand equity is the precise *understanding of the customers' expectations and associations* and the ability to turn this knowledge about customers' anticipation into actual product features.

A particular problem for many companies represents the sharp separation of management tasks related to technology management and brand equity management. This separation is primarily due to the *distinct job specifications*. Whereas technology management requires a thorough understanding of specific technological problems and hence a scientific background, brand equity management rather requires know-how in socio-economic fields. Moreover, due to the distinct different education of technology managers and brand equity managers and marketing personnel they generally show considerable differences in their world-outlook. These diverging attitudes present a considerable potential for dispute and therefore hinder the efficient use of technological as well as market knowledge within the company and thus the perfect fulfilling of customer expectations. The upcoming sections point out the specific problems

---

193 For a detailed discussion see case study Cisco Systems in chap. II.3 and in particular section II.3.3.

companies encounter in combining technology and brand equity management tasks and the specific problems arising from the hierarchical structure of companies that has the aim to allow for co-ordination, motivation, communication, etc. of the distinct functions and tasks within the organisation. Section IV.4.4 finally shows how companies can align their brand equity and technology strategies with the help of the concept of the balanced scorecard extended in order to integrate brand equity and technology management.

Brand Equity Management and Technology Management: Two Distinct Tasks of Equal Importance

Technology management and brand equity management are mostly completely separated in divisions which only sporadically team up. This strict separation of technology management tasks which are in general primarily administered in the research and development departments, and brand equity management that is often seen as a pure marketing activity. Although most companies have realised the utmost importance of customers, and in particular lead users, in unveiling new ideas and thus as a means of generating innovation, R&D departments often still *overemphasise the role of autonomous technological innovation* due to their superior knowledge about the technologically feasible, as well as their extreme concentration on technological problems. On the other hand, the marketing activities of companies in industries characterised by a high technological intensity often merely concentrate on promoting and selling the products coming out of the product development process. Even though companies try to better integrate the knowledge of the marketing department about exact market needs and customers' expectations, the consultation of the market based knowledge often occurs only when the specifications of the new product have already been set and considerable amounts of resources have been invested.

This *extreme technology bias* in the product development process becomes clearly apparent in the findings of the Conference Board presented by Cooper (2001). According to the findings, 46% of the resources invested by companies in the product development process are spend on new product developments which do not meet the company's commercial expectations or never make it to the market.[194] The principal reasons of the failure of new products has been found to be primarily attributable to poor integration of market knowledge in the development process. As pointed out in figure IV.17, four out of five reasons for the

[194] For a detailed discussion of apparent problems in the product development process and their causes see Cooper, R. G. (2001) chap. 1-2.

failure of new products are directly or indirectly related to marketing deficiencies and problems.

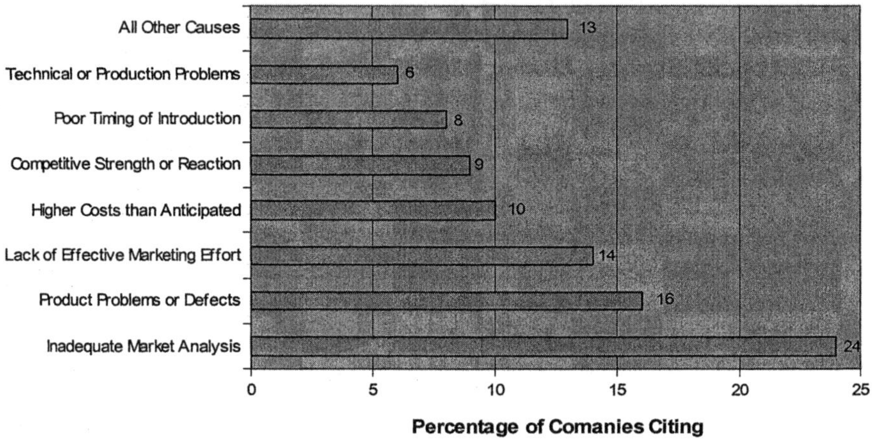

Source: Cooper, R. G. (2001), p. 25.

Figure IV.17: Principal causes of new product failures

Conversely, brand equity management should not be perceived as a new fancy name substituting for the terms advertisement and sales efforts. Whereas adverting and sales activities primarily concentrate on shaping, sharpening, and altering customers' expectations, increasing the notoriety of a certain trademark, as well as informing potential customers about the existence of a certain offer and its characteristics. Brand equity management, on the other hand, concentrates on *growing, maintaining, and fostering any of the five dimensions* of brand equity: (1) Brand loyalty; (2) brand awareness; (3) brand quality; (4) brand associations; and (5) other proprietary brand assets. Advertisement and sales efforts, thus, only present a means of influencing certain subordinate parameters, e.g., notoriety of trademark, customer awareness, or conveying product information.

Brand equity management should hence aim at integrating the company's technological competencies and market knowledge in order to *maximise the value brand equity generates* for customers as well as for the respective company.[195] As has been stressed in the previous chapters, brand

[195] Brand equity provides value to customers by enhancing customers' interpretation and processing of information, confidence in the purchasing decision, as

equity primarily presents a *promise given to customers* and thus brand equity management primarily has to *ensure the accomplishment of the expectations of customers* in order to maintain and further grow brand equity. Advertising and sales efforts which primarily concentrate on influencing the customers expectations and delivering supplementary information, present only one of various aspects of brand equity management. More importantly, *brand equity management has to be a the core of a company's product development process* not only to ensure the *choice of the best protection mode at the right time* for new intangible technological and market based assets along the development process, but also to ensure that the *new products meet or even surpass the expectations customers* associate with a given brand.

As has already been discussed in chapter III.3.3, the *optimal protection mode* of intangible technological assets depends on multiple factors, e.g., nature of immaterial asset, its position in the technology life-cycle, and the geographic dispersion of the exploitation and utilisation of the asset in questions. Moreover, the company has to bear in mind in its choice of protection mode as well as in the potential patent application not only technical and legal aspects, as is mostly done, but also economical and social factors.[196] Concerning the choice of the best time to file for intellectual property protection, e.g., patent or trademark rights, intellectual property rights for technological assets are usually filed shortly after their unveiling in order to reduce the risk of leakage and/or increase imitation costs.[197] Conversely, trademarks are registered towards the end of the product development process, shortly before market launch. Thus, whereas creative efforts and investments, e.g., R&D expenditures, can be expected to be almost immediately reflected in the filing of intellectual technological property rights, e.g., patent filings, we *hypothesise that technological innovation are reflected in the registration of intellectual property rights for market based assets, e.g., trademarks, only after a certain time lag*. The length of the time lag is thereby determined by the length of the product development cycle. Furthermore, intellectual property rights for market based assets are usually filed for a certain

well as use satisfaction. Conversely, the value of brand equity for the company is manifested in the increased efficiency and effectiveness of marketing programs, increased brand loyalty, possibility to charger higher prices and thus achieve higher profit margins, increased brand extensions and trade leverage which last but not least translate into a competitive advantage. Cp. chap. IV.2.

[196] For a detailed discussion of the shortcomings of patent rights and possible problem solutions see chap. IV.1.2.2.

[197] Cp. Hall, B. H., Griliches, Z. et al (1986); Pakes, A. & Grilichez, Z. (1984).

product group or new product generation incorporating various technological findings and not for each individual technological finding as it generally is the case with intellectual technological property rights.

Besides these *intellectual property management tasks* of the choice of the most adequate protection mode and point of time of intangible property filing for the respective intangible asset, brand equity management also has to maximise the information customers can obtain from the brand. By building on the discussion of von Weizäcker (1986), who has further developed the mathematical theory of communication and established a definition which specifies information as a composition of novelty and confirmation, the central problems of brand equity management can be pointed out. The preceding chapters have stressed the important role of *brand equity as a transmitter of information* about the offer's qualities sold under a certain brand name and hence reduces customers uncertainty and risk in the purchasing decision. The *degree of information* the receiver, in this case the customer, can obtain from a certain signal varies, according to von Weizäcker (1986), in relation to the proportion of *novelty and confirmation* of the signal.[198]

As visualised in figure IV.18, the degree of information carried by a certain signal increases towards a maximum by decreasing confirmation and increasing novelty. However, once the *maximum* is reached, a further increase in novelty and thus decrease in confirmation would reduce the degree of information and finally would lead at the extreme left of the figure to the destruction of information and consequently causing chaos. Thus, an excess of novelty or confirmation can cause the destruction of the information bearing role of the signal, and hence brand equity. An overload of novelty destroys the information bearing role of the signal as a reassurance. Conversely, an excess of confirmation impedes the alignment and change of the signal and thus results in the deterioration of the information carried by the signal.[199]

The seminal findings of von Weizäcker clearly reveal the difficulty brand equity management faces in *balancing the share of novelty and confirmation* in order to maximise the degree of information the customer can obtain. In this respect established brand equity represents a certain transmitter of information about the corresponding offer. If, however, the actual offer sold under the brand does not correspond at all to the

---

[198] Von Weizäcker has used in his discussion the terms "Bestätigung" standing for confirmation, stability, reliability, redundancy, and rigidity, and "Erstmaligkeit" standing for the amount of first-appearance and novelty. Cp. von Weizäcker, E. U. (1986), pp. 112-113.

[199] Cp. von Weizäcker (1986), pp. 82-111.

previously expected (100% novelty, 0% confirmation) the customer is confused and the information bearing role of the brand and hence brand equity is reduced if not destroyed. On the other hand, if the offer only confirms the expectations the customers' associate with a certain brand (0% novelty, 100% confirmation), brand equity will deteriorate since the offer will not adapt to the changing needs and wishes of the customers and thus becomes obsolete. Consequently, brand equity management has the task to find the *optimum of novelty and confirmation in the company's offers, and in particular new product developments, in order to maximise the information transmitted* by the brand.

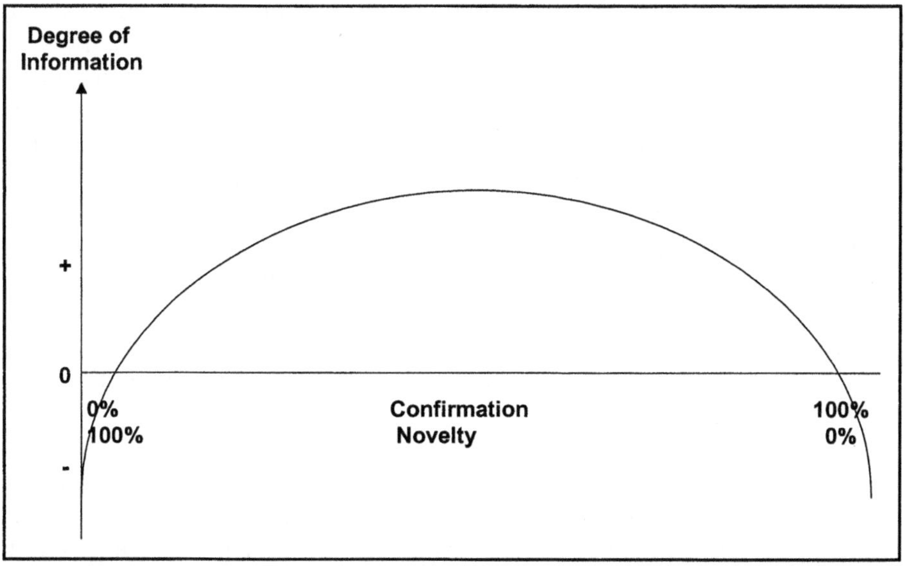

Cp.: von Weizäcker (1986), p. 99.

Figure IV.18: Degree of information subject to novelty and confirmation

The next section points out specific managerial tools that have the aim to help companies to better align their brand equity and technology strategies in determining the optimal constellation of novelty and confirmation in new product developments for maximising brand equity, as well as in circumventing the principal pitfalls of brand equity management. The upcoming paragraphs concentrate in particular on the balanced scorecard system. An adaptation of the concept is presented that puts the management of brand equity and technological assets at the centre of corporate strategy. Thus, the presented enlarged concept provides a management tool for the efficient long-term management of market based and technological intangible assets.

IV.4.4 Tools for Aligning Brand Equity and Technology Strategies

The process of aligning brand equity and technology strategies is basically about allowing for an *optimal flow of information* within the organisation. In general companies own considerable technological competencies as well as market knowledge about their respective fields of activity. Companies, however, often face considerable problems at merging market based and technological knowledge located within different departments at various levels in the company. Furthermore, an *excessive hierarchy* which is claimed to hinder the efficient flow of information within companies,[200] considerably complicates the alignment of technology and brand equity strategies. Consequently, in order to allow for an optimal flow of information within the organisations, companies have to pay attention not to built up too much hierarchical and bureaucratic barriers. An organisational structure that appeared to allow for a good communication between the individual business units, concentrating on technological problems, and lines of businesses which are in charge of specific market segments, is the organisational structure of Cisco Systems. As pointed out in chapter II.3, Cisco organises itself in 3 lines of businesses (LOBS) and about 30 business units. The technological research and development carried out in the individual business units is heavily influenced by the LOBS which have a good knowledge about the actual and potential needs and wishes of Cisco Systems' customers.

Whereas the organisational structure of a company usually reflects the history, culture, and activities of the particular organisation and thus remains specific to the company, the upcoming sections point out the general managerial tool of the *balanced scorecard* for brand equity management. The presented concept will enable companies' to align brand equity and technological strategies on a process level without obliging the companies to realise far-reaching organisational changes. However, before implement a close integration of brand equity and technology strategies companies should make sure to perfectly understand the actual importance customers ascribe to a specific brand name in the purchasing decision process. Hence, before presenting the extended balanced scorecard concept for the alignment of brand equity and technology strategies, the tool of conjoint analysis for the unveiling of the strategic importance of brand equity is presented in the following paragraph.

Conjoint analysis which are in particular in consumer goods industries a popular and well established marketing tool for guiding strategies for

[200] Cp. Grindley, P. C. & Sullivan, P. H. (1998), pp. 84-99.

marketing communication, are often disregarded in industrial goods and service industries.[201] The method of conjoint analysis allows for a thorough investigation of customers' purchasing decision process with regards to product characteristics and brands by using multivariate techniques.[202] Thus, conjoint analyses present a good tool for unveiling the qualities of products and services that are most important to customers and have found broad application in new product evaluation, repositioning, competitive analysis, pricing, and market segmentation. Moreover, the concept can be used in the product development process to unveil the importance customers' attribute to certain product qualities and characteristics. On the same line of argumentation, the method can be used to evaluate the actual importance customers ascribe to a specific brand name in the purchasing decision process. Consequently, companies can *disclose the utility customers obtain from attaching a certain brand name to a specific product and how the brand influences their purchasing decision and the mark-up they are prepared to pay* for a certain brand. Thus, conjoint analysis present a tool for the analysis of the importance customers' attribute to brand equity, e.g., as a means to reduce the risk inherent in the purchasing decision process, and hence if a close integration of brand equity and technology strategies has the potential to generate a strategic advantage and consequently *if the company should implement the extended balanced scorecard concept* presented below.[203]

Balanced Scorecard for Brand Equity Management

This section points out how companies can use the general management concept of the *balanced scorecard*, designed for the efficiently accomplishment of strategy oriented goals, for aligning and optimising brand equity and technology management. Before elaborating the specific use of the balance scorecard for brand equity management, its principal

---

[201] Cp. Green P. E. & Srinivasan, V. (1990).

[202] Conjoint analyses investigate survey data with the help of multivariate technique and reveal the principal factors influencing the customers' purchasing decision process. The data used in the analyses is collected through confronting potential customers with a set of products with different combinations of the various possible characteristics which the customers have to rank the alternatives according to their likelihood of purchase. Cp. Keller, K. L. (2000), pp. 986-987. For a detailed discussion of the general method of conjoint analysis see Green, P. E. & Wind, Y. (1975); Green, P. E. & Srinivasan, V. (1978).

[203] For a discussion of the role of brand equity in customers' purchasing decision process according to the underlying characteristics of products and services see chap. III.3.1.2.

ideas and aims underlying the general concept, the general functioning and design of the balanced scorecard are described. Building upon the general management model the *brandscorecard* concept which has been developed by Linxweiler (2001), is illustrated. The brandscorecard represents a basic instruction for companies of how to analyse and assess their brands and how to deduce a general brand strategy from the company's existing vision. Finally, it is pointed out how companies can use the concept of the brandscorecard to align and integrate their technology and brand strategies. The chapter finally closes with an upshot in section IV.4.5.

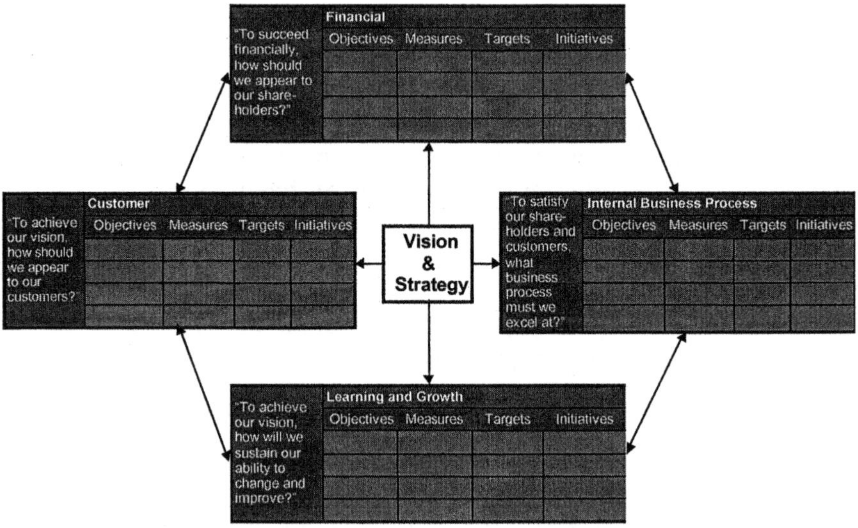

Source: Kaplan, R. S. & Norton, D. P. (1996), p.76.

Figure IV.19: The four perspectives of the balanced scorecard

The balanced scorecard systems that has principally been developed by Kaplan & Norton, has been set out to enable management to better *link the company's long-term strategy with its short-term actions* by supplementing traditional financial measures with criteria measuring performance.[204] As visualised in figure IV.19, the *four perspectives of the balanced scorecard* are the traditional financial view, and the three additional performance measures of customers, internal business processes, and learning and growth. Consequently, the balanced scorecard gives conclusive answers to the four principal questions:

[204] Cp. Kaplan, R. S. & Norton, D. P. (1992, 1996, 2001).

1. *Customer perspective*: How do customers perceive us?
2. Company *internal perspective*: What must we excel at?
3. *Learning and growth perspective*: How can we sustain our ability to change and improve?
4. *Financial perspective*: How does our company appear to shareholders?[205]

Building upon the four perspectives, the balanced scorecard introduces in companies four *new management processes* that have the aim to associate long-term strategic objectives and short- and medium-term activities. These management processes are according to Kaplan & Norton: (1) Translating the company's vision; (2) communicating and linking; (3) business planning, and (4) feedback and learning (see figure IV.20). The first process has the aim to translate the often extremely general strategy statements into clear and measurable strategy objectives. During the second process, the strategic objectives are communicated throughout the organisation and the objectives of the individual departments and business units are linked to the corporate strategic aims. The third process, business planning, allows for the selection, integration, and co-ordination of business and financial plans that takes the company towards its long-term strategic goals. Finally, as pointed out in figure IV.20, the last process of feedback and learning reviews if the company, its business units and departments, as well as employees have attained their set targets in each of the four scorecard perspectives and evaluate the pursued strategy with regards to the realised performance. Consequently, the balanced scorecard allows for the modification of the pursued strategy according to perceived short-term results and hence allows for real-time learning.[206]

The general concept of the balanced scorecard, as briefly depicted above, is broadly used in companies to align management processes and to bring the whole organisation into line with the set long-term strategic goals. The balanced scorecard concept has, due to its origins, a strong financial controlling view. However, as Linxweiler (2001) has pointed out, the concept can, by placing the brand at the centre of all entrepreneurial and customer orientated economic consideration, be adjusted in order to *better account for the outmost strategic role of brands*. The so developed *brandscorecard* concept presents a general instruction of how to analyse and evaluate brand equity, and how to derive strategies from the so

[205] Cp. Kaplan, R. S. & Norton, D. P. (1992).

[206] For a detailed discussion see Kaplan, R. S. & Norton, D. P. (1996); Linxweiler, R. (2001), chap. 4-5.

formulated visions and goals. The subsequent paragraphs briefly outline the brandscorecard concept developed by Linxweiler (2001) and finally show how the technological perspective can be integrated in the model.

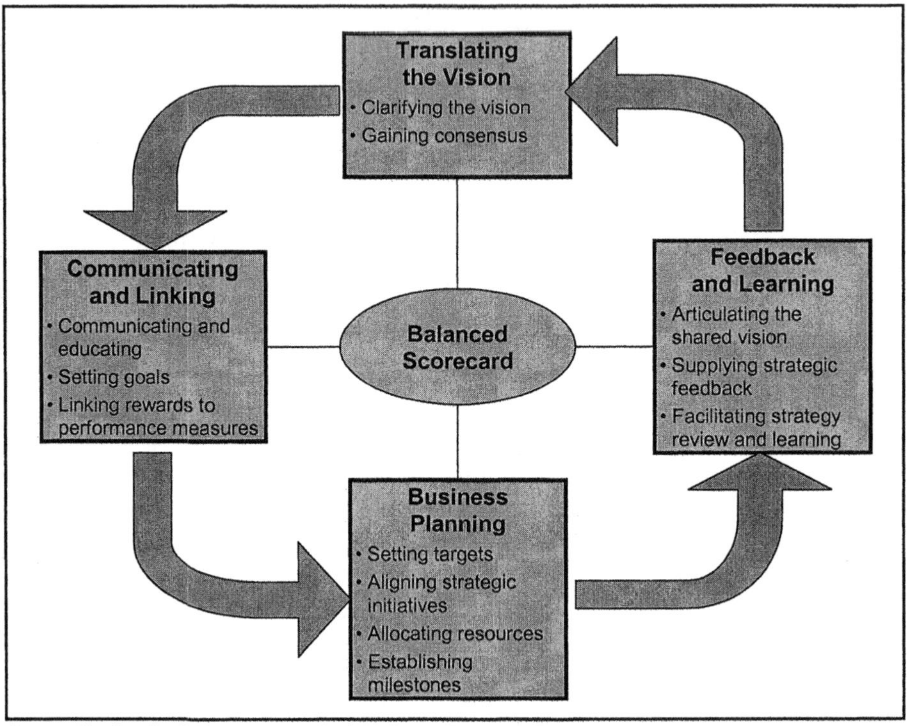

Source: Kaplan, R. S. & Norton, D. P. (1996), p. 77.

Figure IV.20: The four management processes

The principal aim of the brandscorecard is the development of brand concepts and strategies, as well as their efficient implementation through the four management processes of the balanced scorecard, as pointed out below (cp. figure IV.20). Consequently, in this brand focused concept corporate visions are translated into actual strategic goals whose current status of implementation is permanently observable through comparing the set targets with the established system of performance measures. Just as the balanced scorecard, the brandscorecard concept builds upon the two dimensions of management processes and performance measure perspectives. However, whereas the management processes of the balanced scorecard and the brandscorecard concept are identical, the perspectives of the brandscorecard are more brand focused and specific to the individual company. Thus, the higher-ranking brand relevant perspectives, i.e., customer, brand, company, trade/competition, and environment, are broken down in sub-ranges (see figure IV.21).[207]

Figure IV.21 visualises the perspectives of the brandscorecard which can be further divided into subdivisions of the company, e.g., R&D, production, administration, marketing, etc. For the individual perspectives strategic objectives and corresponding performance measures have to be set from which again specific initiatives and targets are drawn (cp. figure IV.20). The corresponding perspectives, strategic objectives and performance measures, as well as initiatives and targets have to be established for each individual brand and/or company.

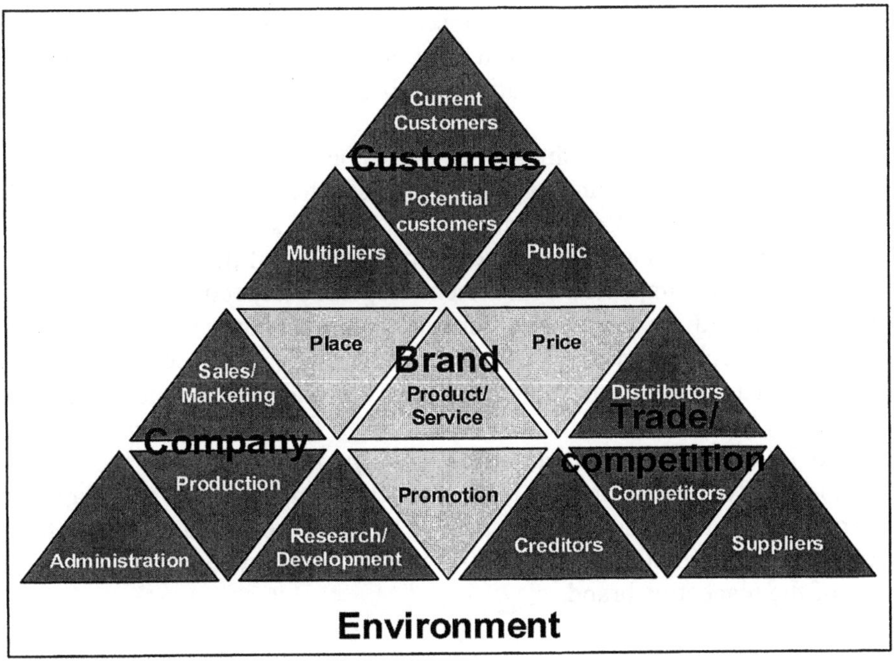

Source: Linxweiler, R. (2001), p. 124.

Figure IV.21: Perspectives of the brandscorecard

Thus, the brandscorecard concept assists companies in developing and implementing brand strategies and hence in managing brand equity. However, how can companies active in technology intensive industries *incorporate the technological perspective in the overall concept of the brandscorecard*? As already mentioned above, the perspectives of the *brandscorecard can be further divided into subdivisions* of the company

[207] For a detailed discussion see Linxweiler, R. (2001), chap. 7.

such as for the R&D or production division and thereby integrate a technological perspective. In order to even better take into account the technological perspective in the company's brand strategy, technological aspects should be included at the level of success-factors in the brandscorecard concept. As shown in figure IV.21, the brand perspective consists of the four domains: Place, price, promotion, and product/service. Each of the domains can be further subdivided into its most important aspects or success-factors.[208] At this level *technological perspectives can be integrated as central success criteria* in the brand management system, e.g., cash flow generated by new products introduced during the last three years, number of product improvements introduced ahead of competition over the past three years, etc. Consequently, by introducing technology relevant performance measures in the brandscorecard concept, a company can account for the strong relationship between technological innovation and brand equity.

A last possibility which may present the most adequate option for companies active in technology intensive industries, is the *extension of the brandscorecard by a technological perspective.* As shown in figure IV.22, the brand remains one of the principal perspective of the scorecard system that is, however, amplified by the technological perspective that is of equal importance and thus accounts for the complementary nature of brand equity and technological assets. The technological perspective is again subdivided into different strategic objectives and performance measures. As clearly pointed out by Linxweiler (2001), the brandscorecard concept has to be seen as an *individualised concept* that takes into account the uniqueness of each brand. Hence, each company has to adapt the brandscorecard and define the specific perspectives, strategic objectives, and performance measures according to the specific personality, qualities, etc. of the respective brand.

[208] Cp. Linxweiler, R. (2001), chap. 8.1.

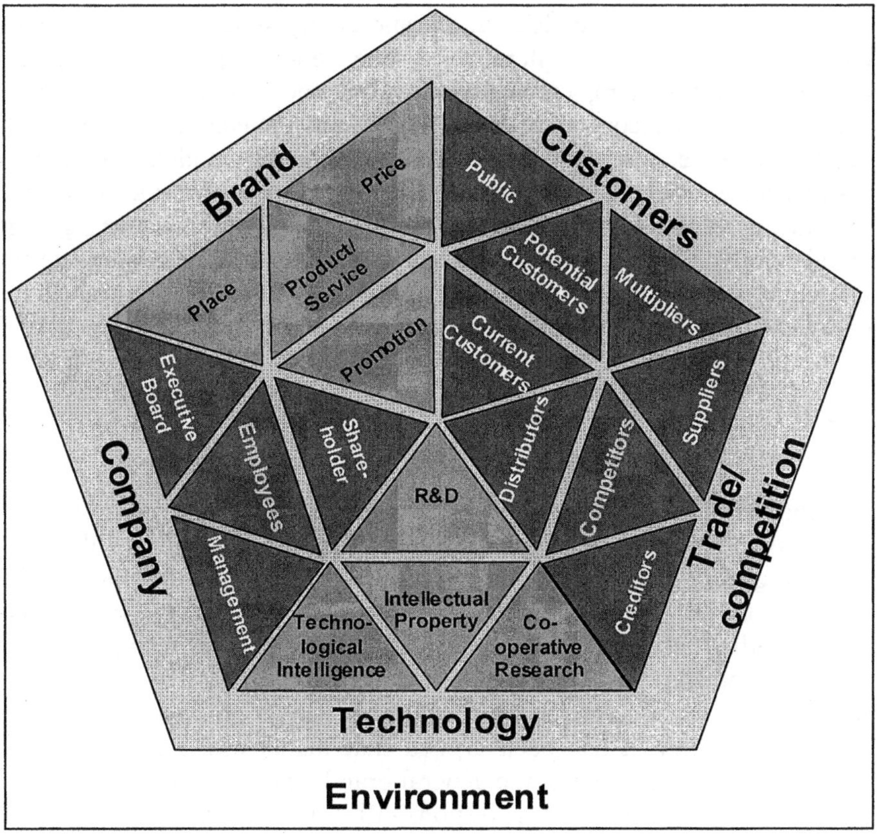

Figure IV.22: Integration of technological perspective in the brandscorecard

In conclusion, the *balanced scorecard concept*, originally developed by Kaplan & Norton, which has been adjusted by Linxweiler in order to better account for the outmost strategic importance of brand equity, can be further improved so as to take into consideration the complementary nature of brand equity and technological assets. The so developed concept thus takes into consideration the complementary nature of brand equity and technological competencies, by at the same time profiting of the advantages of the balanced scorecard concept,[209] and thereby allows for a

[209] The balanced scorecard concept has found broad use in companies due to its specific advantages: e.g., it not only takes into account higher-ranking goals such as ROI and/or cash-flow but also lower-ranking quantitative as well as qualitative performance measures, it narrows the gap between strategic and operative management and thus not put control at the centre but rather strategy and vision, the concept concentrates on rather mid-term and long-term

close integration of technology and brand equity strategies. Consequently, companies can, by implementing the above presented extended brandscorecard system, efficiently develop and put into practice brand strategies which incorporate the principal perspectives influencing brand equity. The extended brandscorecard concept enables a close alignment of brand equity and technology strategies, keeping track on the progress of the various initiatives and the attainment of the set targets, e.g., growing brand equity, increasing appropriability of the returns generated through intangible technological assets, etc., and thus ensures the accomplishment of the company's higher-ranking financial results.

IV.4.5 Upshot VII: Organising for an Effective Brand Equity and Technological Management

As chapter IV.3 has already made clear, brand equity represents a significant strategic advantage whose importance grows along the technology-life-cycle. However, in order to be able to appropriately manage brand equity, brand as well as technology management responsibility has to be appropriately assigned within the company. Three principal models for the integration of technology and/or brand equity management at the organisational level have been pointed out in chapter IV.2. In addition, it has been argued that managerial responsibility for corporate brands, as well as the general brand strategy should be located at corporate level whereas the responsibility for product brands is best allocated at the divisional level. In order to uphold or even extend existing brand equity, as well as to provide for new possibilities to grow new brand equity in new fields of corporate activity, a company has to provide for sufficient investments in technological innovation. It has been argued that best knowledge about technological development on the individual product level is available at the divisional level. Consequently, managerial responsibility, as well as decision making and financial power concerning projects aiming at the incremental improvement of established offerings in order to foster existing brand equity should be located at the divisional level. On the other hand, projects seeking to unveil technological innovation of considerable magnitude that may have the potential to

corporate objectives but, nevertheless, does not neglect the short-term, operative processes, it allows for a permanent tracking of financial results and monitoring of the most important activities and thus the progress of the set off initiatives and allocated resources, it enables companies to alter their strategies and hence to reflect real-time learning, etc. Cp. Kaplan, R. S. & Norton, D. P. (1992, 1996); Linxweiler, R. (2001), chap. 5.

created brand equity in distinct fields of corporate activity should rather be centrally financed and controlled, as well as carried out in the central R&D department.

A major problem of companies appears to be the integration of technology management and brand equity management. The difficulty arises from the distinct activities that necessitate extremely different competencies of the respective employees. Moreover, in most companies brand equity functions are completely separated from technology management functions in clearly separated divisions. This strict separation and the insufficient co-operation of the divisions has been identified as the principal reason for the failure of new product developments. Thus, in order to better allow for the accomplishment of the customers' expectations and needs, as well as to maximise the information transmitted by the brand to actual and potential customers, a better alignment of companies' technology and brand equity strategies is needed.

At the corporate level the integration of technological and brand equity strategies often appears extremely difficult. This problem can be solved by implementing the brandscorecard concept. As has been shown, the balanced scorecard concept which is broadly known to allow for the linking of companies' long-term strategies with short-term action, can be amended so as to better account for the strategic importance of brand equity as well as the complementary nature of technological assets and brand equity. Through the establishment of clear and uniform strategic goals, derived from the company's existing brand vision and brand strategy, specific action can be initiated, and the pursuit and the attainment of the set targets can be permanently monitored on the basis of key performance measures. The expanded brandscorecard concept thus enables companies to define specific strategic goals with the help of the existing brand vision and strategy, accomplish the corresponding activities, control the implementation as well as the effectiveness of the taken action and if necessary realign strategic initiatives and/or reallocate resources. Thus, by integrating the brand and technological perspectives in the general concept of the balanced scorecard, a management tool has been developed that allows for the alignment of technological and brand equity strategies at the process level and which takes the strategic importance of brand equity and technological assets into consideration.

V Econometric Analysis

Building on our empirical and theoretical foundations of the preceding chapters this empirical section endeavours to verify the underlying theoretical assumptions established in chapter III by means of econometric analysis. As already pointed out in chapter I.2.1, up until now only one statistical investigation of the relationship between patent filings, R&D expenditures, and company size, on companies' trademark deposits has been conducted by Allegrezza & Guarda-Rauchs (1999). This study, based on data on Benelux companies, has revealed by logit regression analysis a significant correlation between R&D expenditures and trademark registrations that is comparable in magnitude to the relationship between companies' R&D expenditures and patent filings ascertained by various econometric studies.[1]

Building on these initial findings we further broaden the field of investigation by using a sample containing the world's most R&D intensive multinational companies from various countries within the Triad zone and active in several different industries.[2] The point in common among all the companies included in our sample is that they are all *multinational manufacturing companies* active in *technology-based industries*. Hence, the sample does, for instance, not include pure service companies nor enterprises predominantly active in the food industry.[3]

Chapter V.1 points out the methodological proceeding and specifies several hypothesis on the basis of our theoretical discussion in chapter III and IV, as well as the research focus pointed out in chapter I which have the objective to clarify and direct our econometric investigation. These hypotheses are analysed and the results of the different regression analysis are tested and outlined in sections V.2.2 and V.2.3. The chapter closes in section V.3 with a discussion of the general results and the impact of our findings on companies' strategic planning and the theory of appropriation in general. Finally, indication for the scope of further empirical research in the field of the appropriation of intangible assets and in particular the specific role of brand equity within this field is given.

---

[1] For a detailed description of the various investigations see chap. I.2.1.

[2] The composition of the final research sample has been influenced by the INTERIS database available at the Centre for International Management and Innovation at the University of Hohenheim.

[3] For a comprehensive description of the sample see chap. V.1.2.

However, before specifying our research hypotheses and conducting the specific econometric analyses, we specify our methodological proceeding and the set of data used in the subsequent econometric investigations. Predominantly we point out the specific sources of data and the method used in its ascertainment, as well as the final composition of our sample. Moreover, the exact object and scope of the investigations are clarified before the methods used in the subsequent statistical evaluations are discussed.

V.1 Methodology

V.1.1 Data Sources and Ascertainment

The sample is composed of data from various different sources. The most important source of data represented the *INTERIS database* available at the Centre of International Management and Innovation at the University of Hohenheim. This database contains basic company figures as well as detailed figures on the companies international operations and R&D expenses of the 53 largest and most R&D intensive multinational enterprises (MNEs) of the Triad countries for the years 1980 to 2000. The INTERIS database, a continuous empirical research program at the Centre for International Management and Innovation, has considerably influenced the structure and composition of the sample used in the econometric analysis and delivered considerable data concerning the companies operating profits as well as R&D expenditures for the years 1983 to 1997.[4] In the case of incomplete data sets of specific companies the relevant database was supplemented by figures published in the 'Manual of Multinational Enterprises'[5] and/or company reports. The INTERIS database does, however, not contain any data on the companies' patent and trademark filings over the specific period. General data on companies' patent filings and trademark registrations at the different national as well as supranational patent offices was

[4] The period of investigation was determined by the availability of representative patent and trademark data. Pre 1983 EPO patent data has been adulterated due to the companies' conversion process of intellectual property filings from the different national patent offices towards the EPO. On the other hand, due to PCT filings a certain delay of approximately 2.5 years has to be respected until the EPO data has been updated, so that the latest data available at the time of ascertainment has been patent filings of the companies in 1997.

[5] Stafford, D. C. & Purkis, R. H. A. (1989); Stopford, J. M. (1992).

provided by the online-database 'QUESTEL-ORBIT' which has been available at the Fraunhofer-Institute (FHG-ISI) at Karlsruhe.[6]

For the analysis, data on the respective companies' patent filings and trademark registrations at the European Patent Office (EPO) and at the World Intellectual Property Organisation (WIPO) appeared to be most adequate. A patent *filing at the EPO* is only beneficial, due to the prevailing cost structure, if the company has the intent to file for patent protection of its innovation in at least three countries of the European Union. Moreover, because of the considerably higher cost and the broader geographic validity, the filing of a patent at the EPO can be appraised as an *indicator of high patent quality*.[7] Our investigation has used direct patent filings as well as filings according to the patent co-operation treaty (PCT)[8] of the sample companies at the EPO under the group or respective subsidiary names over the period from 1983 to 1997. Last but not least, by using data on patent filings at the European level, the national bias which is brought about by companies higher patent registrations at the corresponding national patent office, is presumed to be considerably reduced.[9] This is in particular due to the existence of patent offices on the individual national levels. Accordingly, the patent data search was performed on the 'EPAT' database containing data on patent filings at the EPO.

The ascertainment of the companies' trademark registration was carried out on the 'TMINT' database containing data on international trademark registrations under the Madrid Agreements at the WIPO. The WIPO trademark registrations had to be preferred to trademark filings at the EPO because data on EU trademark registration had not been available for the relevant time period. The TMINT database, however, does not contain reliable figures on international trademark registrations of companies not having a subsidiary within a country having signed the Madrid Agreements. Furthermore, even companies owning a subsidiary in one of the participating countries, but headquartered in a country not having jointed the Madrid agreements, are reluctant to register trademarks at the WIPO because the subsidiary has to be the legal owner and user of the registered trademark in order to uphold the trademark in the long-run. Thus, figures on trademark registrations at the WIPO of companies headquartered outside the Madrid Agreement countries, i.e.,

---

[6] For more information about the provider, as well as the provided databases see www.questel.orbit.com.

[7] Cp. Schmoch, U., Grupp, H. et al. (1988), pp. 30-44.

[8] For a detailed discussion of PCT applications see chap. III.3.3.

[9] Cp. Schmoch, U., Grupp, H. et al. (1988), chap. 2.

USA or Japan, do not give a realistic estimate of the companies' registrations of international trademarks. Consequently, in assuming that for these companies the German market represents the most important national market outside their domestic market, we have alternatively searched figures on trademark registrations of US and Japanese companies at the German Patent Office (DPA) available on the 'DMARK' database (cf. figure V.2 and table V.1).[10]

Even though the patent and trademark databases are regularly updated and basically contain the complete set of EPO, WIPO, and DPA registration figures, certain company names have not been recognised by the database or the patent filings and trademark registrations of companies with identical names could not be unequivocally allocated to one or the other company.[11] These companies had to be eliminated from our sample so that the final sample size has been reduced to 33 companies for which complete data on international trademark registrations and patent filings for the years 1983 to 1997 has been available. Moreover, information about trademark filings is only documented in the respective databases with the according registration date, however, no date of trademark filing is available. Thus, in order to be able to readily compare trademark and patent placements in our subsequent analysis the trademark data has been lagged by one year since the average period between trademark filing and registration is assumed to be in the order of magnitude of 12 months.

V.1.2 Choice of Object and Scope of Investigation

As pointed out above, the basic structure of our sample was determined by the INTERIS database of the Institute of International Management and Innovation. The INTERIS database comprises data on 53 R&D intensive multinational enterprises and has delivered extensive data on the companies' basic financial figures as well as R&D expenditures on an annual basis for the years 1983 to 1997. The final composition of the sample has been reduced to 33 companies from the Triad regions

[10] Other studies facing comparable problems with the data concerning the trademark registration of US and Japanese companies have used identical approaches. Cp. Blind, K., Edler, J. et al. (2001), pp. 53-93.

[11] The non-recognition of certain company names, e.g., IBM or Johnson & Johnson, may be due to flaws in the database and or problems of treatment of special characters. A specific example of two companies active under an identical company name represents the Germany Merck KGaA and the US Merck Corp.

because of shortcomings of the patent and trademark databases with respect to certain companies as well as of the non availability of general company figures over the observation period due to M&A activity and business reorganisation. For a description of the composition of our final sample according to the included companies' principal field of activity and home region see figure V.1 and V.2 respectively, and for a complete list of the companies included in our sample see table V.1.

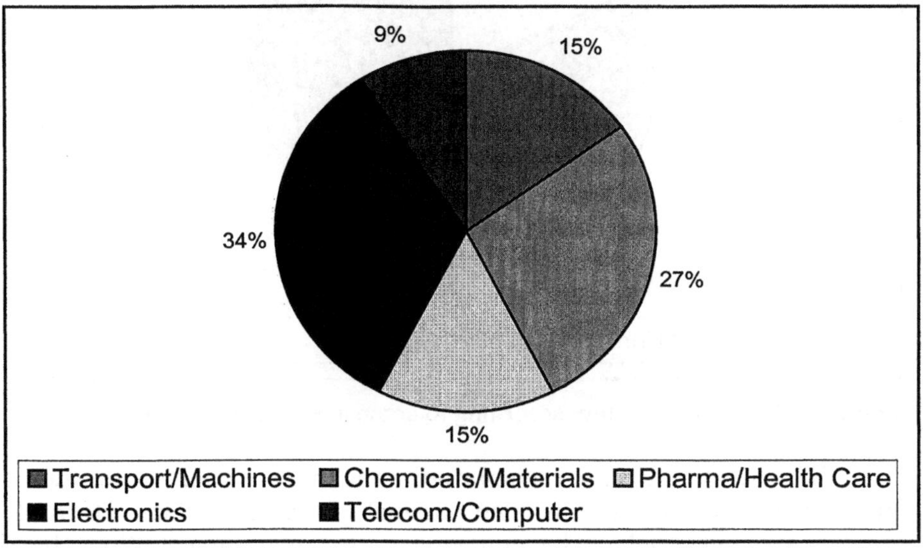

Figure V.1: Sample structure according to companies principal field of activity

The companies' annual patent registrations at the EPO have been searched in the EPAT database and classed into technology sectors according to the four-digit international patent classification code (IPC). The four-digit IPC classes have been further allocated to five general technology fields according to the systematic of OST/INPI/ISI[12]: Electronics; instruments; chemicals and pharmaceuticals; process technology; and engineering. Because of the double counting of patents placed in several different patent classes, the allocation of total patent filings to the respective technology field has been perceived according to the percentage distribution of patents placed in each technology field. Moreover, in order to facilitate and optimise the patent search, the allocation of patent filings according to IPC classes have been grouped

[12] The OST/INPI/ISI classification scheme has been elaborated by Fraunhofer-ISI, the French patent office (INPI), and the Observatoire des Science et Techniques (OST).

into five year periods and subsequently apportioned to the individual years in relation to the company's total patent filings in the specific year.

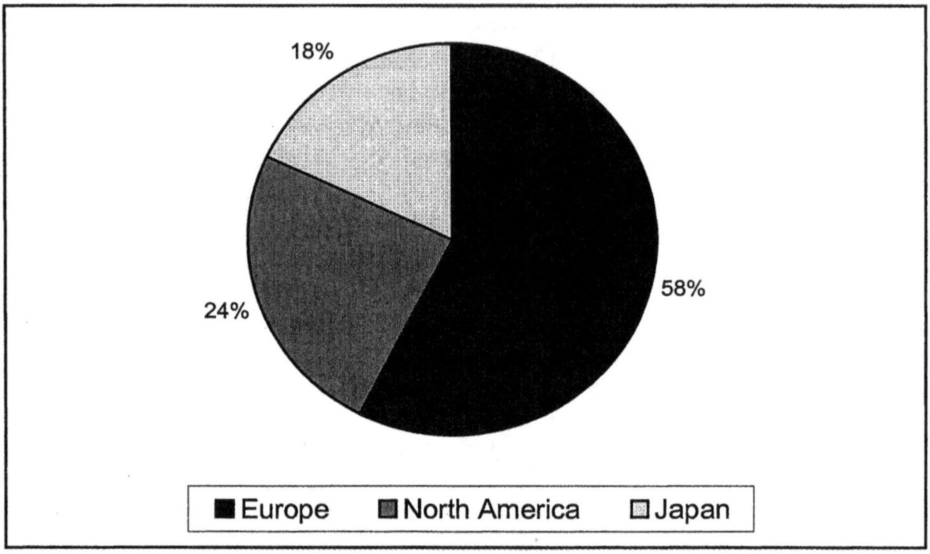

Figure V.2: Sample structure according to companies' home region

In the case of trademark registrations an identical search strategy as in the case of patent filings has been pursued in the TMINT and DMARK databases, respectively. The companies' trademark registrations have been searched according to their recording in the International Classification of Goods and Services (ICGS) which differentiates between 42 trademark classes, for each of the five year periods. The 42 ICGS trademark classes have been grouped into five technology fields, identical to those defined in the systematic of OST/INPI/ISI, however, with the additional field of services.[13]

Thus, of the 33 multinational companies included in the sample 34% are predominantly active in the electronics industry, 27% in the field of chemicals and materials, 15% in the pharmaceutical and health care, 15% in the field of transportation and machines, and a final 9% of the companies are primarily active in the telecommunication and computer industry (cf. figure V.1). For these 33 companies complete data on

[13] The ready availability of reliable data on trademark registrations for the use in services has motivated the use of trademark registration figures for the output measurement of companies' innovative activities in the field of services. Cp. Blind, K., Edeler, J. et al. (2001), pp. 53-93.

annual international patent filing and trademark registration in total and in the individual technology fields for the time period from 1983 to 1997 have been ascertained. Moreover, for most companies detailed figures on annual R&D expenditures, operating profits, and net profits have been available. The complete list of companies included in our econometric investigations is given in table V.1.

Table V.1: Companies included in the investigation

Company name	Natio-nality	Industry	Turnover 1999 (US$ millions)	R&D Intensity
ABB	CH	Transport/Machines	27,875	7.5%
Akzo Nobel	NL	Chemicals/Materials	14,507	5.0%
Alcatel	F	Electronics	23,144	9.2%
Allied Signal	US	Electronics	23,805	3.8%
BASF	D	Chemicals/Materials	29,627	4.5%
Bayer	D	Chemicals/Materials	27,463	7.8%
Bosch	D	Electronics	28,053	6.9%
Daimler Benz	D	Transport/Machines	150,768	3.8%
Dow Chemicals	US	Chemicals/Materials	18,985	4.5%
Du Pont	US	Chemicals/Materials	26,997	6.0%
Ericsson	S	Telecom/Computer	25,287	15.4%
Ford Motor	US	Transport/Machines	163,032	4.4%
General Electric	US	Electronics	111,155	1.5%
General Motors	US	Transport/Machines	167,857	4.1%
Glaxo Wellcome	UK	Pharma/Health Care	13723	14.9%
Hitachi	JP	Electronics	78,161	6.2%
Hoffmann La Roche	CH	Pharma/Health Care	17,271	13.7%
Krupp	D	Chemicals/Materials	29.950	1.6%
Kyocera	JP	Chemicals/Materials	14,131	5.8%
Matsushita	JP	Electronics	74,860	6.5%
Motorola	US	Electronics	31,022	11.1%
NEC	JP	Telecom/Computer	46,630	7.3%
Nokia	FIN	Telecom/Computer	19,875	10.2%
Novartis	CH	Pharma/Health Care	20,341	13.1%
Novo Nordisk	DK	Pharma/Health Care	5,345	5.8%
Pfizer	US	Pharma/Health Care	14,174	19.6%
Philips	NL	Electronics	31,623	7.9%
St. Gobain	F	Chemicals/Materials	13,301	9.8%
Sharp	JP	Electronics	17,108	7.7%
Siemens	D	Electronics	68,944	7.3%
Sony	JP	Electronics	62,857	5.9%
Sulzer	CH	Transport/Machines	4,156	4.3%
Thyssen	D	Chemicals/Materials	N.A.	N.A.

V.1.3 Theoretical Concept and Derived Hypotheses

Before analysing our data set in section V.2, we point out the theoretical concept developed in chapters III and IV, for which already initial empirical evidence has been presented in chapter II. However, in the subsequent econometric investigation a rather *integrated view of the company* and its activities is taken and not, as in chapters II and IV, a detailed examination of one isolated major technological innovation and associated brand equity over a prolonged period. From this integrated model which is explained in more detail in the following paragraphs, certain research hypotheses are drawn in section V.1.3.2. These research hypotheses, generally concerning relationships between individual variables quantifying certain issues, are investigated by multiple regression analysis and the corresponding results are tested for statistical significance and their general meaning is interpreted. The various regression analyses and significance tests are described and results evaluated in sections V.2.2 and V.2.3 after a brief descriptive analysis of our sample in section V.2.1.

V.1.3.1 Underlying Theoretical Concept and Its Operationalisation

As illustrated in chapter III and IV, new idiosyncratic intangible technological assets are of utmost strategic importance for companies in the currently prevailing economic order. These intangible assets show, however, the characteristics of public goods and thus are subject to considerable problems concerning the appropriation of their returns in the absence of legal rights of protection. Intellectual property rights have the aim to enable a company to exclude third parties from using the subject matter of its rights and thus appropriate the associated economic returns. Nevertheless, as various empirical studies have revealed, mere patent protection of technological innovation does not enable a company to satisfactorily appropriate the returns of the immaterial asset in question. Moreover, not all innovations are protectable by patent rights nor are companies willing to disclose critical information about their technological achievements which is obligatory for obtaining patent right protection.[14]

Various authors have already stressed the importance of *complementary assets* in the appropriation of the returns from immaterial

[14] For a detailed discussion of the different classes of intangible assets within business enterprises see chap. III.

technological assets. However, these authors have principally focused their discussion on complementary technological assets and have entirely neglected the importance of *market-based complementarities* and in particular brand equity.[15] Furthermore, no large-scale econometric analysis has been undertaken to empirically validate the established theories of complementary assets, so far. This is in particular attributable to problems of operationalisation and thus accurately quantifying the various effects.

The econometric analysis builds upon the broad econometric findings on the ascertained relationship between R&D expenditures as a measure of innovative input on the one hand, and patent filings as a measure of innovative output on the other. Even though figures on R&D expenditures have been heavily criticised and do certainly not account for the entire input in the creation of innovative output, they represent up to date the only available and reliable measure.[16] Hence, because of the unavailability of alternative and more accurate measures, we use *corporate R&D expenditures* as an *approximate measure of the company's investment in intangible technological assets*. In the same line of argumentation, we use *patent filings* as a measure of the companies' *output of innovative, intangible technological assets*.[17]

These almost 'standard variables' in econometric analyses in the field of technology and innovation management are amplified by a measure of complementary brand equity. As argued in chapter IV.3 and already empirically proven by case study research in chapter II, established *brand equity* represents an important strategic resource complementing a company's technological capabilities. Moreover, due to brand equity's complementary nature and extreme longevity - if managed adequately - with respect to patent right protection, it enables a company to effectively appropriate the returns of its intangible technological assets in the long-run. However, considerable problems exist in measuring brand equity on a business level and comparable basis. Various different methods of calculating the monetary value of individual brands co-exist which show considerable differences in their findings. In addition, most brand value calculations concentrate on individual product brands and do

---

[15] For a detailed discussion of complementary assets see chap. IV.1 and IV.2.

[16] For a detailed discussion of the problematic of R&D expenditure as an input measure see chap. III.2.1.

[17] For a detailed discussion of the shortcomings and limitations of patent rights in measuring a company's innovative output see chap. III.2.

not give a measure of the overall value of brand equity within a company.[18]

Due to the unavailability of a direct, precise, and comparable measure of companies' overall brand equity, we have to use corporate trademark registrations as an alternative measure. Nevertheless, companies' trademark registrations, although observed on a supranational level which are valued as a quality indication, can at best be seen as a second best measure in the absence of another, more accurate index.[19]

As argued in chapter IV.3, companies do usually follow a combined strategy of one dominant corporate brand and individual, complementary product or even product generation trademarks. Thus, we contend that a certain technological innovation which may lead to a new product or considerable product improvement, will lead to the registration of an individual product trademark. On the other hand, the improved performance of the product or the new innovative product increases and/or upholds the overall brand equity associated with the corporate name by satisfying customer expectations. Consequently, although data on the overall brand equity value has not been available for all companies in our sample and can thus not be investigated in a large sample as such, we can measure a company's output of completely new or considerably improved products within the observed period of time by trademark registration which will contribute to the overall brand equity held by a company. Hence, in our econometric investigation we only take into account the legal aspects and largely *neglect the reputational aspects* of brand equity (cf. figure III.18) because of the perceived problems of measurement. Data on trademark registration thus represents at best a rough indicator of incremental brand equity enhancements, however, in the absence of a more precise index, such an approximate measure has to be preferred to no indication at all.[20] For the few companies for which exact data on corporate brand equity has been available, an analyses of the influence of the companies' relative technological strengths on their brand equity is executed.

However, as has already been stated, the model analysed in our econometric investigation deviates from the model of complementary

---

[18] The Interbrand and Financial-World surveys do only determine the value of individual brands, but do not give a ranking of the overall value of brand equity held by an individual company. Cp. Badenhausen, K. (1996); Interbrand (1999a); Khermouch, G., Holmes, S. et al. (2001).

[19] For a detailed discussion of the measurement of the various concepts see chap. V.2.2.

[20] Cp. Schmookler, J. (1962); Carmines, E. G. & Zeller, R. A. (1979), pp. 9-16.

brand equity established in chapter IV with respect to the level of investigation. Whereas the model of chapter IV describes the relationship between technological innovation and brand equity in an isolated technological field, the econometric investigation takes an *integrated view of the company* and thus regards the relationship between a company's R&D expenditures, patent filings, and trademark filings as a whole. This integrated view of the econometric investigation is due to the unavailability of exact and reliable data on the level of isolated activities of a company in specific technological fields.[21]

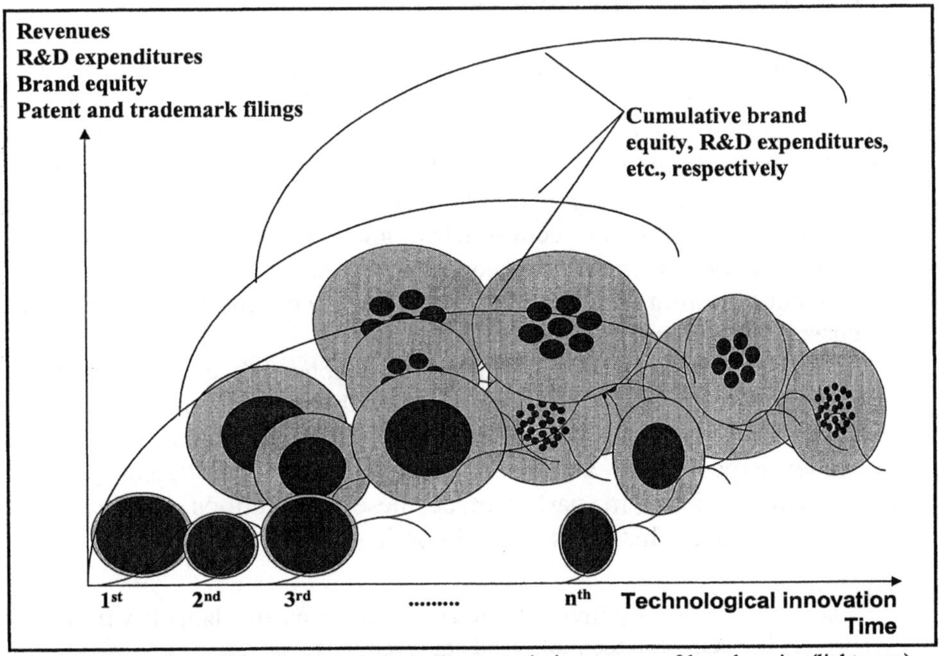

The (visible) surface of the circles represents the strategic importance of brand equity (light grey) and technology assets (dark grey). The lines represent the cumulative expenditures on R&D, as well as cumulative stock of brand equity and patent and trademark filings. See chap. IV.3 for a more detailed description.

Figure V.3: Integrated view of econometric investigation

As figure V.3 illustrates, the subsequent investigation does not analyse the activities of a company in one isolated technological field as done in chapter IV (cp. figure IV.11), but rather takes an integrated view of the company. Consequently, this econometric analysis investigates the

[21] Another possibility to investigate in detail the relationship between R&D expenditures, technological innovation and brand equity presents case study research which has been carried out in chap. II.

general relationship between a company's R&D expenditures, its patent filings, as well as trademark registrations and not, as pointed out, the specific relationship between technological assets and market based assets and their strategic role within one isolated technology-life-cycle. Thus, although the unit of analysis is changed, the econometric investigation gives the possibility to draw general conclusions about the model of complementary brand equity in the appropriation of the returns of intangible technological assets.

V.1.3.2 Research Hypotheses

This section specifies various research hypotheses which are deduced from the model described above that build upon the model of complementary brand equity established in chapter IV, the theoretical foundations presented in chapter III, as well as our initial empirical findings presented in chapter II. These research hypotheses have the aim to direct and focus the econometric analysis and are subsequently investigated by multiple regression analyses and the results verified by significance testing in chapter V.2. The econometric findings are discussed and general conclusions are drawn.

As we have argued in the preceding chapter IV, creative activities within companies lead to new innovations that in turn improve existing products or even bear completely new products which better meet customer expectations and needs. Intellectual technological property rights will at least in part protect these innovations which are of intangible nature. This leads to our hypothesis 1:

Hypothesis 1:

The more a company invests in R&D the more patent rights it will place to protect its intangible technological achievements.

These product improvements are generally of technological nature and thus an increase in R&D expenditures can be expected to result in an increase in the company's registration of patent rights in order to protect its intangible technological innovations. Moreover, due to the pronounced shortcomings of patent right protection, companies are assumed to reinforce the appropriability of associated returns of technological innovation by registering complementary trademarks. Consequently, we hypothesise that a company's R&D investments not only results in increased patent filings, but moreover, a change in the level of investment in creative activities and thus an increase (decrease) in a company's R&D expenditures does not only entail a rise (fall) in patent filings but also in trademark registrations.

Hypothesis 2:

Due to the complementary nature of patent and trademark rights, an increase in a company's R&D expenditures not only leads to an increase in patent filings but also entails a rise in trademark registration, and vice versa.

Furthermore, since trademark registrations are supposed to complement patent right protection, we assume that patent registrations and trademark registrations are placed in identical fields of technology. Which leads to hypothesis 3:

Hypothesis 3:

Due to the complementarity of patent and trademark protection not only a positive relationship between patent filings and trademark registrations exists, but moreover trademarks and patents are thereby placed in identical technological fields.

As already hypothesised in chapter IV.4.3, most technological innovation usually occur during early phases of the product development process and are often immediately protected after their unveiling. Thus, companies file for patent protection usually during early phases of the development process and hence considerably before market launch. Conversely, trademarks are only registered towards the end of the product development process, shortly before market launch. Consequently, a time lag between patent filings and trademark registration is assumed.

Hypothesis 4:

Patent protection is sought for shortly after the unveiling of technological inventions, whereas companies register for trademark protection only before market launch of the new product or product generation incorporating the respective technological improvement. Hence, whereas a companies' technological effort and patent right filings are almost simultaneously, a positive time lag between companies' patent filings and the corresponding trademark registrations prevails.

In addition, since complementary brand equity is thought to increase a company's ability to appropriate the returns of its intangible technological assets, and trademark filings are supposed to measure the contribution of new innovations to the company's overall brand equity, a company that registers relatively more trademarks with respect to its patent filings can be expected to better appropriate the returns of its intangible technological assets. Consequently, we hypothesise a positive relationship between companies' relative trademark registration as well as patent filings and a company's achieved profits.

Hypothesis 5:

Due to the complementarity of patent and trademark protection, a company that files relatively more trademarks and patents can generate higher profits than a company that registers relatively less patents and hence trademarks.

For the few companies for which comparable figures on overall brand equity value have been available, we investigate the relationship between total patent filings over the entire 15 year period and the company's overall value of brand equity. It can be claimed that the more expertise a company has in certain technology field the better it satisfies customer expectations with respect to competitors and thus the more valuable its brand equity. A company's relative technological advantage can be measured by the revealed technological and market based advantage, RTA and RMA (cf. formula V.4 a and b) which is hypothesised to correlate positively with the value of the company's overall brand equity. This leads to hypothesis 6:

Hypothesis 6:

The more pronounced a company's relative technological advantage in a certain field the more valuable its corporate brand equity.

The upcoming section outlines the method of statistical evaluation and the different tests of validity used in our analysis before presenting the statistical investigation of our sample. Furthermore, before exploring the sample by multiple regression technique in section V.2.2, we explore the sample by descriptive statistics and present some initial findings in section V.2.1. The general findings of our econometric investigation are finally discussed in chapter V.3.

V.1.4 Method of Statistical Evaluation and Statistical Validity of Results

The data set described in section V.1.2 has been transformed into a panel-data structure in order to facilitate the analysis of the relationship between the various variables and test the significance of the results (for a detailed list of variables see table V.2).[22] The aim of the econometric analyses is to test the underlying theoretical assumptions as well as the more general model which has been deduced from the model of complementary brand equity presented in chapter IV.3. For that reason six research hypotheses have been deduced in the preceding paragraphs

[22] For our data analysis we have used the statistical programme STATA which necessitates a panel data structure in the long format. Cp. Kohler, U. & Kreuter, F. (2001), chap. 8.6.2.

from the underlying theoretical foundations and the model of complementary brand equity. These research hypotheses, as well as the initial findings of the case study research are verified in the subsequent econometric investigation. For this purpose the use of multiple regression analysis appeared to be most adequate which has the general form shown in formula V.1.

Formula V.1: General form of multiple regression analysis

$$y_{it} = b_0 + b_1 x_{1it} + b_2 x_{2it} + ... + b_n x_{nit} + e_{it}$$

In formula V.1 the dependant variable, y, is assumed to be determined by the explanatory variables, x. Although various different explanatory and dependent variables are used in the subsequent analyses, intellectual property filings, i.e., trademark and patent registrations, present in general dependant variables whereas R&D expenditures, industry of activity, etc. represent explanatory variables. The variable *e* denotes the random error or the so called residual which represents the difference between the actual and predicted value of the dependant variable, y. Due to the panel structure of our data set, each variable has a value for each company i, i = 1,....,n, in various years t, t = 1,...., n. A full list of the variables used in our statistical investigations and their respective category is given in table V.2.

Validity and Reliability of Econometric Results

As in the case of case study research, the quality of an econometric analysis is determined by its *reliability* and *validity*. With respect to econometric analysis reliability describes the extend to which a test yields the same results on repeated trials. [23] Although the goal of error-free measurement is sought for, it is impossible to attain in scientific research, or as Carmines & Zeller (1979) have stressed:

> *"The amount of chance error may be large or small, but it is universally present to some extent. Two sets of measurement of the same features of the same individuals will never exactly duplicate each other."*[24]

[23] Cp. Carmines, E. G. & Zeller, R. A. (1979), chap. 1.
[24] Carmines, E. G. & Zeller, R. A. (1979), pp. 11-12.

Table V.2: Description of data set

Variable[1]	Category
LnRD	Natural log of R&D expenditures
LnOprofit	Natural log of operating profits
LnMTot	Natural log of total trademark registrations
LnPatTot	Natural log of total patent filings
LnPatElec	Natural log of patent filings in the field of electronics
LnPatInst	Natural log of patent filings in the field of instruments
LnPatChem	Natural log of patent filings in the fields of chemicals & pharmaceuticals
LnPatProc	Natural log of patent filings in the field of processes
LnPatMach	Natural log of patent filings in the field of machines and machine tools
LnMElec	Natural log of trademark registrations in the field of electronics
LnMInst	Natural log of trademark registrations in the field of instruments
LnMChem	Natural log of trademark registrations in the field of chemistry & pharmaceuticals
LnMProc	Natural log of trademark filings in the field of processes
LnMMach	Natural log of trademark filings in the field of machines & machine tools
LnMServ	Natural log of trademark registrations in the field of services
IndTranMach	Dummy: 1 if company's main activities located in transportation & machinery industry otherwise 0
IndChemMat	Dummy: 1 if company's main activities located in chemical & materials industry otherwise 0
IndPharma	Dummy: 1 if company's main activities located in pharmaceuticals & health care industry otherwise 0
IndTelecom	Dummy: 1 if company's main activities located in telecommunications & computer industry otherwise 0
NatUS	Dummy: 1 if company headquartered in North America otherwise 0
NatAS	Dummy: 1 if company headquartered in Asia otherwise 0
Cons	Intercept of regression line
lagX_n	Indicates that the corresponding variable X has been lagged by n years

1) Variables have been observed on an annual basis (t) for the years 1983-1997 and for the individual companies (i).

On the other hand, a certain result must not only be reliable but more importantly it has to be valid. In this respect *validity* describes if the measure is in effect measuring what it is expected to quantify. Generally validity can be distinguished into criterion- and content-related, as well as construct validity. In this respect criterion-related validity refers to the accuracy of the relationship between a quantitative measure and an external issue, and is usually estimated by the size of the correlation between the independent and dependant variables. Content validity, on the other hand, concerns the validity of a certain empirical measure in reflecting a specific domain of content and thus depends on the accuracy of the used measure in appraising and quantifying a certain subject matter. Finally, construct validity determines the extent to which certain empirical measures relate to each other consistent with a theoretical hypothesis concerning the interrelation between the various indicators. Consequently, the determination of the construct validity *necessitates a theoretical model* underlying the empirical investigation, an empirical analysis of the hypothesised relationship, and the interpretation of the results of the empirical investigation with respect to the clarification of the initial theoretical concept.[25]

The subsequent econometric investigation endeavours the statistical verification of the theoretical model illustrated in the chapters III and IV. From the theoretical framework central research hypotheses have been deduced in section V.2 which are subsequently investigated by multiple regression analysis. The statistical reliability and validity of the analysed relationships is evaluated by various *significance tests* that indicate the quality of the obtained results. In particular, two different tests of significance are used, one to evaluate the overall statistical significance of the conducted regression analysis which will be done by the so called F-test, and a second test to analyse the significance of the individual correlation coefficients which will be done by either t-test or z-test analysis (see formulas V.2 and V.3).[26]

Formula V.2: General test of significance: F-test

$$F_v = \frac{ESS/k}{RSS/(n-k-1)} = \frac{R^2/k}{(1-R^2)/(n-k-1)}$$

The F-test defined in formula V.2 will be used to assess whether the explanation by the *regression equation as a whole* is statistically significant at a given level of confidence,[27] where ESS is the explained sum of squares, RSS is the residual sum of squares, k is the number of explanatory variables, R^2 is the coefficient of determination, and n-k-1

[25] For a detailed discussion of the various forms of validity see Carmines, E. G. & Zeller, R. A. (1979), chap. 2.

[26] Cp. Barrow, M. (1988), chap. 6; Dougherty, C. (1992), pp. 110-113, 148-166; Sachs, L. (1992), chap. 3.5; Mittelhammer, R. C., Judge, G. G. et al. (2000), chap. 4.

[27] The confidence level is defined as 1 – significance level, where the significance level represents the probability of rejecting the null hypothesis (ρ=0) when it is in fact true.

defines the appropriate degrees of freedom (υ_1 = k and υ_2 = n-k-1) for *n* observations.[28]

Formula V.3: Test of significance of individual coefficients: t-test and z-test

$$a)\ t_{\mathrm{v}} = r\sqrt{\frac{n-k-1}{1-r^2}}\ ;\ \text{or}\ b)\ z = \frac{x_i - \bar{x}}{s}$$

In order to test the statistical significance of the *individual coefficients* of the different regression analysis, a standard t-test, or in the case of panel-data analysis a z-test, will be performed. In formula V.3 a) and b) the variable r denotes the correlation coefficient at n-k-1 degrees of freedom, x_i is an individual observation on the variable x, and x bar and s represent the mean and the standard deviation, respectively. The so calculated t- or z- and F-values are compared with the corresponding critical values with υ degrees of freedom at a given confidence level.[29] If the calculated test-values exceed the critical values (positively or negatively) the null hypothesis, ρ=0, must be rejected and thus the coefficient is significantly different from zero.[30]

Nevertheless, it has to be kept in mind that the investigated sample represents, as do most socio-economic data samples, merely a *subset* of a much larger population. Thus, the coefficients of our analyses are different from their real value which would be found by analysing the data on the entire population. However, since such an analysis is impossible due to the lack of available data, one has to use a sample of *random observations*. In our case the constitution of the sample was determined by the INTERIS database which includes the world's largest and most R&D intensive multinational enterprises and thus can be judged to be of random nature with respect to the aim of our investigation.[31]

---

[28] In the case of panel data regression a Wald Chi squared test is performed instead of the standard F-test.

[29] The critical F and t values are obtained from the respective standardised tables, see Barrow, M. (1988); Sachs, L. (1992); Dougherty, C. (1992).

[30] The null hypothesis, ρ = 0, assumes no relationship between the different variables, and the alternative hypothesis, $\rho \neq 0$, assumes a correlation coefficient different from zero.

[31] However, due to the nature of the INTERIS database a bias towards large and R&D intensive multinational corporations exists.

V.2 Statistical Analyses

V.2.1 Descriptive Statistics

This section analyses the complete data set by descriptive means. This initial descriptive statistical section already points out some interesting findings that are of relevance for the field being analysed by our research. Moreover, general trends in the various industries analysed are depicted. Building on these descriptive investigations, sections V.2.2 and V.2.3 conduct multiple regression analyses as well as test the obtained results in order to verify the statistical correctness of the established theoretical model. Finally, in chapter V.3 the general findings of the econometric analysis are discussed and conclusions are drawn.

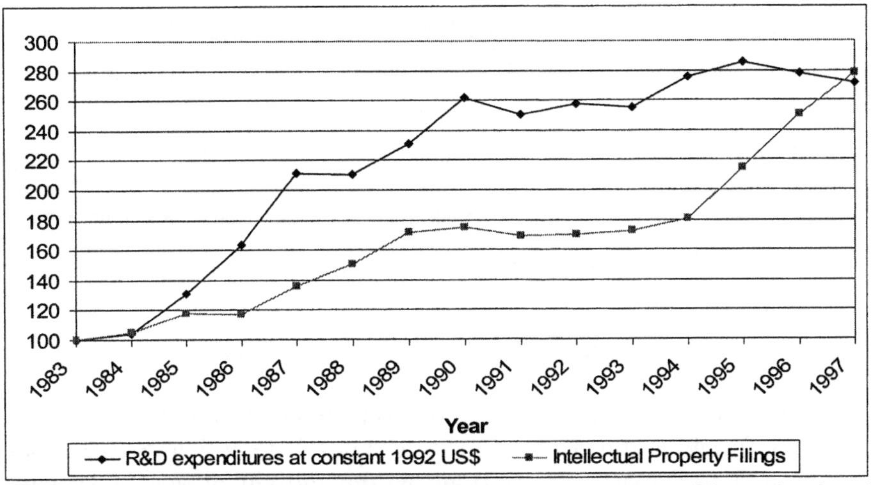

Basis: R&D expenditures at constant 1992 US dollars and cumulated patent filings and trademark registrations for n = 26.

Figure V.4: Index of R&D expenditures and intellectual property filings[32]

The preceding theoretical discussion has pointed out the increasing importance of intangible technological assets for business enterprises. This rising importance of intangible technological valuables is accounted for by the considerable rise in R&D expenditures as well as patent filings and trademark registrations of the companies included in our sample. As figure V.4 visualises, the cumulative R&D expenditures of the sample companies have risen between 1987 and 1993 by more than 300% and

[32] R&D expenditures at constant 1992 US dollars. Cp. NSB (2000).

intellectual property filings more than doubled over the 15 year period.[33] This strong increase in corporate investment in creative activities and the strong rise in annual intellectual property right placements clearly indicate the mounting importance of intangible valuables for corporate thrive. The strategic magnitude becomes even more explicit by regarding the mean R&D expenditures which amounted in 1997 to some US$ 2.4 billion per annum.

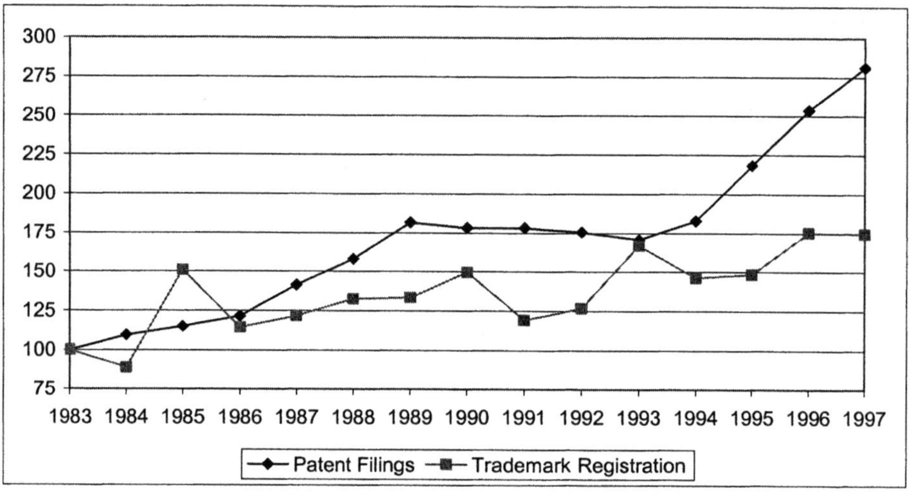

Basis: Patent filings and trademark registrations for n = 33.

Figure V.5: Index of patent filings and trademark registrations

So far, however, we have only considered cumulative intellectual property filings of the companies but did not differentiate between patent filings and trademark registrations in the individual years. As can be seen in figure V.5, patent filings have risen considerably faster than trademark registrations over the period from 1983 to 1997. Whereas trademark registrations have only increased by 80%, patent filings have risen by more than 180%. However, the magnitude of increase in patent filings and trademark registrations has been almost identical until 1994 and only during the last three years of our investigation the annual increase in patent filings has considerably exceeded the per annum rise in trademark registrations (cf. figure V.5).

[33] For the period 1987 to 1997 complete data on corporate R&D expenditures, patent filings and trademark registrations for 29 companies has been available.

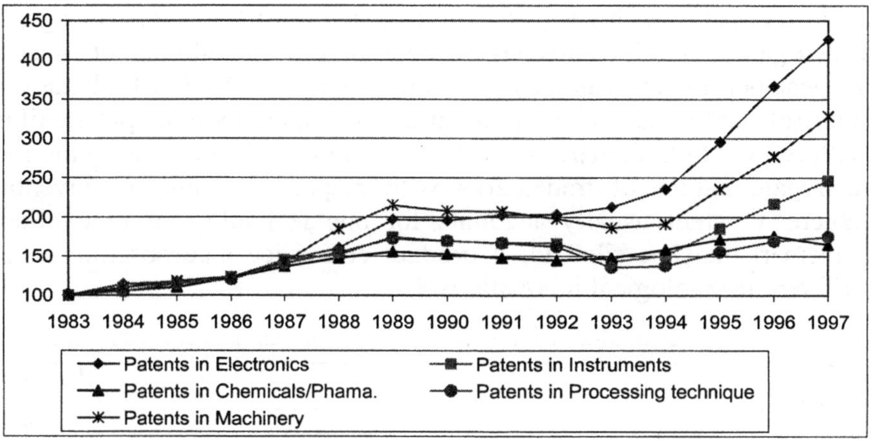

Basis: patent filings allocated to the different technology fields according to the systematic established by OST/INPI/ISI for n = 33.

Figure V.6: Index of patent filings within the five different technology fields

By differentiating patent filings according to the five technology fields defined by OST/INPI/ISI we can see that in particular the number of patent filings within the technology fields of electronics, as well as machines and tools have experienced an above average increase in patent filings. On the other hand, patent filings in the technology fields of instruments and particularly chemicals and pharmaceuticals, as well as processing technique have risen far below the average growth rate in patent filings (cf. figure V.6). With respect to absolute patent filings within each technology field the companies included in our sample filed in the technology fields of electronics and chemicals & pharmaceuticals 37% and 23% of total patent filings, respectively. In contrast, in the fields of machinery, instruments, and processing technique only 15%, 13%, and 12% have been placed. These relatively low total patent filings may be due to the structure of our sample, where 34% of all companies are active in the electronics industry, 27% in the chemicals and materials industry, 15% in the pharmaceuticals and health care industry, 15% in the transportation and machinery industry, and a final 9% in the telecommunication and computer industry (cf. figure V.1). Moreover, the companies' reserve with respect to patent filings in the field of processes can also be due to the low effectiveness companies associate with intellectual property rights, and in particular patents, in this field.[34]

[34] For a detailed discussion of the effectiveness of patents in different technology fields see chap. III.3.3.

Furthermore, with respect to total patent and trademark filings, the investigated 33 companies have filed a total of 135,000 patents over the 15 year period whereas they have only registered 13,500 trademarks in total (cf. table V.3). The significantly higher numbers of patent filings with respect to trademark registration are assumed to be due to the more aggregate nature of trademarks with respect to technical invention. Where a patent usually accounts for one technological innovation a trademark may be filed for a product or service incorporating several different technological innovations.[35]

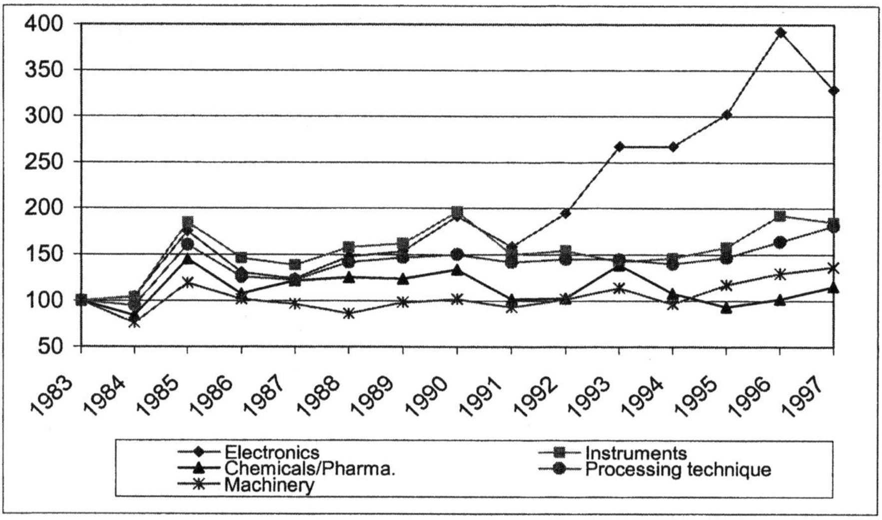

Basis: trademark registrations within the different technology fields excluding trademark filings in the field services for n = 33.

Figure V.7: Index of trademark filings within the five technology fields

A comparable development within the different technology fields in annual trademark registrations can be perceived as in the case of patent filings described above. As figure V.7 illustrates, trademark registrations in the field of electronics have increase strongest by almost 230% over the investigated time period, followed by trademark filings in the technology field of instruments and processing technique with an increase of 85% and 81% respectively (see figure V.7). Trademark registrations in the fields of machines and machine tools, as well as chemicals and pharmaceuticals show the lowest increase in annual registration figures over the 15 years period. Nevertheless, it has to be

[35] For a detailed discussion see chapter IV.3.

stressed that trademark registrations in the field of chemicals and pharmaceuticals account for more than 51% of total trademark registrations, followed by trademarks placed in the field of electronics which still account for 20% of total trademark registrations of all 33 companies over the entire period (cf. table V.3).

So far, we have only considered trademark registrations within the five technology fields of electronics, instruments, chemicals and pharmaceuticals, processing technique, and machinery and have neglected trademark registrations in the field of services. Although, the total number of trademarks placed in the service sector only account for 8% of total trademarks registered by the sample companies over the entire period, the relative increase in service trademarks has exceeded by far any of the five technology fields (cf. figure V.8 and table V.3).

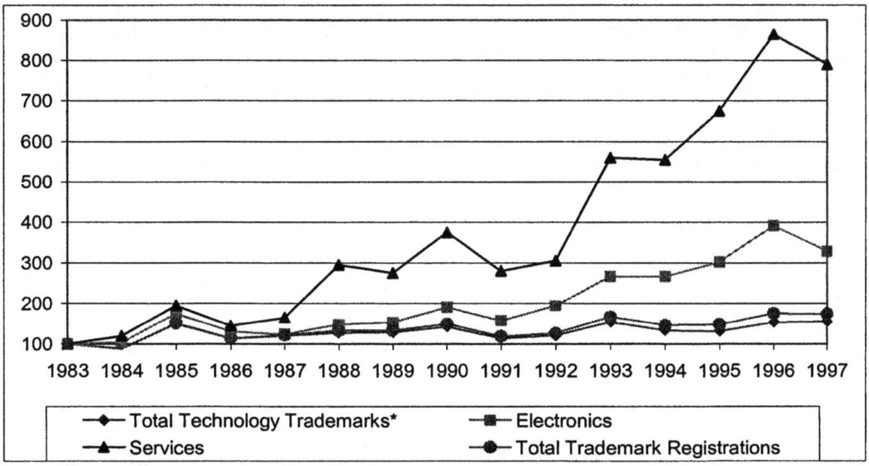

Basis: trademark filings in the respective fields for n = 33.
*) Trademark filings in the five technology fields, excluding trademarks filed in services.

Figure V.8: Index of total trademark registrations vs. trademarks in services

As can be seen in figure V.8, trademark filings in the field of services has increased by almost 700% from 1983 to 1997, whereas total trademark registrations have only risen by 75% and technology trademarks (excluding service trademarks) by merely 55%. This enormous increase in the registration of service trademarks reflects the surge of the companies' activities in the field of services, the lack of alternative intellectual property rights for the protection of innovative services, e.g., patents, and the increased strategic importance of services in differentiating oneself from competitors, as well as creating or reinforcing customer loyalty.[36]

Nonetheless, one has to remember that total annual number of service trademark registrations is still relatively low and total service trademarks only accounted for 14% of total trademark registrations of the sample companies in 1997. However, taking into consideration that in 1983 only 3% of the companies' trademark registrations were placed in the field of services and that in 1997 the number of registrations of service trademark has already exceeded the number of trademark registrations in the field of instruments, machines and tools, as well as processing technique clearly shows the importance of trademarks for services as well as the considerable growth rate in this specific field (cf. table V.3).

Table V.3: Total and relative patent filings and trademark registration

Technology Field	Absolute Patent Filings			Relative Patent Filings			Absolute TM Registrations			Relative TM Registrations		
	'83	'97	'83-'97	'83	'97	'83-'97	'83	'97	'83-'97	'83	'97	83-97
Electronics	1667	7100	51498	31%	47%	37%	88	289	2671	13%	25%	20%
Instruments	756	1864	17875	14%	12%	13%	26	48	602	4%	4%	4%
Chemicals/ Pharma..	1460	2405	31257	27%	16%	23%	407	469	6921	62%	41%	51%
Processing Technique	758	1329	16510	14%	9%	12%	58	105	1220	9%	9%	9%
Machines/ Tools	737	2419	20815	14%	16%	15%	58	79	909	9%	7%	7%
Services	-	-	-	-	-	-	20	158	1140	3%	14%	8%
Total	5378	15117	137955	100%	100%	100%	657	1148	13463	100%	100%	100%

A last interesting point, we want to stress in this descriptive part of the statistical analysis, is the considerable difference in the growth of trademarks placed in the field of services according to the companies' geographical origin. As illustrated in figure V.9, trademark registrations in the field of services have increased substantially by the end of the 1980s. The US companies in our sample show until 1992 considerably higher growth rates in the registrations of service trademarks. These

[36] Cp. Goldfinger, C. (1994), pp. 25-40; de Chernatony, L. & McDonald, M. (1998), chap. 6; Blind, K., Edler, J. et al. (2001), pp.53-61.

findings correspond with the findings of Goldfinger (1994), who argued that the USA had had a considerable advance with respect to the EU and Japan concerning the development of new services.[37] However, since 1992 the growth in the registrations of service trademarks by Asian companies has exceeded by far the increase in the registration of US and EU based companies included in our sample. Moreover, by 1997 the growth rate in the registration of service trademarks at the EPO of EU based companies surpassed the rate of growth of the US companies (cf. figure V.9).

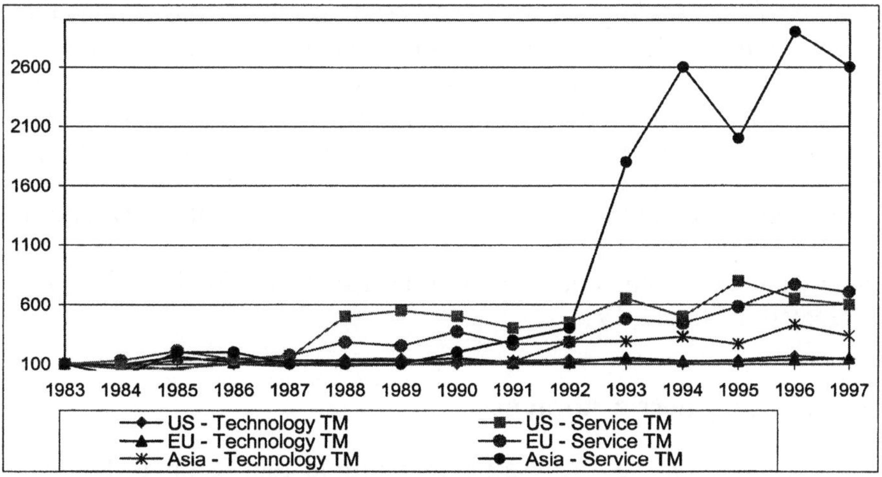

Basis: trademark filings in services and technology classes for n = 33.

Figure V.9: Index of trademark registration in services of companies headquartered in different regions

These findings clearly show an increasing importance of services for even large manufacturing firms. Moreover, the apparent lead of US based companies in the field of services, as claimed by Goldfinger (1994), has significantly declined or has even been reversed by European and Asian companies according to our findings. On the other hand, the number of trademark registrations has not only considerably increased in the field of services over the years, but also in technology fields. Although the average growth rates of trademark registrations in the investigated technological fields have been considerably lower than in the field of services, companies headquartered in Asia have nevertheless increased their registrations of trademarks in technological classes by

[37] Cp. Goldfinger, C. (1994), pp. 29-40.

more than 240% and EU based and US based companies still by 40% and 50% over the 15 year period, respectively.

Although our initial analysis is merely of descriptive nature, it already reveals some interesting findings. Most importantly, the assumption of the preceding theoretical chapters that companies increasingly invest in the generation of intangible technological assets, as well as the central importance of intellectual property rights and in particular patents and trademarks in the protection of their outcomes is confirmed by the presented findings. Furthermore, with respect to trademark registrations companies have in particular increased their recordings in the field of services. This finding clearly endorses the results and arguments of various authors which discovered an increasing importance of services in the activities of manufacturing companies.[38] In the upcoming section these initial general findings are further investigated and the above presented hypothesis, derived from our theoretical model established in the previous chapters, are analysed. The fundamental aim of the following econometric investigation is to empirically test and thus validate the theoretical assumptions underlying the model of complementary brand equity, as well as a first examination of the model presented in chapter IV.3.

V.2.2 Econometric Analyses

This section analyses by means of multiple regression technique the prevailing relationships between trademark registration, R&D expenditure, patent filings, and the economic returns of the companies' business activities. In the econometric analysis we proceed in the following way. First we analyse on the basis of the overall sample, irrespective of the principal activities and thus industry of the different companies, the general link between intellectual property filings and R&D expenditures and the consistency of patent and trademark filings within the different technology fields. Following the cross-sectional analyses we focus on the different industries and investigate the different trends prevailing within the various industries and compare the perceived results.

[38] Cp. Goldfinger, C. (1994); Sirilli, G. & Evangelista, R. (1998); de Chernatony, L. & McDonald, M. (1998), chap. 6; Blind, K., Edler, J. et al. (2001), pp. 53-56, 89-91.

V.2.2.1 Cross-sectional Analyses

This section explores the sample as a total, not taking into account the companies' different activities, in order to analyse the general relationship between trademark registrations and R&D expenditures, as well as patent filings. However, before analysing the various relationships, we have to *determine the exact time lags* prevailing between R&D expenditures and trademark registrations as well as patent filings on the one hand, and between patent filings and trademark registration on the other.[39] The determination of the existing time lag between R&D expenditures, patent filings and trademark registrations is ascertained by *stepwise* data analysis which necessitates a pooling of the data.[40] This analysis was performed individually for the relationships between trademark registrations and R&D expenditures, patent filings and R&D expenditures, as well as trademark registrations and patent filings. In our analysis we have used the natural logarithm of the values since we mean to investigate the relationship between the variations in the different variables and not the absolute figures.[41] For the stepwise analysis we have utilised trademark registrations as the dependent variable and lagged the explanatory variables, i.e., R&D expenditures and patent filings, by one, two, three, and four years respectively and eliminated successively the least significant relationships by using a 5% significance level of exclusion. The same investigation has been performed with total patent filings as the dependent variable and R&D expenditures as the explanatory variable, in order to analyse the delay between R&D expenditures on the one hand and patent filings on the other.

Our results indicate a *time* lag between *R&D expenditures and trademark registrations* of three years, and a time lag between *patent filings and trademark registrations* of one year. These results are statistically significant at a 98% confidence level. Moreover, the stepwise data analysis revealed that there exists no time lag between *R&D expenditures and patent filings* which is significant at 98% confidence level and hence *approves hypothesis 4* of chapter V. Our result of no time lag between R&D and patent filings corresponds with

[39] See chap. IV.4.3.1.

[40] The stepwise analysis has been performed for n = 27 and n = 32.

[41] We assume that the various relationships between trademarks, patents and R&D expenditures are of exponential nature which can be linearised through taking the natural logarithms of the various variables. Cp. Dougherty, C. (1992), pp. 121-127.

the findings of Hall, Griliches et al. (1986), who have found a *contemporaneous relationship between R&D and patenting*.[42] These outcomes clearly reflect the different natures of patents and trademarks. Whereas patents are usually filed immediately after technological invention, and thus with no or only a short time lag between R&D spending and patent filing, trademarks are filed not until shortly before the market launch of the new or improved product, and thus with a considerable time delay to initial R&D spending.[43]

On the other hand, the discrepancy between the contemporaneous relationship between R&D expenditures and patent filings on the one hand, and the delay between patent filings and trademark registration of one year, as well as R&D expenditures and trademark registration of three years, cannot be explained by general logic. The only explanation available may be a certain inaccuracy of the results due to the pooling of the R&D, patent and trademark figures of the 33 companies which are active in various different industries. Thus, these findings that cannot be satisfactorily explained by our research sample and have not been touched upon yet in alternative studies, clearly calls for further research. However, in order to account for the differences prevailing between the various industries, stepwise analyses on the individual industry level are performed in section V.2.2.2.

Taking theses results into account, we examine the prevailing cross sectional relationship between patent filings and trademark registrations on the one hand, and R&D expenditures on the other. Table V.4 presents the results of the different regressions performed with the logarithmic values of the different variables. For the explanatory variable the associated standard errors and z-statistics are reported along with the according regression coefficients. Regression 1 indicates a positive relationship between the variations in trademark registrations and the variations in R&D expenditures and patent filings. In this regression analysis trademark registrations have been lagged by three years, according to the above presented results. Moreover, regression 2 clearly points out a positive correlation between variations patent filings and variations in R&D expenditures on a contemporaneous basis.

The results of the regression 1 and 2 which are both highly significant at a 99% confidence level according to the performed F-test, clearly

[42] See also Pakes, A. & Grilichez, Z. (1984).

[43] These results correspond to the findings of our case study research. In the case of Bayer APIRIN, R&D efforts and the technological invention occurred before the registration of the associated trademark which has been registered shortly before market launch. Cf. chap. II.2.

support *hypothesis 1* established in section V.1.3, stating that a positive link between a company's R&D expenditures and its patent filings and trademark registrations. Moreover, our central assumption of the complementarity of trademark and patent right protection is confirmed by regression 1 which shows a strong positive correlation between trademark registration and patent filings. However, it has to be stressed that while the relationship between R&D expenditures and patent filings appears to be of simultaneous nature, a time lag of three years between a company's investment in R&D, as well as a delay of one year between patent filings and the registration of the according trademarks has been accounted for.

Table V.4: Results of regressions 1 and 2

Regression 1				Regression 2			
Dep. Var.: lnMTot				*Dep. Var.: lnPTot*			
# of obs.: 370		Adj. R^2: 0.1929		# of obs.: 469		Adj. R^2: 0.4084	
Variable	Co-efficient	Std. Err.	z-Stat.	Variable	Coefficient	Std. Err.	z-Stat.
laglnRD_3	0.3548**	0.0742	4.78	lnRD	0.7501**	0.0459	16.35
laglnPTot_1	0.1489**	0.0631	2.36	cons	-0.0968	0.3532	-0.27
Cons	- 0.6877	0.4754	-1.45				

Two asterisks indicate a confidence level of 95%; one asterisk indicates a confidence level of 90% and thus, the coefficient is significantly different from zero at the 5% or 10% significance level, respectively.

In table V.5 the results of the regressions 3 and 4 are presented. These regression analyses examine the overall relationship between the dependent variable total trademark registration (lnMTot) and the identical explanatory variables that were already used in regression 1 and 2 which are, however, supplemented by dummy variables for the individual company's main field of activity and their geographic origin.[44] In order to avoid problems of colinearity, companies headquartered in the EU, as well as companies principally active in the electronics industry, are taken as references. In regression 3 the influence of R&D expenditures, patent filings, the companies geographic origin, as well as the companies' main field of activity on the registration of trademarks have been analysed. Subsequently regression 4 reveals the relationship between R&D expenditures, geographic origin, and industry with the variations in patent filings.

The results of the multiple regression 3 shown in table V.5 confirm our strong and highly significant results of a positive correlation between

[44] For the complete list of variables see table V.2.

the variations in trademark registrations on the one hand, and patent filings and R&D expenditures on the other, that have already been pointed out in regression 1. Furthermore, a negative relationship between a company's location in the USA or Japan with respect to companies headquartered in Europe and the companies' trademark registrations is ascertained. These results which are statistically significant at a 95% confidence level, may indicate that although we have used data on trademark registrations at the European Patent Office and the German Patent Office for those companies with headquarters in countries not participating in the Madrid Agreements, a certain bias in favour of EU based companies still prevails. Or, alternatively, that companies headquartered in the EU register significantly more trademarks than companies based in the USA or Japan. With respect to differences in trademark registrations prevailing between the various industries investigated, the results of regression 3 indicate that companies in the telecommunications and computer (IndTelecom), as well as in the transportation and machinery industry (IndTranMach), register considerably less trademarks than companies in the electronics industry which are used in our analysis as a reference. On the other hand, companies principally active in the chemicals and materials (IndChemMat), as well as in the pharmaceuticals and health care industry (IndPharma) register considerable more trademarks than companies active in the electronics industry. These inter-industry differences are statistically significant at a 90% or 95% confidence interval, respectively. The sole exception presents the pharmaceuticals and health care industry, where the significance test did not confirm the perceived higher propensity of trademark registrations of pharmaceutical and health care companies with respect to electronics companies (cf. table V.5).

With respect to patent filings, the positive and statistically significant contemporaneous relationship between patent filings and R&D expenditures could be confirmed by regression 4 in table V.5. In addition, the results of regression 4 show that the geographic location of the different companies, as well as the field of activity, does not have a strong influence on the patent activities of the companies. The only exception presents the transportation and machinery industry, where companies file noticeably less patents than in any of the other four industries investigated and the result is significant at a 95% confidence level (cf. table V.5). Thus, with respect to patent filings, we can conclude that no significant differences between companies from different nationalities prevail and that the only industry that diverges significantly from the general pattern of patent filings is the transportation and machinery industry.

By comparing the coefficient of determination adjusted for the number of explanatory variables included in the model, better known as the value of adjusted R^2, we can ascertain a considerable increase in the value of the adj. R^2 from regression 1 to regression 3.[45] Thus, by introducing dummy variables for the companies' home region and main field of activity the fit of the model can be increased considerably from approximately 20% of the variations in trademark registrations explained by the explanatory variables in regression 1 (table V.4) to a 60.40% of the variations in regression 3 (table V.5). By comparing the results of regression 2 and 4 of table V.4 and V.5, an identical development can be ascertained. As can be seen, the variations in R&D expenditures explain 40.84% of the variations in patent filings, by adding dummy variables for the companies' geographical origin and main field of activity the adj. R^2 increases by a considerable 10 percentage points.

Table V.5: Results of regressions 3 and 4

Regression 3				Regression 4			
Dep. Var.: lnMTot				*Dep. Var.: lnPTot*			
# of obs.: 370		Adj. R^2: 0.604		# of obs.: 469		Adj. R^2: 0.5082	
Variable	Coefficient	Std. Err.	z-Stat.	Variable	Co-efficient	Std. Err.	z-Stat.
laglnRD_3	0.4128**	0.0721	5.73	LnRD	0.7589**	0.0465	16.31
laglnPTot_1	0.1687**	0.0609	2.77	NatUS	- 0.0841	0.3990	-0.21
NatUS	- 1.1211**	0.3088	-3.63	NatJP	- 0.3927	0.4716	-0.83
NatJP	- 1.0731**	0.3658	-2.93	IndTranMach	- 1.2128**	0.5227	-2.32
IndTranMach	- 0.9379**	0.4103	-2.29	IndChemMat	- 0.0598	0.4354	-0.14
IndChemMat	0.6414*	0.3413	1.88	IndPharma	- 0.2902	0.5287	-0.55
IndPharma	0.4675	0.4106	1.14	IndTelecom	- 0.1915	0.6095	-0.31
IndTelecom	- 1.5233**	0.4716	-3.23	cons	0.1951	0.4904	0.40
Cons	- 0.6787	0.5221	-1.30				

Two asterisks indicate a confidence level of 95%; one asterisk indicates a confidence level of 90% and thus, the coefficient is significantly different from zero at the 5% or 10% significance level, respectively.

The regression analyses depicted in table V.6, has investigated if an increase in patent filings in a specific technology field induces an

[45] Since the coefficient of determination, R^2, will always increase by adding further explanatory variables to a regression equation even if the correlation coefficient of the variable is small and not significant. The adjusted value of R^2 tries to take the number of explanatory variables included in the regression equation into account. Cp. Dougherty, C. (1992), pp. 161-166.

increase in trademark registrations placed in the corresponding technological field. Such an identical development would reinforce the assumption and first empirical findings of regression 1 and 3 of the complementarity of patent and trademark protection. In these regressions a time lag of three years between R&D expenditure and trademark registration and of one year between patent filing and trademark registration has been accounted for. The detailed results of the regression analyses 5 to 10 can be found in table V.6 and V.7.

Table V.6: Results of regressions 5 to 8

Regression 5				Regression 6			
Dep. Var.: lnMElec				*Dep. Var.: lnMInst*			
# of obs.: 370	Adj. R^2: 0.5781			# of obs.: 370	Adj. R^2: 0.2543		
Variable	Coefficient	Std. Err.	z-Stat.	Variable	Coefficient	Std. Err.	z-Stat.
laglnPElec_1	0.0975*	0.0573	1.70	laglnPInst_1	- 0.0013	0.0367	-0.03
laglnRD_3	0.2598**	0.0623	4.17	laglnRD_3	0.0768*	0.0385	2.09
IndTranMach	- 1.1090**	0.3385	-3.28	IndTranMach	- 0.4899*	0.2844	-1.72
IndChemMat	- 0.8218*	0.3001	-2.73	IndChemMat	- 0.1543	0.2371	-0.65
IndPharma	- 0.8979**	0.3920	-2.29	IndPharma	0.0842	0.2850	0.30
IndTelecom	- 1.1891**	0.3718	-3.20	IndTelecom	- 0.4656	0.3271	-1.42
NatUS	- 1.1636**	0.2437	-4.78	NatUS	- 0.4462**	0.2129	-2.10
NatJP	- 0.5006*	0.2880	-1.74	NatJP	- 0.5033**	0.2515	-2.00
Cons	- 0.0894	0.4089	-0.22	cons	0.1405	0.2889	0.49
Regression 7				Regression 8			
Dep. Var.: lnMChem				*Dep. Var.: lnMProc*			
# of obs.: 370	Adj. R^2: 0.7389			# of obs.: 370	Adj. R^2: 0.4949		
Variable	Coefficient	Std. Err.	z-Stat.	Variable	Coefficient	Std. Err.	z-Stat.
laglnPChem_1	0.2638**	0.0507	5.21	laglnPProc_1	0.0852*	0.0454	1.87
laglnRD_3	0.0877*	0.0460	1.91	laglnRD_3	0.1462**	0.0394	3.71
IndTranMach	- 0.1618	0.4248	-0.38	IndTranMach	- 0.5756*	0.2837	-2.03
IndChemMat	1.1531**	0.3574	3.23	IndChemMat	0.4181*	0.2413	1.73
IndPharma	1.5762**	0.4462	3.53	IndPharma	- 0.2901	0.2907	-1.00
IndTelecom	- 0.0351	0.4910	-0.07	IndTelecom	- 0.6180*	0.3389	-1.82
NatUS	- 0.2210	0.3208	-0.69	NatUS	- 0.5534**	0.2170	-2.55
NatJP	- 0.6232*	0.3770	-1.65	NatJP	- 0.6419**	0.2561	-2.51
Cons	- 0.4377	0.4136	-1.06	cons	- 0.2045	0.3224	-0.63

Two asterisks indicate a confidence level of 95%; one asterisk indicates a confidence level of 90% and thus, the coefficient is significantly different from zero at the 5% or 10% significance level, respectively.

As can be seen in tables V.6 and V.7, in all but one multiple regression patent filings lagged by one year are positively correlated with trademark registrations. The intensity of the positive correlation which are all statistically significant at a 95% or 90% confidence level, vary between 0.26 in technology field chemicals and pharmaceuticals and 0.08 in the technology field processing technique. The negative relationship between patent filings and trademark registrations in the technology field instruments is extremely small with a correlation coefficient of -0.0013 and moreover, the relationship is not statistically significant from zero (see regression 6 in table V.6).

Table V.7: Results of regression 9 & 10

Regression 9				Regression 10			
Dep. Var.: lnMMach				*Dep. Var.: lnMServ*			
# of obs.: 370	Adj. R^2: 0.3927			# of obs.: 370	Adj. R^2: 0.4011		
Variable	Co-efficient	Std. Err.	z-Stat.	Variable	Co-efficient	Std. Err.	z-Stat.
laglnPMach_1	0.1104**	0.0403	2.74	laglnRD_3	0.4396**	0.0444	9.90
laglnRD_3	0.0773*	0.0411	1.88	IndTranMach	-0.7009**	0.3113	-2.25
IndTranMach	0.0249	0.2654	0.09	IndChemMat	-0.3861	0.2621	-1.47
IndChemMat	0.2346	0.2237	1.05	IndPharma	-0.6009*	0.3158	-1.90
IndPharma	-0.1464	0.2811	-0.52	IndTelecom	-0.7066*	0.3633	-1.95
IndTelecom	-0.3944	0.3155	-1.25	NatUS	-0.7324**	0.2379	-3.08
NatUS	-0.5754**	0.2028	-2.84	NatJP	-0.6353**	0.2812	-2.26
NatJP	-0.6801**	0.2416	-2.82	cons	-1.7069	0.3808	-4.48
Cons	-0.0659	0.3220	-0.20				

Two asterisks indicate a confidence level of 95%; one asterisk indicates a confidence level of 90% and thus, the coefficient is significantly different from zero at the 5% or 10% significance level, respectively.

With respect to the ascertained relationships between trademark registrations in the respective technology field and general R&D expenditures that have been lagged by three years, all investigations show a strong positive and statistically significant correlation. The correlation coefficients vary between 0.43 in the case of trademark registrations in the field of services and 0.07 in the case of trademark registrations in the technology fields of machinery and machine tools, and instruments (cf. tables V.6 and V.7). Furthermore, in all technology fields companies headquartered in the USA or Japan have filed fewer trademarks than companies based in the EU which have been taken as reference in our investigations. The results thus clearly support hypothesis 2 stating a complementary nature of trademark registration and patent filings, empirically shown by the positive influence of the variation in patent filings in one given technology field on the variation in trademark registration in the identical technological field.

Concerning the propensity to patent of the companies active in the different industries our results indicate that companies that are predominantly active in the electronics industry that functions as the reference industry in our analyses, register considerably more trademarks in the field of electronics than companies focused on any other industry. Regarding trademark registrations in the field of instruments, companies active in the pharmaceutical and health care industry filed most trademarks followed by electronics companies and companies active in the field of chemicals and materials. With respect to trademark registrations in the technology fields chemicals and pharmaceuticals companies principally active in these fields have placed most trademarks. More surprisingly, however, companies predominantly active in the field of chemicals and materials have placed most trademarks in the field of process technology followed by electronics and pharmaceutical and health care companies (cf. regression 7 and 8 in table V.6). Transportation and machinery manufacturing companies, as well as companies active in the field of chemicals and materials show a higher propensity to register trademarks in the field of machines and machine tools than electronics, pharmaceutical and health care, or even telecommunication and computer companies. With respect to services electronics companies file most trademarks followed by chemicals and materials, pharmaceutical and health care, transportation and machinery, and finally telecommunication and computer companies.[46]

In summary, the above presented results clearly confirm the assumption of the complementary nature of patent and trademark protection. Moreover, it could be shown that the intangible outcomes of investments in research and development activities are not only protected by the filing of patents but also by the registration of trademarks. However, whereas a contemporaneous relationship between R&D investments and patent filings has been ascertained, a time lag between R&D expenditures and trademark registrations has been found. In addition, due to the risk of auto-correlation[47] in our multiple regressions,

[46] Concerning the statistical significance of the discussed correlation coefficients see tables V.6 and V.7. According to the Wald Chi Squared test, the multiple regression analyses 5 to 10 are all statistically significant at a 98% confidence level.

[47] Problems of serial- or auto-correlation may be caused by the mutual influence of R&D expenditures on patent applications as well as trademark registrations. Thus, the explanatory variables R&D expenditures and patent application are correlated and consequently the value taken by the disturbance term in any observations is not determined independently of its values in all other observations. Cp. Dougherty, C. (1992) pp. 216-225.

we have carried out further regression analyses investigating the relationship between the dependent variable trademark registrations and either R&D expenditures or patent filings independently. The results of these additional regression analyses are in general consistent with the results outlined above. However, the results generally show higher correlation coefficients, as well as a higher statistical significance, as in the combined analyses. Furthermore, the results of our regression analyses 3 to 10 indicate considerable differences in the companies' behaviour in trademark registration across the different industries. Hence, the next section individually explores the relationship between trademark registrations on the one hand, and patent filings and R&D expenditures on the other hand, in the various industries.

V.2.2.2 Industry Analyses

Building on the findings of the cross sectional analyses outlined above, we will separately analyse in this section the five different industries in which our sample companies are predominantly active in order to reveal inter-industry differences in the companies' behaviour in registering for trademark protection. Thus, we perform a stepwise analysis with a 5% significance level of exclusion for all five industries to uncover the precise time lags prevailing between R&D expenditures, patent filings, and trademark registrations in the specific industry. Building on these results we then examine the relationships between trademark registrations, patent filings, and R&D expenditures in each of the industries. However, in order to avoid problems of serial correlation we perform individual regression analyses investigating the influence of variations in the explanatory variables, patent filing and R&D expenditures, on the dependent variable trademark registrations.[48]

Electronics Industry

According to the method described in section V.2.2.1, we determine the optimal time lag prevailing between R&D expenditures and patent filings on the one hand, and trademark registrations on the other in the electronics industry.[49] The stepwise analyses which was performed at a 5% significance level of exclusion, revealed a time lag between R&D expenditures and trademark registrations of two years and no time lag

[48] Due to the smaller industry samples the problem of serial-correlation is more pronounced than in the case of the cross-sectional analysis.

[49] The stepwise analysis was carried out with patent and R&D data which has been lagged by 1, 2, 3 and 4 years, respectively.

between patent filing and trademark registrations. Taking these findings into consideration, we next investigate in a multiple regression analysis the relationships between the dependent variable trademark registrations and the explanatory variables patent filings, R&D expenditures, and the companies' nationality.

Table V.8: Relationship between trademark registration, patent filings and R&D expenditures in the electronics industry

Regression 11				Regression 12			
Dep. Var.: lnMTot				*Dep. Var.: lnMTot*			
# of obs.: 129	Adj. R^2: 0.5995			# of obs.: 165	Adj. R^2: 0.5427		
Variable	Coefficient	Std. Err.	z-Stat.	Variable	Coefficient	Std. Err.	z-Stat.
LaglnRD_2	0.7016**	0.1125	6.24	lnPTot	0.3093**	0.0736	4.21
NatUS	-1.6606**	0.5536	-3.00	NatUS	-2.1221**	0.5678	-3.75
NatJP	-1.2187**	0.5115	-2.38	NatJP	-1.5400**	0.5258	-2.93
Cons	-1.6561*	0.9202	-1.80	cons	1.815**	0.5525	-3.29

Two asterisks indicate a confidence level of 95%; one asterisk indicates a confidence level of 90% and thus, the coefficient is significantly different from zero at the 5% or 10% significance level, respectively.

The results of regression 11 and 12 depicted in table V.8 show a positive and statistically significant relationship between the variations in the explanatory variables R&D expenditures and patent filings and variations in the dependent variable trademark registrations. In regression 11 a time lag between R&D expenditures and trademark registrations of two years has been taken into consideration. In the case of the relationship between patent filings and trademark registrations, shown in regression 12, a contemporaneous relationship was assumed. Furthermore, our results indicate that electronics companies headquartered in the USA and Japan register considerably less trademarks than EU based companies. All correlation coefficients, as well as the overall regression equation are statistically significant according to the performed tests.

Chemicals and Materials Industry

In the case of the chemicals and materials industry a contemporaneous relationship between trademark registrations and R&D expenditures, as well as patent filings appeared to present the best fit between the dependant and the explanatory variables. The multiple regression results clearly indicate a positive and highly significant correlation between patent filings, as well as R&D expenditures on the one hand, and trademark registrations on the other.

In comparison to the results of our investigation in the electronics industry, the chemicals and materials industry shows a lower correlation between trademark registrations and patent filings, as well as R&D expenditures. However, concerning the relation between the individual coefficients in the chemicals and materials industry, the relationship between trademark registrations and patent filings appears more pronounced than the link between trademark registration and R&D expenditures (cf. table V.9). In the electronics industry in contrast, R&D expenditures have shown a higher correlation coefficient than patent filings (cf. table V.8). Concerning the influence of the national origin on trademark registrations in the chemicals and materials industry only Japanese chemicals and materials companies appear to register significantly less trademarks than their European counterparts.

Table V.9: Relationship between trademark registration, patent filings and R&D expenditures in the chemicals & materials industry

Regression 13				Regression 14			
Dep. Var.: lnMTot				*Dep. Var.: lnMTot*			
# of obs.: 135	Adj. R^2: 0.6000			# of obs.: 135	Adj. R^2: 0.7281		
Variable	Coefficient	Std. Err.	z-Stat.	Variable	Coefficient	Std. Err.	z-Stat.
lnRD	0.1544*	0.0827	1.87	lnPTot	0.2899**	0.0734	3.95
NatUS	-0.2732*	0.5738	-0.48	NatUS	-0.4117	0.3535	-1.16
NatJP	-2.7163**	0.5115	-2.38	NatJP	-1.9399**	0.5231	-3.71
Cons	-2.2583**	0.5772	3.91	cons	1.7813**	0.3977	4.48

Two asterisks indicate a confidence level of 95%; one asterisk indicates a confidence level of 90% and thus, the coefficient is significantly different from zero at the 5% or 10% significance level, respectively.

Transportation and Machinery Industry

According to the results of the stepwise analyses in the transportation and machinery industry, a lag of one year between R&D expenditures and trademark registration and a delay of four years between patent filing and trademark registration prevails.[50]

[50] Generally it is assumed that patents are filed immediately after the unveiling of a new technological invention and thus a short or no time lag is expected between investments in R&D and patent filing. On the other hand, trademarks are only filed shortly before market launch and thus considerably later than associated patents. The discrepancy between the expected and the revealed time lags between R&D, patents placements and trademark filings cannot be readily explained and clearly calls for further research.

As the results of regression 14 and 15 in table V.10 show, the positive relationships between trademark registrations and patent filings, as well as R&D expenditures has been confirmed by the findings in the transportation and machinery industry. In the case of the transportation and machinery industry the variations in trademark registrations are stronger influenced by variations in patent filings than by R&D expenditures although the coefficient indicating the relationship between R&D expenditures is relatively strong and statistically significant at the 95% confidence level.

Table V.10: Relationship between trademark registration, patent filings and R&D expenditures in the transportation & machinery industry

Regression 15				Regression 16			
Dep. Var.: lnMTot				*Dep. Var.: lnMTot*			
# of obs.: 62	Adj. R^2: 0.3194			# of obs.: 55	Adj. R^2: 0.4352		
Variable	Coefficient	Std. Err.	z-Stat.	Variable	Coefficient	Std. Err.	z-Stat.
laglnRD_1	0.5238**	0.1383	3.79	laglnPTot_4	0.6598**	0.1549	4.26
NatUS	-1.4195**	0.5869	-2.42	NatUS	-1.0191*	0.5582	-1.83
NatJP	dropped			NatJP	dropped		
Cons	-1.600	1.0023	-1.60	Cons	0.7384	0.7426	-0.99

Two asterisks indicate a confidence level of 95%; one asterisk indicates a confidence level of 90% and thus, the coefficient is significantly different from zero at the 5% or 10% significance level, respectively.

With respect to the previously analysed industries the transportation and machinery industry shows the strongest link between trademark registrations and patent filings (cf. table V.10). Concerning the influence of the companies nationality on trademark registrations in the transportation and machinery industry, the US companies appeared to register significantly less trademarks than the European companies which have been used as reference in our regression. The dummy variable NatJP, indicating the bearing of Japanese companies in registering for international trademark protection with respect to European companies, had to be dropped due to the low number of Japanese companies active in the transportation and machinery industry that have been included in our sample.

Pharmaceuticals and Health Care Industry

The pharmaceuticals and health care industry that generally is perceived as an industry in which patents are relatively effective in protecting technological innovation, appeared to be the industry with the highest total trademark filings in our sample. According to the results of the analyses of the prevailing time lags a contemporaneous relationship between patent filing and trademark registration exists. However, concerning the relationship between R&D expenditures and trademark registrations no unequivocal result could be found. According to performed stepwise analysis two different time lags, of contemporaneous nature and of t-2, between R&D expenditures and trademark registrations appeared to be of equally good fit.

Table V.11: Relationship between trademark registration, patent filings and R&D expenditures in the pharmaceuticals & health care industry

Regression 17a				Regression 17b			
Dep. Var.: lnMTot				*Dep. Var.: lnMTot*			
# of obs.: 61	Adj. R^2: 0.3487			# of obs.: 71	Adj. R^2: 0.4269		
Variable	Coefficient	Std. Err.	z-Stat.	Variable	Coefficient	Std. Err.	z-Stat.
LaglnRD_2	0.2879	0.1730	1.66	lnRD	0.4064**	0.1425	2.85
NatUS	-0.5380	1.266	-0.42	NatUS	-0.4863	1.3198	-0.37
NatJP	dropped			NatJP	dropped		
Cons	1.2829	1.2669	1.01	cons	-0.3684	1.1163	-0.33

Regression 18			
Dep. Var.: lnMTot			
# of obs.: 75	Adj. R^2: 0.7656		
Variable	Coefficient	Std. Err.	z-Stat.
LnPTot	0.7656**	0.1535	4.99
NatUS	-0.3684	0.9638	-0.38
NatJP	dropped		
Cons	0.7100	0.8580	-0.83

Two asterisks indicate a confidence level of 95%; one asterisk indicates a confidence level of 90% and thus, the coefficient is significantly different from zero at the 5% or 10% significance level, respectively.

Consequently, we performed two independent regression analyses, one to investigate the relationship between trademark registrations and R&D expenditures on a contemporaneous level and the other taking a time lag of two years into account. The regression results shown in table V.11 clearly illustrate, that no time lag between R&D expenditures and trademark registrations has to be assumed. The results of the regression analysis performed with R&D expenditures lagged by two years are not statistically significant and moreover, the general test of significance of the entire regression equation had to be rejected. On the other hand, the results of the regression analysis carried out on the assumption of a contemporaneous relationship between the dependent and explanatory variables are highly significant and the Wald Chi^2 test confirms the statistical significance of the overall regression equation at a 98% confidence level.

Comparing the results of the analysis of the pharmaceutical and health care industry with the outcomes of the chemicals and materials industry, it appears that not only the perceived time lags are quite similar in the two industries but also the calculated correlation coefficients. In the case of pharmaceuticals and health care companies the simultaneous link between trademark registrations and patent filings appeared to be more pronounced than the relationship between trademark registrations and R&D expenditures (see the respective coefficients in regression 17b and 18 shown in table V.11). With respect to the pharmaceuticals and health care companies' nationality no significant difference in the registration behaviour of trademarks has been ascertained. The variable NatJP had to be dropped in the analyses due to the low number of observations.

Telecommunication and Computer Industry

The last industry represented in our data sample is the telecommunication and computer industry. However, due to the low number of observations, merely 3 of the 33 companies are located within the telecommunication and computer industry, the regression investigation did not yield statistically significant results. Moreover, due to the low number of observations not only the individual regression coefficients turned out to be not statistically significant at the 10% significance level, but moreover, the general test of significance determining the overall statistical significance of the regression analysis did not pass the significance test at the 90% confidence level.

Thus, in summary, the results of the individual industry analyses have confirmed the findings of the cross-sectional analyses of section V.2.2.1. As shown above, across all investigated industries a positive and statistically significant relationship between the variations in trademark registrations on the one hand, and R&D expenditures and patent filings on the other, has been found. Hence, an increase/decrease in R&D expenditures and/or patent filings is reflected in an increase/decrease in trademark registrations. These findings clearly support hypotheses 2 and 3 outlined in section V.1.3.2 hypothesising a positive correlation between the dependent variable trademark registrations and the dependent variables R&D expenditures and patent filings, due to the direct link between technological innovation and trademark registration, and the complementary nature of the two different modes of protection.

However, concerning the strength of the correlation between trademark registrations on the one hand, and patent and R&D expenditures on the other, as well as the perceived optimal time lags prevailing between the dependent and the explanatory variables, considerable differences between the four investigated industries have been observed. With regard to the existing time lags, the chemicals and materials, as well as the pharmaceutical industries have shown a contemporaneous relationship between the dependent and the explanatory variables. In contrast, in the electronics, as well as the transportation and machinery industry, a time lag of two years between R&D expenditures and trademark registrations has been revealed.

Concerning the influence of R&D expenditures as well as patent filings on trademark registrations considerable differences between the various industries have been perceived. The relationship between R&D expenditures and trademark registrations, for example, has been considerably stronger in the electronics industry than the link between patent filings and trademark registrations. In contrast, the industry analyses revealed a stronger link between patent filings and trademark registrations than between R&D expenditures and trademark registrations in the chemicals and materials, the pharmaceutical and health care, as well as in the transportation and machinery industries. Moreover, by comparing these results concerning the influence of variations in R&D expenditures and patent filings on variations on trademark registrations with the results of the investigation of Levin, Klevorick et al. (1987), it becomes apparent that in particular those industries that rate patents as an efficient protection mechanisms, i.e., chemicals, materials, and pharmaceuticals, show a stronger influence of patent filings than R&D expenditures on variations in trademark registrations on the company level.[51]

On the other hand, industries that rate patents, according to the results of Levin, Klevorick et al. (1987), as not very effective, i.e., industries in the field of electronics (e.g., computer, communication equipment, and measuring devices), show a stronger correlation between R&D expenditures and trademark registrations than between patent filings and trademark registrations. This clearly indicates that trademark registrations do not only complement patent right protection, but also other means of protection, e.g., trade secrecy and lead-time advantages. Consequently, by regarding trademark registrations one may obtain a *more complete picture* of a companies' creative activities than merely considering patent filings as the only available and reliable measure of companies' innovative output. This may particularly be true for those

[51] The results of the investigation of Levin, Klevorick et al. (1987) are presented in table III.4.

fields where patent rights are not perceived as an efficient protection mechanism, e.g., process and service innovation.

V.2.2.3 Analysis of the Impact of Patent Filings, Trademark Registrations on Companies' Brand Equity and Operating Profits

This section aims to analyse the influence of complementary trademark registrations on companies' ability to appropriate the returns of investments into creative activities, e.g. R&D. According to the theory developed in chapters III and IV, a company that complements its patent rights by trademark registrations can better appropriate the returns of its intangible technological assets which can be seen as a direct outcome of its investments into R&D activities, and thus generate a relatively higher profit. Moreover, we investigate the influence of a company's relative technological advantage on the monetary value attributed to its corporate brand. However, in these analyses we had to use a reduced sample because of the unavailability of exact and comparable data on the value of the companies' overall brand equity.[52] Moreover, data on the companies' operative cash flows has not been available, so that we alternatively use figures on the companies' operating profits on an annual basis.[53]

Profit Impact of Patent Filings and Complementary Trademark Registrations

As argued in chapter IV.3, a company that complements its patent right protection by trademark registrations is assumed to be able to better appropriate the returns of its intangible technological assets and hence the returns of its R&D investments. Consequently, hypothesis 4 in section V.1.3.2 assumes a positive correlation between the number of trademark registrations, as well as patent filings and the heights of the profits the company can reap of its activities. Moreover, since R&D

[52] Due to the different methods of calculating the monetary value of brands, as well as the focus of most brand equity investigations, our sample was reduced to 11 companies for which comparable data on brand equity was available. Cp. Khermouch, G., Holmes, S. et al. (2001), pp. 44-55.

[53] Cash flows figures are usually used in analyses of companies' profit situation since cash flows are less influenced by politic manipulations, cp. Wöhe, G. (1993), pp.851-854. In our analyses we use operating profits which account for net profits less taxes, as well as below-the-line expenditures and earnings. For a detailed discussion see Carlton, D. W. & Perloff, J. M. (1994), pp. 333-336.

investments are seen as a direct source of technological innovation that confer a company a strategic advantage which may be protected by intellectual property rights and/or alternative methods, e.g., lead-time advantages and trade secrecy, they are assumed to have a positive influence on the profits a company can generate.

However, before analysing the prevailing correlation between a company's operating profits on the one hand, and patent filings, trademark registrations, and R&D expenditures on the other, we have to determine the prevailing time lags between R&D expenditures, as well as intellectual property filings and operating profits. It is assumed that a certain time lag between R&D expenditures as well as intellectual property filing and their influence on the operating profit prevails. According to the stepwise analysis performed on cumulative data, we have to account for a time lag of four years between R&D expenditures as well as patent filings and operating profits. Thus, a change in R&D expenditures and patent filings is reflected in a change in operating profits four years later. Moreover, this result clearly confirms the findings of the contemporaneous relationship between R&D expenditures and patent filings outlined in section V.2.2.1. Conversely, a change in trademark registrations is reflected in a change in operating profits in the subsequent year which again indicates that trademarks are filed only shortly before the market launch of the respective technological invention.

As shown in regression 19 in table V.12, all explanatory variables, i.e., trademark registrations, R&D expenditures, and patent filings, show a *positive relationship* to the dependent variable operating profits. Thus, an increase in R&D expenditures, patent filings and/or trademark filings will, ceteris paribus, lead to an increase in the company's operating profits. The correlation coefficients are all significant at the 95% or 90% confidence levels, respectively. Furthermore, according to the performed Wald Chi^2 tests the overall regression analyses are all statistically significant at the 99% confidence level. Concerning inter-industry and regional differences, our investigations have shown that no statistically significant differences between the various industries and regions exist. Moreover, according to the adjusted coefficients of determination of the various regressions, variations in R&D expenditures show the highest adj. R^2 value with respect to variations in the operating profits of the sample companies, followed by patent filings and trademark registrations. These results thus reflect the fact that investments into R&D not only create intellectual capital which is by definition protected by legal property rights, e.g., patents and trademarks, but also further immaterial assets and human capital based valuables that have a significant influence on the profit earning potential of the company.[54]

Table V.12: Influence of patent filings and complementary trademark registrations on companies' operating profits

Regression 19				Regression 20			
Dep. Var.: lnOprofit				*Dep. Var.: lnOprofit*			
# of obs.: 310	Adj. R^2: 0.4892			# of obs.: 427	Adj. R^2: 0.1834		
Variable	Co-efficient	Std. Err.	z-Stat.	Variable	Co-efficient	Std. Err.	z-Stat.
laglnMTot_1	0.0791*	0.0448	1.77	laglnMTot_1	0.1898**	0.0402	4.70
laglnRD_4	0.2963**	0.0652	4.54	IndTransMach	0.0821	0.5019	0.16
laglnPatTot_4	0.1291**	0.0533	2.42	IndChemMat	-0.5112	0.4177	-1.22
Cons	4.4960**	0.3698	12.16	IndPharma	-0.2854	0.5017	-0.57
				IndTelecom	-0.8233	0.6066	-1.36
				cons	6.8731**	0.2977	23.09
Regression 21				Regression 22			
Dep. Var.: lnOprofit				*Dep. Var.: lnOprofit*			
# of obs.: 310	Adj. R^2: 0.5341			# of obs.: 328	Adj. R^2: 0.3473		
Variable	Co-efficient	Std. Err.	z-Stat.	Variable	Co-efficient	Std. Err.	z-Stat.
laglnRD_4	0.4510**	0.0549	8.22	LaglnPatTot_4	0.2766**	0.0451	6.14
IndTransMach	-0.2626	0.2669	-0.98	IndTransMach	0.1388	0.4270	0.33
IndChemMat	0.0838	0.2329	0.36	IndChemMat	-0.1480	0.3560	-0.42
IndPharma	0.0919	0.2693	0.34	IndPharma	-0.0534	0.4256	-0.13
IndTelecom	-0.7735	0.3198	-2.42	IndTelecom	-0.7843	0.5131	-1.53
Cons	4.3566**	0.4310	10.1	cons	6.0171**	0.3402	17.69

Two asterisks indicate a confidence level of 95%; one asterisk indicates a confidence level of 90% and thus, the coefficient is significantly different from zero at the 5% or 10% significance level, respectively.

In conclusion it can be confirmed that an increase in a company's R&D expenditures leads to an increase in patent and trademark filings which are complementary modes of protection. Furthermore, an increase in R&D expenditures generates intangible assets that increase a company's profit earning potential. These intangible assets generated through investments in R&D are partially protected by patent and/or trademark rights that in turn increase a company's ability to appropriate the returns of its innovative intangible assets that is reflected in a positive relationship between the variations in patent filings, as well as trademark registrations and the variations in the companies' operating profits. Building on these findings we investigate in the subsequent section the relationship between a company' revealed technological

[54] For a detailed discussion see in particular III.2.1.1 and figure III.10.

advantage and market based advantage on the one hand, and the accumulated value of brand equity on the other.

Impact of a Company's Revealed Technological and Market Based Advantage on Brand Equity Value

This final section of the econometric analysis endeavours to examine the relationship prevailing between a company's investments into R&D and relative technological, as well as market based advantage on the one hand, and the overall value of its brand equity on the other. However, as already stressed above, no reliable and comparable data on the value for all sample companies' brand equity has been available. Consequently, our initial sample has been further reduced to 10 companies for which data on corporate brand equity value has been available. This analysis uses data on the company's brand equity in the year 2000 according to Interbrand's brand value calculations.[55]

Formula V.4: Revealed technological (RTA) and market based advantage (RMA)

$$\textbf{a)}\ RTA_{ix} = \frac{\sum_{t=1}^{n} P_{ix} \Big/ \sum_{t=1}^{n} P_{x}}{\sum_{t=1}^{n} P_{i} \Big/ \sum_{t=1}^{n} P} \quad ; \quad \textbf{b)}\ RMA_{ix} = \frac{\sum_{t=1}^{n} TM_{ix} \Big/ \sum_{t=1}^{n} TM_{x}}{\sum_{t=1}^{n} TM_{i} \Big/ \sum_{t=1}^{n} TM}$$

However, in this econometric investigations of the relationship between a company's brand value and patent right filings and trademark registrations, the *revealed technological*, as well as *market-based advantage* of the companies are used and not, as in the preceding analyses, the logarithms of the absolute patent and trademark filings. The revealed advantages of the companies are calculated according to equations shown in formula V.4 a) and b), where P and TM denote patent filings and trademark registrations of company i in technology field x over the period of time t_1 to t_n, respectively.[56] Thus, the revealed advantage represents a company's relative patent / trademark strength in

[55] Cp. Khermouch, G., Holmes, S. et al. (2001), pp. 44-55.
[56] Cp. Almeida, P. (1996).

a particular technology field with respect to its relative stake in total patent / trademark registrations (cf. formula V.4).

Consequently, by calculating the RTA and RMA for each company, we obtain the companies' relative patent and trademark strengths over the entire period of investigation in the particular technology field x by taking the companies relative patenting strength into consideration. Hence, by using figures on the companies' RTA / RMA we adjust for the companies' overall size. Furthermore, since most companies show a rather strong position in a limited number of technological fields we use the RTA and RMA figures of the technology field, where the respective company showed a particular strength.

Table V.13: Relationship between brand equity value and RTA and RMA

Regression 22			
Dep. Var.: BrandEquity			
# of obs.: 10		Adj. R^2: 0.0959	
Variable	**Coefficient**	**Std. Err.**	**t-Stat.**
RTA	6.8366	9.9762	0.69
RMA	0.4241	3.6134	0.12
Cons	0.0304	16.9651	0.00

Two asterisks indicate a confidence level of 95%; one asterisk indicates a confidence level of 90% and thus, the coefficient is significantly different from zero at the 5% or 10% significance level, respectively.

As the results presented in table V.13 show, a positive relationship between a company's RTA and RMA and the value of its brand equity has been ascertained. However, the results of regression 22 are not significant due to the ascertained high standard errors, and according to the coefficient of determination adjusted for the number of explanatory variables merely 9.56% of the variations in the dependent variable are explained by variations in the explanatory variables. Furthermore, according to the performed F-test the overall regression is not statistically significant. These problems of statistical significance and low fit of the model can be attributed to the *extremely low number of observations*.

In summary we can affirm that although a positive correlation between the companies' revealed technological, as well as market-based advantages and the overall value of companies' brand equity has been discovered, the findings are not unanimous and statistically significant at a 90% significance level. Thus, in order to achieve significant and conclusive results about the influence of manufacturing companies' patent filings and trademark registrations and thus generation of new intangible technological assets on a company's overall brand equity, further econometric investigations are needed that have to be carried out on the basis of a larger data sample. This in turn necessitates the availability of comparable and exact data on the brand equity value of companies' overall brand equity and not only of individual, isolated product brands as they can be found nowadays in various publications.

V.3 Discussion and Findings

The previously described econometric analyses have revealed some interesting findings concerning the general theoretical assumptions established in chapter III, as well as the model of complementary brand equity established in chapter IV. However, as has already been pointed out in section V.1.3, in the econometric investigation a rather integrated view of the company had to be taken and not, as in the case of chapter IV, an isolated view on a single technological innovation. This section summarises the findings of the econometric investigations with respect to the hypotheses formulated in section V.1.3, discuss their general implication with regard to previously performed investigations, points out the major shortcomings, and indicates the scope of further research in the general field of the appropriation of the returns of intangible technological assets, and in particular the specific role of brand equity within this field of economic research.

As has already been pointed out throughout our discussion in section V.2, hypotheses 1 to 3 and 5 have been clearly confirmed by the econometric findings. Not only a positive correlation between a company's R&D expenditures and intellectual property filings has been confirmed by the analyses, as pointed out in hypothesis 1, but also a strong complementary relationship between patent filings and trademark registrations, as stated in hypothesis 2, has been found. Furthermore, the assumption of complementarity between patent and trademark protection has been further substantiated by the findings of regressions 5 to 10. These regressions have verified the hypothesis 3, stating a positive correlation not only at the cumulative level, but also within the individual technological fields.

However, the ascertained relationship between patent filings and trademark registrations is generally less pronounced than the correlation between trademark registration and R&D expenditures. This weaker link between patent and trademark placements is in particular pronounced in industries where patent protection has been found not to be as effective as alternative means of protection, e.g., trade secrecy or lead-time advantages. Thus, it can be argued that trademarks may not only be registered for technological innovations already protected by patent rights but they may also complement technological innovations protected by alternative protection modes which cannot be ascertained by simple patent counts but nevertheless are a direct outcome of a company's investment into creative activities (cp. table III.4 and figure III.10). Consequently, trademark registrations may even be a better measure of the output of creative investments, e.g., R&D expenditures, than the measure of patent activity since trademarks also account for intangible assets not protected by patent rights. This may in particular be true in industries where companies perceive patent right protection as not very effective or innovations are not even patentable, e.g., incremental innovation, and thus companies prefer alternative modes of protection, e.g., computer industry.

Furthermore, hypothesis 5, supposing higher profits of companies filing more patent rights and registering more trademark rights, could be validated. As regressions 19 to 22 have revealed, a highly significant and positive relationship between the variations in R&D expenditures, patent filings, and trademark registrations and the variations in operating profits has been ascertained. The last investigation, aiming at the revelation of the prevailing relationship between a company's revealed technological and market based advantage and the company's overall accumulated brand equity, has shown a positive correlation between the dependent variable brand equity value and the explanatory variables RTA as well as RMA. However, due to the considerably reduced sample size and because of the unavailability of comparable and exact data on companies' overall brand equity value, no clear and unanimous conclusion concerning our hypothesis 6 can be drawn.

Concerning the relationship between R&D expenditures, patent filings, and trademark registrations considerable inter-industry differences have been ascertained in the analyses. These differences did not only concern the companies' propensity to file for patent and trademark registration but also the ascertained time lags between investments in R&D, patent filings, and trademark registration. Thus, not only the time lags between R&D expenditure and trademark registration but also between patent filing and trademark registration varied considerably between the different industries. Nevertheless, it can be said that whereas a contemporaneous relationship between R&D expenditures and patent filings exists a positive time lag between patent filings and trademark registration can be assumed. Thus, hypothesis 4 has been validated by the empirical findings. The considerable variations across the different industries, in particular with respect to the exact time lags, however, clearly call for further empirical investigation.

With regard to previously performed empirical investigations of the role of market-based complementarities in the field of technological innovation the here presented econometric analyses represent so far the most extensive investigation of the prevailing relationship between the explanatory variables R&D expenditures and patent filings on the one hand, and trademark registrations as the dependent variable, on the other. Moreover, considerable shortcomings of the investigation of Allegrezza & Guarda-Rauchs (1999) have been eliminated. So, the statistical investigations build upon an extensive theoretical basis that has been established in the previous chapters and for which already initial empirical evidence has been presented in the case studies of chapter II. Furthermore, the econometric analyses do not, as in the case of Allegrezza & Guarda-Rauchs (1999), use categorical and binary data gathered in telephone surveys about companies' patent or trademark registrations at the level of a national patent office,[57] but rather uses detailed figures of the sample companies' patent and trademark registrations at the supranational level.

Nevertheless, due to ascertained problems of operationalisation and unavailability of comparable and exact data, our econometric analyses did not take brand equity as a whole into consideration but entirely neglected the reputational aspects of brand equity which are of particular importance with respect to the strategic role of brand equity.[58] Moreover, although central assumptions underlying our theoretical model of complementary brand equity have been validated, our ultimate model of chapter IV.3 could not be tested and may not even be testable by econometric investigation per se. This is due to problems of measuring *qualitative factors* such as perceived quality of customers, customer loyalty, or general associations associated with brand equity. Accordingly, Nonaka (1991) has stated:

> *"In most companies, the ultimate test for measuring the value of new knowledge is economic – increased efficiency, lower costs, improved R&D. But in the knowledge creating company, other more qualitative factors are equally important."*[59]

Thus, in the era of the knowledge based economy econometric investigations by themselves cannot be considered as sufficient, but have

---

[57] Allegrezza, S. & Guarda-Rauchs, A. have used variables that are mostly categorical or ordinal and thus only take into consideration if or if not a company has field for trademark or patent protection at the Benelux Trademark Office.

[58] For a detailed definition of brand equity see chap. III.3.1.2 and IV.2.1.

[59] Nonaka, I. (1991), p. 103.

to be complemented by empirical investigations better accounting for more qualitative factors, e.g., detailed case study research.

In spite of the above presented limitations of econometric investigations more quantitative as well as qualitative research is needed to better understand and thus account for inter-industry differences concerning the strategic role of the various forms of intellectual property right protection in appropriating the returns of intangible assets and the ascertained differences in the time lags between R&D expenditures, patent filings, and trademark registrations. Moreover, with regard to the model of complementary brand equity established in chapter IV.3 further econometric investigation of the role of the different dimensions of brand equity may be of special interest. Of particular concern may be the investigation of the influence of established trademarks which are ascertained by customers as particularly innovative, on companies' expenses on marketing and communication by the introduction of subsequent technological innovations. However, one has to be careful not to ascertain marketing and communication expenses as investments in the creation of a sustainable comparative advantage, as done by Erickson & Jacobson (1992), since such expenditures can easily be imitated and thus do not meet the criteria of strategic relevance as pointed out in chapter IV.1. Moreover, marketing and communication expenses on either the company or product level are not easily available and more importantly are not readily comparable since certain companies assign distribution and/or promotion costs to marketing expenditures whereas other companies perceive marketing expenditures as being only advertisement expenditures.

VI General Summary and Conclusion

In the era of the *knowledge based economy* company specific intangible assets as well as intangible market based assets are of utmost strategic importance. Moreover, in order to be able to successfully compete in the current economic order which is furthermore characterised by increasingly shorter product- and technology-life-cycles as well as rising globalisation, companies have to ensure an effective appropriation of the returns generated by their intangible assets. This is the more important for companies active in *technology intensive industries* since these companies have to invest increasing amounts of money in the generation of technological innovation which create customer utility, and hence positively differentiate their products and services from those of competing companies. On the other hand, however, these companies active in technology based industries are confronted with the problem of the public good characteristics of these technological assets and the associated *problem of appropriation*. Moreover, in reality legal property rights such as patents and even alternative modes of protection, e.g., trade secrecy, lead-time advantages, etc., are not a guarantee for a perfect appropriation of the returns generated by immaterial technological assets in the long-run as is often claimed by economic theory. Various empirical investigations have revealed that intangible property rights thought for the protection of technological innovation, e.g., patent rights or petty patents, are usually obviated long before their official expiration. Consequently, companies in technology intensive industries face, on the one hand, rising investments in technological assets and, on the other hand, encounter the problem of excluding third parties from free-riding on their innovative investments and thus to appropriate a better part of the returns generated by their assets. This leads to a certain reluctance of companies to invest private resources in the generation of new intangible technological assets which, however, puts the company's ability to successfully compete in the knowledge based economy in peril.

Building on these apparent deficiencies in protecting technological assets, our research has investigated the *role of complementary brand equity* in the appropriation of the returns generated by immaterial technological assets that has been almost entirely neglected, so far. In order to direct and focus our research, a general research question as well as hypothesis have been established in chapter I. The subsequent chapter II, depicting the case studies Bayer Aspirin and Cisco Systems, has further clarified and specified the research focus taken, as well as presented some initial empirical evidence. Although the two cases show considerable differences with regard to the period and unit of analysis as well as industry of investigation, both cases have clearly pointed out the utmost strategic importance of brand equity in technology intensive industries as well as the close and complementary relationship of technological and market based assets.

Further, motivated through the findings revealed by case study research and the initial recognition of the neglect of the role of market based brand equity in the *appropriation of the returns generated by immaterial technological assets*, chapter III has established the theoretical foundations necessary for a thorough analysis of relationship between technological and market based assets and the strategic role of brand equity in the efficient and effective appropriation of the returns stemming from technological assets. Chapter III has focused on depicting the general characteristics of intangible assets and in particular intangible technological assets, general sources of technological assets, as well as most important protection modes. The subsequent chapter IV has, by building upon the empirical and theoretical foundations laid in chapter II and III, pointed out the strategic role of immaterial technological assets and investigated the strategic role of complementary brand equity in the effective protection of technological assets in the long-run. The theoretical discussion of chapter IV has finally led to the development of the *model of complementary brand equity* for the sustainable appropriation of the returns of intangible technological assets in chapter IV.3. The model has consolidated the theoretical and empirical findings of the preceding chapters and depicted the changing strategic importance of technological and market based assets and thus their role in the appropriation of the returns generated by technological innovation. Chapter IV closes in section IV.4 with a discussion of the organisational implications, points out the different integration strategies at the organisational level, as well as shows how companies can integrate brand equity and technology management at the process level with the help of the concept of the balanced scorecard. The so developed extended concept provides a basis for implementing strategies that account for the utmost strategic importance of brand equity and the complementary nature of market based and technological assets.

Finally, chapter V has endeavoured the statistical verification of the theoretical assumptions underlying the model of complementary brand equity established in chapter IV.3 and a first investigation of the established model by taking a rather integrated view of the company. For this purpose several research hypotheses have been formulated with the aim to focus and direct the econometric analyses. These research hypotheses have been subsequently examined by multiple regression analysis and the overall results discussed in chapter V.3.

VI.1 Discussion of Methodological Proceeding

Concerning the chosen methodological proceeding, our discussion has not regarded brand equity from a pure marketing perspective such as defined by Keller (1993) but rather stressed the influence of product characteristics determined by technological assets on the formation and preservation of brand equity. The intend of the here presented research project has been the analysis of the role of brand equity in the appropriation of the returns of intangible technological assets, the revealing of the importance of incremental technological innovation in upholding and growing established brand equity, as well as the role of existing brand equity in acquiring and building new technological assets. These fields of research have been largely neglected in the discussion of the appropriation of returns form technological assets and in the general discussion of brand equity, so far.

The fact of the lack of an existing theoretical framework and extensive empirical evidence onto which our discussion could have fallen back considerably influence our methodological proceeding. Thus, in order to clarify our precise research intent, we have outlined after a short introduction in chapter I the case studies Bayer Aspirin and Cisco Systems in chapter II. The principal purpose of the two case studies has been to introduce into the field and further clarify the intend of our research by presenting some initial empirical evidence. Therefore, both case studies have been chosen with the objective to evidently point out the complementary nature of technological and market based assets, as well as the outmost importance of brand equity in appropriating the returns of intangible technological assets. Chapter III has subsequently illustrated the present status of the ongoing discussion in the field of intellectual property management as well as intangible assets and intangible technological assets in particular, and establishes conceptual definitions which have the aim to increase the general comprehensibility of the discussion. Building upon the general discussion of the characteristics of intangible assets, how such assets can be generated and protected in business enterprises of chapter III, chapter IV has taken up a strategic point of view and integrated the brand equity perspective in the general discussion of the protection of immaterial technological assets for the appropriation of the economic returns generated by these assets. The discussion has finally led to the establishment of the model of complementary brand equity for the sustainable appropriation of intangible technological assets in chapter IV.3. The succeeding chapter IV.4 has pointed out some important organisational implications. Last but not least, chapter V investigates by multivariate technique a sample of 33 multinational companies with the aim to empirically substantiate the theoretical framework underlying the newly developed theory.

Consequently, due to the lack of an extensive discussion and existing theoretical framework chapter III was meant to lay the basic foundations for our discussion of chapter IV and in particular chapter IV.2 and IV.3. Furthermore, in order to validate and underpin the theory developed in chapters IV.2 and IV.3 we complemented the initial empirical evidence presented in the cases studies by an extensive econometric investigation analysing the theoretical foundations underlying our theoretical model developed in chapter IV.

Finally, the discussion has assumed a rather rational behaviour of customers resembling that of a homo-economicus and has put less weight on the psychological and socio-economic aspects of brands, e.g., as a vehicle to communicate the affiliation to a certain social class and/or as a means of expressing a certain lifestyle or mental attitude. This proceeding was chosen since the focus of the research has been the investigation of the strategic role of brand equity for companies active in industries characterised by a high importance of technological competencies and innovation. Hence, it was put forward that the customers' purchasing decision process in such industries is stronger influenced by the actual and potential capability characteristics of the products than by pure psychological aspects. Nevertheless, psychological aspects of brands do play an important role in most if not all markets. However, in markets for complex products, e.g., products with a high technological component, perceived risk of customers with regard to product quality, and in particular technological uncertainty, may be particularly high and thus the aspect of brands as a quality insurance may be more important in the customers purchasing decision than pure psychological aspects. On the other hand, in the case of relatively simple products where the quality and properties of the product can be assessed before purchase or are predetermined by legal standards and regulations, e.g., textiles, mineral water, writing paper, brand equity may not be of importance at all or may have an extremely high psychological aspect.[1] Furthermore, the importance of the psychological aspect also depends on the specific market, i.e., pure consumer market, e.g. mineral water, business-to-business, e.g., raw-steel, or somewhere in-between, e.g., computer processors. It is generally assumed that pure psychological aspects are of highest importance in the purchasing decision process in pure consumer

[1] For a detailed discussion see chapt. III.3.1.2.

markets and lowest in markets characterised by business-to-business relationships, although no clear-cut delimitation can generally be drawn.[2]

Nonetheless, psychological principals, such as, for example, how the choice of a name affects brand recall and recognition,[3] apply equally to all products and markets and thus are also, undisputedly of importance for companies primarily active in technology intensive industries. However, given that psychological aspects are assumed to only be one aspect of minor importance of various factors influencing brand equity in industries that are primarily driven by technological development a further scholarly piece on the psychological aspects of brands would have evidently gone beyond the scope of our research. Moreover, an extensive discussion of these psychological aspects of brands, although primarily concentrating on consumer goods markets, already exists in the marketing literature.[4] However, it may be of future interest to analyse the transferability of these aspects on the purchasing decisions in business-to-business relationships where, in contrast to end-consumer markets, the purchasing decision process is usually not a single-persons but rather multi-person process.

VI.2 Résumé of Research Finding and Implications

VI.2.1 General Summary of Findings

The general discussion on brand equity has already indicated the extreme persistence of market based assets and their strategic role for business enterprises.[5] Although the discussion has so far primarily focused on consumer goods industries and has almost entirely neglected technology based industries, the findings of the case studies presented in chapter II have substantiated the general research hypothesis formulated in chapter I. Chapter I.2.2 presupposes a strategic advantage of those companies in technology intensive industries endowed with brand equity in the

---

[2] See for example Doole, I. & Lowe, R. (2001), chap. 10; Jeannet, J. P. & Hennessey, H. D (2001), pp. 186-215.

[3] See for example Alba, J. W. & Chattopadhyay, A. (1985); Keller, K. L. (1993).

[4] See for example Zeithaml, V. A. (1988); Sujan, M. & Bettman, J. R. (1989); Bettman, J. R., Johnson, E. J. et al. (1991); Hoyer, W. D. & MacInnis, D. J. (2001).

[5] Nickel (2000), for example, has shown the extreme fidelity of consumers with regard to certain brands and thus persistence of market based brand equity if managed appropriately. He points out that consumers often stick to the brand which they have bought in their youth, through out their life.

appropriation of the returns generated by intangible technological assets in the long-run with regard to those companies not having established brand equity at their disposal.

Motivated by these findings a thorough analysis of the characteristics of intangible assets has been undertaken. This theoretical discussion emphasised the *public good characteristics* of immaterial assets which presents the core problem in the appropriation of the returns stemming from such assets. Thus immaterial assets generally show the characteristic of non-excludability, non-rivalry, and high fixed costs in their production and hence third parties, not having contributed to the creation of the intangible asset in question, cannot or only under high cost be excluded from the exploitation of the asset. Even though these characteristics equally apply to all intangible assets *various classes of intangible assets* have been identified with regard to the spread of the underlying knowledge, the degree of codification of the knowledge, as well as the degree of legal appropriability. The established classification categorising intangible assets in the three classes: (1) *Human capital*; (2) *intangible assets*; and (3) *intellectual capital or property* has the aim to establish a uniform and coherent definition contributing to the clarification of the ongoing discussion in the general field of intellectual property management, as well as to facilitate and clarify the theoretical discussion of the subsequent chapters.

With regard to the *generation of intangible technological assets* two general sources for companies have been identified: The company internal value chain, and the company's external environment. With regard to a company's internal sources of intangible assets two distinct forms have to be distinguished: (1) *Learning by doing without searching*; and (2) *searching without doing*. Whereas the second form has been broadly discussed in the scientific literature in the past, the role of companies' routine activities in the generation of intangible assets has been largely neglected, so far. Despite the neglect, such routine activities have a considerable *cumulative influence* on the overall stock of intangible assets within companies as well as on the maintenance and enhancement of companies' portfolio of immaterial technological assets. As has been pointed out, this important role of routine activities is due to the characteristic of *non-abrasion in use* of intangible assets and the *process of learning and unlearning* which is of particular meaning with respect to the generation of human capital based assets.

Concerning *external sources of intangible assets* the three principal sources have been investigated: (1) Acquisition of intangible assets by *licensing*; (2) integration of intangible assets by *merger and acquisition* or *employee recruitment*; as well as (3) *co-operative forms* of intangible asset creation. Although these sources of intangible assets are extremely important for companies in order to remain at the technological forefront in diverse fields of technological expertise, it has to be remembered that a company generally needs a *minimum of internal technological competence and expertise* in order to be able to fall back on these external sources. Furthermore, the accessing of external sources of immaterial assets shows some severe shortcomings and problems of which the most important are: (1) The inability to transfer human capital based and even intellectual asset over open markets; (2) the immanent risk of becoming dependent on external sources of intangible assets; (3) the evocation of the not-invented-here-syndrome that may result in a decline in the motivation of the company's employees; (4) the risk of specialist employees carrying important human capital based assets leaving the acquired company post acquisition; and (5) the risk of loosing company specific intangible assets in co-operative arrangements and thus the danger of the company of being bereaved of its competitive advantage.

Moreover, the discussion of the different sources of intangible assets has clearly revealed the *importance to differentiate between the different classes of intangible assets*. It has become apparent that companies have to follow different strategies in order to generate or acquire assets allocated in the various classes, i.e., human capital based, intangible assets, or intellectual property. This finding has been further reinforced by the results of the discussion of the different possibilities to protect and thus enable a company to appropriate the returns generated by the intangible asset in question. The discussion of chapter III.3 has focused on the most important and broadly known modes of protection of immaterial assets which are: Patent rights, trademarks, trade secrets, lead time advantages, and complementary resources. The investigation has revealed that the *choice of protection mode* is primarily influenced by the nature of the respective intangible asset, the position of the technological asset in the technology-life-cycle, and the degree of the international diversification of the use and commercialisation of the asset in question.

Building on the discussion of chapter III the subsequent chapter IV has analysed the *strategic role of intangible assets* and in this respect the specific role of complementary brand equity in technology intensive industries. Intangible assets are in general of particular strategic importance due to the inherently high ambiguity surrounding these assets, the complementary nature of most technological assets, the possibility to protect these assets by property rights that have the potential to thwart an attempt of direct imitation or replication in the short-run, as well as the possibility to uphold and reinforce these barriers to imitation. However, one has to take into consideration that ambiguity and legal protection do, at least in the case of patent protection, substitute each other and thus an increase in legal protection by means of filing a patent considerably lowers the ambiguity surrounding the subject matter of the patent. Moreover, the accomplishment of the *criteria of strategic relevance*, i.e., creating a customer value, non-substitutability, non-imitatability, and scarcity, does not as such enable a company to generate a certain economic rent with the asset in question. The asset has furthermore to accomplish the *criteria of profitability* which is determined by the appropriability of the returns generated by the asset in question.

Consequently, a company not only has to own a sustainable strategic advantage in order to ensure its profitability and thus continued existence but has also to make sure that it is able to *appropriate* the returns generated by its sustainable strategic advantage. Furthermore, companies have to take a rather *holistic view of the appropriation* of intangible assets and thus not only focus on the safeguarding of actual strategic resources but also include the optimisation, enrichment, safeguarding, stocktaking, evaluation, and surveillance of the company's actual and future intangible resources.

Concerning the *role of brand equity*, chapter IV.2 has further specified the definition given in chapter III.3 which defines brand equity as the *combination of the legal and reputational aspects* surrounding trademarks and brand names. Thus, brand equity combines *highly tacit reputational aspects* and *legal aspects* of intellectual property rights and hence is surrounded by extremely high barriers to imitation. In addition, the reputational aspects of brand equity can be further differentiated in: (1) Brand loyalty; (2) brand awareness; (3) perceived quality; (4) brand associations; and (5) further proprietary brand assets which further increase complexity enfolding brand equity. Consequently, established brand equity is an *important strategic asset* associated with high ambiguity and legal barriers that make imitation for competitors extremely difficult if not impossible.

With regards to the *generation of brand equity* it has been revealed that brand equity cannot be established in technology based industries by mere marketing expenditures but has to be built by an *objective technological advantage* generating a perceivable consumer benefit. Companies having successfully built brand equity subsequently have a strategic advantage due to the consumer lock-in which is generated through the information customers hold about the brand and hence the associated products and services. These switching costs of consumers are particularly pronounced in *technology markets* since high perceived risks for customers exist due to information asymmetries and bad choice leading to important consequences. Nevertheless, established brand equity has to be continuously fostered in order to bestow its holder with a lasting competitive advantage. As has been shown, *brand equity presents a guarantee or promise* given and thus in order to uphold or even increase brand equity a company's offering has to fulfil and/or even surpass the pledges given by the brand. Thus, if managed appropriately brand equity presents an *extremely persistent strategic advantage* of utmost importance in repeated sales.

Furthermore, the discussion has revealed that brand equity is most easily built by *first-mover firms*. This is due to their *temporary monopoly position* during which customers accumulate information about the product and/or service sold under the specific brand. Moreover, by simply being a pioneer, companies benefit of a favourable image. Consequently, innovations are extremely important in the generation of brand equity and moreover, patents, trade secrecy, etc. are of utmost importance in providing the innovator with a temporary monopoly position enabling the company to *pre-empt market entry* and thus efficiently establish brand equity and gain a *lead on the learning-curve*.

Building on the findings of the previous chapters, chapter IV.3 has established a *model of complementary brand equity for the sustainable appropriation of intangible technological assets*. The model reveals the *changing strategic roles* of technological and market based assets in the appropriation of the returns generated by an initial technological innovation along the technology-life-cycle. If a company does not account for the variation in the strategic importance of technological assets and brand equity it may miss an opportunity to build a persistent competitive advantage in early phases of the technology-life-cycle which in turn considerably reduces its ability to appropriate the returns of its initial innovation in later phases. Consequently, companies have to build brand equity in *periods of technological strength* that balances out the loss of strategic advantage due to the inventing around, expiration, or even imitation of the subject matter of patents in subsequent phases of the technology-life-cycle. Moreover, brand equity established with the help of a technological advantage is not only of strategic importance in selling products and services to end consumers, but also in recruiting and retaining highly skilled employees, and/or entering co-operation agreements. However, companies always have to bear in mind that brand equity represents a *promise or even guarantee given to customers, employees, co-operation partners*, etc., that has a significant influence on the decision making process if the decision maker is confronted with high risks and uncertainty ex-ante decision. Thus, in order to maintain and/or foster brand equity a company and its offerings have to fulfil or even surpass the pledges given by its brand. Moreover, it has been shown that in this process of fulfilling and surpassing expectations induced by a certain brand, *technological innovation* and in particular *continuous incremental innovation* are of utmost importance.

Furthermore, to ensure sufficient innovation, required to maintain established brand equity and to build new brand equity in distinct fields of corporate activity, companies have to effectively *allocate managerial and legal responsibility* with respect to brand equity and related investment in technological innovation. Due to the close relationship of brand equity and technological innovation, companies have to ensure that responsibility, as well as decision making power concerning investment in technological development projects and associated brand equity is allocated at the respective organisational level where the *best knowledge about the individual concerns exist*. Thus, with regard to brand management and technological innovation which have the aim to *improve existing products and foster established brand equity*, managerial responsibility and decision making power should be allocated at the divisional level. On the other hand, projects aiming at completely *new fields of corporate activity* that rather show the characteristics of basic research, and may have the potential to *create considerably new brand equity*, and hence substitute for activities approaching the end of the life-cycle, should be allocated at the corporate level. A third important possibility has been identified which concerns projects at the cross-divisional level. As has been shown, such *cross-divisional projects* are of key importance in pooling know-how of the various divisions of a company, enabling the pursuit of projects that may surpass the financial possibilities of the individual division and/or the avoidance of parallel research. Finally, companies have to efficiently integrate the brand equity and technological perspectives, account for the utmost strategic importance of brand equity, as well as for the complementary nature of brand equity and technological assets. In this respect three principal integration strategies have been pointed out: (1) Integration of brand equity management functions across the different hierarchical levels; (2) an integration of technology management functions across the different hierarchical levels; and (3) an integration of brand equity and technology management functions. It is put forward that a pure integration of the brand equity (1) and technology management functions (2) across the different hierarchical levels is not sufficient and has to be enlarged by an integration of the brand equity and technology management functions (3) so as to account for the complementary nature of market based and technology assets. Finally, it is pointed out how companies can accomplish an integration of brand equity and technology management at the process level through the implementation of the developed extended brandscorecard concept which builds upon the system of the balanced scorecard of Kaplan and Norton.

The principal theoretical assumptions underlying the model of brand equity presented in chapter IV.3 have been verified by *econometric investigation* outlined in chapter V. Although the statistical analysis only took the legal aspects of brand equity into consideration and largely neglected the reputational aspects, the *complementary nature of patent filings and trademark registration* could be substantiated. Moreover, a clear positive relationship between companies' investments in the creation of intangible technological assets, i.e., R&D, and the registration of trademark rights has been ascertained, validating the assumption that *trademarks do play an important role in protecting intangible technological assets*. Last but not least, a clear positive link between companies' patent filings and trademark registration, on the one hand, and companies' net profits on the other, has been revealed. However, considerable differences regarding the propensity to file for patent protection and to register trademarks, the ascertained time lag between patent filing and trademark registration, as well as the correlation between patent filing and trademark registration between the different industries have been ascertained. In addition, the inability to quantify certain issues, as well as the lack of exact and comparable data on the company level have strongly limited our attempt to investigate the model established in chapter IV.3. Thus, the results of the case study research and econometric investigation, as well as the theoretical discussion clearly call for further research in the field of brand equity and the appropriation of the returns generated by intangible technological assets.

In conclusion, the discussion has clearly shown that *brand equity classifies as an important strategic resource in technology intensive industries* which enables a company to effectively and efficiently appropriate the returns of its initial technological innovation in the long-run. Furthermore, the role of brand equity increases along the technology-life-cycle, if managed appropriately, and may even outweigh the losses of competitive advantage experienced by the company due to the imitation, replication, and/or even theft of a its intangible technological assets. Thus, companies active in technology intensive industries have to ensure the establishment of complementary brand equity which combines high legal barriers to imitation and ambiguity, creating a considerable customer lock-in and thus presents a *formidable market entry barrier*, enabling the initial innovator to effectively appropriate the returns of its technological innovation in the long-run.

VI.2.2 Implications for Research and Practice

The presented discussion of the appropriation of the returns generated by immaterial technological assets and in this regard the investigation of the specific role of brand equity, as well as the empirical findings outlined, have various implications on research and practice. Concerning *scientific research* the presented theoretical discussion and empirical investigations show considerable implications for: a) the field of *intellectual property management* and in particular the classification of intangible assets within business enterprises and sources of intangible assets; b) the field of *technology management* by establishing routine activities as an important source of technological expertise complementing R&D activities; c) the general discussion of the *appropriation of the returns of intangible assets* by enlarging the discussion in the field of complementary brand equity and demonstrating the complementary nature of patent and trademark rights; and finally d) the domain of *brand equity* by revealing the close relationship of a company's specific technological expertise and brand equity and the assets specific strategic roles within the technology-life-cycle.

1. The discussion has shown that a *classification of intangible assets* according to the spread of knowledge, the codification of the knowledge, and hence the legal appropriability is of utmost importance in the discussion of intellectual property management. Thus, the definition of human capital, intellectual assets, and intellectual capital or property and their classification in *non-appropriable*, *restricted appropriable*, and *legally appropriable* intangible assets established in chapter III.1.2 not only contributes to the general debate by establishing a clear and coherent definition of the terms used, but also clarifies and facilitates the subsequent theoretical discussion. Moreover, the necessity and importance of the established definition became particularly apparent in the extensive discussion of the various sources of intangible technological assets, as well as legal and organisational protection modes.
2. The thorough discussion of the various *sources of technological assets*, within as well as outside of the company, establishes learning by doing through companies' routine activities as an equally important source of technological expertise as R&D activities, particular important in mature industries. Thus, the discussion attempts to point out the deficiency of the past theoretical discussion by predominantly focusing on R&D activities as the principal creative activities within companies to generate technological expertise and invention and entirely neglecting

the important role of routine activities in creating predominantly human capital based assets. Moreover, company *expenditures on learning activities* which usually take the form of expenditures on the training and formation of the company's employees, is not accounted for in companies' R&D expenditures. Consequently, the *accuracy of R&D figures* as an input measure for companies investments in activities creating new technological insight and invention has to be thought over and the complementation of these figures by companies' expenditures on employee formation and training needs further discussion.

3. The principal contribution of the presented research has to be seen in the field of the general discussion of the *appropriation of the returns generated by intangible technological assets*. Although various authors have pointed out the apparent problems of business enterprises in the appropriation of the returns of intangible assets, the severe shortcomings of patent rights in efficiently protecting these intangible assets and thus enabling their holder to appropriate a better part of the returns generated by the assets, as well as the central importance of this topic for the overall discussion in the field of innovation management and the knowledge based economy, no investigation of the *role of market based assets* within the field of the appropriation of intangible technological assets had been undertaken. The presented theoretical discussion and empirical investigation has clearly revealed the extreme importance of brand equity in enabling companies active in technology intensive industries to effectively appropriate the returns of the initial technological innovation. Thus, brand equity clearly classifies as an *innovation specific complementary asset* that the innovator can easily and at low cost establish and which subsequently puts imitators at a persistent strategic disadvantage. Furthermore, brand equity combines high ambiguity and high legal protection not limited in its duration and thus presents an strategic advantage that fulfils the criteria of non-imitability, non-substitutability, generating high customer value, and being extremely scarce. Consequently, it has been concluded that established brand equity presents an extremely important *sustainable competitive advantage* whose importance increases along the technology-life-cycle and thereby enables a company to reap a better part of the returns generated by its initial technological advantage. Moreover, due to the proven *complementary nature of brand equity* and intangible technological assets the singular use of patent figures for the output measurement of investments in innovative activities in technology based companies has to be put in question. According to the presented results trademark filings classifies as an equally important output measure in technology based industries since it does not only

account for patentable innovations but also takes human capital based and intangible assets into consideration which are, by definition, not included in patent counts. Moreover, the ongoing discussion of the severe shortcomings of the actual system of legal rights on intellectual property in particularly emphasising the pronounced and apparent deficiencies of patent right protection of technological innovation has to be though over. So far, authors have in general merely focused in their discussion on one isolated intellectual property right or mode of protection. However, as the discussion has clearly revealed, the *individual modes of protection* as well as the *different intellectual property rights complement each other* and thereby considerably reduce the limitations associated with the individual mode or intellectual property right. However, in order to be able to take advantage of these complementarities one has to take a more strategic and not, as mostly done so far, only legal regard. Consequently, in order to efficiently evaluate the effectiveness of intellectual property rights in protecting a company's intangible assets the discussion has to be broadened and has to take the complementary nature of the various intellectual property rights as well as alternative modes of protection into consideration. The mere analysis of the advantages and disadvantages of isolated protection modes or even intellectual property rights has been shown to be insufficient and to lead to the wrong conclusions.

4. Concerning the specific field of *brand equity management* the previous discussion has revealed an important role of technological assets in creating and maintaining market based brand equity. So far, the discussion of the strategic role of brand equity has predominantly focused on consumer goods industries and has largely omitted the investigation of the technology intensive industries. The presented discussion has revealed how companies in technology intensive industries can efficiently *establish and foster brand equity* as well as how the *strategic role of brand equity evolves along a specific technology-life-cycle*. In addition, the role of technological innovation has been identified as an important initial source of brand equity and in this regard the protection of the technological asset through, for example, patent rights, trade secrecy, etc., in order to provide the company with a temporary monopoly position supporting the establishment of brand equity. Furthermore, through a temporary monopoly position on its technological innovation the company can gain a lead on the learning-curve that puts actual and potential competitors at a considerable disadvantage. Last but not least, technological innovation and in particularly incremental innovation do

play an important role in *upholding and fostering of established brand equity* in the long-run.

With regard to the practical situation, the discussion has shown various interesting implications for business enterprises in technology intensive industries. Of particular interest for business enterprises may be, for example: a) The examination of *how companies can build and maintain brand equity* and in which particular *circumstances brand equity presents a strategic advantage*; b) which role brand equity plays in *recruiting and retaining specialist employees* or in entering *co-operative agreements* with the aim to access complementary technological expertise; c) how to *organise for efficient brand equity management*; and d) how to *account for the strategic importance and complementary nature of technological assets and brand equity in the company's strategy.*

1. The discussion has revealed the importance of a *superior product and/or service* and thus a technological advantage the company in question holds with respect to its competitors. Consequently, companies in technology based industries cannot build persistent brand equity by mere marketing activities since, if the product or service offered does not meet the promises made by the brand, customers will no longer believe the affirmations made by the company and/or brand. Thus, superior product perception built by subjective claims and advertising which are not substantiated by the actual product or service offer, are extremely short lived and may even turn into a persistent disadvantage. Moreover, brand equity is of particular importance in *markets characterised by high uncertainty and risk.* In such an environment brand equity presents an important source of information that has a considerable influence on the decision making process. Consequently, established brand equity presents an *important strategic advantage* which customers, employees, as well as partner companies perceive as a promise or guarantee given, that has to be met in order to uphold and grow brand equity.
2. Brand equity does not only present an important asset in the market for a company's products and services but also in recruiting and retaining specialist employees. *Brand equity conveys important information* about the potential employer that is of extreme importance in the labour market characterised by high uncertainties and risk of the potential employee about the potential employer. Thus, favourable associations held by potential and actual employees about the company and/or its products and services may communicate information influencing the employees final decision. The same is true for *co-operation agreements and network relationships*. Brand equity built by a company's superior

expertise in a certain technology field or market transfers important information about the potential partner company ex-ante co-operation which cannot be obtained in another way. Consequently, brand equity presents an important lever in co-operation negotiations and the ability to enter co-operation agreements with companies being in a leading position and hence bestows the respective company with a strategic advantage in accessing external sources of technological expertise.

3. Another important topic the discussion has touched upon is the efficient *organisation of brand management* within corporations. As has been pointed out, companies have to differentiate between *legal and managerial responsibilities* of brand management. Whereas legal responsibilities such as the registration of new trademarks, contractual decisions about in- and/or out-licensing, etc. can be allocated at the corporate level, managerial responsibly usually associated with marketing and sales functions should rather be located where the best knowledge about the product and/or service in question is available, i.e., divisional level. Furthermore, due to the close interrelation of brand equity and *technological innovation*, responsibly and decision making power about projects in technology fields aiming at the improvement of existing products and thus the perpetuation of established brand equity should be allocated at the respective divisional level where the best knowledge about customers' expectation exists. Conversely, research projects aiming at new fields of technological expertise endeavouring to establish new brand equity in distinct fields of corporate activity should rather be allocated at the corporate level.
4. Finally, three principal integration strategies have been discussed at the organisational level. Moreover, it has been pointed out how the concept of the *balanced scorecard* can be adapted so as to account for the strategic importance of brand equity as well as the complementary nature of technological and market based assets. Through the establishment of clear and uniform strategic goals, derived from the company's existing brand vision and brand strategy, specific action can be initiated, and the pursuit and the attainment of the set targets can be permanently monitored on the basis of key performance measures. The expanded brandscorecard concept thus enables companies to define specific strategic goals with the help of the existing brand vision and strategy, accomplish the corresponding activities, control the implementation as well as the effectiveness of the taken action, and if necessary realign strategic initiatives and/or reallocate resources. Hence, it reveals a possibility how companies can integrate their technology and brand equity management at the process level. However, although the balanced scorecard is nowadays in widespread use and extensive

experience about the applicability and usefulness of the basic brand scorecard concept exists, the extended brand scorecard system still has to proof its practicability and benefits within companies. It may be of particular interest for future research to investigate the specific problems and advantages accompanying the implementation of the concept in specific companies and thus to modify, specify and further develop the management system.

VI.3 General Conclusion and Scope for Further Research

The aim of the undertaken research project has been the investigation of the role of brand equity in the appropriation of the returns of intangible technological assets. For this purpose a thorough look has been taken upon intellectual property management and innovation management, investigating the characteristics of intangible assets, the specific sources of technological assets, as well as the most important protection modes available. Building upon these theoretical foundations the strategic role of intangible assets in general, and technological assets as well as brand equity in particular, has been analysed. The theoretical discussion and empirical investigation have finally led to the formulation of the model of complementary brand equity for the sustainable appropriation of the returns of intangible technological assets.

With regard to the *general research question* as well as *hypothesis* established in chapter I, a close relationship between a companies technological proficiency and brand equity has been discovered. It has been shown that company specific technological assets generating a perceivable customer benefit are of utmost importance in establishing and maintaining complementary brand equity. Due to brand equity's characteristics of combining high ambiguity and legal protection it presents a formidable and extremely sustainable competitive advantage putting actual and potential competitors at a considerable disadvantage. In addition, it has been shown that the loss of strategic advantage due to the imitation and replication of a company's initial technological advantage is substituted for by the rising importance of brand equity along the technology-life-cycle. Consequently, complementary brand equity can be said to enable a company, if managed appropriately, to efficiently and effectively appropriate the returns generated by its initial technological innovation in the long-run and hence is of greatest strategic importance for companies in technology intensive industries. Thus, the *general research hypothesis* formulated in chapter I.2.2, stating a close relationship between a company's technological assets and the possibility to establish brand equity, as well as an important strategic role of established brand equity in the appropriation of the returns generated by technological assets, has been validated by our discussion and empirical findings.

Although the field of research pointed out in chapter I has been extensively investigated certain questions and findings transcending the scope of the presented research call for further investigation. In the field of technology management these lie with respect to the findings pointed out in sighting and developing more accurate and comparable in- and out-put measures of technological innovation at the corporate level. Moreover, an improved understanding of the inter- and intra-industry differences in company's propensity to patent and register trademarks is needed in order to be able to better interpret the general output of companies' creative activities. With respect to brand equity and in particular brand equity's role in the appropriation of the returns of technological assets further empirical validation is needed. However, due to the ascertained problems of quantification of certain facts as well as the lack of accurate and comparable data further research should not only focus on the econometric investigation of the presented model but also include more qualitative methods such as case study research.

With the presented empirical findings and theoretical discussion we hope to have contributed to a better understanding of how companies can achieve effective appropriation of the returns generated by technological assets in the long-run as well as the strategic role of brand equity in technological intensive industries which presents a starting point for future research in this field.

Bibliography

Aaker DA (1989) "Managing Assets and Skills: The Key to a Sustainable Competitive Advantage." *California Management Review* Winter: 91-106

Aaker DA (1990) "Brand Extension: The Good, the Bad, and the Ugly." *Sloan Management Review* Summer: 47-56

Aaker DA (1991) *Management des Markenwerts*. New York, Campus Verlag.

Aaker DA (1992) "The Value of Brand Equity." *Journal of Business Strategy* **4**: 27-32

Aaker DA (1996) *Building Strong Brands*. New York, Free Press

Aaker DA (1997) "Should you take your brand to where the action is?" *Harvard Business Review* **75**(5): 135-143

Aaker DA and Jacobson R (1994) "The Financial Information Content of Perceived Quality." *Journal of Marketing Research* **31**: 191-201

Abernathy W. J. and Clark KB (1985) "Innovation: Mapping the winds of creative destruction." *Research Policy* **14**: 3 - 22

Afuah A (1998) *Innovation Management: Strategies, Implementation, and Profits*. New York, Oxford University Press

Alba JW and Chattopadhyay A (1985) "Effects of Context and Part-Category Cues on Recall of Competing Brands." *Journal of Marketing Research* **22**: 340-349

Albert MB, Avery D et al. (1991) "Direct validation of citation counts as indicators of industrially important patents." *Research Policy* **20**: 251-259

Allegrezza S (1998) "To Patent or Not to Patent." *ECO-CEPS* **1**: 5-6

Allegrezza S and Guarda-Rauchs A (1999) "The determinants of trademark deposits: an econometric investigation." *Economie Appliqué* **2**: 51-68

Allen D (2000) "Living the Brand." Design Management Journal **11**(1): 35-40

Almeida P (1996) "Knowledge Sourcing By Foreign Multinationals: Patent Citation Anlysis In The US Semicondutor Industry." *Strategic Management Journal* **17**: 155 - 165

Alstaedter R (1997) *100 Jahre Acetylsalicylsäure*. Leverkusen, Bayer AG - Geschäftsbereich Consumer Care

Amit R and Schoemaker PJH (1993) "Strategic Assets and Organizational Rent." *Strategic Management Journal* **14**: 33 - 46

Anderson P and Tushman ML (1990) "Technological Discontinuities and Dominant Designs: A Cyclical Model of Technological Change." *Administrative Science Quarterly* **35**: 604-633

Arora A (1995) "Licensing Tacit Knowledge: Intellectual Property Rights and the Market for Know-how." *Economics of Innovation and New Technology* **4**: 41-59

Arrow KJ (1962a) *Economic Welfare and the Allocation of Resources for Invention*. The Rate and Direction of Inventive Activity: Economic and Social Factors, Princeton, Princeton University Press

Arrow KJ (1962b) "The Economic Implications of Learning by Doing." *Review of Economic Studies* **29**: 155-173

Arrow KJ (1969) "Classification Notes on the Production and Transmission of Technological Knowledge." *The American Economic Review* **52**: 29 - 35

Arundel A and Kabla I (1998) "What percentage of innovations are patented? Empirical estimates for European firms." *Research Policy* **27**: 127-141

Atuahnene-Gima K (1992) "Inward Technology Licensing as an Alternative to Internal R&D in New Product Development: A Conceptual Framework." *Journal of Product Innovation Management* **9**: 156-167

Badenhausen K (1996) "Blind Faith." *Financial World* **165**: 50-65

Barney JB (1986) "Strategic Factor Markets: Expectations, Luck and Business Strategy." *Management Science* **32**: 1231 - 1241

Barney JB (1991) "Firm Resources and Sustained Competitive Advantage." *Jounal of Management* **17**(1): 99-120

Barrow M (1988) *Statistics for Economics Accounting and Business Studies*. London, Longman

Basberg BL (1987) "Patents and the Measurement of Technological Change: A survey of the Literature." *Research Policy* **16**: 131-141

Baumol WJ (1993) *Entrepreneurship, Management, and the Structure of Payoffs*. Cambridge, Massachusetts, MIT Press

Bayer (1983) *Aspirin ein Jahrhundertpharmakon*. Leverkusen, Bayer AG

Bayer (1996) Schmerz zwischen Steinzeit & Moderne. Leverkusen, Bayer AG

Begg D, Fischer S et al. (1991) *Economics*. London, McGraw Hill

Bennett PD (1988) *Marketing*. New York, McGraw-Hill

Berkowitz L (1993) "Getting the Most From Your Patents." *Research Technology Management* March-April: 26-31

Bermann D (2001) Lucent sucht erneut Käufer für Konzernsparte. *Handelsblatt*.

Besen SM and Raskind LJ (1991) "An Introduction to the Law and Economics of Intellectual Property." *Journal of Economic Perspectives* **5**: 3-27

Bettman JR, Johnson EJ et al. (1991) Consumer Decision Making. *Handbook of Consumer Behaviour*. T. S. Robertson and H. H. Kassarjian. New Jersey, Prentice-Hall: 50-84

Bierly P and Chakrabarti A. (1996) "Generic Knowledge Strategies in the U.S. Pharmaceutical Industry." Strategic *Management Journal* **17**: 123-135

Bird M, Channon C et al. (1970) "Brand Image and Brand Usage." *Journal of Marketing Research* **7**: 307-14

Blind K, Edler J et al. (2001) Description of a Database of 250 Innovative Service Companies and Analysis of Their Patenting Activities. Karlsruhe, FhG-ISI: 53-93

Bohle F (1988) 100 Jahre Forschung und Fortschritt: Bayer Pharma 1988. Leverkusen, Bayer AG - Sektor Pharma

Bound J, Cummins C et al. (1984) Who Does R&D and Who Patents? *R&D, Patents, and Productivity*. Z. Griliches. Chicago, University of Chicago Press: 21-54

Brooking A (1996). *Intellectual Capital*. London, Thomson Business Press

Brooking A (1997) "The Management of Intellectual Capital." *Long Range Planning* **30**(3): 364-365

Buckley PJ and Carter MJ (2000) "Knowledge Management in Global Technology Markets." *Long Range Planning* **33**: 55-71

Buckley PJ and Casson M (1996) "An Economic Model of International Joint Venture Strategy." *An Economic Model of International Joint Venture Strategy*: 849-876

Bunnel D (2000) *Making the Cisco Connection: The Story behind the Real Internet Superpower*. New York, John Wiley & Sons

Buzell RD and Gale BT (1987) *Das PIMS-Programm: Strategien und Unternehmenserfolg*. Wiesbaden, Gabler

Cantwell J and Piscitello L (1999) "The Emergence of Corporate International Networks for the Accumulation of Dispersed Technological Competencies." *Management International Review* **39**(1): 123-147

Carlton DW and Perloff JM (1994) *Modern Industrial Organization*. New York, HaperCollins

Carmines EG and Zeller RA, Eds. (1979) *Reliability and Validity Assessment*. Quantitative Applications in the Social Sciences. Newbury Park, Sage

Caves RE (1971) "International Corporations: The Industrial Economics of Foreign Investment." *Economica* **38**: 1-27

Caves RE., Whinston MD et al. (1991) "Patent Expiration, Entry, and Competition in the U.S. Pharmaceutical Industry." *Brookings Papers: Microeconomics*: 1 - 66

Chesbrough HW and Teece DJ (1996) "When Is Virtual Virtuous? Organizing for Innovation." *Harvard Business Review* January-February: 65 - 73

Chesnais F (1996) Technological agreements, networks and selected issues in economic theory. *Technological Collaboration*. R. Coombs, A. Richards, P. P. Saviotti and V. Walsh. Cheltenham, Edward Elgar: 18-33

Cheung SNS (1982) "Property Rights in Trade Secrets." *Economic Inquiry* **20**: 40-53

Christensen CM, Suárez FF et al. (1998) "Strategies for Survival in Fast-Changing Industries." *Management Science* **44**(12): 207-220

Cisco (1998) Cisco Systems Im Profil. Hallbergmoos, Cisco Systems GmbH: 1-10

Clark K (1987) Investment in New Technology and Competitive Advantage. *The Competitive Challenge*. D. J. Teece. Cambridge MA, Ballinger Publication: 59-81

Clark KB and Griliches Z (1984) Productivity Growth and R&D at the Business Level: Results from the PIMS Data Base. *R&D, Patents, and Productivity*. Z. Griliches. Chicago, University of Chicago Press: 393-416

Coase RH (1937) "The Nature of the Firm." *Economica* **4**: 386-405

Cockburn I and Griliches Z (1988) "Industry Effects and Appropriability Measures in the Stock Market's Valuation of R&D and Patents." *AEA Papers and Proceedings* **78**: 419 -423

Cohen WM and Levinthal DA (1989) "Innovation and Learning: The Two Faces of R&D." *The Economic Journal* **99**: 569 - 596

Cohen WM and Levinthal DA (1990) "Absorptive Capacity: A New Perspective on Learning and Innovation." *Administrative Science Quarterly* **35**: 128 - 152

Conrad CA (1983) "The Advantage of Being First and Competition Between Firms." *International Journal of Industrial Organization* **1**: 353-364

Cook TE (1988) *International Mergers & Acquisitions*. New York, Basil Blackwell

Coombs R, Richards A et al. (1996a) Introduction: technological collaboration and networks of alliances in the innovation process. *Technological Collaboration*. R. Coombs, A. Richards, P. P. Saviotti and V. Walsh. Cheltenham, Edward Elgar: 1-17

Cooper RG (2001) *Winning at new Products: Accelerating the Process from Idea to Launch*. Cambridge, MA

Coyne KP (1986) "Sustainable Competitive Advantage - What it is, What it Isn't." *Business Horizons* January-February: 54-61

David PA (1993) Intellectual Property Institutions and the Panda's Thumb: Patents, Copyrights, and Trade Secrets in Economic Theory and History. *Gloal Dimensions of Intellectual Property Rights in Science and Technology*. M. B. Wallerstein, M. E. Mogee and R. A. Schoen. Washington, D. C., National Academy Press: 19-61

Davidson JH (1976) "Why most new consumer brands fail." *Harvard Business Review* **54**(March-April): 177-122

De Chernatony L and McDonald M (1998) *Creating Powerful Brands*. Oxford, Butterworth Heinemann

De Pay D (1996) Schutzrechte und Schutzrechtspolitik. *Handwörterbuch der Produktionswirtschaft*. W. Kern. **2**: 1830 -1840

Demsetz H (1967) "Toward a Theory of Property Rights." *American Economic Association* **57**: 346-359

Demuth A (1999) "Corporate Branding schafft Wettbewerbsvorteile in globalisierten Märkten." *Frankfurter Allgemeine Zeitung* **84**: 33

Deutsches Patent- und Markenamt (2000) Gebrauchsmuster, DPMA. 2000

Deutschman A (1994) "The Managing Wisdom of High-Tech Superstars." *Fortune* October **17**: 97-103

Dierickx I and Cool K (1989) "Asset Stock Accumulation and Sustainability of Competitive Advantage." *Management Science* **35**(12): 1504-1511

Dimitriadis S (1994) *Le Management De La Marque: Vecteur de croissance*. Aix-en-Provence, Les Editions D'Organisation

Doole I and Lowe R (2001) *International Marketing Strategy: Analysis, Development and Implementation*. London, Thomson Learning

Dosi G (1982) "Technological paradigms and technological trajectories." *Research Policy* **11**: 147-162

Dougherty C (1992) *Introduction to Econometrics*. New York, Oxford University Press

Drucker PF (1998) "Wissen - die Trumpfkarte der entwickelten Länder." *Harvard Business Manager* **4**: 9-11

Dunning JH (1994) "Multinational enterprises and the globalization of innovatory capacity." *Research Policy* **23**: 67-88

Durand T (1988) "Management pour la technologie: de la théorie à la pratique." *Revue Francaise de Gestion* November/December: 5-14

Durand T (1998) The Alchemy of Competence. *Strategic Flexibility: Managing in a Turbulent Environment.* G. Hamel, C. K. Prahalad, H. Thomas and D. O'Neal, John Wiley & Sons: 303-330

Durand T (2000) "L'alchimie de la compétence." *Revue Francaise de Gestion*: 84-102

Durand T and Guerra-Vieira S (1997) Competence-Based Strategies when Facing Innovation: But what is Competence? *Strategic Discovery: Competing in New Arenas*. H. Thomas and D. O'Neil, John Wiley & Sons: 79-97

Dyer JH (1997) "Effective Interfirm Collaboration: How Firms Minimize Transaction Costs and Maximize Transaction Value." *Strategic Management Journal* **18**(7): 535 - 556

Economist (1998) "A Viking with a compass." *The Economist* 6th June: 76-77

Edvinsson L and Malone MS (1997) *Intellectual Capital*. London, Pitakus

Edvinsson L and Sullivan PH (1996) Developing an Intellectual Capital Management Capability at Skandia. *Technology Licensing: Corporate Strategies for Maximizing Value*. R. L. Parr and P. H. Sullivan. New York, John Wiley & Sons: 261 - 265

Egginton DA (1990) "Towards Some Principles for Intangible Asset Accounting." *Accounting and Business Research* **20**(79): 193-205

Eisenhardt KM (1989) "Building Theories from Case Study Research." *Academy of Management Review* **14**: 532-550

Ellsworth RK (1998) "Identifying the economic value of trade marks." *Trade Mark Yearbook*: 74-76

EMDS Group (1999) Die beliebtesten Arbeitgeber. *Wirtschaftswoche Online*

Engelsman EC and Van Raan AFJ (1993) "International Comparison of Technological Activities and Specialisations: A Patent-based Monitoring System." *Technology Analysis & Strategic Management* **5**: 113 - 136

EPO (1994) *Utilisation of Patent Protection in Europe*. Munich, Eposcript

Erickson G and Jacobson R (1992) "Gaining Comparative Advantage Through Discretionary Expenditures: The Returns To R&D And Advertising." *Management Science* **38**(9): 1264-1279

Ernst H (1998) "Industrial research as a source of important patents." *Research Policy* **27**: 1-15

Ernst H (1999) "Führen Patentanmeldungen zu einem nachfolgenden Anstieg des Unternehmenserfolges? Eine Panelanalyse." *ZFBF* **51**(12): 1146-1168

Esch FR (2000). *Moderne Markenführung*. Wiesbaden, Gabler

Farquhar PH (1989) "Managing Brand Equity." *Marketing Research* **1** (September): 24-33

Fellman MW (1998) "Just the name, thanks: Why Beemer bought Rolls." *Marketing News* September 14: 6

Foray D (1995) Knowledge Distribution and the Institutional Infrastructure: The Role of Intellectual Property Rights. *Intellectual Property Rights and Global Competition*. H. Albach and S. Rosenkranz. Berlin, Sigma: 77-117

Fornell C, Robinson WT et al. (1985) "Consumption Experience and Sales Promotion Expenditure." *Management Science* **31**(9): 1084-1105

Freeman C (1974) *The Economics of Industrial Innovation*. Harmondsworth, Penguin

Freeman C (1994) "The economics of technical change." *Cambridge Journal of Economics* **18**: 463-514

Freeman C and Soete L (1997) *The Economics of Industrial Innovation*. Cambridge, MA, MIT Press

Freter H and Baumgarth C (2000) Ingredient Branding - Begriff und theoretische Begründung. *Moderne Markenführung*. F. R. Esch. Wiesbaden, Gabler: 289-315

Friedman DD, Landes WM et al. (1991) "Some Economics of Trade Secret Law." *Journal of Economic Perspectives* **5**: 61-72

Galbraith JR (2000) *Designing the Global Corporation*. San Francisco, Jossey-Bass

Galimberty I (1993) Large Chemical Firms in Biotechnology: Case Studies on Learning in Radically New Technologies. *SPRU*. Brighton, University of Sussex: 335

Gallini NT (1992) "Patent policy and costly imitation." *Rand Journal of Economics* **23**(1): 52-63

Gambardella A (1992) "Competitive advantages from in-house scientific research: The US pharmaceutical industry in the 1980s." *Research Policy* **21**: 391-407

Gassmann O and v. Zedtwitz M (1996) *Internationales Innovationsmanagement*. St. Gallen, Franz Vahlen

Geroski P (1995) Markets for Technology: Knowledge, Innovation and Appropriability. *Handbook of the Economics of Innovation and Technological Change*. P. Stoneman. Cambridge, MA, Blackwell: 90-131

Gerybadze A (2004) *Technologie und Innovations Management*. München, Verlag Vahlen

Gerybadze A (1995) *Strategic Alliances and Process Redesign*. Berlin, Walter de Gruyter

Gerybadze A (1997a) Globalisierung von Forschung und wesentliche Veränderungen im F&E Management internationaler Konzerne. *Globales Management von Forschung und Innovation*. A. Gerybadze, F. Mayer-Krahmer and G. Reger. Stuttgart, Schäffer-Poeschel: 17-37

Gerybadze A (1997b) Kompetenzverteilung und Integrationskonzepte für Wissenszentren in transnationalen Unternehmen. Stuttgart, University of Hohenheim

Gerybadze A (1998) "Technological Competence Assessment within the Firm: Applications of Competence Theory to Managerial Practice." *Discussion Paper on International Management and Innovation* **98-03**

Gerybadze A (1999) *Managing Technology Competence Centers in Europe*. Antwerpen, Maklu

Gerybadze A, Meyer-Krahmer F et al., Eds. (1997) *Globales Management von Forschung und Innovation*. Stuttgart, Schäfer Poeschel

Gerybadze A and Reger G (1998) "Globalization of R&D: recent changes in the management of innovation in transnational corporations." *Research Policy*

Ghemawat P (1986) "Sustainable advantage." *Harvard Business Review*: 53 - 58

Glass B (1990) "Patently Unfair?" *Info World* **29**: 56-62
Goebbels R (1997) "Le Capital Marque." *ECO-CEPS* **2**: 3-4
Goebbels R (1998) "Propriété Intellectuelle: Indication à l'Innovation et à la Diffusion de la Technologique." *ECO-CEPS* **1**: 3-4
Goldfinger C (1994) *L'Utile et le Futile: L'économie de l'immatériel*. Paris, Editions Odile Jacob
Goshal S and Nohria N (1993) "Horses for Courses: Organizational Forms for Multinational Corporations." *Sloan Management Review* Winter: 23-35
Graham MB (1985) "Corporate Research and Development: The Latest Transformation." *Technology in Society* **7**: 179-195
Granstrand O (1999) *The Economics and Management of Intellectual Property*. Cheltenham, Edward Elgar
Granstrand O and Sjölander S (1990) "Managing innovation in multi-technology corporations." *Research Policy* **19**: 35-60
Granstrand W and Sjölander S (1990a) "The Acquisition of Technology and Small Firms by Large Firms." *Journal of Economic Behaviour and Organization* **13**: 367-386
Grant RM (1996a) "Prospering in Dynamically-competitive Environments: Organizational Capability as Knowledge Integration." *Organization Science* 7(4): 375 - 387
Grant RM (1996b) "Toward a Knowledge-Based Theory of the Firm." *Strategic Management Journal* **17**: 109-122
Grant RM (1997) "The Knowledge-based View of the Firm: Implications for Management Practice." *Long Range Planning* **30**(3): 450-454
Grant RM (1998) *Contemporary Strategy Analysis*. Oxford, Blackwell
Graves L (1998) "American Brand-stand." *MC Technology Marketing Intelligence*: 56
Graves L (1998a) "Cisco's shot across the bow." *MC Technology Marketing Intelligence* **18**(11): 24-38
Green PE and Srinivasan V (1978) "Conjoint Analysis in Consumer Research: Issues and Outlook." *Journal of Consumer Research* **5**: 103-123
Green PE and Srinivasan V (1990) "Conjoint Analysis in Marketing: New Developments With Implications for Research and Practice." *Journal of Marketing* **54**: 3-19
Green PE and Wind Y (1975) "New way to measure consumers' judgements." *Harvard Business Review* **53**: 107-117
Griliches Z, Ed. (1984) *R&D, Patents, and Productivity*. Chicago, Chicago University Press
Griliches Z (1984a) Introduction: R&D, Patents, and Productivity. *R&D, Patents, and Productivity*. Z. Griliches. Chicago, University of Chicago Press: 1-19
Griliches Z (1984b) Market Value, R&D, and Patents. *R&D, Patents, and Productivity*. Z. Griliches. Chicago, University of Chicago Press: 249-252
Griliches Z (1989) "Patents: Recent Trends and Puzzles." *Brookings Papers on Microeconomics*: 291-330
Griliches Z (1990) "Patent Statistics as Economic Indicators: A Survey." *Journal of Economic Literature* **28**: 1661-1707

Griliches Z and Mairesse J (1984) Productivity and R&D at the Firm Level. *R&D, Patents, and Productivity*. Z. Griliches. Chicago, University of Chicago Press: 339-374

Grindley PC (1990) "Winning standards contests: using product standards in business strategy." *Business Strategy Review* **1**: 71-85

Grindley PC (1995) *Standards Strategy and Policy: Cases and Stories*. Oxford, Oxford University Press

Grindley PC and Nickerson JA (1996) Licensing and Business Strategy in the Chemicals Industry. *Technology Licensing: Corporate Strategies for Maximizing Value*. R. L. Parr and P. H. Sullivan. New York, John Wiley & Sons: 97-120

Grindley PC and Sullivan PH (1998) Irreconcilable Differences? Managing the Knowledge Creating Interfaces. *Profiting from Intellectual Capital: Extracting Value from Innovation*. P. H. Sullivan. New York, John Wiley & Sons: 84-99

Grindley PC and Teece DJ (1997) "Managing intellectual capital: Licensing and cross licensing in semiconductors and electronics." *California Management Review* **39**: 8-41

Grossman GM and Helpman E (1990) "Comparative Advantage and Long-Run Growth." *American Economic Review* **80**(4): 796-815

Grupp H and Schmoch U (1999) "Patent statistics in the age of globalisation: new legal procedures, new analytical methods, new economic interpretation." *Research Policy* **28**: 377-396

Güldenberg HG (1999) Marken bieten strategische Vorteile. *Frankfurter Allgemeine Zeitung*. Frankfurt. **228/39:** 14

Güldenberg HG (1999a) "Der volkswirtschaftliche Wert und Nutzen der Marke." *Gewerblicher Rechtsschutz und Urheberrecht* **10**: 843-847

Güldenberg HG (2000) Die Gretchenfrage: Global? Lokal? Oder im Trend - "glokal"? *Frankfurter Allgemeine Zeitung*. Frankfurt: B2

Gupta AK and Govindarajan V (2000) "Knowledge Flows within Multinational Corporations." *Strategic Management Journal* **21**: 473-496

Hagedoorn J (1993) "Understanding the Rationale of Strategic Technology Partnering: Interorganizational Modes of Cooperation and Sectoral Differences." *Strategic Management Journal* **14**: 371 - 385

Hagedoorn J and Narula R (1996) "Choosing Organizational Modes of Strategic Technology Partnering: International and Sectoral Differences." *Journal of International Business Studies* **27**: 265 -284

Hagedoorn J and Schakenraad J (1991) The Role of Interfirm Cooperation Agreements in the Globalisation of Economy and Technology. Brussels, Commission of the European Communities: 1-207

Hall BH, Griliches Z et al. (1986) "Patents and R&D: Is there a lag." *International Economic Review* **27**(2): 265-283

Hall R (1992) "The Strategic Analysis of Intangible Resources." *Strategic Management Journal* **13**: 135-144

Hall R (1993) "A Framework Linking Intangible Resources and Capabilities to Sustainable Competitive Advantage." *Strategic Management Journal* **14**: 607-618

Hall R (1997) Complex Systems, Complex Learning, and Competence Building. *Strategic Learning and Knowledge Management*. R. Sanchez and A. Heene. Chichester, John Wiley & Sons: 39-64

Harhoff D, Narin F et al. (1997) "Citation Frequency and the Value of Patented Information." *Discussion Paper* **97-27**

Harrigan KR (1988) "Joint Ventures and Competitive Strategy." *Strategic Management Journal* **9**: 141-158

Haspeslagh PC and Jemison DB (1991) *Managing Acquisitions: Creating Value Through Corporate Renewal*. New York, Free Press

Hatch MJ and Schultz M (2001a) "Are the Strategic Stars Aligned for Your Corporate Brand?" *Harvard Business Review* February: 128-134

Hatch MJ and Schultz M (2001b) "Den Firmennamen zur Marke machen." *Harvard Business Manager* **4**: 36-43

Hauser JR and Simme P (1981) "Profit Maximizing Perceptual Positions: An Integrated Theory for the Selection of Product Features and Price." *Management Science* **27**(1): 33-56

Hausman J, Hall BH et al. (1984) "Econometric Models for Count Data with an Application to the Patent-R&D Relationship." *Econometrica* **52**(4): 909-938

Hayek FA (1945) "The Use of Knowledge in Society." *The American Economic Review* **35**: 519 - 530

Henderson R. and Cockburn I (1994) "Measuring Competence? Exploring Firm Effects in Pharmaceutical Research." *Strategic Management Journal* **15**: 63-84

Henderson RM and Clark KB (1990) "Architectural Innovation: The Reconfiguration of Existing Product Technologies and the Failure of Established Firms." *Administrative Science Quarterly* **35**: 9-30

Hirschleifer J (1971) "The Private and Social Value of Information and the Reward to Inventive Activity." *American Economic Review* **61**(4): 561-574

Horstmann I, MacDonald G et al. (1985) "Patents as Information Transfer Mechanisms: To Patent or (Maybe) Not to Patent." *Journal of Political Economy* **93**: 837-858

Hoyer WD and MacInnis DJ (2001) *Consumer Behaviour*. New York, Houghton Mifflin

Hymer SH (1990) The Large Multinational "Corporation": An Analysis of some Motives for the International Integration of Business. *Multinational Corporation*. M. Casson, Hants: 3-31

Interbrand (1999) "Why do Brands Matter? Because They Create Value." *www.interbrand.com*

Interbrand (1999a) "How Interbrand compiled The World's Most Valuable Brands." *www.interbrand.com*

Jacobsen R (1988) "The Persistence of Abnormal Returns." *Strategic Management Journal* **9**: 415 - 430

Jaffe AB (1986) "Technological Opportunity and Spillovers of R&D: Evidence from Firms' Patents, Profits, and Market Value." *The American Economic Review* **76**(5): 984 - 1001

Jaffe AB, Trajtenberg M et al. (1993) "Geographic Localization of Knowledge Spillovers as Evidence by Patent Citations." *Quarterly Journal of Economics* August: 577-598

Jarillo JC (1988) "On Strategic Networks." *Strategic Management Journal* **9**: 31 - 41

Jeannet JP and Hennessey HD (2001) *Global Marketing Strategies*. Boston, Houghton Mifflin Company

Jennewein K (1997) Les effets de la libéralisation du secteur des télécommunications en Europe et les limites de la politique concurrentielle européenne. Grenoble, Université Pierre Mendès France

Johanson U (1999) Characteristics of Intangibles - Proposals Generated from Literature and Experienced Swedish Firms, School of Business, Stockholm University

Kamien MI and Schwartz NL (1974) "Patent Life and R&D Rivalry." *The American Economic Review* **64**(1): 183 - 187

Kapferer JN (1999) *Les Marques, Capital De L'Entreprise*. Paris, Editions d'Organisation

Kapferer JN and Thoening JC, Eds. (1994). *La Marque: Moteur de la compétitivité des entreprises et de la croissance de l'économie*. Paris, Ediscience

Kaplan RS and Norton DP (1992) "The Balanced Scorecard - Measures that Drive Performance." *Harvard Business Review* (January - February): 71-79

Kaplan RS and Norton DP (1996) "Using the Balanced Scorecard as a Strategic Management System." *Harvard Business Review* (January-February): 75-85

Kaplan RS and Norton DP (2001) *The Strategy Focused Organization: How Balanced Scorfecard Companies Thrive in the New Business Environment*. Boston, Harvard Business School Press

Katopis C (1997) "Patents vs. Patents? Policy implications of recent patent legislation." *St. John's Law Review* **71**: 329-376

Katz ML (1986) "An Analysis of Cooperative Research and Development." *Rand Journal of Economics*: 527-543

Katz ML and Shapiro C (1986) "How to License Intangible Property." Quarterly Journal of Economics: 567-589

Katz R and Allen TJ (1982) "Investigating the Not Invented Here (NIH) syndrome: A look at the performance, tenure, and communication pattern of 50 R&D Project Groups." *R&D Management* **12**(1): 7-19

Kaul I, Grunberg I et al. (1999a) Defining Global Public Goods. *Global Public Goods: International Cooperation In The 21st Century*. I. Kaul, I. Grunberg and M. A. Stern. Oxford, Oxford Uni Press: 2-19

Keller KL (1993) "Conceptualizing, Measuring, and Managing Customer-Based Brand Equity." *Journal of Marketing* **57**: 1-22

Keller KL (2000) Kundenorientierte Messung des Markenwerts. *Moderne Markenführung*. F. R. Esch. Wiesbaden, Gabler: 965-987

Kerin RA and Sethuraman R (1998) "Exploring the Brand Value - Shareholder Value Nexus for Consumer Goods Companies." *Journal of the Academy of Marketing Science* **26**(4): 260-273

Khermouch G, Holmes S et al. (2001) "The Best Global Brands." *Business Week* August **6**: 44-55

Killing P (1980) "Technology Acquisition: License Agreement or Joint Venture." *Columbia Journal of World Business* (Fall): 28 - 46

Kim WC and Mauborgne R (1999) "Strategy, Value Innovation, and the Knowledge Economy." *Sloan Management Review* Spring: 41-54

Kitch EW (1977) "The Nature and Function of the Patent System." *Journal of Law and Economics* **20**: 265-290

Kitch EW (1980) "The Law and Economics of Rights in Valuable Information." *The Journal of Legal Studies*: 683-723

Kline SJ and Rosenberg N (1986) An Overview of Innovation. *The Positive Sum Strategy: Harnessing Technology for Economic Growth*. R. Landau and N. Rosenberg. Washington, D. C., National Academy Press: 275-305

Kodama F (1995) *Emerging patterns of innovation: sources of Japan's technological edge*. Boston, MA, Harvard Business School Press

Kogut B and Zander U (1992) "Knowledge of the Firm, Combinative Capabilities, and the Replication of Technology." *Organization Science* **3**(3): 383-397

Kohl F (1997) 100 Jahre Acetylsalicylsäure: ein Sieg der pharmazeutischen Chemie. *PZ Magazin*. **32:** 11-22

Kohler U and Kreuter F (2001) *Datenanalyse mit Stata*. Wien, R. Oldenbourg Verlag

Kortum S and Lerner J (1999) "What is behind the recent surge in patenting?" *Research Policy* **28**: 1-22

Krugman PR and Obstfeld M (1994) *International Economics: Theory and Policy*. Berkeley, CA, Harper Collins

Kunisch R (2000) Markenkosmetik. *Frankfurter Allgemeine Zeitung*. Frankfurt: B6

Kuznets S (1962) *Inventive Activity: Problems of Definition and Measurement*. The Rate and Direction of Inventive Activity: Economic and Social Factors, Princeton, Princeton

Lane V and Lacobson R (1995) "Stock Market Reactions to Brand Extension Announcements: The Effects of Brand Attitude and Familiarity." *Journal of Marketing* **59**: 63-77

Lawless MW and Fisher RJ (1990) "Sources of Durable Competitive Advantage in New Products." *Journal of Product Innovation Management* **7**(1): 35-44

Lei DT (1997) "Competence-building, technology fusion and competitive advantage: the key roles of organizational learning and strategic alliances." *International Journal of Technology Management* **14**: 208-237

Lei DT, Hitt MA et al. (1996) "Dynamic Core Competencies through Meta-Learning and Strategic Context." *Journal of Management* **22**(4): 549-569

Lei DT and Slocum JW (1992) "Global Strategy, Competence-Building and Strategic Alliances." *California Management Review* **34**: 81 - 97

Leonard-Barton D (1995) *Wellsprings of Knowledge: Building and Sustaining the Sources of Innovation*. Boston, MA, Harvard Business School Press

Levin RC (1988) "Appropriability, R&D Spending, and Technological Performance." *AEA Papers and Proceedings* **78**: 424 - 428

Levin RC, Klevorick AK et al. (1987) "Appropriating the Returns from Industrial Research and Development." *Brookings Papers on Economic Activity* **3**: 783-820

Lieberman MB (1989) "The Learning Curve, Technology Barriers to Entry, and Competitive Survival in the Chemical Processing Industries." *Strategic Management Journal* **10**: 431-447

Lieberman MB and Montgomery DB (1988). "First Mover Advantages." *Strategic Management Journal* **9**: 41-58

Liebeskind JP (1996) "Knowledge, Strategy, and the Theory of the Firm." *Strategic Management Journal* **17**: 93-107

Liebeskind JP, Oliver AL et al. (1996) "Social Networks, Learning, and Flexibility: Sourcing Scientific Knowledge in New Biotechnology Firms." *Organization Science* **7**: 428-443

Linxweiler R (2001) *BrandScoreCard: Ein neues Instrument erfolgreicher Markenführung*. Groß-Umstadt, Sehnert

Lippman SA and Rumelt RP (1982) "Uncertain imitability: an analysis of interfim differences in efficiency under competition." *The Bell Journal of Economics* **13**: 418-438

Lundvall BA (1998) "Why Study National Systems and National Styles of Innovation." *Technology Analysis & Strategic Management* **10**(4): 407-421

MacMillan I, McCaffery ML et al. (1985). "Competitors' Responses to Easily Imitated New Products - Exploring Commercial Banking Product Introductions." *Strategic Management Journal* **6**: 75-86

Madhok A and Osegowitsch T (1998) "Technology Flows Across Firms and Nations: The International Organization of the Biotechnology Industry." *Organizational Science* **9**: 326-339

Magee SP (1977) "Multinational Corporations, the Industry Technology Cycle and Development." *Journal of World Trade Law* **11**: 297 - 321

Majer W (2000) Langer Atem. *Frankfurter Allgemeine Zeitung*. Frankfurt: B3

Mann CC and Plummer ML (1991) *The Aspirin Wars: Money, Medicine, and 100 Years of Rampant Competition*. Boston, Harvard Business School Press

Mansfield E (1984) R&D and Innovation: Some Empirical Findings. *R&D, Patents, and Productivity*. Z. Griliches. Chicago, University of Chicago Press: 127-148

Mansfield E (1985) "How Rapidly Does New Industrial Technology Leak Out." *The Journal of Industrial Economics* **34**: 217-223

Mansfield E (1986) "Patents and Innovation: An Empirical Study." *Management Science* **32**(2): 173-181

Mansfield E, Schwartz M et al. (1981) "Imitation Costs and Patents: An Empirical Study." *The Economic Journal* **91**: 907-918

Markides CC (1999) "A Dynamic View of Strategy." *Sloan Management Review* Spring: 55-63.

Marseille J (1999) “Aspirine - La potion magique.” *Enjeux* Mars: 133-135

Mascarenhas B and Aaker DA (1989) “Mobility Barriers and Strategic Groups.” *Strategic Management Journal* **10**: 475-485

McTavish JR (1987) “What's in a Name? Aspirin and the American Medical Association.” *Bulletin of the history of medicine* **61**: 343-366

Menke-Glückert W (1998) Berlin: Baby Benz faces the moose. *Europe*. Washington: 40-42

Mirow M (2000) Wertsteigerung durch Innovation im globalisierten Unternehmen. Feldafing

Mittelhammer RC, Judge GG et al. (2000) *Econometric Foundations*. Cambridge, Cambridge Uni Press

Mokyr J (1998) “Science, Technology, and Knowledge: What Historians can learn from an evolutionary approach.” *Papers on Economics & Evolution* **9803**: 1-31

Morin J (1988) *L'Excellence Technologique*. Paris, Pubi-Union

Mossinghoff GJ (1984) “The Importance of Intellectual Property Protection in International Trade.” *Boston College International & Comparative Law Review* **7**: 235-249

N.A. (1994) “"Feindvermögen": Im Januar 1918 mit einem Federstrich alles verloren.” *Bayer Intern* **12/94**: 3-4

N.A. (1995) OTC Market Report - Update USA: 1-3

N.A. (1996) Aspirin - Das Medikament des 20. Jahrhunderts. *Focus*. 5/1996: 118-119

N.A. (1997) Aspirin: Das Neue im Bewährten. *Insider's Markenarchiv*: 24-26

N.A. (1998) “Une super aspirine.” *Sciences et Avenir* Juillet: 36

N.A. (1998a) Europaparlament: Copyright muss auch im Internet gelten. *Handelsblatt*: 1

N.A. (2000) “Urteile für die Markennameninhaber.” *Spiegel Online*

N.A. (2001a) Lucent-Übernahme für 40 Milliarden Dollar? *Spiegel Online*

N.A. (2001b) Nortel baut nach Milliardenverlust weitere Stellen ab. *Handelsblatt*

Nalebuff B and Brandenburger A (1996). *Coopetition-kooperativ konkurrieren*. Frankfurt, Campus-Verlag

Narin F, Noma E et al. (1987) “Patents as Indicators of Corporate Technological Strength.” *Research Policy* **16**: 143-155

Narin F and Olivastro D (1992) “Status Report: Linkage between Technology and Science.” *Research Policy* **21**: 237-249

Nelson RR (1959) “The Simple Economics of Basic Scientific Research.” *The Journal of Political Economy* **67**(3): 297 - 306

Nelson RR (1982) “The Role of Knowledge in R&D Efficiency.” *The Quarterly Journal of Economics* **97**: 453-570

Nelson RR (1991) “Why do Firms Differ, and How Does it Matter.” *Strategic Management Journal* **12**: 61 - 74

Nelson RR and Winter SG (1982) *An Evolutionary Theory of Economic Change*. Cambridge, MA, Belknap Harvard Uni. Press

Nickel V (2000) Sparsam, aber treu. *Frankfurter Allgemeine Zeitung*. Frankfurt: B4

Nilsson EA (1995) "Innovating-By-Doing: Skill Innovation as a Source of Technological Advance." *Journal of Economic Issues* **29**(1): 33-46

Nonaka I (1991) "The Knowledge-Creating Company." *Harvard Business Review* November-December: 96-104

Nonaka I (1994) "A Dynamic Theory of Organizational Knowledge Creation." *Organization Science* **5**: 14-37

Nonaka I and Takeuchi H (1995) *The Knowledge-Creating Company: How Japanese Companies Create the Dynamics of Innovation*. New York, Oxford University Press

NSB (2000) Science & Engineering Indicators 2000. Arlington, National Science Foundation

OECD (1999) *OECD Science, Technology and Industry Scoreboard: Benchmarking Knowledge-based Economies*. Paris, OECD Publications

OECD and Eurostat (1998) *Services: Statistics on International Transactions 1987-1996*. Paris, Eurostat

Ordover JA (1991) "A Patent System for Both Diffusion and Exclusion." *Journal of Economic Perspectives* **5**: 43-60

Ouchi WG (1980) "Markets, Bureaucracies, and Clans." *Administrative Science Quarterly* **25**: 129 - 140

Ouchi WG and Bolton MK (1988) "The Logic of Joint Research and Development." *California Management Review* **30**(3): 9 - 33

Pakes A and Griliches Z (1984) Patents and R&D at the Firm Level: A First Look. *R&D, Patents, and Productivity*. Z. Griliches. Chicago, University of Chicago Press: 55-72

Parkhe A (1993) ""Messy" Research, Methodological Predispositions, and Theory Development in International Joint Ventures." *Academy of Management Review* **18**(2): 227-268

Parr RL (1996b) Central Control of Technology Licensing. *Technology Licensing: Corporate Strategies for Maximizing Value*. R. L. Parr and P. H. Sullivan. New York, John Wiley & Sons: 121-134

Parr RL and Sullivan PH, Eds. (1996) *Technology Licensing: Corporate Strategies for Maximizing Value*. New York, John Wiley & Sons

Parr RL and Sullivan PH (1996a) The Future of Intellectual Capital Management. *Technology Licensing: Corporate Strategies for Maximizing Value*. R. L. Parr and P. H. Sullivan. New York, John Wiley & Sons: 267-275

Patel P and Pavitt K (1990). "The Importance of the Technological Activities of the World's Largest Firms." *World Patent Information* **12**: 89-94

Patel P and Pavitt K (1995) Patterns of Technological Activity: their Measure and Interpretation. *Handbook of the Economics of Innovation and Technological Change*. P. Stoneman. Cambridge, MA, Blackwell: 14-51

Patel P and Pavitt K (1996) "Technological Competencies in the World's largest Firms: Characteristics, Constraints and Scope for Managerial Choice." *Research Policy*

Patel P and Pavitt K (1997) "The technological competencies of the world's largest firms: complex and path-dependent, but not much variety." *Research Policy* **26**: 141-156

Patel P and Vega M (1999) "Patterns of internationalisation of corporate technology: location vs. home country advantages." *Research Policy* **28**: 145-155

Pavitt K (1982) "R&D, patenting and innovative activities." *Research Policy* **11**: 33-51

Pavitt K (1990) "What We Know about the Strategic Management of Technology." *California Management Review* (Spring): 17 - 26

Pavitt K (1991) "What makes basic research economically useful?" *Research Policy* **20**: 109 - 119

Pearce R and Papanastassiou M (1999) "Overseas R&D and the strategic evolution of MNEs: evidence from laboratories in the UK." *Research Policy* **28**: 23-41

Pettis CR (1995) "The Relationship of Corporate Brand Strategy and Stock Price." *Morgan Stanley U.S. Investment Research* June 13: 20-23

Pettis CR (1995a) *TechnoBrands: How to Create and Use "Brand Identity" to Market, Advertise and Sell Technology Products.* New York, Amacom

Pettis CR (1995b) "The Importance of Brand to the Success of Technology Companies." *Morgan Stanley U.S. Investment Research* March 6: 24-26

Pfaffmann E (2001) *Kompetenzbasiertes Management in der Produktentwicklung.* Wiesbaden, DUV

Picot A (1998) Wissensmanagement und Wissenslogistik in Unternehmen und Märkten. München

Picot A, Reichwald R et al. (1996) Die grenzenlose Unternehmnung. Wiesbaden, Gabler

Pindyck RS and Rubinfeld DL (1992) *Microeconomics.* New York, Maxwell Macmillan

Pisano GP (1990) "The R&D Boundaries of the Firm: An Empirical Analysis." *Administrative Science Quarterly* **35**: 153-176

Pisano GP (1991) "The Governance of Innovation: Vertical integration and collaborative arrangements in the biotechnology industry." *Research Policy* **20**: 237 - 249

Pisano GP and Wheelwright SC (1995) "The New Logic of High-Tech R&D." *Harvard Business Review* September-October: 93-105

Porter ME (1985) *Competitive Advantage: Creating and Sustaining Superior Performance.* New York, Free Press

Porter ME (1991) "Towards a Dynamic Theory of Strategy." *Strategic Management Journal* **12**: 95-117

Porter ME (1996) "What is Strategy?" *Harvard Business Review* November-December: 61-78

Powell WW (1990) "Neither Market Nor Hierarchy: Network Forms of Organization." *Research in Organizational Behaviour* **12**: 295 - 336

Powell WW (1998) "Learning From Collaboration: Knowledge and Networks in the Biotechnology and Pharmaceutical Industry." *California Management Review* **40**: 228-240

Powell WW, Koput KW et al. (1996) "Interorganizational Collaboration and the Locus of Innovation: Networks of Learning in Biotechnology." *Administrative Science Quarterly*: 116-136

Prahalad CK and Hamel G (1990) "The Core Competence of the Corporation." *Harvard Business Review*: 79 - 91

Quélin B (1997) Appropriability and the Creation of New Capabilities Through Strategic Alliances. *Strategic Learning and Knowledge Management.* R. Sanchez and A. Heene. Chichester, John Wiley & Sons: 139-160

Quintas P, Lefrere P et al. (1997) "Knowledge Management: a Strategic Agenda." *Long Range Planning* **30**(3): 385-391

Ransley DL and Gaffney RC (1997) "Upgrading your Patenting Process." *Research Technology Management* **40**: 41-46

Rao AR and Monroe KB (1989) "The Effect of Price, Brand Name, and Store Name on Buyers' Perceptions of Product Quality: An Integrated Review." *Journal Marketing Research* **26**: 351-357

Reed R and DeFilippi RJ (1990) "Causal Ambiguity, Barriers to Imitation, and Sustainable Competitive Advantage." *Academy of Management Review* **15**(1): 88-102

Rhône-Poulenc (1995) Rhodine - Usines du Rhône. *L'Album Rhône-Poulenc.* Paris: 23-27

Richards I, Foster D et al. (1998) "Brand Knowledge Management: Growing Brand Equity." *Journal of Knowledge Management* **2**(1): 47-54

Roberts EB (1999) Global Benchmarking of the Strategic Management of Technology. Cambridge, MA, MIT: 1-32

Roberts EB and Berry CA (1985) "Entering New Businesses: Selecting Strategies for Success." *Sloan Management Review* **26**(3): 3-17

Robinson WT (1988) "Sources of Market Pioneer Advantages: The Case of Industrial Goods Industries." *Journal of Marketing Research* **25**(February): 87-94

Robinson WT and Fornell C (1985) "Sources of Market Pioneer Advantages in Consumer Goods Industries." *Journal of Marketing Research* **22**(August): 305-317

Roeb T (1994). Markenwert: Begriff, Berechnung, Bestimmungsfaktoren. Aachen, Universität Siegen: 292

Romer PM (1986). "Increasing Returns and Long-Run Growth." *Journal of Political Economy* **94**(5): 1002-1037

Rosenberg N (1974). "Science, Invention and Economic Growth." *Economic Journal* **84**: 90-108

Rumelt RP (1987) Theory, Strategy, and Entrepreneurship. *The Competitive Challenge.* D. J. Teece. Cambridge, MA, Ballinger: 137-158

Rutledge J (1998) "How to protect brand value." *Forbes* **162**(12): 154

Sachs L (1992) *Angewandte Statistik: Anwendung statistischer Methoden.* Berlin, Springer Verlag

Sahl C, Xuyen GNS et al. (1998) "Combien Coûte un Brevet." *ECO-CEPS* **1**: 19-23

Sanchez R and Heene A (1997) A Competence Perspective on Strategic Learning and Knowledge Management. *Strategic Learning and Knowledge Management*. R. Sanchez and A. Heene. Chichester, John Wiley & Sons: 3-15

Sanders BS (1962) *Some Difficulties in Measuring Inventive Activity*. The Rate and Direction of Inventive Activity: Economic and Social Factors, Princeton, Princeton University Press

Sattler H (1999) Praxis von Markenbewertung und Markenmanagement in deutschen Unternehmen. Jena, PricewaterhaouseCoopers: 1-17

Saviotti PP (1998) "On the Dynamics of appropriability, of tacit and of codified knowledge." *Research Policy* **26**: 843 - 856

Scherer FM (1965) "Firm Size, Market Structure, Opportunity, and the Output of Patented Inventions." *American Economic Review* **55**(5): 1097-1125

Scherer FM (1984) Using Linked Patent and R&D Data to Measure Interindustry Technology Flows. *R&D, Patents, and Productivity*. Z. Griliches. Chicago, University of Chicago Press: 417-461

Scherer FM (1988) "Corporate Take-overs: The Efficiency Arguments." *Journal of Economic Perspectives* **2**(1): 69-82

Schmalensee R (1982) "Product Differentiation Advantages of Pioneering Brands." *American Economic Review* **72**: 349-365

Schmoch U (1990). *Wettbewerbsvorsprung durch Patentinformationen*. Köln, TÜV Rheinland

Schmoch U, Grupp H et al. (1988) *Technikprognosen mit Patentindikatoren*. Köln, TÜV Rheinland

Schmookler J (1962) *Changes in Industry and in the State of Knowledge as Determinants of Industrial Invention*. The Rate and Direction of Inventive Activity: Economic and Social Factors, Princeton, Princeton University Press

Schnaars SP (1986) "When Entering Growth Markets, Are Pioneers Better Than Poachers?" *Business Horizons* **29**(March-April): 27-36

Schrader S (1991) "Informal technology transfer between firms: Cooperation through information trading." *Research Policy* **20**: 153 - 170

Schrage M (1999). "You're so money: When products don't matter." *MC Technology Marketing Intelligence* **19**(2): 21

Schreiner C (1999) *100 Jahre Highlights*. Leverkusen, Bayer AG - Geschäftsbereich Consumer Care

Seibert G and Wandelberger E (1988) Lexikon 2000. A. P. Zeller. Weinheim, Zweiburgen Verlag. **9**

Senker J (1995) "Tacit Knowledge and Models of Innovation." *Industrial and Corporate Change* **4**(2): 425-447

Shane S (1998) "Luck, Knowledge, and the Discovery of Entrepreneurial Opportunities." *Draft Version - not published*: 1-48

Shapiro C (1985) "Patent Licensing and R&D Rivalry." *The American Economic Review* **75**(2): 25 - 30

Siegel IH (1962) *Scientific Discovery and the Rate of Invention*. The Rate and Direction of Inventive Activity: Economic and Social Factors, Princeton, Princeton University Press

Sirilli G and Evangelista R (1998) "Technological innovation in services and manufacturing: resuts from Italian surveys." *Research Policy* **27**: 881-899

Sloman J (1991) Economics. New York, Harvester Wheatsheaf

Smit M (1999) Ingredient Branding. *Co-Branding: The Science of Alliance*. T. Blackett and B. Boad. London, MacMillan Business: 66-83

Solow RM (1997) *Learning from "Learning by Doing"*. Stanford, CA, Stanford Uni. Press

Solt ME (1993) "SWORD Financing of innovation in the biotechnology industry." *Financial Management* (22): 173-190

Srivastava RK, Shervani TA et al. (1998) "Market-Based Assets and Shareholder Value: A Framework for Analysis." *Journal of Marketing* **62**: 2-18

Stafford DC and Purkis RHA (1989) *Directory of Multinationals*. New York, Macmillan Publishers

Stefan M (2003) *Technologische Diversifikation von Unternehmen*. Wiesbaden, Gabler

Steward TA (1994) "Your Company's most valuable asset: Intellectual Capital." *Fortune* **3**: 29 - 33

Steward TA (1997) *Intellectual Capital: The New Wealth of Organizations*. London, Nicholas Brealey

Stiglitz JE (1999a) Public Policy for a Knowledge Economy, World Bank

Stiglitz JE (1999b) Knowledge as a Global Public Good. *Global Public Goods: International Cooperation In The 21st Century*. I. Kaul, I. Grunberg and M. A. Stern. Oxford, Oxford Uni Press: 308-325

Stopford JM (1992) *Directory of Multinationals*. New York, Stockton Press

Stopford JM and Wells LT (1972) Developing an Organization for Multinational Business. *Managing the Multinational Enterprise*. J. M. Stopford and L. T. Wells. New York, Basic Books: 9-19; 201-202

Suárez FF and Utterback JM (1995) "Dominant Designs and the Survival of Firms." *Strategic Management Journal* **16**: 415-430

Sujan M and Bettman JR (1989) "The Effectws of Brand Positioning Strategies on Consumers' Brand and Category Perceptions: Some Insights From Schema Research." *Journal of Marketing* **26**: 454-467

Sullivan PH (2000) *Value-Driven Intellectual Capital: How to Convert Intangible Corporate Assets into Market Value*. New York, John Wiley & Sons

Sullivan PH and Edvisson L (1996) A Model for Managing Intellectual Capital. *Technology Licensing: Corporate Strategies for Maximizing Value*. R. L. Parr and P. H. Sullivan. New York, John Wiley & Sons: 249-260

Sveiby KE (1997) *Wissenskapital - das unentdeckte Vermögen: Immaterielle Unternehmenswerte aufspüren, messen und steigern*. New York, Verlag Moderne Industrie

Teece DJ (1977) "Technology Transfer by Multinational Firms: The Resource Cost of Transferring Technological Know-How." *The Economic Journal* **87**: 242 - 261

Teece DJ (1981) "The Market for Know-How and the Efficient International Transfer of Technology." *Annals* **458**: 81-96

Teece DJ (1986) "Profiting from technological innovation: Implications for integration, collaboration, licensing and public policy." *Research Policy* **15**: 285 - 305

Teece DJ (1988) Technological change and the nature of the firm. *Technical Change and Economic Theory*. G. e. a. Dosi. London, Frances Pinter: 256-281

Teece DJ (1998) "Capturing Value from Knowledge Assets: The New Economy, Markets for Know-How, and Intangible Assets." *California Management Review* **40**: 55-79

Teece DJ (2000) "Strategies for Managing Knowledge Assets: The Role of Firm Structure and Industrial Context." *Long Range Planning* **33**: 35-54

Teece DJ (2000a) *Managing Intellectual Capital: Organizational, Strategic, and Policy Dimensions*. New York, Oxford Uni. Press

Teece DJ, Pisano G et al. (1997) "Dynamic Capabilities and Strategic Management." *Strategic Management Journal* **18**: 509 - 533

Theile K and Burr, W (2000) "Ingredient Branding: Perspectives and Problems of Brand Development in Business to Business and End-User Relations." *Advances in Business Marketing and Purchasing* **9**: 443-465

Thurow LC (1997) "Needed: A New System of Intellectual Property Rights." *Harvard Business Review* September-October: 95 - 103

Tibesar A (1996) Marques et Stratégies d'Innovation dans les Entreprises Industrielles Luxembourgeoises. *Un Quart de Siècle de Droit Benelux des Marques*. B. B. D. Marques. Den Hague: 195-210

Tibesar A (1997) "Marques et Protection de l'Innovation dans les Entreprises Industrielles Luxembourgeoises." *ECO-CEPS* **2**: 10-14

Tibesar A (1998) "Les Entreprises Industrielles Luxembourgeoises Face à la Propriété Intellectuelle." *ECP-CEPS* **1**: 24-27

Tidd J, Bessant J et al. (1997) *Managing Innovation: Integrating Technological, Market and Organizational Change*. Chichester, John Wiley & Sons

UNCTAD (1999) *World Investment Report*. New York, UN Publication

van Reekum AH (1999) Intellectual Property and Pharmaceutical Innovation. Ridderkerk, Rijksuniversiteit Groningen

Vernon R (1966) "International Investment and International Trade in the Product Cycle." *Quarterly Journal of Economics* **80**: 190 - 207

von Hippel E (1982) "Appropriability of Innovation Benefit as a Predictor of the Source of Innovation." *Research Policy* **11**: 95-115

von Hippel E (1986) "Lead Users: A Source of Novel Product Concepts." *Management Science* **32**(7): 791-805

von Hippel E (1987) "Cooperation between rivals: Informal know-how trading." *Research Policy* **16**: 291-302

von Hippel E (1988) "Trading Trade Secrets." *Technology Review* February-March: 58-64

von Hippel E (1988a) *The Sources of Innovation*. Oxford, Oxford Uni. Press

von Weizäcker EU (1986) Erstmaligkeit und Bestätigung als Komponenten der pragmatischen Information. *Offene Systeme I: Beiträge zur Zeitstruktur von Information, Entropie und Evolution*. E. U. von Weizäcker. Stuttgart, Klett-Cotta: 82-113

Voss CA (1985) "The Role of Users in the Development of Applications Software." *Journal of Product Innovation Management* **2**: 113-121

Wermelskirchen S (1999) Kraft des Namens. *Wirtschaftswoche*. **47:** 154-160

Wernerfelt B (1984) "A Resource-based View of the Firm." *Strategic Management Journal* **5**: 171-180

Williamson OE (1979) "Transaction-Cost Economics: The Governance of Contractual Relations." *The Journal of Law and Economics*: 233-261

Winter SG (1987) Knowledge and Competence as Strategic Assets. *The Competitive Challenge*. D. J. Teece. Cambridge, MA, Ballinger: 159-184

Wöhe G (1993) *Einführung in die Allgemeine Betriebswirtschaft*. München, Vahlen

Wortmann M (1990) "Multinationals and the internationalization of R&D: New developments in German companies." *Research Policy* **19**: 175-183

Wright BD (1983) "The Economics of Invention Incentives: Patents, Prizes, and Research Contracts." *The American Economic Review* **73**: 691 -

Xuyen GNS (1998) "Comment Obtenir un Brevet Européen." *ECO-CEPS* **1**: 11-16

Yamin M (1996) Understanding 'strategic alliances': the limits of transaction cost economics. *Technology Collaboration*. R. Coombs, A. Richards, P. P. Saviotti and V. Walsh. Cheltenham, Edward Elgar: 165-179

Yin RK (1994) *Case Study Research: Design and Methods*. Thousand Oaks, Sage Publications

Yip GS (1995) Creating Global Marketing. *Total Global Strategy*. G. S. Yip. New Jersey, Prentice Hall: 123-149

Young S and Feigin B (1975) "Using the Benefit Chain for Improved Strategy Formulation." *Journal of Marketing* **39**: 72-74

Zander U and Kogut B (1995) "Knowledge and the Speed of the Transfer and Imitation of Organizational Capabilities: An Empirical Test." *Organization Science* **6**(1): 76 - 92

Zeithaml VA (1988) "Consumer Perceptions of Price, Quality, and Value: A Means-End Model and Synthesis of Evidence." *Journal of Marketing* **52**: 2-22

Zündorf U (2001) *100 Jahre Aspirin: The future has just begun*. Leverkusen, Bayer AG

Printing and Binding: Strauss GmbH, Mörlenbach

GPSR Compliance

The European Union's (EU) General Product Safety Regulation (GPSR) is a set of rules that requires consumer products to be safe and our obligations to ensure this.

If you have any concerns about our products, you can contact us on ProductSafety@springernature.com

In case Publisher is established outside the EU, the EU authorized representative is:

Springer Nature Customer Service Center GmbH
Europaplatz 3
69115 Heidelberg, Germany

Batch number: 10725973

Printed by Printforce, the Netherlands